William Henry Taylor

The Book of Travels of a Doctor of Physic

Containing his Observations made in certain Portions of the two Continents

William Henry Taylor

The Book of Travels of a Doctor of Physic
Containing his Observations made in certain Portions of the two Continents

ISBN/EAN: 9783337209988

Printed in Europe, USA, Canada, Australia, Japan

Cover: Foto ©Andreas Hilbeck / pixelio.de

More available books at **www.hansebooks.com**

THE

BOOK OF TRAVELS

OF

A DOCTOR OF PHYSIC.

CONTAINING HIS

OBSERVATIONS MADE IN CERTAIN PORTIONS
OF THE TWO CONTINENTS.

PHILADELPHIA:
J. B. LIPPINCOTT & CO.
1871.

PREFACE.

The kind reception accorded to a short series of newspaper letters of mine, describing a portion of the tour to which this volume relates, leading me to infer that a comprehensive narrative might meet with favor, it is now presented, with the hope that I am not counting unduly on the forbearance of the public.

I am fully sensible of the difficulty of giving interest to the relation of what has already been told a thousand times. To obviate this difficulty to some extent, I have endeavored to view the scenes I have to describe from a standpoint and in a manner different from what has been usually chosen. I have looked at them a-slant and a-squint, and out of the corner of my eye, as it were. This may have given my pictures sometimes an appearance of distortion. The distortion is only apparent, however, and the reader may assure himself that what I describe is presented faithfully as I saw it. Where I have been compelled to make statements which it was out of my power to verify for myself, I have resorted to the best authorities. Whatever information, therefore, is to be gathered from the book may be relied upon as accurate.

But my chief dependence for conferring novelty and interest upon the work has been by making it a personal narrative. To relate the incidents of travel and to describe men and manners rather than things, has been my object. The book, therefore, necessarily contains much about myself individually, and it has much besides about myself that is not necessary, but which is, I trust, not offensively obtruded. I have occasionally, too, wandered clean away from the main subject; but, as these little excursions are made with the worthy object of relieving the aridity of drier details, they should not be too harshly judged. By proceeding in this way, then, while I am quite sure that I have not made a very instructive book, I permit myself to hope that I have made a reasonably entertaining one.

Though the book is announced specifically as the work of a medical man, the reader need not fear that he will be troubled with much of a professional nature,—with little more, indeed, than brief notices of the claims of such places as are of repute as sanitary resorts.

I am constrained to ask the critical reader to be considerate towards the many faults in the execution of the work, which he will no doubt discover, seeing that it had to be done under pressure of a variety of pursuits not friendly to correct and tasteful composition.

It is my sorrowful office to add here that, while engaged with the last pages of this book, I was called upon to deplore the death of the companion in the journey of which it is the record. He returned from Europe with little, if any, improvement of health, and passed the ensuing winter in Florida,—his sojourn there apparently benefiting him. The amelioration was but transient; he soon grew worse. When the summer came, he went to the Virginia Springs. Worn as he was, yet I scarcely thought when I grasped his fevered hand and looked into his thin face a short while before he set out that it was for the last time. I saw him no more, however. At the Springs he failed rapidly. Exerting his almost exhausted strength he regained his home, where, lingering for a very little while, he died. He had made the preparation of a Christian for the change, and departed in peace of soul and mind and body. So has passed away the friend to whose liberality I am indebted for the opportunity of beholding the scenes I herein attempt to portray, and with the memory of whom all my future recollections of them must be sadly blended.

RICHMOND, VA., May 13th, 1871.

CONTENTS.

CHAPTER I.

Shows why and when the Doctor went forth upon his Travels, and how he got as far as Cuba—Of the Circumstances of his Disembarkation at the City of Havana, and an Account of the Hotel El Telegrafo 9

CHAPTER II.

Exhibits some of the Characteristics of the City of Havana . . 18

CHAPTER III.

Which is Recreational, Ecclesiastical, Sepulchral, and Meteorological 31

CHAPTER IV.

Containing Matter of direful Belligerency relevant to the Great Rebellion in Cuba—Of the Rise and Exaltation of the Voluntaries, and of the astounding Feats of Arms that they performed . . 43

CHAPTER V.

Tells how we plowed the Main from Cuba's Tepid Isle to old Romantic Spain—Our Joys and Woes in transitu, and Portraits of our Partners thereof, with Notes on Things Nautical, Medical, Philological, etc. 56

CHAPTER VI.

Of our Landing in Europe, and of the beggarly Reception we met with—Of the Fonda de America of Cadiz—Of the City of Cadiz—Of its Cathedral—Of the State of Politics in Cadiz, and how the Patriots of that City became involved in Difficulties with the Central Government, and by what Means they gained a happy Issue out of them—Of the fostering of the Tender Passion by the Gaditanos, and of the surpassing Charms of the Cadiz Lad.es . 75

CHAPTER VII.

Containing some Account of Railroad Economics in Spain—Of the City of Seville, the Character of its Inhabitants, and its Commercial Status, Present and Prospective—Of the Cathedral, the Alcazar, the House of Pilate, the Paintings, and the Tobacco Factory, and of the ruined City of Italica 86

CHAPTER VIII.

How we retrace our Steps to Cadiz and go thence to Malaga—How we put up at the Fonda de la Alameda and make awful Discoveries of what is in the Pot—A general Description of Malaga, with the Incidents of our Stay there—How we go from Malaga to Granada and get Experience of Travel by Diligence . . . 100

CHAPTER IX.

Granada—Of the Hotel de Washington Irving, and the Landlord of that Hostel and his all-accomplished Son-in-Law—Of the Alhambra—Of the Generalife 110

CHAPTER X.

Of what other Things are to be seen in Granada, especially the Cathedral and the Carthusian Convent—Of the sociable and edifying Nature of our Indoor Life there—How we returned to Malaga, with the unpropitious Circumstances of the Journey, and how we were comforted on the Way 126

CHAPTER XI.

Of the Steamer Jackal, and of our Voyage in her to the Rock of Gibraltar—Of Gibraltar and its Features, Military and Civil . 136

CHAPTER XII.

How we extended our Observations into Heathenesse, and of the strange Things we there saw 149

CHAPTER XIII.

Of what Manner of Men the Spaniards are, and a Political Prelection concerning the Reconstruction of Spain 166

CHAPTER XIV.

Of our pleasant Voyaging from Gibraltar to Malta—Reflections on the Character of the English People—How I displayed and magnified our Country's Greatness in the Belles-Lettres—How we reached the City of Valetta, with various Matters to its Disparagement 177

CHAPTER XV.

Of the ominous Bark wherein we set sail for Italy, and of a very distressful Accident that happened to me, and of the unrighteous Accusations made against me therein — Of our Transshipment into another Bark, and the fresh Tribulations engendered thereby — how we sped triumphantly past Scylla and Charybdis and got safely to Naples—With brief Descriptions of the Places we saw on our Way 196

CHAPTER XVI.

How we had Difficulty in setting up our Staff in Naples, and of the Place where it was finally set up—Of Naples in its out-of-door Aspects 206

CHAPTER XVII.

Naples within-doors 216

CHAPTER XVIII.

Of sundry noted Places in the Neighborhood of Naples—The Tomb of Virgil—The Lake Agnano—The Grotto of the Dog—The Solfatara—Monte Nuovo—The Grotto of the Sibyl—The Lake Avernus, and the Town of Baiæ—Together with Contributions towards the Biography of a certain ardent Follower of Science . 226

CHAPTER XIX.

Containing the Character of Pliny the Elder, and an Account of the City of Pompeii, Past and Present 244

CHAPTER XX.

How we journeyed to the Eternal City, and of our Besetments and Contentions and Strivings by the Way, and how hard it was to make good our Lodgment therein 257

CHAPTER XXI.

How we strove to do our Duty by the manifold Sights to be seen at Rome, and of the Expert whose Aid we invoked—Containing also an Exposition of the Science and Art of Topography as applied there, with Descriptions of some of the principal Churches, and Notes on the Vatican 271

CHAPTER XXII.

The Relics of the Ancient City 285

CONTENTS.

CHAPTER XXIII.

Of Rome in its Modern Relations; its Squares, Fountains, Picture-Galleries, Palaces, etc.; including Short Disquisitions on Art and Co-tenancy—Of certain Great Rejoicings going on thereat, and a Vision of the Woman of Babylon—Concluding with the Sorrowful Story of good little Santy Tudwolley 297

CHAPTER XXIV.

Relates how we went from the Eternal City to Civita Vecchia by Rail, and how we there took Shipping for Marseilles—Of our Bark, her interior Economy, and how she was navigated to her Port, and the Quality of the Skipper thereof 311

CHAPTER XXV.

A Brief Mention of the City of Marseilles, and how Hostilities broke out between us and the Hotel of Peace—A Cursory View of Paris, interspersed with Episodic Observations upon, first, the Excellences of the Military Law; and second, the Inconveniences of Sunday-Clothes 323

CHAPTER XXVI.

How we went from Paris to Calais, and how we passed over the English Channel with due Observance and landed at Dover—How we went to London—A Cursory View of London, with some Facts that militate against the Assertion that the English are a Nation of Shopkeepers 343

CHAPTER XXVII.

How we set out for Liverpool to embark for America, and of the agreeable Companion we journeyed with—A few Observations on Liverpool—A Glimpse of Ireland, and the Passage Home, with an Account of the Principal Passenger and of my Shipwreck, and the Conclusion of the Volume 357

THE BOOK OF TRAVELS

OF A

DOCTOR OF PHYSIC.

CHAPTER I.

Shows why and when the Doctor went forth upon his Travels, and how he got as far as Cuba—Of the Circumstances of his Disembarkation at the City of Havana, and an Account of the Hotel El Telegrafo.

In the latter part of 1868, a gentleman of Richmond, Virginia, with whom I had been traveling in Minnesota, during the summer, as physician and companion, proposed to me to accompany him on a winter tour. He was suffering from a pulmonary affection, and he intended to visit Florida, Cuba, and Southern Europe, in the hope of deriving benefit from their milder climates. It had long been a darling wish of my heart to see Europe, and I had been three or four times on the point of having the wish gratified, but lawsuits and marriages and other calamities that had befallen friends with whom I had arranged to go, had prevented the execution of the design, and at length the war and its consequences seemed to have destroyed the chance of it altogether.

It will readily be believed, therefore, that I embraced the opportunity now offered with alacrity. I immediately set about making the necessary preparations,—stirring up my debtors with great sharpness, somewhat augmenting the number and importance of my creditors, and bidding adieu to my friends; who, for the most part, transformed what ought to have been a sorrowful scene into one of joy, by ice-cream and oysters, and donations of pocket-handkerchiefs and chewing-tobacco. Surely, nothing can be more soothing than parting from real friends. Blessings on mine, for they are among the best in the world. They have never failed to facilitate my departure, and I hope soon to afford myself the pleasure of parting from them again.

I was without encumbrance of wife or sweetheart or children, to be raising objections and bellowing after me; was disfranchised, and so relieved of all solicitude concerning the welfare of my country; and all my patients, in anticipation of the journey, had been either killed by their diseases or cured by my judicious treatment—except a few old chronics, whose only chance for salvation depended on their never beholding me again. In short, I was ready to go at once, and in condition to stay just as long as it suited the humor of my companion.

On the first of December, then, we set out, and, lingering for a time in Florida, finally embarked at Cedar Keys, in a little tergiversatory steamer with a hard-swearing captain, in which, by slow degrees, we were rolled out of the country. On the last night of the trip the steamer surpassed herself in churning us up. Bilious through and through, I hailed the dawn of the last day of 1868 with feelings of supreme delight; and, rising before the sun, found that we were steaming along the Cuban coast. It was just far enough from us to have itself clothed in a thin veil of haze, and thus veiled presented in the morning light a more picturesque and pleasing sight than if it had been altogether unclouded. The mountains and hills that rise and loom loftily as the land recedes from the sea give it a bold and majestic appearance, while, at the same time, the eye is refreshed by the sight of villages and plantations, which, combined with the tropical fertility that marks the country and the air of prosperity that, whether imaginary or real, is spread over it, endue the prospect with peculiar impressiveness and beauty.

At half-past seven we stood confronting Morro Castle, —having come to a stand-still in obedience to the law of the land, which requires all vessels to stop and undergo examination before being allowed to enter the harbor. A glorious display of bunting got up by the occupants of the castle, which was intended to notify the citizens of Havana of our arrival, ensued; and being found to be all right, as far as could be ascertained at this early stage, we were permitted to proceed. Passing through the narrow throat of the harbor, which is completely commanded by fortifications, we began to sail up the beautiful bay, cheered by blasts of martial music from the castle, in which the ice-horny twang characteristic of much of the music of these parts strikingly predominated. And now came to us, as we moved along, boat after boat, containing all sorts of officials, demanding all sorts of papers and requiring all sorts of information—a part of the excellent system adopted by the Spanish government to facilitate commercial intercourse, and which causes the haven of Havana to rebellow with the blasphemies of tars.

Spanish officials as a class are dreadfully afraid of being overreached, and are especially dubious of Americans—our people having among them a great, though not overgood, reputation for the possession of astonishing acumen. As an instance of their cautiousness, I was told that an American company had proposed to the government of New Granada to catch all the alligators from the Magdalena River gratis, for the sake of their hides—these alligators being of an impudent, homicidal breed that were continually walking out upon land, waylaying and consuming children. But the wise men and counselors of New Granada, pondering deeply upon the proposition, opined that there was more in these hides than met the eye; and considering, further, that the fathers and grandfathers of the young people for generations had been eaten without any notable inconvenience resulting, they declined to accept the offer.

Scrupulous and punctilious at all times, the Cuban authorities were now a hundredfold more vigilant than ever, suspecting everybody and everything; for the rebellion was raging in the inaccessible depths of the island; some battles had been fought between the loyalists and rebels, in which one of the latter was known to be killed, and one of the former admitted to be wounded; and every nation of the earth was believed to be surreptitiously inching its talons thitherward for their engobblement.

In addition to the official boats, bumboats—perfect little floating shops, with fruits, cigars, etc. for sale—also came flocking around; and boats with the hotel-runners, clamorous and pertinacious, with the banners of their respective establishments floating gloriously over them, pursued us indefatigably. Nothing more than verbal communication was allowed to be held with them. A bumboatman, inspired by a respect for law as praiseworthy as it is rare, even declined to pass a pear up to the commander till permission from the authorities should be obtained. The commander refused to ask it with amazing warmth, and went without the pear. Presently the authorities, for their own behoof, called the boats nearer, and got therefrom a most sumptuous repast of oranges and bananas and sardines and wine and cigars, and thus intercourse to this extent was established. An exorbitant number of these officials, enough to watch every hole and corner of the ship, were aboard of us. They were in the uniform of their order, consisting of a Panama hat and long-tailed linen coat with faint blue stripes and black cuff-pieces, and they were men of portly presence and good appetite. Their vigilance was excruciating, and thoroughly disgusted our officers and crew.

In about three hours after dropping a final anchor, the authorities decided that our four passengers had possibly not come there to take the city, and might be allowed to land without bringing irretrievable disaster upon the body-politic. In the mean time, while they were arriving at this conclusion, we employed ourselves in contemplating the scene

The approach to Havana and the view of it from the water is famous the world over for its beauty. The loveliness of its situation, the picturesqueness of its buildings and their strange kind of architecture, make of it at all times a pleasing and interesting sight; while the extreme brilliancy of the morning sun under which we now beheld it threw over all a sort of romantic air which enraptured the eye and engaged the attention, so that even three hours enforced gazing upon it was not altogether intolerable. The harbor is more than two miles in length and wide in proportion, being a paragon of harbors for commodiousness and safety and beauty; its main drawback being that it does not smell good—so I have been told, though candor compels me to say that though I have snuffed at it time after time with great care, I have not been able to detect this fault. The handiwork of man does much to enhance the interest of the scene. The ships of every nation on the globe are seen here packed in masses at the wharves or scattered singly all about the harbor; and as you stand on the deck of your vessel and look around the spirit is refreshed by the sight of a floating dry-dock, several warehouses, the roof of the Tacon Theatre, the opening of the city sewers, an orphan asylum, a hospital, the jail, and fortifications of divers forms in sundry places.

Among the boats my companion had descried that bearing the banner of the Hotel El Telegrafo, and in it the commissioner or interpreter pertaining to that hostelry. The interpreter recognized him simultaneously, or rather a little antecedently; and a joyful recognition it was, for the interpreter remembered that last year he had spent five months in Havana, and a great many dollars among the corps of the Telegrafo. In this boat we embarked and sailed to the passengers' landing-place under the surveillance of a myrmidon of the law.

On reaching the shore we were subjected to the indignity of having to open our trunks with our own hands, and then of having them heartlessly rummaged before our eyes. With feelings of indignation not untinctured with trepidation we saw our dirty clothes turned heels over head, our paper collars finger-marked, the photographs of our beloveds leered at, and my bundle of smoking-tobacco punched through and through in many places. It was demanded of me whether I had letters to any one on the island; to which I returned a negative response. I was also interrogated in Spanish touching my possession of a pistol. Now I had a *revolver* at that moment in the pocket of my overcoat, which was slung over my arm; but I am a poor, diffident creature, and fearing that pistol and revolver might not be transmutable terms in Spanish, I was afraid that I might exhibit my ignorance by producing one when asked for the other, and so responded strictly to the point, disclaiming any such possession. No plunder worth taking being found in our trunks, they were restored to us, and we were then thrust into the clutches of one from whom to escape scathless is impossible.

This is a saucy little functionary, who sits in a cage and presides over the incomings and outgoings of wayfarers, no one being allowed to pass or repass without being lightened for the journey. At the first pop he stole two dollars apiece from us, and then fastened upon our passports; and all the satisfaction we could get was a scrap of trilingual paper called a landing-permit, of which I will merely say that if its Spanish and French are as awfully execrable as its English, it should be used as a gun-wad for the summary execution of the ungrammatical villain who concocted it;—this was all we got for our two dollars, except the information that he intended to have four dollars more out of each of us before we got out of that island. In consideration of these facts, it will excite no wonder in any well-balanced mind to be told that during our sojourn in Cuba we were rankling with rebellion and spent night and day in calling down benedictions upon the rebel cause.

Escaping from the custom-house, we were put into a vehicle by the interpreter and hurried to the hotel, where the entire establishment, from the landlord down to the second assistant cook and bottle-washer, in honor to my companion, turned out to receive us. Great was the rejoicing over us; we were promised the best apartments in the house,—which being, however, at that time in occupation, we were temporarily put into one of the worst; water, soap, and towels were dealt out in profusion; and in due course, renewed, regenerated, and disenthralled, we were taking our ease in our inn.

The Hotel El Telegrafo is situated in the extra-mural portion of the city, opposite the parade-ground; so that the eyes of its guests can be gladdened by the sight of the process of developing the inchoate son of Mars into a perfect man of war; and is hard by the Havana Railroad depot; so that their ears can be easily split by the everlasting howlings that burst from the whistles of the locomotives congregated there—for surely no railroad in all the world doing a like amount of business, nay, doing a hundred times as much, makes a fuss comparable to theirs. Their locomotives are American built, provided with whistles the most disastrous to the auditory apparatus that science has hitherto devised, and they begin to shriek hours before daybreak, which they steadily continue in long, loud, and tremendous blasts till the time arrives to begin again next morning. Could the rebels have captured this railroad and rooted it up it ought to have been a matter for general gratulation, for it is difficult to understand how any real peace can exist while it survives. The hotel is under the dominion of Don Juan Miguel Castañeda, a venerable old fellow, the soul of courtesy—unhappily ignorant of English, but who walks about equipped with an interpreter and looks after the comfort of his patrons;—and woe be to any domestic complained of to Don Juan, for he is incontinently seized and cast out with wrath and violence. Under his management the Telegrafo has got to be esteemed as perhaps the best hotel in Havana. It is kept clean—a thing much to be desired and something rare in Spanish countries. Bedbugs are slain wherever caught, and, marvelous to tell, no flea dared molest us during our stay. The intellect even of our era of enormous mental energy has failed to evolve any more reliable device against mosquitoes than the netting used by the fathers, which enables us in our agony to substitute suffocation for venesection—this is liberally provided by Don Juan, and hence it must be admitted that he has done his duty in this particular also, so that it is by no connivance of his that they sometimes make his house too hot to hold its inmates.

The chambermaids in this hotel are all of the masculine gender. The one presiding over our apartment was a lean African youth of Cimmerian darkness, very attentive and sociable, and seemingly of rebel proclivities in politics, from the zest with which he would shout out *vivas* of Cuban independence in a low voice when he deemed no loyal ear was listening. His name was either Benito or Bonito,—a distinction involving a notable difference; the former signifying Benedict, and consequently being a very judicious and tasty prenomen, while the latter is the Spanish synonym for pretty, and in the present instance could not be applied without arousing in the mind of the recipient, if he possessed a spark of sensibility, the most poignant realization of unworthiness. Being myself somewhat fastidious in philological matters, I considered the subject, and, concluding that Benito was the true appellation, adopted it in my communications with him. My companion, however, who cared not a straw for the niceties of language, but concerned himself only with the æsthetics of elocution, always called him Bonito (or more strictly Bone-eater), this being susceptible of a more emphatic cadence, and so better fitted for exclamatory pronunciation than the other form. Benito was filled with a laudable thirst for knowledge, aspiring to proficiency in the English tongue because of a burning desire to get to the United States,— the great impulse driving him to make this hegira, according to his own declaration, being an unquenchable longing to exercise the elective franchise. His aspiration was encouraged by various guests, who taught him a great many English words, which he learned readily, for he had an eminent genius for philology. But his teachers were mostly of a facetious order of intellect, and, ignoring the refinements of the language, stored him with extremely plain Anglo-Saxon words and idioms, so that I fear me mightily that when he comes to our land and begins conversation upon the model set him by his instructors he will serve to point the apologue of the boys and frogs, realizing that what was sport to them is death to him.

In Havana the custom is for two meals a day—breakfast between nine and ten, dinner from four to six. On rising in the morning the hotel bestows upon you gratis a cup of coffee; at night you can obtain a cup of excellent chocolate, for which you will be charged, unless you

swear that you won't pay for it, when Don Juan will
gracefully strike it from the bill. Between meals ravenous people sit down to a formal lunch; all the lady-
boarders do this — the abstemious content themselves
with an orange, or banana, or a slice of pineapple, these
fruits being kept always set forth in the office for the
public accommodation, where can also be found a chunk
of charcoal glowing in a silver-plated fire-dish, for the
benefit of smokers. The bill of fare is as lengthy and
variegated as any gourmand need wish, but the style of
cookery is rather disappointing. To get vegetables you
must be content to have them fished out of an *olla*, which
is a conglomerate boil of almost every culinary element
in the animal and vegetable kingdoms, from sausage to
cabbage. The dessert is simple, consisting generally of
fruit-jellies, though sometimes you will be furnished with
cakes which are radically defective in what constitutes
cake according to our views of the structure of cakes, and
with a kind of soapsuds pudding which will cause you
to mourn over the misuse of the good things of this
world, and possibly make you overflow with bile. Good
table-wine is provided at every meal, and at the end of
it you can have your coffee. Now, in common with the
generality of my countrymen, I like when breakfasting
to drink my coffee *pari passu* with the mastication of my
food; but the waiter never succeeded in thoroughly comprehending and conforming to this anomaly, and every
morning it required a new and reiterated expression of
my desire to have it respected and obeyed. In justice to
Don Juan's cooks, it is but fair to add that the appetite
is so demoralized by the fierce heat of Havana that the
eater may be easily led to blame his provender when he
should rather denounce his recreant stomach and liver.

CHAPTER II.

Exhibits some of the Characteristics of the City of Havana.

THOUGH it does not cover an inordinate amount of ground, Havana is large in point of population, which numbers near two hundred thousand. A wall of ponderous stones, begun more than two hundred years ago and a hundred years in building, now broken down in many places and going to decay, divides the city into two parts, called respectively the Old City and the New. The former, which borders the bay and is the great business quarter, is a crowded, compactly built, dismal assemblage of houses, permeated by streets narrower than many of the alleys in other cities, which cross at right angles, and from which ascends an aroma of villanous pungency. After looking and smelling around here no one will be surprised that yellow-fever and cholera make terrible ravages among the Habaneros. There is the merest apology for a sidewalk, and, as the streets are generally thronged with passengers and vehicles, pedestrianism is not pleasant. Owing, however, to the urbane willingness of the people to walk in the middle of the street, collisions are not frequent, between passengers, at least; though between passengers and vehicles they are common enough. In a heavy shower the water rolls down these narrow thoroughfares in a sluice, and dogs, babies, and the infirm must get within-doors or be washed away.

The stores, which are very numerous in this quarter, are for the most part sad-looking, disheartening strongholds, with iron gratings over the windows; but they are well supplied with goods of every description; and so accommodating are the shopkeepers, and at the same time such able financiers, that they can sell their merchandise below cost and still realize a handsome profit. Coffee-houses and cigar-stands abound here, and, indeed, are superabundant in every part of the city. Almost every establishment in Havana dependent upon the public patronage solicits it through the medium of some figurative epithet emblazoned on its sign. Thus "The Nymphs" is a dry-goods store; "The Industry" deals in hardware and perfumery; and at "The Elegance" you can obtain old barrels and trash in heterogeneous variety. Some of them are hallowed by scriptural appellations; for instance, I noted "The Resurrection Coffee-house," "The I Am Saloon," and "The Immaculate Conception College for Young Ladies."

In the New City the streets are generally much wider, and the aspect of affairs more lively. This quarter is, however, somewhat hotter than the Old City, from whose streets much of the glare of the sun is kept by the approximation of the houses. But, on the other hand, it is quieter, far better ventilated, and decidedly less high-scented. Stores are numerous here, too, and cheek-by-jole with private residences. Indeed, the commingling of shops and dwellings is the rule all over Havana. There is no fashionable quarter, and it is impossible to judge of one's *ton* by the locality in which he resides. The style of architecture is striking. The prevailing taste is for a building of two stories, very seldom three, and often only one in height, with walls of amazing thickness, doors massive and studded with big-headed bolts, windows with iron gratings of the most substantial pattern, and the whole concern apparently got up expressly to laugh a siege to scorn. The houses are generally large, plain, and hard-looking even to meanness, giving the town a rather depressing air of antiquity. The roof is flat, and frequently adorned with battlements and with ornaments of the minaret or ten-pin species—the officinal designation of which I am not in a position to determine. Over the outer walls is plastered an elaborate coating of stucco, which is daubed with vast flakes of yellow and blue paint or whitewash—commemorative, I suppose, of the gold and azure wherein their old friends the Moors took such rare delight. The street fronts of many of the houses are constructed with arcades, or covered ways,—a thrice-blessed architectural device, for it enables one to promenade the highways to a considerable extent protected from the rays of the sun, which is a matter of the primest importance in this incandescent climate. The proprietor deems it no derogation from the dignity of his mansion to rent out the lower part for shops; and if he owns a horse, the noble animal is provided with apartments in the dwelling along with the rest of the family. There is generally a court inclosed by the building, which is set off by shrubbery, and around it runs line upon line of corridors up to the roof, which itself forms a commodious area for drying clothes. To keep cool seems to be a cardinal aim with the inhabitants, and in constructing their dwellings everything is subordinated to it except the equally strong disposition which every man has to make his house truly his castle. Window-glass is eschewed to a great extent, the floors are tiled, and every means is employed to cajole the breezes to play about the habitation. The combined result of these two motives is that a Havana house may be a very ungainly structure to behold, but yet one of the most agreeable to abide in. To the longing for refrigeration is sacrificed some of the delicate desire for privacy which characterizes the dwellers in temperate climes, so that in many residences the interior of the apartments, bed-chambers inclusive, is left perfectly patent to the public gaze; and many a time in my nightly wanderings have I been privileged, poor, ignorant bachelor that I am, to get an inkling of the mysteries of love-making, and had my soul refreshed with glimpses of domestic joys by beholding, to use the words of an old bard who was a great favorite of mine in my earlier years,—

"The neat little girl a-mending of her clothes,
And the good little boy a-reading of his book."

For the recuperation of the parboiled citizens there are two or three parks. In the Old City there is the Plaza de Armas, fronting the captain-general's palace—shady, but small and rather strongly flavored; having stone benches, which are much used as beds by the weary loafers belonging to this quarter.

In the New City there is a very fine park, called, till

within these latter days, the park of Isabella II., from a statue of that unlucky potentate which adorned it. But one of the first acts of Captain-General Dulce after his landing being to stretch forth his hand and jerk her Majesty up by the roots, it was during my stay in Havana anonymous. The statue was a sweet effigy, with a benignant countenance, into which I used to gaze with a continuous benevolent grin and an occasional wink of respectful admiration; and it was with something of a love-lorn feeling that I passed by one morning and beheld the tracks of the cart-wheels that had borne the old lady away in the silent watches of the night to the lumber-house. I inquired diligently concerning the disposition made of her, but whether she had been preserved intact or been ungallantly ground up into fertilizer I could by no means ascertain. Notwithstanding its bereavement of its statue, a number of fountains, parterres, and shade-trees, with iron benches under them, suffice to make it a most pleasant resort; and every evening it is thronged with the Habaneros, who come to enjoy the agreeable promenade it affords and to listen to the music of the military bands. For their accommodation a public-spirited individual keeps here a multitude of chairs, which he lets at five cents the sit; and seated upon one of them I have again and again solemnly speculated upon the length of time it would take an enterprise of this sort among us to become bankrupt,—allowing, as seems not unreasonable, that the proprietor would incur a deficit of two-thirds of his legitimate revenues nightly by clandestine occupation on the part of his white fellow-citizens, and that in about a week his whole stock would be transmuted into firewood by the men-and-brethren. I loved to linger there in those balmy evenings, where I could sit by the side of the lovely señoritas, and though debarred from converse with them could yet listen to the sweet flow of their beautiful language and to the fascinating crunches of their little teeth upon the peanuts and sugar-candy, which they come down upon with powerful gusto.

As it is too warm to walk with comfort, except in the morning and evening, and as the accommodations for pedestrians are rather of the worst, the custom of riding is almost universal. Accordingly, there is an infinite number of vehicles, which carry passengers about the city at a very cheap rate. They are usually drawn by a little horse of the Cuban breed, which, possessing the same unhappy tendency to immortality that distinguishes our mules, is driven without mercy to the bitter end, which generally comes to him in the bull-ring, where he is at the last sent to participate in the fight and die the death of a hero. The coachmen themselves are identical with those who scourge all the other cities of the earth,— defiers of all laws, human and divine, which they either break to flinders outright, or else hideously warp, to the serious loss and excessive fermentment of their helpless victim.

One class of these vehicles is peculiar, and is certainly a sight most rare and curious to see; it is the *volante*. To obtain a realization of a volante, take the body of a one-horse chaise, beat on it, stamp on it, and pound down on it with rocks and paddles till it is flattened to one-half of its primal height; next attach to it a pair of shafts three times as long at least as any which the most daring intellect among our coach-makers would not shudder to imagine; and then clap on a pair of the largest-sized wheels that can be got for love or money, letting them stick out well to the rear; at the extreme terminus of the shafts hitch your animal; if you can afford the expense, have another animal hitched outside the shafts; and on this one, or, if merciless necessity forbid the team, then on the single one, perch a darkey rigged in boots most gloriously bedaubed with silver-plated medallions and curlycues, and so fearfully and wonderfully made that their tops can readily carry three days' rations—and you will have a critically correct reproduction of the aristocratic turn-out of Havana. Ensconced in this you bounce pleasantly hither and thither like a trap-ball, and can, nay, must in the narrower streets, go straight ahead, for to turn a corner is with them one of the most delicate of manipulations, unless they have all out-doors to do it in. This is the style in which the ladies love to go when they do their shopping, and such is the veneration in which these wonderful contrivances are held that their owners will not degrade them by putting them in a stable or coach-house, but keep them ostentatiously displayed in their front parlors.

A walk through the streets of Havana furnishes one with a good many objects of interest. There is something of excitement in it, too; for the break-neck velocity with which the vehicles are driven along these narrow ways forces the pedestrian to exercise the discernment of the hawk and the agility of the antelope to keep from under their wheels. The drivers are perfectly reckless, and I am convinced that their recklessness is strongly tinctured with malice prepense. I verily believe that they strive to run over the foot-passengers; and in my own case—may confusion confound them for it!—they succeeded. On the very day of my arrival I was cast down and wellnigh destroyed by a volante which bore down upon me with the utmost wrath and violence while I was standing on a corner with my whole heart and soul absorbed in the attempt to decipher a theatre bill. My stock of Spanish objurgations was at that period limited to one which I had picked up on my way over from Florida, of so appalling a character that, as I afterwards learned, no decent person would have uttered it for the world. This objurgation I hurled at the driver with all my strength, whereat he laughed derisively and went thundering on.

In the streets you will see multitudes of venders of multifarious articles, many of them conveying their wares in immense hampers slung over the backs of horses. The kind and quality of their commodities they announce in syllables of dolor lengthily yelled forth of the saddest and most lugubrious cast. From them can be procured everything required to supply the daily wants of a family,—fruits, chickens, eggs, and sugarcane—which last article is sucked in enormous quantities by the citizens. You will also very likely meet with large droves of cows, accompanied by their calves, coming into town to be milked at the doors of their patrons— a plan worthy of all commendation and imitation, since it allows every consumer to water his milk to suit his own taste. Another thing that you will be sure to see, is a long string of horses advancing towards you overwhelmed and almost hidden in extraordinarily voluminous loads of green fodder, giving you a capital idea of how Birnam wood came to Dunsinane; and you will furthermore see a good many clumsy carts drawn by oxen, which will afford you the opportunity of comparing the Cuban method of applying ox-power with ours—their method being to gear the ox so that he pushes with his forehead instead of pulling with his shoulders as with us, and is said to be much the more consonant with the ox's own views on this important matter; while any tardiness of locomotion is forestalled by a substantial stick with a sharp nail in the end of it, which is poked into him with all the fervency and zeal which is uniformly displayed by folks hereabouts when operating on the feelings of their fellow-creatures. You will also be able to realize the immense business that is done in the sale of lottery-tickets. A great many persons gain their livelihood exclusively by peddling these tickets, and you will encounter them everywhere, equipped with great sheets of tickets and a pair of shears, ready to snip off as many as you want.

Lastly, in the survey of the streets, here, there, and everywhere you will be assailed by beggars till you are constrained to believe that if the number of persons engaged in a pursuit furnishes any indication of its prosperousness, mendicancy is one of the most lucrative and desirable avocations that can be followed in Havana.

Along these highways there flows a continuous tide of people with complexions of milk-and-cider mixed in various proportions; every one, with scarcely an exception, smoking a cigar or cigarette, and dressed in costume to suit the climate. Some go in their shirt-tails, and some few without any shirt at all. The ladies' dresses I cannot undertake to describe, being but poorly versed in the technology of the subject, but I observed that they were furnished with the most portentous trails, which sweep the streets effectively as they amble along; and I have often chuckled most self-satisfactorily as I beheld them raking up the hundreds of old cigar-stumps that strew the path, to think I was not a husband or a father compelled to equip them with dry-goods for this purpose. With the most deprecatory deference I would add, after having seen the ladies of Spain, that in my humble judgment the Havana fair ones are demoralized both in dress and looks below the standard of their trans-Atlantic fellow-countrywomen—which, however, I hasten to attribute to the malefic influences exerted upon them by proximity to the United States. On the other hand, by the benefic influences from the same quarter they are moralized in comportment far above them—no winks, blinks, or grins being bestowed upon strange gentlemen out-of-doors (at least, none were bestowed upon me) by a lady of Havana. As far as I could discover—and as a traveler after information I felt it to be my duty to exhaust all reasonable means, such as staring at them till they blushed, and the like, to ascertain the fact—their discretion in public would not shame that of a daughter of the Puritans under the same circumstances.

As for the male element of the population, I think the same influences that have operated against the appearance and improved the morals of the ladies have injured the manners of the other sex. They do not exhibit altogether as much of that lofty courtesy which distinguishes the gentlemen of Spain. Nevertheless, they are extremely polite, offering you anything in their possession that you happen to express an admiration for. I know of no quicker mode for a strict-constructionist to acquire a fortune than by circulating among them, praising their property, and taking them at their word. They cherish many of the other traits that mark the fatherland. They have the national tendency to procrastination, *mañana* (to-morrow) being a word that the stranger soon learns from the everlasting repetition of it. They are the same rigorous believers in the power of the *vis medicatrix naturæ*, by which the hides of men and beasts are in their judgment enabled to withstand an unlimited amount of pounding; and it would be hard to say whether father or son is the more expert in passing off counterfeit money. Among the trading portion of the community there is a profound knowledge of the subtleties of prevarication.

I was assured by one who knew them well, and my own experience bears out the assurance, that in dealing with them the only way to get your rights is to outlie them; if you are a mediocre liar, or, worst of all, if you are a plain sticker to the truth, you have no resource but in their mercy, and their stock of this is small and of poor quality.

Their mode of life in Havana is to stew all day and cool off in the evening by riding or promenading in the parks, or collecting together in the coffee-houses to drench themselves with iced drinks; and as there are no reading-rooms, no Young Men's Christian Associations, and, in fact, scarcely any place at which to spend an evening except the coffee-houses and theatres, these institutions are enormously patronized. The coffee-houses are the great rendezvous for acquaintances and cities of refuge for married men. The people of Havana smoke as incessantly as Vesuvius, every man, many a woman, and nearly every child being a votary of the weed. Their conversation—that of the lower orders, at any rate—is full of strange oaths, some of them awful to think of, and it is the universal habit when it is wished to attract any one's attention, instead of calling out like a Christian, to hiss like a goose.

The most active phase of Havana life, perhaps, is to be viewed in the markets and on the wharf; in other places and under other circumstances the people appear more or less listless, their energy being vaporized out of them by the heat. There was a market-house or bazaar —and a very substantial and commodious structure it was—back of our hotel, in which I was fond of lounging in order to be refreshed by the bustle prevailing there. There was a spacious court inclosed in a quadrangular range of little shops, where all manner of commodities were offered for sale, and in which hat- and shoe-making and other manufacturing pursuits were carried on in all their branches. It pleased me to stand by and contemplate a brother bachelor reasoning with the fire of a Demosthenes for a reduction in the price of a chicken-leg,—a chicken is sold both by wholesale and retail here,—or to observe a father making the family marketing as he bore away his beans, his lottery-tickets, his calendar of saints'-days and drawing-days, his fine-tooth comb, and his fish—all wrapped up in a pocket-handkerchief.

On the wharf it is brisk indeed. It could not be otherwise, for mariners are a fearfully exacting people, and whoever has to work at their behest must do it with all his heart and soul and strength, under penalty, in case of default in the least degree, of being cursed out of his wits, and possibly of being knocked on the head in the bargain. To economize space, the vessels are moored with their bows to the wharf, where they lie packed in crowds. Merchandise of every description is strewed around, and the shouting of the captains and the grunting of the stevedores give special animation to the scene. It is recorded by Mr. Knickerbocker, the historian, that the early Dutch settlers of the New Netherlands were wont to import tiles from Holland. In my investigations about here I discovered that the people of Havana also import tiles. Why they do it I did not ascertain, though I am very sure it is not for lack of dirt to make them with.

To conserve the peace of the city they have a body of police armed with cutlasses. These are rather ferocious in look, but fortunately, perhaps, for the welfare of the public are of somnolent tendencies and pass a good part of their time in nodding. As a rule, in making an arrest their duty is held not to be fully discharged without a few whacks with the cutlass; but they use the flat of it, and, provided the malefactor evinces an aptitude for the reception of wholesome correction by jumping around and bellowing, he may chance to get to the bar of justice unscathed, except by a thorough good paddling. If, however, he show himself sullen and insensitive, they try the edge on him.

As a Southerner, I was naturally interested in noting the condition of the negroes here. It appeared to me that they were treated remarkably well. Before I visited Cuba it was my impression—and doubtless it is that of many Americans—that they were subjected to great hardships and even cruelties; but, as far as I could learn from observation and inquiry, such was not the case. It was even the reverse. They had a great many privileges —some of them very valuable ones—secured by law; more than were granted to the slaves in our Southern States. I know that they walked about unjostled and undisturbed, enjoying unquestioned equally with the whites the right to walk in the middle of the streets and to get run over by carriages. The fact is, the dividing line between white and black on this island is not always to be easily drawn, and the races are consequently placed nearer on an equality than they can practically be with us. As a natural result, the negroes are happy and contented, and will probably remain so till some philanthropist comes along and gives them the fatal information that they have "rights."

The negro men are robust, hearty-looking fellows, and many of the women are positively elephantine with fat; and it is one of the common and striking sights of Havana to see one of these expansive African matrons floundering along the highways with a long-nine stuck in her mouth and rigged out in the height of fashion, with a broad scarf drifting from her shoulders, and a trail whose length has been adjusted in liberal proportion with her own width. It is said that this sublime fatness is due partly to the nourishing juices imbibed in the suction of sugar-cane, but in a far greater degree to the nutrient virtues of dirt-casing,—in proof of which it is affirmed that if the subjects are scoured they dwindle visibly, and if the operation is persisted in they finally perish from a general wasting away. But the most wonderful thing about the colored persons is to hear them speak Spanish. I am aware that travelers before me have marveled to hear the children in France discoursing French so glibly. This is doubtless extremely curious; but to hear a nigger talk Spanish—ah! it is overwhelming!

The 6th of January is an anniversary pregnant with joy to every colored soul, for on that day they are temporarily emancipated; and the result is as if the powers of darkness were all turned loose and the city of Havana is upheaved from its foundations. The day is celebrated firstly as a festival of the church, and secondly to commemorate the overthrow of a mighty African potentate who, as tradition hath it, did long syne lord it abominably over his virtuous and unoffending subjects. Early in the morning, in taking my accustomed airing, I was driven by a shower for shelter into the portico of the Tacon Theatre. Immediately there came upon me a great band of the emancipated, and hemming me in they forthwith struck up one of the national airs of Guinea, with an instrumental accompaniment upon appliances which I had never known before employed to aid the cadences of music's glorious swell. There were horse-hair fiddles and shoe-string bows, sugar-cane fifes, drums made of hollow logs, and an anonymous instrument formed by inclosing pieces of demolished cups and saucers in a shot-bag—the whole reinforced by the ice-horny bugles of their adopted country. The effect of this combination was indescribably grand. Never hitherto had I fully realized the power of a harmony of discords. I began to think I was running crazy. An ingenious idea struck me. I at once began to distribute five-cent pieces liberally, and so precipitated matters, bringing out the worst they could inflict and hurrying it to a crisis; and after enduring ten minutes of inexpressible auditory agony I was allowed to depart. They and their compatriots spent the rest of the day in constant repetitions of these scenes, waylaying and surrounding unhappy passengers in the streets, and dazing them into yielding up their last real, or laying siege to the hotels and harrowing the money out of the pockets of the guests collected in the balconies. Banding together in orchestras, with the like rare instruments to those which I have specified, men and women, with countenances adorned with a handful or two of flour, and rallying round a leader all gloriously bedight with feathers and skins of varmints, voyaged hither and thither through the town, stopping at every propitious spot to chant the songs and perform the dances of their fatherland—giving a woful revelation of humanity when unregenerated by the right of suffrage. Some of them of graver demeanor went about singly, distributing printed papers containing high-strung poetical laudations of their excellent qualities, for which a pecuniary recognition was expected; and others, musical, but respectable and segregate, walked into the stores with bugles and without ado blew so wild and hope-destroying a blast that the inmates wailed forth a beseeching goose-hiss with one accord and cried their mercy with a donative.

Their extravagances on these occasions are endured with great loving-kindness and patience by the citizens, but overmuch joy at times brings some of them within purview of the cutlasses of the police; and on the night of this day I beheld the counterfeit presentment of some puissant Ethiopian original, clad in a royal robe of red and with an ample ruff of turkey feathers round his neck, puffed up into the insanity of arguing a point of municipal law with one of the custodians. In deference to the day, however, the custodian was magnanimous, and merely gave him a thump in the back which would have dislocated the spine of any other than an African magnate, and bade him go home, instead of paddling him off to the calaboose, as he would have done under any less genial circumstances.

In return for the beneficent treatment they experience, the colored people do the citizens a good service by gathering up the cigar-stumps that might else breed a pestilence, and drying, powdering, and consuming them in the shape of cigarettes.

It is generally known that the Coolies form a respectable element in the servile population of Cuba. They are pretty plentiful in Havana. I studied them with considerable interest, and, as the question of Chinese labor has become one of some moment in our own country, I will briefly sum up my observations made upon them in that city. I found them to be a quiet, unobtrusive people, attending to their own business and meddling with nobody else's concerns, walking along the streets with their shirt-tails clean out of their breeches and with their eyes cast down, seemingly profoundly pondering upon what they are engaged in at the time, and maintaining an eagle watch for cigar-stumps, in lust of which they rival them of Africa. Best of all, they abound in the rare and inestimable trait in the character of a servant, unselfish desire to please the master—hanging themselves promptly as soon as they cease to give satisfaction.

CHAPTER III.

Which is Recreational, Ecclesiastical, Sepulchral, and Meteorological.

I HOPE the reader will steadfastly keep in mind the fact that when I travel it is for information. By remembering this he can creditably account for some of my proceedings that might otherwise bear a sinister interpretation. It was this motive that induced me to attend a bull-fight,—not from any approbation of bull-fights *per se*, but because I could not feel that my thirst for knowledge was adequately slaked till I had seen so pronounced a feature of the Spanish civilization. Thanks to the humanizing influences of our own Christian country, where a purer public sentiment has substituted man-fights for bull-fights, the better class of the people of Havana have come to discountenance the national sport, and it is esteemed rather discreditable to be seen at the exhibition. The lower orders, however, still enjoy it with all the zest of the natives of Spain.

It took place on a Sunday, which is the sensational day; bull-fights, cock-fights, operas, and, in fine, all the best things coming off on Sunday—by which and the raising of flags the Sabbath is almost solely reverenced and distinguished from the other six days of the week; for as to shutting up shop, abstaining from secular pursuits, and turning the thoughts heavenward upon the day of rest, it is not the fashion. The announcement stated that "six famous bulls, Yankees and natives of the country," would fight in honor of the volunteers; and the management went on to declare that "it would be ungrateful if it did not say, in view of the legitimate rights proclaimed in this noble land, *Viva España! Viva*

Cuba! Glory to General Dulce!"—a sort of patriotic outburst then dreadfully common, and figuring on every printed thing, from the theatre-bills to an advertisement of a corn-plaster.

My companion, myself, and a general of the armies of the Union, who was a guest with us at the hotel, went together to the Plaza de Toros, where was a large and appreciative audience collected to see the fight, among whom were nearly all the Americans in Havana. Three or four ladies were also present, who, to their honor be it recorded, were soon made sick at the stomach and had to be carried off. The remainder of the assembly was composed mainly of riffraff, inclusive of several of the heroic volunteers, who were very likely dead-heads, and flitted around with their guns slinging about, capped and on the half-cock. According to the published programme, Captain-General Dulce had promised to honor the occasion with his presence, and on his appearance the band was to burst out with the great national hymn of Riego, but he failed to turn up In default of him, therefore, we feasted our eyes on the president of the bull-ring, a respectable-looking, dignified old wretch, who sat in state on his throne, and whose word was law.

The Plaza de Toros is a large amphitheatre, with a fine arena and tiers of seats admirably arranged for seeing. It has no roof, and hence the prices of admission are graded according as you sit on the shady or the sunny side, being one dollar for the former and sixty cents for the latter. There is also a kind of boxes, which are choice places and put at a still higher rate. Finding these very commodious, we usurped and ensconced ourselves in one of them, although we had taken only dollar tickets, and occupied ourselves in scanning and criticising the audience while waiting for the entertainment to begin.

The mode of conducting the performance is about as follows: First, there is a tremendous smash of melody by the band, and while it is riving the ears in sunder the offensive division of the *dramatis personæ*, consisting of villainous-featured men and sorry and sorrowful-looking steeds, enter the arena and perambulate about it to exhibit their good points—forming as damnable a cortége as needs to be beheld; the *matador*, or murderer, availing himself of the occasion to appear before his worship the president of the bull-ring and with the most stately obsequiousness make annunciation to him of the doughty deeds he means to do; the which his worship bids him go and do in gracious phrase, and, presenting him with a sword, dismisses him with a benediction; whereupon the serio-comical cortége files out. Presently there is a blare of a trumpet, and in a bull comes plunging. He goes rearing and ramping around, and is excited to deeds of daring by colored cloths continually flaunted into his eyes. It affords some sport to see him chase the bannermen; but they easily evade him by getting behind the barriers arranged for their protection, and they succor one another by attracting his attention in a new direction by a flirt or two, for he is green enough to allow himself to be diverted from his object in this way. Two or three horses, whose days of usefulness as beasts of burden or of draught have passed away, are now ridden blindfolded into the arena—the aim of their riders being to place them where they can be most commodiously tossed and gored by the bull. And now one of these unfortunate creatures has his bowels jerked out of him with tremendous applause. This is the fun of the thing. In general, the poor horse shows very little emotion. Doubtless, compared with what he has undergone during his lifelong vassalage to the coachmen of this town, a rake with a bull's horn is but a gentle titillation. He knows that " peace waits him on the shores of Acheron," and thither he departs without unnecessary comment. In order to stimulate the bull to put forth more determined efforts, a man goes in front of him and by a dexterous movement inserts a long dart covered with pieces of colored paper into each shoulder. Six of these darts are planted in him before he is done with; and when extra stimulation is required, the darts have fireworks attached to them, which, fizzing and exploding around the bull's head, drive him raving distracted. Great is now the havoc among the horses, and proportionately great is the applause among the enraptured spectators.

The last scene is a single combat between the matador and the bull, in which the man, armed with his sword, essays to kill the animal. Equipped with a colored cloth, the matador draws the bull towards him by waving it in his face, and as he rushes the man nimbly moves aside and at the same time aims the point of the weapon at the vulnerable spot where the head and body unite. His miss-licks excite manifestations of supreme contempt from the assembly, but the successful blow is hailed with deafening acclamations, and the remains of his antagonist are ignominiously dragged off by a pair of gaudily-bedizened mules to the sound of triumphal music and sold for butcher's meat.

At our own entertainment, where "six famous bulls, Yankees and natives," figured, one fought indifferently, two well, and two very well, while one, who was of the Falstaffian breed that esteems discretion to be the better part of valor, would not fight at all. This one was dragged and beat and kicked out laden with the contempt and scorn of an outraged people, and, having saved his pusillanimous beef, no doubt lives to this day, an object of contumely and derision to all high-toned bull-fighters. An old rebel-gray-colored bull performed prodigies of valor, and from the way in which he upset his assailants I had great hopes of seeing the final departure of some of them from amongst us; but, like the brave fellows whose uniform he wore, the superior resources of his enemies were too much for him, and he had to succumb. In especial he uplifted and utterly overthrew one of the devils on horseback, and, having him fixed under the prostrate horse, he did poke him about and stir him up right merrily till his countenance did pale with dismay, and this for a long time despite the furious flaunting of all the banners. He also disarmed and put to flight the matador, who preserved his vitality only by the desperate expedient of falling flat before him and allowing him to pass over rough-shod. In fact, he inflicted such a stigma upon this matador that in obedience to the public voice this puissant performer was dismissed in disgrace and a rival matador appointed in his place, who, knowing the scientific touch, did the business of the rebel bull, and those that came after him, with cleverness and speed. I believe I must acknowledge that at each of these incidents the current of my feelings flowed in unison with that of the citizens there assembled, who would have been pleased above measure had either the horseman or the matador, or both of them, tasted of death. Five or six horses were transferred during the conflict from Havana to another and a better place, and it is with profound regret that I make the additional statement that not a man was seriously injured.

On this occasion a boy about twelve years old (who, if he had been a son of mine, I do assert, should have been spanked with astonishing vim and fury for disgracing his good old father by being in such company) solicited leave to insert a pair of the darts into the shoulders of one of the bulls. This performance, as far as my inexperienced judgment enlightens me, is not inferior in danger to any exploit of the bull-ring, for in executing it it is necessary to stand face to face with the exasperated animal without a weapon or deluding banner, depending for safety solely upon agile movement. The boy accomplished the daring feat most dexterously. Amidst a long, wild, and enthusiastic shout he was caught up in the arms of the people and placed before the president, who greeted him with words of congratulation and commendation, and with much emotion gave him his paternal blessing. A career with so glorious a beginning argues a not less glorious ending, and I do not feel that I am over-confident in predicting that, stimulated by the overwhelming applause he received that day, he will be urged on till he is found worthy to be decorated with the noblest insignia his fraternity can be graced with — the iron bracelets and the collar that fastens with a screw behind.

The audience, on the whole, comported themselves very well. They early established an understanding with the performers, advising them what to do, and cursing them heartily when they failed to do it. They were unsparing critics and ravenous for fireworks, for the application of which they ofttimes clamored when the bull was getting along sufficiently well without them.

The amiable old president conformed to all their wishes as far as he could, making his subordinates torment the bulls to the utmost of their ability and eviscerate as many horses as the management could possibly afford to lose; and in short, did everything in his power to enhance the agreeableness of the occasion.

Although Havana taken as a whole possesses characteristics of great interest to a stranger, there are not very many individual objects of special attractiveness. Among these few the Cathedral is paramount. Its foundations were laid two hundred years ago, and it was carried leisurely along towards completion for near seventy years. It is a large stone structure, of a massive style of architecture, shaped into rude symmetry. Within it looks somewhat desolate and faded, and, like all Catholic cathedrals, is at all times hazy and odorous with the fumes of incense. In the centre of the high altar is a statue of the Immaculate Conception, and around the sides of the church are several altars adorned with religious paintings, before which the faithful can frequently be seen making adoration.

The celebration of high mass in this Cathedral is very pompous—a military band performing the national air being introduced to aid the effect—and the impression it makes is grand and solemn. Every Sunday morning I attended the Cathedral, and, though I had an ulterior object in view in which I was each time disappointed, I was always more than recompensed for any inconvenience incurred in going thither. This Cathedral, like the churches in Europe, lags terribly in the march of progress in the matter of accommodations for worshipers, there being no seats provided. Those who go up to the sanctuary habitually take a piece of carpet or a rug to squat on during their devotions, but straggling sinners who have not had the foresight or opportunity to make this provision must either lean against a pillar or kneel on the cold, hard pavement, at the risk of corns on their knees and rheumatism all through them. This arrangement, however objectionable in other respects, has the crowning advantage at least of affording no facilities for nodding, so that the attention is kept alive from first to last. It would be still more commendable did it have the affect of fixing the attention exclusively upon the services; but the congregation is almost entirely composed of the softer sex,—the men having wofully backslidden, and preferring the cock-pit to the church of Sundays,—and they, instead of steadfastly looking after their salvation, are immensely given to gaping and staring about at their brother-worms—especially at such stray ones as are made conspicuous non-conformists by their ignorance of the formulary:—all of the congregation doing this except the colored element, which seems rapt in an ecstasy, and swerves its eyes not one iota from the fugleman. These tastefully-draped female figures gracefully kneeling here and there, the solemn ceremonial of the altar, the band of priests and children ministering around it, and the music, now soft and touching and again loud and triumphant, form a picture striking and beautiful, seeming as if it were some skillfully composed dramatic tableau.

But, independent of any claim upon the traveler's notice which its religious uses or architectural features may endue it with, the Cathedral has another and a peculiar and sacred interest. To its guardianship are consigned the remains of the great Columbus. To see the place where these relics are deposited was the ulterior object of my visits to which I have above alluded. But, as I have said, I was every time foiled, for I could not get near enough during the services, without elbowing myself into the front rank of the kneeling worshipers and standing there like the chief of sinners towering among the saints. I poked and peered about as much as I decently could, till I perceived that I had come to be looked upon as an idle scoffer,—though, indeed, I was no such base thing,—and finally desisted lest some true believer should mash my nose and black my eyes for an audacious heretic. I tried during the week-days, but the Cathedral was always closed, and I did not know how to proceed to get in. One day, however, I found an intelligent colored brother engaged in whitewashing the walls of the curate's establishment adjoining the church, and to him I imparted my desires with great fluency, having compiled the necessary phrases with much care from the Spanish dictionary. He responded in terms which I was not prepared to hear, and consequently did not comprehend. An agonizing scene ensued. First there were mutual misunderstandings, and then high words passed between us,—for the practice seems to be universal to regard a person to whom the vernacular is unintelligible as somewhat deaf, and in order to put him *en rapport* with the speaker it is thought to be necessary to bawl the words at him. By dint of stupendous intellectual struggles I gathered the information that the church would be opened at *doce y media*—that is, half-past twelve o'clock. As it wanted two hours or more to that time, I spent the intermediate period in prowling about the neighborhood. When the stated hour arrived I again repaired to the Cathedral, but not a door was open. The brother of the whitewash brush was still there, and I went to him with a reproachful look. A dreadful hullabaloo began. The only intelligible inference I could draw from it was that he had told me *dos y media*—half-past two—instead of *doce y media;* but I was too much disgusted by the ambiguity of the Spanish tongue to be disposed to broil in the sun for two hours more, and so returned to my hotel.

But I could not bear to leave America without a sight of the tomb of its immortal discoverer; and so, on the very last day of my stay in Havana, I went again to the Cathedral resolved to get in or perish in the attempt. The doors were shut as usual, but I marched boldly into the curate's house. There was no one there to oppose or to assist me, and I steered my way along with burglarious sagacity until I found a door communicating with the interior of the Cathedral. Through this I passed and beheld a lofty scaffolding on which men were mounted engaged in decorating the church for an approaching holyday, and laughing and talking in a very matter-of-fact and undevout manner. They paid no heed to me, and I walked on, and then at last I stood before the place where rests the sacred dust, and reverentially laid my hands upon the marble tablet that marks it.

The cavity containing the remains is on the left-hand

side of the high altar as you enter from the front, in a
line with the statue of the Immaculate Conception, and
is closed with a slab of white marble about two feet and
a half square, having sculptured upon it a bust of Columbus in a medallion resting upon a quadrangle carved
into various nautical emblems, overlying which is the
following inscription :

> "¡ O restos e imagen del grande Colon,
> Mil siglos durad guardados en la urna
> Y en la remembrancia de nuestra nacion !"

> "O relics and image of the great Columbus,
> A thousand years endure preserved in this urn
> And in the remembrance of our nation !"

The main object of our expedition being to obtain for
my companion the benefit of favorable climates, my
attention was naturally directed somewhat closely to
this subject, and I made some observations which it is
my purpose to briefly present whenever in the course of
this work I shall have to describe our sojourn in any
place of repute as a residence for invalids.

Of the climate of Cuba outside of Havana I know
nothing, for during my stay on the island I remained in
the city—the vexatious police restrictions on travelers,
engendered of the insurrection, and my companion's
assurance, from former experience, that there were no
accommodations fit for a sick man in the interior, damp-
ing any desire for wandering. Havana itself, however,
has a pre-eminent reputation as a winter residence for
consumptives. In my opinion it does not altogether
deserve it. It is generally agreed that the principal
benefit that accrues to a sufferer from this malady by the
change to a warmer climate is from the opportunity
thereby afforded for taking exercise, from which the cold
and inclement weather of his own country debars him.
But excessive heat is as an effectual restrainer upon exercise as excessive cold, and in some respects is the greater
evil of the two, for the latter is susceptible of being mod-
erated by the mere act of exercise itself into a tonic agent,
while it is hard to make by any expedient anything better
than a debilitant of the other. Besides, undue heat en-

feebles the digestive apparatus, the proper performance of whose functions is a matter of the first importance to the consumptive. Now, if at any place we see a man on a scaffold laying bricks with an umbrella hoisted to save himself from sun-stroke in the depth of winter, we have reasonable grounds for inferring that that place is warm—that, in fact, it is quite warm. Such a sight can occasionally be seen in Havana in January. Very early in the morning it is pleasant, but from about nine o'clock till near nightfall whoso perambulates the city, unless he be already kiln-dried, is like to return with an addled head. During this baking-time the heat is tempered by the sea-breeze, which blows from about ten till four. It is soothing, and indeed indispensable, to sit where it can fan you; but sitting and getting fanned all day is not exercise as commonly understood. There is, however, no disposition to take any other kind, nor, if there were, could it be gratified without the adventurer being the worse for it. All this part of the day, therefore, is apt to be wearisome, and if its monotony can be broken at all it must be done not by active but passive means. The arrival of evening is hailed with unequivocal satisfaction, for it brings relief. Nothing can be balmier than these evenings, but their balminess, great as it is, does not compensate a man—unless he be a very lazy one—for the waste of the intervening day.

There is not much more inclination for food than for exercise. Under the demoralizing influence of the heat the stomach gets to be trifling and unreliable, indisposed to take in anything to do, and doing what little it takes in a slovenly manner. I was very seldom blessed with a satisfactory state of hungriness. Even whisky loses its beneficent powers, and instead of acting as the great consoler stirs up bile and inward strife; and, as befell the Ettrick Shepherd with the jaundice, "you begin to hate and be sick o' things that used to be maist delightfu'—sic as the sky, and streams, and hills, and the ee and voice and haun and breast o' woman." Stanch and solid men become infected with a hankering after lollipop, swigging sugar-water, lime-juice, and white-of-egg (which constitute a *panale*)—an indication of a serious depravation of taste. And so, what with very little going into the body and everything capable of evaporation or filtration transpiring and percolating out of it, the sojourner presently finds himself in a wishy-washy, unstable, dish-raggy state, such as bodes no good to an invalid.

The mean winter temperature of Havana, as shown by the thermometer, is 71°. Many persons are misled by this expression of "mean temperature," understanding it as in some degree tantamount to uniform temperature. Nothing can be more erroneous. Sixty degrees in the morning and evening—which would be felt to be unpleasantly cool in Havana—and 93° at noon—which is abominably hot anywhere, will give a mean for the day of 71°; but it is evident that the latter figures furnish an inadequate criterion for judging the character of the temperature of such a day. Seventy-one degrees is a sufficiently genial temperature, but it is very far from representing the real, practicable bearableness of an Havana winter, for during the greater portion of the great majority of days the thermometer will be found to rise very much higher than this. Of inclement weather there is none to hurt. Rain is welcome, for it tends to cool the air and revives the oppressed spirits. After a prolonged shower it was sometimes but little hotter than one of our fourth-of-Julys. I had no experience with the "Northers" which occasionally blow here, and are regarded with abhorrence by sick people.

The following summary of the state of the weather during our stay in Havana will enable the general reader to form some idea of the character of the climate. It is not drawn up with the scientific precision of the meteorologists, and because it is not I flatter myself that it is much less likely to mislead and will prove more serviceable. Out of thirty-one days, seventeen were clear and warm—and when I say warm I mean uncomfortably warm; five were cloudy and warm; one was drizzly and warm; five were cloudy and comparatively pleasant; two were drizzly and mild; and one was cloudy and so cool as to enable me to wear a waistcoat and cravat. During this time there were three good rains in the night, and on one of the cloudy days there was a fine shower, and on two of them heavy rains. Out of the thirty-one days, therefore, there were twenty-three on which it is safe to say that such natural and rational exercise as walking about the city was nugatory as a hygienic resource, or injurious and even dangerous on account of the heat; while the tempting coolness of some of the rest was made unavailable for this purpose by the drizzle on which the coolness itself depended.

Now in justice to the climate of Havana I ought to add that my companion was himself partial to it, and, as he had the advantage of being an invalid, his opinion is entitled to much weight. But, in the first place, he was no enthusiastic admirer of exercise under any circumstances and was abundantly content to do without it altogether; and, in the next, it was manifest to me that he suffered from the heat and its concomitant effects. Besides, it must be borne in mind that there is a salamander sort of people who rejoice in hot weather and thrive in it, and if my companion really felt better in Havana he must have been one of this kind; while, on the other hand, there is a cold-blooded class who cannot abide high temperatures and are exalted in proportion to the downfall of the thermometer—to which class I belong. And this leads me to say that it would be well for an invalid contemplating a journey to Cuba to subject himself to a preliminary self-examination, and if he find that roasting and parboiling agree with him he will be perhaps benefited by going thither; if, on the contrary, these processes stew the grease out of him and render him soft and mushy, it will probably be to his interest to stay away.

In short, then, I dislike Havana as a residence for consumptives because the climate is so hot as to be enervating—destroying the disposition for wholesome exercise and curtailing the opportunities for enjoying it; and because it hinders the nutritive functions of the patient. To Americans it presents other objections independent of sanitary considerations which I need not enlarge upon—such as difference of language and customs, which is a matter of no small import to a sick person. Except in the novelty of its scenes and the animation of a large city, I do not perceive that it offers any advantages over Florida,—and these are points not of paramount hygienic importance,—while in all essential particulars it is, in my opinion, inferior to that State.

CHAPTER IV.

Containing Matter of direful Belligerency relevant to the Great Rebellion in Cuba—Of the Rise and Exaltation of the Voluntaries, and of the astounding Feats of Arms that they performed.

WHILE all the other Spanish-American possessions have torn themselves away from the mother-country and exchanged monarchy for anarchy, Cuba, more wise till recently, firmly retained her allegiance. Faithful among the faithless, her faithfulness was munificently recognized by the bestowal of the proud title of " The Ever-faithful Isle." This is her official designation, and under it she has been robbed and domineered over to this day.

Certain bold and eager spirits, chafed at the idea of being forever the plundered and the oppressed, and very likely desirous of doing a little plundering and oppressing for their own behoof, have from time to time struck a feeble blow for freedom—and then been garroted in the presence, and generally with the approbation, of their fellow-sufferers. And so the ever-faithful isle continued faithfully to allow its citizens to be shoved out of the way for their cousins over the water who were too no-account to be trusted with anything to do at home, and toiled and toiled for dear old broken-down and greedy Spain. I am far from censuring its people for this tame submission, because I am satisfied that for some folks dependence upon even a bad government is better than the best independence they can achieve and manage for themselves. But the revolution in the old country occurring, the general upturning thereby occasioned presented an opportunity to the bold and eager spirits I have mentioned that they could not neglect, and almost simultaneously it was noised abroad in Havana that a band of patriots had raised the standard of revolt in the fastnesses of the Oriental department where nobody could get at them, and were resolved to defend it to the last. The band was swelled by recruits, each one demanding and obtaining an officer's commission, so that in a little while the new organization was one of the most thoroughly officered in the world, and required only private soldiers to assume a decidedly offensive attitude.

And now news was received that the rebels were committing frightful devastations in the interior—smoking up all the cigars and turning the negroes free, who immediately began sucking all the sugar-cane—an occupation in which they take a fiendish delight. The death-blow thus being struck at the main staples of the island, infused prodigious alarm into the authorities and caused them to put forth vehement exertions to avert it. Prayers were offered up, orders were issued to the custom-house and passport officials to let no man enter in or go out of Cuba without making him bitterly regret that he ever undertook it, and many dozens of troops, in detachments one after another, were dispatched to the theatre of war. What the hostile forces did when they met the public never knew till they read it in the New York papers; for news does not circulate freely in Havana, and in order to know what is going on in the city curious persons subscribe to an American journal.

At this juncture Captain-General Lersundi reigned in Cuba. He had been very popular, but being surmised to be an adherent of the expelled queen he was now in less favor with the public. Sudden and radical changes in a government are terrible shocks to office-holders, and it is no more than common charity on such occasions to give them time to cogitate before requiring them to explicitly define their position. It appears that Captain-General Lersundi was not explicit, and hence incurred distrust; but he nevertheless gave evidence of his fidelity to the interests of Spain by doing all in his power to suppress the rebellion. He had, however, more to encounter than he had means to cope with. It demanded all the regulars he had to hunt the rebels and stay the ravage of cigars and sugar-cane; and squad after squad were sent forth to get upon the scene of action, if they could find it, till at last the city itself was left almost defenseless. In this state of affairs, lest the rebels lying dormant in the metropolis should rise triumphantly and take it, he resorted to an expedient which, though frequently adopted, has seldom been found to work altogether satisfactorily—he called for volunteers to protect it. And this was the origin of that formidable organization which afterwards became a very Frankenstein, threatening to destroy those who had evoked it into being. He had invited the wolves to protect the sheep.

To the call of their country the bull-fighters, the deadbeats, the blood-tubs, and the other braves of Havana made a gallant response. They rallied round the flag by hundreds. They were enrolled, rigged out in all the glorious panoply of war brand-new and resplendent, and organized into companies. The parade-ground in front of our hotel was plowed up by the tread of the awkward squad, and the air of the vicinity and the ears of the slumberers thereabouts were vexed every morning before daybreak by the blasts of the shrill bugle. Speeches were made to the volunteers,—or "voluntaries," as they were called in Havana English,—odes were addressed to them, and entertainments given in their honor. Every Sabbath morning they turned out in bulk, in full glory, to be reviewed by the captain-general, and on these occasions the noise of their drums and horns was as terrible as an army with banners. The cynosure of all observers, in soldier clothes and adorned with bees-waxed and sand-papered accoutrements, with the *entrée* to the bull-ring and free liquor, and with all his country's wishes blest, sure nothing could be more delightful and honorable than to be a voluntary.

For a length of time things went on in this peacefully-obstreperous way—the voluntaries for some unexplained reason comporting themselves with much decorum. In the mean while Captain-General Lersundi had been recalled and Dulce appointed in his stead. The latter was long in coming, for though it was of great importance that he should reach Cuba as soon as possible, it was no less important as a point of etiquette that he should zigzag out of his course to partake of dinner with the dignitaries of all the Spanish dependencies he could find on the way. At last he was signaled from the Morro. I went down to the wharf to see him land. His reception, apart from the usual military fuss and flurry, was not demonstrative, for he was not much desired by the people, and was less so when it was known that he had brought with him the bishop nicknamed Pimpernel (or some such thing)—a personage very obnoxious, and who had been banished by Lersundi for refusing to allow that potentate's ears to be tickled by the salutatory pealing of the church-bells in his progresses through the island. Of course the voluntaries were out in full force and feather, as, led by that love of strut and show which is one of the deadly sins of volunteer nature, they would have been all the same to receive my Lord Beelzebub. Artillery thundered, and the banging and clanging of drums and ice-horns will long to be remembered There was a goodly assemblage of spectators, composed almost exclusively of loafers and negroes, who were perched on sugar-hogsheads; and lined the streets. As the procession marched in quick-time past me I uplifted my opera-glass to scrutinize it critically; but just as I had drawn a fair bead on Dulce some supple-jack of a fellow punched one of its eyes out, and I had to devote all the rest of the time to groping for it under the feet of the crowd, so that I missed the best part of the show. However, I saw them carry him to his palace, which was very near by, and there they left him.

Captain-General Dulce immediately issued a proclamation. Its tenor was extremely liberal, apparently. It guaranteed freedom of worship—to Catholics; and liberty of the press on all subjects except prohibited topics. It respectfully asked the rebels to surrender, and wound up with "*Viva España!* Your Captain-General, Dulce." He also straightway instituted some reforms in matters which the lax rule of his predecessor had neglected, to the detriment of the body politic. His principal move in this direction I have already had occasion to mention, —namely, the rooting up of the marble embodiment of her Majesty Isabella II. Besides this great feat, he rechristened certain parks and places whose names savored of the abominations pertaining to royalty. His fair show exalted him a little in the popular favor, and he had a tolerable prospect of a somewhat successful administration.

But in less than three weeks after Captain-General Dulce had assumed the reins of government trouble began to come thick upon him. One night during a performance at the Villanueva Theatre something was said or done that grievously worked up the loyal bile of the voluntaries who happened to be present; and without much preliminary ado they opened fire on nobody in particular but anybody in general. A sort of free-shooting ensued among the audience. Several men were more or less damaged, and a ribbon, said to have been of the rebel colors, was pulled off of a lady's head, and the better part of her hair likewise. A dreadful scene impended, but everybody taking to their heels as fast as they could, it was happily averted.

This incident created tremendous excitement, and the next day the city was in commotion. The voluntaries turned out and paraded the town with screams of "*Viva España!*" till the backs of their coats were soaked through with perspiration. I followed a company of them down to the captain-general's palace, by the side of a warrior whom I took to be the captain's orderly from the big saddle and bridle he lugged on his shoulders, seeking for information but gaining very little. A speech was made to them in the Plaza de Armas, the sentiments of which they applauded with hideous growls of approbation, and then they took a temporary rest and refreshed themselves with bananas and cigarettes.

Upon returning from the Plaza to the hotel I presently beheld a voluntary at the next corner bayoneting a citizen-coachman. This was a most pleasing spectacle, for I had suffered terribly from these coachmen; and so in company with my fellow-guest the general of the United

States army, who had an equal relish for the sight,—he having just before been offered by one of them the alternative of twenty cents over-pay or the city jail,—I hurried down to enjoy the grateful scene. Just at the most interesting part of it up came a body of these same voluntaries and commenced whirling their guns around us as if they were crazy. The general and myself attempted thereupon to go quietly back to our hotel, but were dexterously intercepted by a voluntary, who made dreadful flourishes at us. Now, being notorious for my suavity of deportment and with an antique cotton umbrella in my hand, I do not see how anybody could present a more peaceful and law-abiding appearance than I did, and the general looked to the full as unbelligerent; and so, presuming on this appearance, we continued to go on, when suddenly the voluntary drew his gun from the half to the full cock, and playing the muzzle of it all about our digestive apparatus uttered a series of most ferocious words, of which the only one we could hear distinctly was "*mismo.*" We interpreted this to mean "*mizzle!*"—and mizzle we did, with promptness and dispatch, into an adjacent coffee-house. Our impetuous entrance roused consternation in this quiet retreat, and the inmates, rearing and snorting with terror, shut the doors while we made for a place of safety; and getting at last into the closet where they kept their liquors, we concluded that we could be in no better spot, and remained there till order was restored, when we made the best of our way back to our hotel. As for me, I was mighty circumspect in my movements for the rest of this day; but the general was indiscreet enough to go a-driving in the evening with an American resident-physician, whereby he came to be beset by another voluntary, who treated both of the gentlemen with unparalleled ignominy and contempt—forcing their horse's head back upon his spine till he was in deadly peril of suffocation from the strain on his windpipe, and shocking their modesty to the core by the awfully improper language he used in their presence.

From this time forth was waged a war of extermination between the voluntaries and the patriots in Havana.

It must, I think, be quite refreshing to stand by and see the ruination of a town in which the spectator has no personal interest at stake. The operation itself it has been my fortune to witness more than once, but in every instance my own bodily welfare was so much implicated in what was going on as to rob the scene of its enjoyableness. The contest now inaugurated led me to fancy that this æsthetic spectacle was at length about to be vouchsafed to me; but things were not ripe enough for it, and, after all, I had to go away disappointed.

The tactics adopted by both parties varied from that inculcated in the recognized text-books. The favorite manœuvre of the patriots was for one of them to cock himself on the top of some neutral house, peep over the parapet, and when a voluntary hove in sight to let drive at him, and then tip along the adjoining roofs as fast as his legs could vibrate, and so away. For this proceeding the house was held responsible, and soon the inmates would be astonished to behold the voluntary making for them to satisfy the claims of justice on their unoffending carcasses. And then woe to them; for generally the claims were exacted first and the justice examined (partially) into afterwards. Deplorable would be the nasal venesection and the ocular nigrification, the eradication of hair and the fracturing of teeth; and fortunate was any part of the body susceptible of the reception of a kick that bore not many indelible impressions thereof, and thrice fortunate any corn not irrecoverably shattered by the poundings of gun-stocks. And sometimes, too, on these occasions were done deeds which are not to be spoken lightly of.

As it was thought like enough that there were patriot-guests in our hotel ready to avail themselves of its facilities to slay their enemies in the fashion, Don Juan issued special orders that whoever could be caught at it should be knocked on the head on the spot, and his body thrown out of the window into the faces of the voluntaries as a peace-offering—the great doors being in the mean time shut and barricaded till an explanation could be made and a cartel agreed to.

The voluntaries labored under the disadvantage of

being readily recognized by their uniform, and hence could be killed rationally, systematically, and knowingly; while, on the other hand, all the rest of the community labored under the disadvantage of not having their political complexion so completely unveiled, and hence were apt to be killed without reason, system, or knowledge. In fact, in righting their wrongs, the voluntaries were not overscrupulous *how* they were righted so that they *were* righted; and when shot at were well content if they could shoot at somebody in return, no matter who. Moreover, they were not as perfect marksmen as they may yet become, and when they pulled trigger it usually fared better with the victim than the bystanders. They had, however, the sensitiveness of a first-class shot, and it galled them mightily to fire without effect; consequently their favorite plan was to shoot into a theatre or coffee-house, where there was plenty of people, so that if they missed the man they aimed at they would have the satisfaction of knowing that, at any rate, the bullet had not been thrown away. It soon became pretty well established that non-belligerents were in more danger than any other class of people; and, during the height of the disturbances, for some days you could not poke your nose out of your door without the risk of having it blown off for somebody else's. With all their faults, however, the voluntaries had one trait that savored somewhat of a generous spirit: they always gave a man two chances for his life—to run away or to stand still; and he was allowed to take his choice. If he elected the former, it was held to be the flight of conscious guilt, and they gave him his deserts on the spot; if the latter, he was instantly shot as a contumacious and arrogant rebel, insolently braving the true men.

The row at the Villanueva Theatre occurred on Friday night, and on the Sunday night following the voluntaries took it into their heads to assault the residence of Don Aldama, rebel sympathizer so called, which is almost next door to the Hotel El Telegrafo. The proceeding created a terrible to-do in our neighborhood. The cracking of musketry mingling ominously with patriotic shrieks, and our proximity to the scene threw the hotel into a dreadful state of commotion; for experience had shown that the voluntaries were monstrous uncertain people, and we feared we knew not what would happen to us all. However, we barricaded ourselves in, and felt a measure of hope from the fact that the hotel had furnished no less than six as its quota to these defenders of the country—among whom was our bar-keeper; and it was with feelings of unutterable relief that our party remembered that we had only the day before bought a bottle of his Schiedam schnapps on trust, and so might count on his protection. Some of the boldest essayed to reconnoitre from the windows, but the whiz of bullets past their heads caused them to jerk themselves in and close the blinds speedily; and in the mean time the hotel corps mostly stampeded for the house-top. Among them I encountered our chambermaid Benito making off, his eyes gone clean out of sight and his black countenance almost reconstructed on a white basis; and I did what I could to augment his nimbleness by reminding him of the aid and comfort he had given the rebels by his *vivas* for Cuban independence. One of the corps, Leon by name, our waiter at table, who was in the habit of ever and anon solacing himself surreptitiously with what he called a "yin-cocktl," had glided to a neighboring coffee-house to partake of a glass of his favorite mixture just previous to the inception of the fray, and got back in the nick of time to see the doors slammed to. His petitions for admission were absolutely unheeded,—as would very likely have been Don Juan's himself under the same circumstances,—and Leon had nothing to do for it but to dodge among the columns of the arcade and bear the brunt as best he might till hostilities ceased.

The firing gradually died away, the shrieks became fewer and hoarser, and all was thought to be over, when there came a furious knocking at the gates. The stampede for the house-top was now wellnigh universal, scarcely any one remaining below except a brave lady who had been bedridden for some months, and who doggedly held her ground. At last the knocking assumed such an imperative tone that enough courage was collected from the crowd to open the door. To our great joy the knocker proved to be our own voluntary barkeeper, who, wearied with the toils and glutted with the honors of war, had temporarily withdrawn from the field to repose upon his laurels and smoke a peaceful cigar.

The storm being now much abated, we ventured to go a little distance into the street. There I met Leon murmuring at the way of the world in shutting its doors upon friends in adversity, and presently beheld a spectacle that moved me with sorrow and indignation. It was a son of genius, a light of intellect, in captivity. In other words, a reporter for the papers had been taken up. The offense charged upon him was that he had construed Captain-General Dulce's proclamation of liberty of the press too literally, and had taken the liberty to publish his opinion of the voluntaries, which was one in which the admiration they were wont to hear expressed for their excellent traits was something tempered down. He was the spoil of one of the littlest in physical proportions of the honorable body so wantonly traduced—little, indeed, but a nice little man, as I opine from the stalactitical ornamentations about his nose, which showed that, though too little to be intrusted by his ma with the responsibilities of a pocket-handkerchief, he was entirely too neat to use his coat-sleeve as a succedaneum. It was with heartfelt pride that I listened to my literary brother as he looked down upon the upturned dirty nose of his diminutive captor and defended himself from the accusation—which he did with admirable volubility and a multitude of multifarious gestures. Nothing could be a more potent tribute to the power of humane letters than to see the frame of the hardened little voluntary quivering under the effort to suppress the sniffles aroused by my brother's eloquence. Though I understood never a word of his fluent argument, I felt that it must be irresistible, and so was not surprised when assured by our interpreter that he had cogently and conclusively exculpated himself from all responsibility for the political complexion of his paper, inasmuch as his functions were confined to the purely literary departments of market reports, marine bulletin, and belles-lettres.

Incredibly difficult as it was to do, he succeeded in convincing even the reluctant voluntary of his innocence; and he was, accordingly, allowed to go scot-free—except that his revolver was retained as some compensation for the fruitless trouble to which he had put the conservator of the peace in the investigation of his case:—a very judicious termination of the affair, which no American can reasonably criticise, since its analogue is performed in our courts every day of the year. Forsooth, I myself am intimately cognizant of one such analogue that was adjudicated by the wonderfully exemplary municipality of Lastditch, in which town a worthy dray-driver was arrested on a false charge while pursuing his avocation in the streets, and he and his horse and his dray were all incarcerated therefor, being kept in prison for a night and part of a day; but the next morning, his innocence being made as clear as the noonday sun, he was promptly given his liberty—the which, however, he could by no means compass till he had made satisfaction to the uttermost farthing to the municipality for its provident care in the warehousing of his vehicle and the stabulation of his beast.

We remained in the street before the hotel for some time, when a gentleman came up having a pistol in his hand, which he was good enough to hold right to our eyes so as to satisfy any curiosity we felt respecting its pattern and calibre—at the same time requesting us to be so obliging as to go in the house. To show that we reciprocated his courtesy, we complied with his request on the spot, went in, closed the doors imperviously, and retired to our slumbers, from which we were roused off and on through the night by an occasional volley or howl.

By the blessing of St. Jago, our hotel had escaped a visitation; but on that same night the Louvre Coffeehouse, one of the finest and most frequented in the city, was fired into by a squad of these very singular troops while it was full of innocent and unsuspecting people, and several of them killed and wounded. From all I could hear this was a most dastardly and wanton outrage, and but for the despicable deficiency of the murderers in marksmanship the slaughter would have been much greater than it was.

Early the next morning I sallied forth to note the result of the night's proceedings. I fully expected to see Don Aldama's house battered to pieces and every pane of glass in it shivered; for the voluntaries must have fired upwards of a thousand shots at it, and it is the largest residence in the city, occupying an entire square; so that I know that, even with my limited acquaintance with algebra and geometry, I can demonstrate to a certainty that a man firing at it cannot miss it even if he tries. And yet not a pane of window-glass was broken, and the sole result of this grand fusillade was four or five bullet-marks on the wall, and the slaughter of one horse, who had been slain in the streets by a stray ball. A policeman was also seen lying dead that night in the parade-ground opposite, but as he had walked away by morning it was supposed that he was only dead-drunk. The marksmanship displayed on this occasion, so far as I know, has never been paralleled.

But though the outside of Don Aldama's mansion thus miraculously escaped, it was not so with the inside. The intrepid assailants kept up their efforts unflaggingly till they had put the porter to flight, and then breaking through all opposition which nobody else made, effected an entrance. At once they proceeded to wean back the affections of Aldama's rebellious heart to their allegiance by processes which have been in much vogue with the truly loyal in every age and country. To save him from being further bewitched by the siren notes of rebellion they demolished his pianos;—to prevent him from indulging in treasonable reflections they smashed his looking-glasses. His costly furniture, his noble pictures, things precious and beautiful that he had collected to adorn his home—all these they broke in pieces, they ripped in tatters, they ground to powder. His household gods they overturned and trampled in the dust—and did it all with that zeal and brutishness which men display from whose breasts a mythic patriotism has crowded out the real humanity; for, believe me, my reader, love of country, even when pure and unselfish, is not so noble

as the love of man; and your own heart will tell you, if
it is an uncorrupted one, that an entire patriot—one of
the Brutus stamp, who can deliberately murder his child
or despoil or slay his fellow-men for no other reason than
to show his patriotism—is rather a monster to be denounced than a paragon to be imitated. And so these
lovers of their country destroyed Don Aldama's property
in such quantities and in such modes as must needs con-
strain him, if he spoke his honest sentiments, to acknowledge that the government he had striven to get rid of, if
not the best government he had ever seen, was a confounded sight better than the one he had got for himself
in its stead.

From this time forth till we quitted the island the
voluntaries maintained their exaltation. They wandered
over the town establishing the true political faith with a
zeal and unction which was increased instead of being
diminished by the fact that every day or so some of them
suffered martyrdom at the hands of the infidels. Chock-
full of patriotism and aguardiente, they inflicted a great
many kicks and cuffs on the men and outrages of various
kinds on the women—the most common of which was
the enforcing of both matrons and maids to shout *Viva
España!* The intrinsic perversity of the female temperament often made matters worse for the fair victims
than they might have been, for they were very contumacious in refusing to shout when bid. The consequence
was that they got themselves caught round the neck and
squeezed till the loyal watchword was choked out of
them. Exploits like these brought the voluntaries to be
considered something of a nuisance, and a strong desire
was expressed that they would please to resign. The
theatres were closed, cock-fights and bull-fights suspended, and people, both strangers and citizens, were
leaving by every opportunity. In this condition of
affairs the captain-general resorted to the measure of
rebuking the voluntaries severely for their performances;
in return for which he was cursed most heartily and be-
spattered profusely with the pungent appellations peculiar
to the lower order of Spaniards. He now discovered that
he had no control over them, and endeavored to supplant

them by calling around him the marines and what regulars he could—for which the voluntaries threatened to kill him. It was shrewdly surmised by certain long-headed oracles that the royalist Lersundi had cunningly organized these voluntaries for the express purpose of bedeviling his liberal successor. Whether this was so or no, it is certain that Captain-General Dulce was powerfully perplexed, not to say terrified, by them, and his tribulations were still accumulating when we took our departure.

Since then General Dulce has obtained his recall, and has died: I believe him to have been a very fair-minded and lenient officer, but his administration must have proved anything but pleasant to himself, and appears to have afforded very little satisfaction to anybody else. He thought to govern by reason a people who can appreciate nothing but force; and offended by his lenity a community which sets bulls afire, horns out the insides of horses, and stirs up oxen with a sharp nail. With the further proceedings of the voluntaries and the progress of the revolution since his day my readers are, doubtless, as familiar as I am myself.

CHAPTER V.

Tells how we plowed the Main from Cuba's tepid Isle to old romantic Spain —Our Joys and Woes in transitu, and Portraits of our Partners thereof, with Notes on Things Nautical, Medical, Philological, etc.

IN the midst of the glory of the voluntaries and the tribulation of Captain-General Dulce we packed our trunks and left. By this time scarcely an American sojourner remained in Havana, and when we bade Don Juan Castañeda good-by it was with an emotion of sorrow for the amiable old landlord, as we thought that the goodly stream from which came so great a part of his nourishment was so completely dried up We had taken passage in the Spanish mail-steamer née "Prince Alfonso," but now "Guipuzcoa,"—the metamorphosis of her name being due to the disrepute into which her namesake had fallen in consequence of the casting out of his mother the Queen Isabel,—and on board of her we departed on the 30th of January, bound for Cadiz.

A departure for the old country is an event of great interest to the provincials, and a large concourse of the citizens of Havana, composed mainly of those of low degree, boatmen, wharf-rats, and the like, assembled to give us the benefit of their benediction on our momentous adventure. The ship was surrounded by boats bringing off baggage and passengers, and there was great bustle and animation both inside and outside of the vessel. The friends of the passengers were out in force, many of whom graced the neighboring housetops, whence they waved their handkerchiefs with zeal and vigor; and I was especially struck with one who, his abounding love being too vast to be encompassed in any handkerchief, had provided himself with a sheet or table-cloth, and from his high pinnacle wafted his good wishes after us in volumes. Our company kept their eyes on the shore and reciprocated all these friendly signals heartily, but as for ourselves, having been skinned to the utmost possible limit during our sojourn in the city, we were pretty sure that there was no one present interested in our further welfare, and so we gazed upon the scene with much composure.

At length, when the sun was getting ready to set and we feared that in obedience to the regulations of the port we should have to remain inside the harbor all night, the multifarious formalities necessary to make a valid departure from these coasts were finished up and we started. We fired a gun—the Spanish war-vessel by which we passed lowered her flags in honor to us, or because it was sunset and she wanted to get them out of the dew; we screamed and waved adieus to those on shore, and the populace shrieked and heaved them back to us as we moved along. Spanish navigators consider the tender impulses of humanity on these occasions. To an American or English captain leave-takings are foolishness, and one of them would have cracked on a full head of steam and jerked the tender ties that bound us to those we were leaving behind in two with a snap. But the captain of the Guipuzcoa steamed away slowly and gently, so that we enjoyed the luxury of grief with some comfort and satisfaction. Presently we passed through the throat of the harbor by the Morro, which treated us with silent contempt,—the sentinel not even presenting arms,—and then we were out on the great ocean.

No man that is not more stolid than a chopping-block can see himself thus cast loose from terra firma without some emotion, and many feel a good deal of it, and they who are blessed with the gifts of rhetoric wax eloquently sentimental under it. I have read some dozens of affectingly lugubrious adieus to my native land—most of them inspired by the sinking of the Neversink sand-hills. To the sad souls who penned these farewell tributes, if it be any consolation to them to know it, I can give the assurance that the same feelings are engendered by the disappearance of the Cuban coast as the bark is bearing the voyager away to Europe—the same in kind, but differing in degree. I was affected as America faded from my view; but I forbear to describe what I felt, because everybody who has a book of trans-Atlantic travel has already read an account of the attending psychological phenomena, drawn up by one of the gifted ones just mentioned, and because I was not as much affected as I could have wished, for my sensibility had received its great shock, and been nearly exhausted by it, some time before, at the outer gates of Richmond. It is very comforting to know that the reaction from this state of depression is generally very quick, sudden, and complete. The gleam from the lighthouse on the shore, which was still plainly visible when we retired for the night, solaced us with the feeling that we were not yet quite cut off from communion with our fellow-men, but in the morning all signs of land were gone, and it was as if we were alone in the world.

The Guipuzcoa was a fine, English-built, iron propeller. She was constructed with the view to carrying the largest possible number of passengers, and hence the state-rooms, so far as snug is synonymous with small and close, were of the snuggest description. As a favor, we two had been given one intended to accommodate four persons, with the understanding that in case of a press of passengers we were to receive two more in it. Had they come we must have died. The ship was officered altogether by Spaniards, except that the engineers were Scotchmen—the owners having doubts of the trustworthiness of their fellow-countrymen in matters of steam. A great many attempts, by the way, have been made to inculcate into the minds of Spanish youths a knowledge of the mysteries of this subtle vapor, so as to qualify them to act as engineers. They are painstaking and circumspect while in subordination to their instructors, giving promise of much usefulness in their day and generation, but become tremendously inflated by the dignity of their position when put in absolute command of an engine. With the lofty spirit of their nation, they have a contempt for the servile duties of turning gauge-cocks and the like, which they were forced to perform during their novitiate, and in full belief that the engine is overawed by the grandeur of their presence they sit in majestic state before it and let it work on in blind obedience till they are blown up—whereat they are mightily astonished, not at the magnitude of the display, but at the unheard-of effrontery of the thing.

The captain of the Guipuzcoa was rather a little man, utterly dried up and weather-beaten, and circled amongst us covered with a navy-cap whose top was voluminous and with all the stiffening gone, and whose leather front exactly coincided with his forehead at every point. This was his sea costume, but he was afterwards pointed out to me in Cadiz arrayed in a stove-pipe hat and a dress-coat, by which he was transmogrified beyond recognition. As our acquaintance with him ripened he developed some strange peculiarities and traits of character. The first mate was no less dried up and weather-beaten than the captain, but was mainly noticeable for the familiarity with English which he professed. I had a conversation with him nearly every day when they were getting ready to take their observation of the sun, but all I was ever able to draw out of him was, "Ain't they pretty?"—

referring to the girls aboard—and "mus' go git my sexton. Good-by."

On the morning of the first day out, which was the Sabbath, there were dragged forth from a special closet labeled "*Armeria*," an altar, some cloths, candlesticks, a crucifix, etc., which being set up and arranged in due form in the saloon, mass was celebrated by the ship's padre. The day was a lovely one, and it was spent by the passengers on the upper deck, where they sunned and aired themselves with prodigious gusto. In conformity with a custom of many sapient sea-going folk, most of them had brought their own chairs on board with them, expecting great comfort and advantage from the incumbrance, and they now sat and lolled in supreme bliss; but, as is not uncommon in ocean voyages, the sittings they were then enjoying were almost the only ones they were able to get out of these appliances till they arrived in Europe, for we soon fell into difficulties which caused the chairs to be stowed away in a sort of caboose among certain parrots who were hung up there in tin cages. These parrots were members of the household of some of our passengers and were going along with the rest of the family to the old country. They spoke Spanish fluently and with as much accuracy as even I did myself, and made a great many remarks suggested by the novelty of the situation in which they found themselves. In the course of the day we were refreshed by a glimpse of land, being the island of Nassau, and saw an object floating in the distance bearing a suspicious resemblance to a raft and giving rise to melancholy surmises.

We numbered some seventy or eighty persons, comprising several ladies and children. During the day, in default of anything better to do, I endeavored to ingratiate myself with the parents by teaching two or three babies to say *Viva España!*—my Cuban experience leading me to believe that it was a bit of erudition not unlikely to stand them in good stead thereafter. While I thus trained their intellects, the colored youth who officiated as nurse to them took like heed to their bodies; and in order to prepare them for one of the great objects of their future career he inured them to tobacco by distending his cheeks with the fumes of cigars of quality more awful than any of our oak-leafs, applying his mouth to theirs, and inflating them with smoke till it was a draw whether they would strangle or burst. Contemplating his proceedings for a long time, it struck me that he engaged in them with more relish than trainers of youth are wont to have for their labors, and then I became overwhelmed with the most serious doubts whether he were actuated by the motives for their physical improvement I had attributed to him. In fact, I was convinced he was doing it for the fun of it—that he was perpetrating a joke of the kind called practical upon them—a species of amusement which the wise and good of all ages have frowned upon as being one of the most reprehensible in which our poor, fallen race can indulge.

Though but remotely pertinent to the matter in hand, I am moved to relate here a matter which may prove of benefit to some of my readers—for I am one of them that love to do good, and do not shirk doing it out of season as well as in. What I am going to tell may be depended upon as being absolutely true in all essential particulars.

At one period it befell that a startling mystery overshadowed the citizens of the goodly and enlightened town of Lastditch. Divers sober and discreet persons reported that in passing their ways by night they had beheld in the churchyard of St. Sepulchre's a sheeted ghost wandering among the tombs and gibbering on the walls—most awful for to see. These reports worked up the people mightily. All who were constrained to go by St. Sepulchre's did so terror-stricken and sore dismayed, and all who could turn aside therefrom turned far aside. Thus it went on for a space of time—the papers publishing authentic narratives of eye-witnesses and the people agape with wonder. One night Josiah Goodaig, a citizen of courage and vigor, either by reason of inadvertence or necessity was wending by the haunted ground. Just as he reached the corner of the wall up rose the spectrum, all in white, and gibbering before him—most awful for to see. Josiah Goodaig crouched to the earth with fear and all his courage collected in his finger-ends, near which there chanced to be half of a brick; and so, naturally, this he clutched, and leaping up heaved it with all his might at the spectrum—whereat the spectrum evanished, and Josiah Goodaig fled for life.

Now in Lastditch dwelt a roisterly, joyous youth, and Emmanuel Funniman was his name. There was also a hospital therein, styled the Hospital of the Assassination. From the case-book of that institution I transcribe the following entry:

Name of Patient.	Complaint.	Exciting Cause.	Predisposing Cause.	Treatment.
Emmanuel Funniman.	Side caved in.	Brickbat.	Usurpation of the ghostly office and prerogatives.	Bleeding, cupp g, leeching, blistering, lancing, padding, splinting, bandaging, purgation, salivation, starvation, etc. (not space enough on the line for all of it).

In the course of time Emmanuel was restored to his originally fine physical condition, except that he had a considerable dent in his side and was a litle curved both antero-posteriorly and laterally, and regained his roisterly and joyous frame of mind—only he confined the manifestation of it to verbal expressions, and except at a change of the weather, when he would complain of a sensation of pins and needles in the hollow of the dent and look grum and downcast. He is still frequently to be seen on the streets of Lastditch, and can, if he is so minded, substantiate the facts here related—though, in sooth, he is singularly averse to any mention of the subject.

Let a note be made of this case by all concerned. Of a verity it is pregnant with good for somebody.

In the night following this lovely Sabbath-day the weather changed. The wind freshened and the sea roughened, and this state of things continued to grow worse for the next three days, when it became downright tempestuous. And now, in the words of an old nautical bard,—

"How stormy the winds did blow,
And the ragin' seas did flow !
You'd see the old tars go a-tippin' to the top,
And the landsmen a-layin' down below."

Our craft rolled about terribly. It was impossible to move around, except by the performance of a series of difficult and startling acrobatic feats, while to remain still subjected us to submersion and saturation by the huge waves that ever and anon surged over us. To eat with any satisfaction was out of the question. Plates of garlic soup, decanters of dreadfully mean wine, and pots of scalding hot and highly-colored coffee were constantly capsizing into our laps, and our very bread would be snatched out of our mouths. The poor waiters, obliged to balance the store of solid and liquid victual they bore in their hands, were kept posturing equal to any gymnasts. Plates and dishes and cups and saucers perished by the score. On one occasion a car, used to convey these articles from the saloon to the kitchen, loaded to its maximum, broke from its moorings and demolished its contents with a crash which for a moment led us to believe that of a surety our hour had come. At every roll of the vessel the children bawled with terror, and their yells mingling with the howling of the tempest and the smash of crockery combined to form a scene of appalling grandeur.

During these dreadful days the majority of the passengers reposed themselves below in their berths till the catastrophe of the crockery-box scared them up, when they ranged themselves on the seats on the opposite sides of the cabin, where the confronting rows looked at each other ominously as the one see-sawed away down and the other see-sawed away up. A few only who were men of proof gathered round the social board, and at times a meal had to be pretermitted altogether on account of the impossibility of making the table stay set. The parrots in their caboose grew extremely thoughtful, shook their heads, and said never a word.

To augment the horrors of our situation, that direful malady the sea-sickness broke out amongst us, and such was its malignancy that in less than two days it was epidemic, and nearly every soul of us was laid low by it. I myself had some of its premonitory symptoms. My appetite was taken from me, and from time to time it gave fearful admonitions that it was disposed to "go back" on me and deprive me of my former acquisitions; but by judiciously taking an occasional ounce or so of preventive I was enabled not only to come off with my withers unwrung, but even to triumph superabundantly over the miserable retchers who strewed the ship from stem to stern. Few things afford more heartfelt joy than is experienced by a disinterested spectator as he looks upon a victim of this fell disease in full agony, or as he notes the ghastly subterfuges and evasions by which some strong-minded but weak-stomached sufferer struggles to conceal the fact that the enemy's grip is heavy upon his vitals. All this I enjoyed, but somewhat to my discomfort, nevertheless; for the sounds of their woe ascended continually, disturbing my meditations by day, and, in conjunction with the shaking I got in my berth, effectually breaking up my rest at night; and, moreover, before the epidemic disappeared, the vessel was in little better plight than a pig-pen ravaged by hog-cholera. Fortunately for our sanitary condition a hogshead or two of water would now and then surge down below, washing us out and saving us from an otherwise inevitable quarantine, though at the expense of moist beds and of exhalations whose like have not been smelt since the demolition of the Augean stables.

Among our company was the secretary to my lord the Bishop of Cuba—a pale and delicate-looking gentleman with a melancholy shade upon his face and a black skull-cap upon his head, sent out, peradventure, for recreation and relaxation. But, God wot, of recreation gat he manifold little, though of relaxation he was favored with exceeding overmuch abundance. He was one of the very first as well as the very last victims of the pestilence. He could play excellently well both at cards and on the piano, and during the brief spell of fair weather he played in both capacities to the satisfaction of all concerned. But when the wind began to blow and the sea to flow he was played out. He threw up his cards, and he threw up his whole stock of eatables, and, with the co-operation of the garlic soup which was prescribed to him as a stomachic, it really appeared as if he would throw up every movable thing within him. His was about the worst case I ever had the pleasure of seeing, and I confess that I felt some compassion for him. He had a tendency towards reaction, and at one time rallied sufficiently even to preach us a sermon and to resume his hand at cards; but he was fearfully prone to relapse, and his last state was apt to be as bad as his first. The tenor of the discourse which he preached, as far as I was able to gather it, was that he who is brought low shall be exalted; and he was himself a pregnant commentary upon it, for since none of us had been brought lower than he had, so none of us were by any means so completely "gone up."

Another conspicuous victim was the youthful colored nurse. Retribution came upon him swift and dire for his horrible inflation of the innocents, for he was among the first and worst who were prostrated by the malady; and it was with such satisfaction as the immaculate experience when justice overtakes the guilty that I beheld him on his knees, with the tip of his spinal column and the appurtenances thereunto belonging raised at an angle of forty-five degrees, and his head poked through a hawse-hole, at the point of death. Providence was gracious to him, and he rallied enough to tumble down below, where he remained till near the close of the voyage; and there, in the course of my wanderings about the ship, I occasionally saw him, in his master's stateroom in the midst of the household,—who, sad to say, were but little less afflicted than himself,—sore cast down, with his face in a basin; and sometimes I passed him tottering and tumbling along, looking like an African spectre, gaunt and ghastly, and weary of the world.

Far be from me the presumption of criticising in a matter whereof I know little, but it appeared to me that the navigation of the ship was conducted without all of the advantages afforded by the modern improvements in the art. Every clear morning the mariners on the Guipuzcoa sighted the sun as it rose and marked a line with a lead-pencil on the compass-box; and sometimes made some sort of devices on their shirt-sleeves. These schemes were intended to circumvent the compass, which—in consequence of the variation (which is great in some parts of this course), and because the ship was of iron, and the captain had never allowed himself to be bothered by such nonsense as having his instruments tested and corrected—was disposed to point in any direction that suited its convenience; but by the aid of these marks, in some mysterious manner, they were enabled to navigate the vessel in full confidence and in bold defiance of the magnetic needle. They were also constantly tinkering with their sextants—showing that there was likewise something wrong with this important part of a navigator's armamentarium—screwing and unscrewing them, and blowing into them, and shaking them up to make them work. Howbeit, taking such observations as happened to turn up and steering by compass-box and shirt-sleeves, on we went.

During the second week the weather improved greatly and we had a much more agreeable time than we had been spending hitherto. The invalids came out of their beds, the parrots grew delightfully chatty, and the meals had something like justice done to them. We had unfortunately come away from Havana without our cook, who happened to be ashore when we left; but a deputy was sworn into office in his stead, who discharged the functions of it very acceptably. Breakfast was served at half-past nine o'clock. At this repast we had fish, oranges, kidneys, raisins, beefsteak, bananas, peppermint-drops, sugar-cakes, Catalan wine, tripe, and many other good things—the meal being usually prefaced with garlic soup. At one we had lunch, consisting of lemonade made of rotten oranges, and emulsion of almonds flavored with prussic acid. At half-past four came dinner, which was much the same as breakfast, except that boiled and baked were substituted for fried; and at half-past eight we had tea, coffee, and chocolate, with biscuits made of a porous texture to adapt them for sucking up the fluids.

It so chanced that the Lenten season began while we were still in mid-ocean; but after the effectual cleaning out we had been subjected to by the sea-sickness there was small disposition to its due observance—the company sheltering themselves behind that merciful dispensation of the church which grants to the traveler a large discretion in the matter of eating; and this, too, despite the sermon of the secretary of my lord the bishop delivered on Ash-Wednesday, in which he inculcated abstinence with great earnestness and painted its blessings in glowing colors. He himself, I must state to his credit, followed the precepts he laid down to the letter, observing the appointed fastings with rigor—being much encouraged in the performance of this pious duty by the circumstance that for his soul he could not keep a mouthful of food on his stomach.

The day and nearly all the night was passed by the majority of the gentlemen in playing cards, and generally for money. Their cards were of an outlandish pattern, being figured with swords, cups, etc., instead of the devices with which we are beguiled; and the games they played were great mysteries. One of our particular friends lost some four hundred dollars in gold, and also his senses by being slung backwards off his chair by a lurch of the vessel while he was intently studying the main chance at three o'clock in the morning. The latter item of his losses he gradually regained, but the former was flown forever. The ladies sat and looked at the gentlemen, jabbered with one another, or twiddled with their thumbs; and my companion and myself contemplated all hands and counted off to a nicety on our fingers how many more days there were to be before we would see the blessed land.

As few Americans are fools enough to travel by this route we reaped all the benefits which the rarity of the event naturally gave rise to, being treated with the highest consideration by the officers of the ship and by the passengers. We could not but most favorably contrast the treatment we received from these really courteous people with that which a foreigner generally meets with under similar circumstances among Americans or Englishmen. Their intercourse with us was not mere scraps of formal politeness; they evinced an anxiety to oblige us and make us contented. In generous regard for our isolated situation they conversed with us by the hour (in Spanish), and all hands zealously combining to imbue us with the abstrusities of the language, they patiently caused us to repeat words and phrases till our tongues were ready to cleave to the roofs of our mouths and our jaws were fit to drop. While in Cuba I had learned what Spanish was necessary to procure provisions. This provisional Spanish was all I knew; but this I now bawled out liberally at table. My companion relied exclusively upon English in his communications with the Spaniards. He asked for whatever he wanted in that tongue, and if the waiter failed to comprehend him he repeated his demand in tones rising higher and higher till they amounted to a stentorian roar, and either jarred understanding into the cranium of the waiter or else penetrated into the ears of some distant Anglo-Spaniard, who, for politeness' sake or to keep from being struck deaf by the racket, would act as interpreter. At any rate, he always got what he asked for, and then was wont to laugh derisively at the uselessness of my hardly-acquired scrapings of the pure Castilian.

We lightened the time and derived some whiffs of joyance from the observation of such of our companions as presented any salient points; but, in fact, they were few—the company being made up mostly of plain matter-of-fact people, without distinctive traits of character. It was not uninteresting to behold the bishop's secretary brooding all day long in a corner, from which he never moved except with a galvanic spring to relieve the weight of woe forever pressing upon his stomach. The only other person on board who commanded our special attention was a blustering gentleman of the army, as bold as he was big. He had one of the attributes pertaining to many great men—his appearance showed that he was distinct from the common run of mortals; at the same time he exhibited a characteristic in which great men are apt to be deficient—he was extremely familiar with other people. He was stricken in years, and his hair was oxidized, though at times it had a vivid polish, put upon it either by grease or perspiration, and it was sheared short all over except on the sides of his temples, where large flat tongues of it were plastered hermetically tight against the skin. He shaved now and then, and at such times his face looked morbidly clean and presented a most unnatural contrast with the rest of his carcass; but in a day it became as rough and wiry as a cotton-card. His voice was harsh and blatant, being, in fact, a bray, in which there was less melody than is in the fall of a hodful of brick; and when it was invigorated by the huge quaffs of Catalan wine which he boused prodigiously, it suffocated completely everybody else's. He wore a pair of lurid-red breeches, and a blue coat so beslobbered with gold lace that I esteemed him to be some mammoth pillar of the realm till I was assured by one well versed in the military insignia of Spain that his rank was of the lowest. Notwithstanding his ingratiating manners and his endeavors to be sociable and agreeable, the pleasure of his society was not greatly courted; nor did I perceive that the odor of sanctity was so strong about him that he of all men should have been chosen as a candle-bearer in a certain very solemn religious rite that had to be performed on the voyage, though the padre thought differently. He discharged the duty, however, with wonderfully lofty humility, and looked as saintly a sinner as could have been selected. This buster of a military man, like military men notoriously are, was a profound admirer of the fair sex—his admiration being like his person, great but clumsy; and his amatory accents were no less grating and thunderous than his ordinary utterances. His attentions were assiduous and energetic. On one occasion I beheld him endeavoring to ensconce himself between two ladies, and in order to do it he had to climb over the table. It was perfectly portentous to see the vast expanse of his lurid-red breeches rising gradually in the air, and after rolling around come plumping down between the unfortunate females, cleaving the twain asunder. One of them called him a *borrico* so frequently and so emphatically that I was induced to look the word out in the dictionary. It signifies "jackass."

By reason of my medical character I had the happiness to get on intimate terms with the ship's padre. But as what I am going to say about him consists mostly of notes intended for the edification of my brethren of the

Faculty of Physic, those of the laity who are uninterested or squeamish in our honorable but plain-spoken science are hereby notified, so that they can skip this passage of the narrative. The padre was wretchedly diseased with nothing at all,—a case sufficiently curious but by no means infrequent,—and it was his habit to consult every physician that came within his power concerning his malady. But it seemed that there was an insuperable difficulty in the way of obtaining the benefit of my valuable counsel, for the only language I dared to trust my lips to utter besides English was French, and this he did not understand. In this emergency he hit upon the brilliant expedient of addressing me in Latin. Now the only Latin that I claimed to have any proficiency whatever in was the dialect used by doctors in prescribing calomel, castor oil, salts, etc.—which is of a sort that would cause Cicero to die a-laughing to hear and drive him clean crazy if he tried to comprehend; and besides, even if I happened to know any of the real Roman words, the padre's pronunciation was so different from that which I had been taught to use that we would still remain unintelligible to one another. But lo, the padre took a pencil and wrote what he wished to say on a piece of paper; and, wonder of wonders! I was actually able to guess what he meant—ay, and I replied in kind, and he was able to guess what I meant. It was a delightful discovery. Before this I would cheerfully have sold all my knowledge of the classic language for a sugar sixpence, and now here I was conversing after the manner of the poets, and orators, and warriors, and the mighty men of the days of old, saying, "How de do?" "Cool to-day," "B'lieve I'll turn in," and other delectable things in the grand old Roman way—showing how egregiously I had been mistaken when I thought that the best years of my life had been wasted in acquiring this most indispensable language.

But could I have foreseen what was to befall me I should scarcely have been so jubilant over the revival of learning; for as soon as the padre found that communication was established between us he spread out his case *ab initio ad infinitum usque ad nauseam*, and gave me no rest, but had me talking Latin day and night; being continually suggesting doubts for me to resolve and propounding queries for me to answer. And besides, there are doctrines in medicine which, like certain dogmas in religion, are dependent on faith alone for their reception; and these, when laid before him, he provokingly insisted upon understanding; but which neither his theological Latin, nor my medical Latin, nor the classical Latin common to both of us availed to clear up to the extent of one speck—which was not very surprising, however, seeing that the most cogent and copious English cannot do it. He professed to be afflicted with some kind of abdominal trouble or other—a sort of intestine insurrection, in which his bowels would rise up and hitch themselves together, to the great discomposure of his body and disturbance of his peace of mind; and he showed me the diagnoses and prescriptions of my predecessors, which he had forced them to commit to writing, and which he carefully preserved for his instruction and guidance. However it may be in other matters, in medicine safety does not abide among a multitude of counselors. As a matter of course, these opinions were terribly discordant, and some of them were rather curious. They perplexed the unfortunate subject of them beyond measure, but to this perplexity it was due, no doubt, that he was spared to consult me; for, having studied them till he had no idea what ailed him or what to do for himself, he had not dared to follow any of the directions to their full extent. His last adviser had ordered him when he retired to bed to deposit a bladder full of shot upon his bowels to weight them down, with the assurance that in time their aspiring tendencies would be crushed out of them. Seeing that there was sense and reason in this, the padre had obeyed the injunction faithfully, and lay every night wide awake holding on the bladder to keep it from rolling off and smashing to flinders, and in a kind of chronic nightmare from the pressure. And now, finding this scheme not as successful as he could wish, he sought to obfuscate himself yet further by procuring my advice.

The treatment of such cases is usually beset with difficulties, but I made short work with this one—or, at least, I tried to do so. I told the padre that his bowels might possibly be out of gear, and that if they were, all his other ailments were due to nothing more than the sympathy of other parts with them. "Darn all such sympathy," quoth his reverence in Latin. I prescribed twenty grains of blue mass to begin with. This was a most unfortunate move, for the padre knew nothing in the world about any such substance, and was determined to know everything about it before he trusted any of it in his inside. It booted nothing to translate "blue mass" literally into Latin. Raking and scraping among the *débris* of classic lore with which my mind was incumbered, I got enough of it together to furnish forth an account of the method of manufacture, the uses, and the mode of administration of the remedy. But unluckily, after I had fully described it with infinite labor, all that the padre could be made to understand was that it was a preparation of mercury; and, far more unluckily, he did not know and would not believe that mercury was given but for one malady in the whole nosology, and rose aghast at the idea that I should suppose a man of his kidney to be afflicted with that. For my own sake, therefore, as well as for his, I delved for my trunk in the depths of the ship's hold, and brought therefrom a portion of the drug in question and gave it to him for his examination. Moreover, when by these means he was led to express a partial willingness to believe that it might possibly possess something of virtue, he became tormented with the most agitating apprehension of the effects of such a dose as twenty grains; and so I swallowed a plug of it as big as a bullet before his face to demonstrate its innocuousness. By the time we had reached this point in our proceedings the Guipuzcoa had reached Spain. The consultation was obliged to be terminated, and I parted from him leaving him anxiously balancing the pros and cons of blue mass, and bearing with me the melancholy certainty that all I had accomplished for him was only to add one more winding to the pathological labyrinth in which he was already inextricably involved.

If our days were rather tame aboard this vessel, our nights smacked of vivaciousness. As the shades of evening settled down, the cares of the officers seemed to be lifted up, and they came into the saloon and roused the passengers into jollity. The ship was provided with a piano, a little jangled and stridulous from frequent pickling with brine, but capable of furnishing very passable notes under gingerly manipulation, and the ladies and gentlemen were accustomed to accompany it with the sweet and tender airs that characterize the Spanish ballad music; and to its lascivious pleasings we were also wont to caper every night, wind and weather permitting. Our captain was the master-spirit of the revels. He was an ancient mariner on whom tar and salt had done their worst, and his custom was to co-operate with the piano on the neck of a massive gourd, which he scraped and beat upon with a stick with the hand of a master. He also was able to scream like a pelican, and had given unto him power to laugh similar and equal to any hyena, which gifts be kindly exercised for the entertainment of the passengers. I' faith, he was a right jocund navigator—a passing merrisome person, in sooth. Another trait in his character, most grateful to sea-sick and doubting souls, was that he took in sail when the wind blew; and, moreover, he compassionately allowed the men at the wheel to lighten their toils by the solace of song. Albeit myself the very embodiment of gravity, I was hauled up by this frolicsome old functionary and compelled to display my Terpsichorean skill. The dances in vogue were of the Cuban pattern—a sort of solemn wiggle, composed of little pitty-pat steps, hard to do and very inconsequential when done. Forced to participate, I thought it would do no harm to infuse a little animation into the performance, and so I spiced it with a few extracts from the Old Virginia Breakdown, and fastening a remorseless clutch upon the girls, gave them such a squeezing up and shaking down as made them look wild for an hour afterwards.

I have thus described our week-day life on this voyage. On Sundays we had mass in the morning whenever the vessel was sufficiently steady to suffer the padre to perform his genuflections without capsizing. The rest of the day was consecrated to gambling, and at night we had the usual variety of singing and dancing.

In this goodly company and amid these diverse scenes we spent sixteen days. Early on the morning of the 12th of February we passed in sight of Santa Maria, the southernmost of the Azore Islands—the glimpse of land thus obtained exhilarating all mightily, and inducing the captain that night to dance, sing, scream, laugh, and bang on his gourd with most joyful vehemence. What added to the gratification of this sight was that it showed we were on the right track; and, as the route from St. Mary's to Spain was tolerably short and plain, we were enabled to head in the proper direction and drive on with good assurance of not losing our way. On the 15th, when we came out from dinner, lo, there was land again —like a cloud on the far-off horizon. I have not language to tell my emotions as I gazed upon it, for that was Europe rising before me, and the consummation of the wish of many and many a year was now at hand. As we neared it, it showed itself to be a bold and striking headland, much resembling a Mississippi River bluff. It was Cape St. Vincent, dear to every English heart as marking the scene of the great naval victory of Jervis and Nelson over the Spaniards in 1797. We ran close in to it and skirted the shore, and that night I sat up late watching the lighthouse on the point and refreshing my soul, so long cribbed and cabined, with the delicious hopes of deliverance that the sight inspired.

Next morning land had vanished again, but only for a time. Soon the Spanish shores reappeared, and soon we were in a lovely bay, and before us was sweet Cadiz, beautiful and clad in white, reposing on the sea.

CHAPTER VI.

Of our Landing in Europe, and of the beggarly Reception we met with —Of the Fonda de America of Cadiz—Of the City of Cadiz—Of its Cathedral—Of the State of Politics in Cadiz, and how the Patriots of that City became involved in Difficulties with the Central Government, and by what Means they gained a happy Issue out of them—Of the fostering of the Tender Passion by the Gaditanos, and of the surpassing Charms of the Cadiz Ladies.

ALL the morning there was great commotion on board the Guipuzcoa, for the trunks were being excavated from the hold and all hands were engaged in devising ways and means of cheating the custom-house. The ship, not being able to get to the wharf, was obliged to anchor in the bay, and the commotion was intensified a hundredfold by the arrival of little boats which came off to us in multitudes, waiting for our liberation by the officials to disembark the passengers. When freedom was proclaimed, the fuss and botheration were distracting. Amid the noise and confusion my friend and I saw our trunks spirited away, and, dashing headlong after them, found ourselves in a boat almost sinking with excess of baggage and people. We clung to it, however, and it conveyed us safely to the shore. This system of debarking out in mid-ocean, as it were, and getting to land in a sail-boat at the peril of your life and property, is in vogue in all the Southern European ports, and an abominable one it is.

An immense gathering of Cadiz loafers and dead-beats was waiting on the landing-place to receive us, and apparently the whole guild of beggars had turned out in honor of our advent. These beggars were the most persistent and impudent scamps I ever encountered—their manners assimilating them to highway robbers rather than to the "poor but respectable" persons they would fain be thought. They collared us, and pulled and tugged at our garments as if they intended to pull our very pockets out. In the mean time we had to maintain a lookout sharper than a serpent's tooth upon the vicissitudes which our trunks were undergoing. In such circumstances a man is not apt to feel very charitable. The reverse feeling began to wax hot within us, and finding that our tormentors did not comprehend English well enough to know what "damn," its congeners, auxiliaries, and augmentatives meant, my friend took his cane and I my old cotton umbrella, and by vigorous flourishes contrived to gain some surcease of their demonstrations. On the whole, we had a realizing sense of what it is to be a stranger in a strange land devoid of friends or counselors. We knew not what to say— or rather, how to say it—nor what to do. Our chiefest consolation was that our wives were not with us. My companion had at times mourned that he had not brought his with him, but he was thankful now that he had not; and as for mine—Heaven be praised! I never had one, and wouldn't at this juncture have had one at any price, for she would have been fully equivalent to another trunk, and it was more than we could do to take care of the two we had. What would have become of us is a subject of mere conjecture had not an English-jabbering hotel-runner delivered us by seizing and rushing us to the custom-house.

The custom-house people were very courteous, and as we had, furthermore, cunningly enlisted their gentlemanly instincts in our behalf by the judicious arrangement of our large and not very enticing accumulations of dirty linen, they allowed us to pass out of their formidable portals undeflowered. The citizens of Cadiz have not yet seen occasion for baggage-wagons, so our runner procured us a couple of porters to carry our trunks; and under his guidance we trudged on to the hotel called Fonda de America. We were welcomed with great cordiality by the proprietor and all his staff, and put in the best rooms in the house.

Cadiz is a city of some seventy-two thousand inhabitants, situated on a tongue of land jutting into the sea, which almost surrounds it. The neck connecting it with the main-land is very narrow and consequently offers such facilities to the Gaditanos for cutting themselves off from the world that they have more than once been tempted to shut themselves in and defy outsiders; but where the latter have had control of the water the citizens have found that they were in much the predicament of a rat in a trap beleaguered by his enemies. It is strongly fortified, being inclosed by a granite rampart, which in parts is very wide, forming an admirable promenade, from which there is a lovely view of the harbor with its shipping, and to seaward an impressive one for such as love to solemnize their thoughts by contemplating the great ocean. In its general appearance it resembles Havana, having the same narrow streets, which possess the Bostonian proclivity for all at once splitting in two and coming to an untimely end. By reason of their contracted character these streets enjoy the execrable power of concentrating sounds and making them cavernous and sepulchral in their resonance; and they are made perfectly hideous by the howls of the peripatetic purveyors of fish, eggs, and charcoal. I never will believe that mortal man elsewhere ever was cursed with such outrageous, diabolical, ear-splitting, gall-bursting vocal organs as these perambulators glory in exercising; in comparison, the bellowing of bulls, the braying of asses, the filing of saws, are attuned to heavenly harmonies.

The buildings are mostly tall and white, with the lower windows grated and the upper ones balconied. The town is one of the cleanest I ever saw, and there is a neatness of look about it quite attractive. Still there is a certain gloominess pervading it, arising from a feeling of constriction and confinement which the narrowness of its thoroughfares renders very perceptible to a person accustomed to wide ones. The people are of solemn mien and wonderfully addicted to the wearing of cloaks, and the favorite color of their umbrellas is red. What they do for a livelihood I was not able to ascertain. There was no indication that they do anything. It may not be altogether irrational to surmise, inasmuch as the church-bells were on the ring almost incessantly during our stay among them, that "prayer's all their business, all their pleasure praise." The most flourishing craft decidedly was priestcraft. I encountered members of this fraternity everywhere, from rosy morn till some time after dewy eve, whipping along in their distinctive toggery of black robe cut free and easy, and a hat which it is a detraction from the personal appearance of a useful though perhaps not over-comely piece of hardware to call "shovel." Some of their reverences who were young, had their clothes new, and wore them with as much style as their impracticable fashion permitted; many of the elderly brethren, however, were careless of dress, and their robes looked frowzy and their hats looked seedy.

Our hotel, the Fonda de America, derived its name from the fact that its system of management was not Spanish but French. It was a small establishment, but a good one; in fact, in the matter of its table it pleased me better than any I stopped at in Europe. For its size it was somewhat expensive to keep, for in addition to the other outlays the landlord had to pay four dollars a day house-rent and six hundred dollars a year taxes; and, as it was rather indifferently patronized, I judge it was not very remunerative. On some days we were the only lodgers, and at these times we lost our appetites with apprehension of the probable amount of our bills. In this hotel they spoke every language under heaven— after a fashion; and to conform with them we did the same—after a fashion. To accommodate the division of political sentiment rife in the community there were two dining-rooms—one, the larger and better, furnished with a number of little tables, for the republican eaters, and another, with a single long table, for the monarchists,—it being thought injudicious to hazard a promiscuous gathering where cutlery abounded. This long table I noted particularly and found it forever on the set, with vases of flowers and pyramids of oranges and plates of fruit and nuts invitingly displayed, but never saw a guest at any time partaking of its bounty; whence I drew the inference that the monarchical faction had either died or been killed out, or that they were accustomed to feed under cover of the night from dread of the righteous indignation of the republican party.

The proprietor of the Fonda de America spent the most of his time in figuring at his accounts in the endeavor to strike something like a balance between his income and his outgo; in the intervals of respite from this, assisted by his staff, he stood on the brink of a chasm in the floor of the office and peered fixedly into a vast cistern made in the cellar to hold drinking-water, and with which cistern there was something or other wrong. All the *attachés* of the hotel were singularly courteous and polite, and the chambermaid captivatingly so. I used to pass her every morning while she was washing off the steps, and nothing could exceed the grace with which she would jump up from her knees, wave her scouring-rag, and greet me. She would almost shake to pieces in deprecation when we sought to spare her any little service that it was her province to perform, and it was charming to witness the energy with which she projected her forefingers at us when seeking to convey an idea into our uncomprehending minds—a not uncommon trick with Spaniards under like circumstances, who think, doubtless, that in this way they can job their meaning into a man's skull like so much putty into an auger-hole. I was so affected by her manner that I put myself to learning two or three of the most expressive forms of salutation in order to reciprocate her politeness.

Notwithstanding all I have said in commendation of the Fonda de America, there were numerous objections to it—so numerous, indeed, as to be beyond enumeration; they were its fleas. Looking back by the light of experience I find that when we set foot in Cadiz we had entered the borders of the fatherland of fleas, and never got out of it till we reached Marseilles. At first they were more merciful to me than I had any right to expect, while they were unrelenting towards my companion. In time we were treated with a just impartiality, but at the last our relative inflictions were reversed—he was let off with the abstraction of a few mouthfuls while I was devoured alive. Those domiciled in this fonda I esteem to be the finest in all Andalusia, and so potent were they that for a time they enabled my companion to dispense with the counter-irritant lotions with which he was wont to anoint himself.

Cadiz possesses but few sights. The principal one is the Cathedral. Though I afterwards saw others more magnificent than this and many persons consider it rather an indifferent edifice, yet, as it was the first European cathedral I visited, it made a pleasing impression upon me, which I still retain. There is the solemnizing effect about it which is inseparable from the massive pillar and lofty arch which enter into its architecture. It is adorned by a few pictures, which are not thought a great deal of by connoisseurs, and it has several chapels, not very richly furnished; but there are numbers of wooden saints and apostles which enlist attention by the skillfulness and elaborateness of the carving. Here, in the choir, as in other cathedrals, the holy brotherhood are wont to assemble at stated hours every day and chant praises, prayers, and thanksgivings, in which they are aided and abetted by a band of little boys in girls' clothes of a red or black frock and white josey; and it is not an altogether ungrateful discord to hear the roars and grunts of the old folks mingling with the bleats and blares of childhood. These ministering children, I fear me, are not as reverent nor as free from hankering after the beggarly elements of the world as beseems their function. One big child, about eighteen years old, dogged me all over the church with piteous entreaties for a *cuarto* (half a cent); and a small one, who with the quickness of youth had assimilated some English words, bade me " Goo' morndin," and in the very act of paying his adorations to the high altar solicited my pecuniary commiseration of his necessities.

The beggars, whom we encountered *en masse* when we landed, I afterwards continually met in detail whenever and wherever I walked. Whether the Father of Deceit had blinded them with that most preposterous of all delusions, that I was a foreigner of opulence, or whether they were attracted by that beaming benevolence that bristles all over me, I do not know; but as soon as I stepped out of my hotel they began to gather about me, and when I returned it was generally with a full retinue. It would have been a sight of unquenchable delectation to my friends could they have seen me

sauntering along the streets of Cadiz with my pipe in
my mouth, and adorned with all that dignity and decorum
which I so well know how to assume, enveloped with
ragamuffins of all sizes, sexes, and sorts, smiling upon
them, laughing with them, and treating them with the
utmost urbanity and good-feeling, and never giving them
a cent.

We were hardly settled in the town before we were
pushed into the current of the local politics. The hotel-
runner, who was a Russian filled with love of liberty and
panting for the elective franchise, instructed us and fired
our hearts. He was of the most ardent stripe of politi-
cians, having already shut the mouths of two of his opponents, the monarchists, with an ounce of lead apiece, and
longed and prayed for an opportunity to repeat the
operation on others. He vibrated several times during
our stay back and forth from despair to ecstasy as the
prospect for an internecine war in the streets brightened
and waned. Cadiz, and indeed all Andalusia, was overwhelmingly and vehemently republican, and discreet
monarchists compelled to tarry within its borders set
their houses in order, knowing perfectly well what a day
might bring forth. As the central government was not
unjustly suspected to squint strongly towards the establishment of a monarchy, it and the people of this region
regarded each other with mutual distrust; and when,
some two months before our arrival, the former in its
paternal generosity kindly offered to relieve the latter of
the bother of bearing and the trouble of taking care of
arms, the latter declined the relief tendered. At this the
central government becoming vexed put forth the paternal
authority and demanded the arms, and then the patriots
of Cadiz, including our Russian, rose up and indignantly
refused to surrender them.

Implicit confidence was felt in the efficacy of the master-
stroke of cutting themselves off from the mainland; but
the government had forestalled this by taking possession
of the isthmus and putting a garrison in the town. Besides, they sent a fleet to beleaguer it by sea. In the
face of established Spanish precedent in dealing with
refractory people, the citizens were asked to yield before

being annihilated, and were actually given time to consider the matter. All the persons of means and respectability took advantage of the delay to pack up what movables they could and flee inland. The road was filled with men, women, and children, and household gods, in carts, on donkeys, and on foot; but the true patriots, again including our Russian, undismayed by the pass to which things had come, erected barricades, dodged behind windows, and ascended to the housetops, determined to strike one lick at all events

Mobs of all nations, and even regularly organized bodies of the people of some, are marvelously incredulous of the occurrence of a perfectly patent result till they see it happen. It is this characteristic which has so often led the Poles and Hungarians and Irish, the moment they begin to react from a prostrating blow, to make another effort,—frittering away what little strength they have regained, instead of patiently waiting till they have accumulated enough of it to be available. This incredulous spirit animated the patriots of Cadiz on the occasion in question. They could not realize the certainty that if the affair came to the arbitrament of arms, they would be overwhelmingly defeated and the city battered down, but resolved to try the hazard of the issue with a heroism which would have been near the standard of Greek or Roman praise had any of them owned a cent's worth of the property they magnanimously proposed to stake. We must not withhold from them the merit of personal bravery, for they were fully determined to stand the first volley, and then do as the gallant irregulars have ever done—run away, or perish in the attempt. Indeed, the fervor of some of them led to a preliminary skirmish with a body of the government troops, and I saw two or three houses smartly spluttered with bullet marks, which testified to a vigorous fusillade against the upper windows.

While affairs were rapidly approaching a crisis, the apartments of the American consul were being crammed with persons seeking the protection of the American flag, —which, rebel though some folks think me, I don't mind owning it gives me some pleasure to know is regarded as a potent talisman in other countries besides the United

States,—and that functionary began to find himself smothering under the pressure of the supplicants. Considerations of personal salvation, if nothing else, made it imperative upon him to attempt some solution of the question. Laying hold of his banner he lifted it on high, and boldly marched to the barricades of the patriots. He and his gridiron were received with tremendous cheers of welcome, and being courteously pulled over to the inside of the works he was at once granted an audience with the leaders. In the conference he proposed as a basis of settlement, that instead of surrendering their arms to the government as was demanded, which was an ignominy they could not be expected to submit to, they should surrender them to him, and he would deliver them to the government himself. This singularly ingenious compromise, alike honorable to both parties, was immediately accepted,—but with the distinct understanding that it was not done from any fear of the accidental effusion of blood, nor to avoid the useless destruction of other people's property, but entirely out of regard and affection for their revered exemplar, the great Republic of the West. In obedience to this arrangement the arms were given to our consul, he gave them to the government, and they took excellent care of them; and thus peace was re-established in Cadiz.

It appears from the records that the people of Cadiz have always been of an amatory cast. Some of the Roman writers mention this trait; and Byron, an admirable authority on the subject, dwells upon it. From my own observations, I am constrained to think that the characteristic still applies. "The dark-eyed Girl of Cadiz" who tickled his lordship so hugely when he was in these parts, has left behind her a progeny worthy of their captivating predecessor. I am notoriously cool and cautious in these matters, and hence my assertion ought to have no common weight when I affirm that the ladies of this town are not bad-looking. They know it, too, as appears by the fact that they have an inordinate propensity for prowling around and showing themselves. In Andalusia almost every young woman is handsome; not like it is in other countries, here beauty is the rule, plainness the rare exception. Their complexion is olive, not dark enough to hide but sufficiently to temper most delectably the ruddy tinge that mantles in their cheeks. Their hair is black and glossy and their eyes black and sparkling. They are short in stature and of a most agreeable dumpiness of form, being an exact and comfortable armful. In movement they are distractingly graceful. Above all, they have no false modesty, nor any cumbersome amount of the true, so that an admiring soul can gaze upon them without that chilling fear of big brothers which so cripples the affections in this land of ours. But, unfortunately, lovely as they are, they are sadly ignorant, not knowing the simplest rudiments of English grammar—a deplorable circumstance, grievously diminishing the pleasure they were otherwise so well fitted to bestow.

What I say of the charms of the Spanish ladies applies to them only while they are young; when they become old, the contrast is heart-rending. There is then a perfect smash of their good points, and Father Time, not satisfied with flindering their features, erects upon the ruins a structure the direct opposite of what shone there so gloriously in their youth. Nowhere have I ever seen young women so bewitching; nowhere old ones so—so —well, retaining so much of the witch still.

I was very forcibly struck with the rare courtesy displayed by the ladies of Cadiz towards strangers—in evidence of which I must relate a little incident. While taking my usual saunter one morning, I suddenly heard a female voice exclaiming, in gentle tones, " Oh, monsieur, monsieur, monsieur; come in, come in, come in; come in, monsieur, come in." Now I am none of your conceited young men, quick to infer that every woman's speech concerns me; and having always been treated with marked contempt by the sex am slow to make a personal application of any benevolent expression they may let fall; wherefore I went steadily on. The invitation had been given in very fair English and now it was repeated in French, and this time in a manner which admitted of no doubt that it was intended for me. Turning my head and looking up I beheld two lovely ladies at a window, who having at length attracted my attention, expressed both by words and actions the most hospitable feelings towards me. The sincerity of their desire to welcome me under their roof was beyond all cavil, and it was impossible for me not to be moved by this unwonted mark of esteem. Unfortunately, I chanced to be smoking, and being a person of the most rigid notions of decorum, the bare idea of taking a pipe into the presence of ladies shocked me to the heart—at the same time my regard for good tobacco is not an iota less strong than for etiquette. Under the circumstances, therefore, I felt constrained to decline with many apologies this flattering invitation; but to show my sense of their very great civility, I informed them that I would do myself the honor of calling that evening, and so with mutual benedictions we separated. Most unluckily, that very afternoon we departed from Cadiz, and my promise had to go unfulfilled. Of course I cannot fairly claim that all the ladies of this city manifest this courteousness in quite as active and outspoken a form as these did. It is possible that these were made exceptionally hospitable by propinquity to the Cathedral, for their habitation was almost under the eaves of the sacred edifice, and by the great advantages they enjoyed for communion with the holy brotherhood officiating there.

In respect of the fitness of Cadiz as a winter residence for invalids, I should judge that its completely exposed situation would make it unsuitable. According to that delusive criterion the "mean temperature" it is superior to any place on the European shore of the Mediterranean; but there is full sweep for every wind that chooses to blow upon it, and hence it is subject to sudden vicissitudes of weather, which is one of the worst characteristics that can afflict a climate. Rains, too, are frequent, though they are usually not heavy nor prolonged. We were there during the last two weeks of February, exclusive of four days in Seville. For the first week the weather was variable, with two or three days, not consecutive, very fine; while the intervening ones were cool, and at times cold, with occasional rain. For the last week the weather was uniformly pleasant. Although I cannot recommend Cadiz to the invalid as a permanent stopping-place, a visit to it could do him no harm, but, on the contrary, would most probably prove to be both agreeable and beneficial—and, indeed, in my opinion, when the circumstances of his case will permit it, he will find a brief stay in several places to be more advantageous than a lengthened sojourn in any one of them.

CHAPTER VII.

Containing some Account of Railroad Economics in Spain—of the City of Seville, the Character of its Inhabitants and its Commercial Status, Present and Prospective—of the Cathedral, the Alcazar, the House of Pilate, the Paintings, and the Tobacco Factory, and of the ruined City of Italica.

ALTHOUGH the state of my companion's health inclined him to remain to the southward at this season of the year, he yet felt that it would be a sin and a shame to be so near Seville and not go to it. Accordingly, he determined to venture that far north even at the risk of his life. As it was to be merely an excursion, we left our heavy baggage in the care of the Fonda de America and took only our carpet-bags. There were two routes open to us—by steamer or by rail. We preferred the former, wishing to see the river scenery on the Guadalquivir, but being told that nobody but market folks patronized that line, and that the boat had no accommodations for artistic tourists, and was, besides, absolutely dependent on wind and weather, and, moreover, never scrupled to stop anywhere for any length of time where there was a chance of turning a penny or so in the retail fish business, we concluded to take the railroad. We purchased our tickets —receiving a brass outlandish coin in change instead of a gold one, which we did not detect till we reached Seville, and which the ticket-seller could not identify on presentation when we returned—and got aboard the train.

The cars here are fitted up in the fashion of our hacks,

with linen-covered seats facing one another, slings to hang your arms in, and window-frames that pull up by means of long straps. In these you are securely fastened for weal or for woe till you arrive at a station, when you are temporarily set at liberty; and if you should perchance yearn for a drink of water you can occasionally get it at some of the stopping-places for a cent and a quarter a glass. This system of railroading is general in Europe,—a system which, thanks to our enlightened republican institutions, has never obtained a foothold in our happy land. The locomotives are of the old exploded pattern, resembling a saw-mill on wheels, with a stove-pipe for a smoke-stack, and with the working-gear out of sight, and their whistles are of the most powerful feebleness. The conductor traverses a narrow gangway on the outside of the train, poking his head into the windows to collect the tickets, and his manners are fascinatingly polite. With a most graceful bow he takes the tickets, punches a hole through them with extreme obsequiousness, and tears himself away with "Felicity to you, gentlemen." It is truly delightful to have to commune with so sweet-tempered and pleasant-spoken an official.

The first objects that attract the attention outside of Cadiz are numerous pyramids of salt; for this is a great salt-making region. A few miles farther and we come to San Fernando, whose citizens are furious fliers of kites. The next station is Port St. Mary, a town of some size, whence is procured the water which supplies Cadiz; but, notwithstanding this fact, the commodity is as dear here as anywhere else, maintaining its maximum price of a cent and a quarter a glass. The only other important place before reaching Seville is Xeres, a large and finely situated town, famous as the depot for sherry wine. Along this route the country appears to be rich and the soil is evidently most fertile. Olive-trees are abundant, and if the Spaniards are indeed lazy agriculturists, as has been charged against them, it is not very perceptible hereabouts, for this region bears unmistakable marks of thrift and good culture.

Our observations on these points were mostly made in returning from Seville, for the cars are timed in such a manner as to reach the city late at night; so that at this period of the year the view is shut off about the middle of the journey. The railway time-tables of Spain are made not for a period but for all time. The sun, moon, and stars in their rising and setting may vary with the seasons, but not so they; the schedule once arranged it remains thus forever after. The Spaniard of to-day comes and goes at the hours that his father did before him, and whoever procures a Railroad Guide of the present epoch may bequeath it to his posterity, assured that it will retain its pristine usefulness to the remotest generations.

Debarking at Seville, with considerable effort we scraped together sufficient Spanish to get ourselves deposited in a sort of box and drawn to the Hotel de Londres—a pretty fair inn, where they give you mosquitoes in place of the fleas that are furnished at Cadiz. Their coffee, however, needed tonics, and we would have liked the establishment better had they changed the table-napkins oftener than Stonewall Jackson did his shirt.

Seville is a city of about a hundred and twenty thousand inhabitants. It is situated in the midst of a rich and beautiful plain on the banks of the Guadalquivir River— a stream not very large nor overcrowded with shipping. Its history goes far back, and its associations are numerous and of the most interesting character. The Phœnician, the Roman, the Goth, and the Moor have combined to make its story. Their impress is on it still, and the observant traveler as he notes the traces they have left behind them is irresistibly led to moralize upon the vicissitudes it has undergone. As for me, there is no city which has so excited my mind to sober but not unpleasing reflection, and I shall always regard my visit to it as one of the fortunate events of my life.

The houses of Seville are in the peculiar massive but ornate style of Spanish architecture, with balconied windows or miradors, and are generally rather handsome. The city possesses an assemblage of winding streets, nearly five hundred in number, which are sufficiently narrow, and laid out after a pattern abstruse enough to mystify a Philadelphia lawyer. Along them patter a multitude of

female creatures most lovely to behold, who glance at
you to your extreme peril, and sometimes even wink in a
manner calculated to deceive the very elect. At night
the principal thoroughfares are crowded with pedestrians,
who as they go babbling along furnish a very animated
picture. Then "young-eyed Lewdness walks her midnight
rounds," and at such times in making my solitary prowls
often would my musings on the Phœnicians, Romans,
Goths, and Moors, above alluded to, be incontinently dis-
solved into a vision of New York.

Along these streets patter also, cheek-by-jowl with the
ladies, a multitude of jolly little Andalusian jackasses, which
are the medium of the carrying trade, wheeled conveyances
being rare. The owners of these active little fellows load
them till they are out of sight, and then jumping on ride all
over them, from the tip of their tails to the tip of their noses.
The animals are wonderfully obedient and straightforward,
pursuing the direct tenor of the way the master sets
them, and turning neither to the right nor to the left for
any obstructing footman; so that disastrous collisions
with oil and charcoal, and eggs and wine, would be imminent but for the admonitory shriek of dismay which the
driver wails forth when the quadruped is trying to per-
forate a pedestrian.

A great deal of business is done in Seville in wine, oil,
and oranges; but when I was there times were hard, the
people complaining especially of the intolerable advance
in liquor, which had gone up no less than one hundred
per cent.—being then two cents a drink. It is painfully
evident that the sceptre of commercial greatness, which
Seville held under the Moorish domination and again just
subsequent to the discovery of America, has fallen from
her hands. We met with the sole manufacturer of the
only genuine celebrated "J. C." licorice, who dwells here,
—a pleasant encounter, for my companion had used much
of his product in preparing tobacco, and I had been an
enthusiastic sucker of it before

"Time reft whate'er my soul enjoy'd,
And with the ills of Eld the sweets of Youth alloy'd,"—

and he told us sadly and bitterly how deplorably the

sales of that standard article had diminished. We would fain have consoled him by accounting for the diminution on the ground that the great progress which chemical science has made in America enables our people to manufacture the best of licorice out of molasses; so that it is only the old fogy tobacconists who now use the imported sort. He had not heard of this scientific fact, and retired from the interview overflowing with admiration of the capacity of our people and in despair at what it boded to the "J. C." As it is with licorice, so it is with other of their productions. They do not advance with the times, and, ignorant how art can be made to supplant nature, they allow other countries to surpass them in their own specialties. It is so with wine, more of which can be made in a New York cellar by our improved appliances in a day than by their tardy and antiquated processes they can get from all their vineyards in a year. Recent results obtained with soap-grease give reason for thinking that a fatal blow is impending over their oil, and when, at no distant day, oranges are made by machinery from old rags and decayed vinegar, they will be done for.

To see the sights of Seville to advantage it is necessary to have a guide. I attempted to "do" them on my own responsibility, but with bad success. Why or how it is —whether I am to congratulate myself as possessing the most winning of looks, or whether I am to bemoan myself as presenting the greenest of aspects,—truly I wist not, but certain it is that no sooner did I descend upon Spain than I became the rallying-point for all the vagabonds who caught sight of me. I had hardly ventured out of the shadow of the Hotel de Londres before I was clamped by the seediest-looking villain I ever beheld, who offered to be my cicerone. The only decent habiliments he had on were a pair of boots,—one with no bottom and the other with no top,—and for his salvation it was impossible for him to speak a word of English. I have a kind of fellow-feeling for poverty and he intuitively detected it; so he ruthlessly disgraced me with his company in spite of all my feebly forcible hints, till I fortunately met with my companion out for an airing, who flatly refused to go a step till I had dismissed my "friend,"—as I was mightily mortified to hear him termed. It was hard to do this, the most strenuous verbal efforts accomplishing nothing whatever, and it was only by the *tour de force* of dodging into breakfast that I effected it. After this we procured a genuine and gentlemanly guide, better looking and better dressed than either of us, and went the rounds.

The first place we visited was the Cathedral. Of this far-famed structure no adequate conception can be obtained but by the sight of it. It is a vast quadrangular building of massive, elaborate, and diverse architecture, erected on a site where originally stood a temple of Venus. This was transformed into a Christian church and followed by a mosque, which being burned by an invader was succeeded by another mosque; and this in turn has made way for the present temple—requiring hundreds of years, and labor and money incalculable, to develop it to its present majestic form. The exterior, though not altogether devoid of beauty, is effective rather from its irregularities of style and the rubs and dints which the hand of time has dealt upon it. Within arises column after column of vast proportions, with broad aisles between, sustaining lofty arches of noble workmanship; and the light comes dimly in through stained windows depicting religious subjects—among the finest specimens of painting on glass that have ever been produced. Here are numerous chapels magnificently adorned, and sacred utensils, chalices, crosses, and crucifixes, works in gold and silver and precious stones, of incalculable value. One of the chapels is inclosed with a railing of pure silver. There are carvings in wood representing Scripture scenes, so elaborately done that it tires the imagination to conceive the patient labor it must have required to execute them; while all around are paintings which are esteemed as treasures all the world over wherever art is cultivated. And here have mouldered and are mouldering into dust the bodies of men and women mighty and powerful centuries ago. In one of the chapels is interred King San Fernando who wrested this city from the infidels, and there I read in antiquated Latin the panegyrics on the tombs of Alfonso the Learned, his son, and Beatrice his wife, who went the way of all the earth many and many a day long gone. In this same chapel the fair and unfortunate Maria de Padilla rests secure from the persecutions of her lover the cruel Don Pedro. But to me, as an American, the most interesting of all these monuments to the departed was the simple slab in the floor of the Cathedral over the grave of Hernando, son of Columbus. Upon it is a long inscription, a part of which is the celebrated dictum, "To Castile and Leon Columbus gave a new world;" and it is accompanied by representations of the peculiar-shaped little vessels by which was effected the discovery of America. I feel that I can convey but a poor idea of this perhaps the noblest fane ever erected by man for the worship of the Creator. To me it is far more pleasing than St. Peter's, and I cherish it as a darling reminiscence of my European experiences. It is, indeed, a grand and solemn temple; and bigoted and insensitive must be he who, whatever his creed, can linger in its venerable precincts without finding his soul stirred by some passing thrill of adoration. Even my companion, as matter-of-fact a traveler as needs to be, with the rheumatism staring at him bodily from the cold marble pavement, was touched and remained till he got a little chilly.

Incorporated with the Cathedral is the Giralda—the muezzin tower of one of the former mosques. It has stood the wear and tear of time for near seven hundred years, having been erected in 1196, and yet remains a perfect, beautiful, and curious specimen of Moorish architecture. It rises to the very effective height of three hundred and fifty feet, and is surmounted by a rather heavy weathercock of twenty-eight hundred pounds weight. In the base of it there dwells an interesting family. The top is reached not by the abominable device of a winding stairway, but by a commodious brick walk rising gently along each of the four sides, so that the ascent can be made with very little fatigue. When I ascended it I passed through the interesting family, part of whom were frying meat for the family breakfast, part washing the family clothes, and part rocking the family

baby. I was lost among them for awhile, but they put
me on the right track, and I pursued my course leisurely,
ever and anon stopping at the windows to contemplate
the prospect, till I was about three-fourths of the way up,
when I was rather startled to see a door in the core of
the tower pop open and an old lady pop out with a
broom. This good dame I opine to be the sweeper of
the Giralda; she had a well-furnished apartment, and
was brisk and active despite her high living. Progress-
ing, I finally attained the loftiest practicable point, and
was rewarded by a scene full of grandeur, and beauty,
and vertigo. Nothing could be more delectable than the
view I enjoyed from this sublime perch, albeit somewhat
marred by the moral certainty I was under the whole
time I was thus perched that the entire concern was
tumbling over with me. While inspecting the numerous
bells that hung around, the bell-ringers came to perform
their everlastingly-recurring function. They were one
man and one boy, and did their duty manfully, with
many a gymnastic jump and jerk, keeping all the bells
going simultaneously; and the ding they made up there
was awful. Finding my reason fleeing me, I descended
to terra firma.

Next to the Cathedral in interest comes the Alcazar—
the palace of the old Moorish kings, and likewise dignified
or disgraced by being the residence of several of the
Spanish monarchs. Here Don Pedro, a fellow who
appears to have figured pretty largely almost everywhere in this region, played many of his pranks; and
here the Emperor Charles V. was married. It is a magnificent example of what the Moors could do, but it has
been nearly ruined by "improvements." Many portions
of it have been repainted, regilded, and retiled, by way
of restoration to its primal gorgeousness, some of which
operations have been done well and others outrageously,
the general result being to deteriorate the effect by re-
placing the air of antiquity, which is the great charm of
such a place, by an obtrusive freshness suggestive of a
brand-new establishment. It would be tedious to merely
describe all that is sufficiently interesting when looked at.
One of the noted portions of it is that called "The Hall

of the Maidens"—so called, according to our guide, because here were every year brought a hundred virgins, from among whom the king was empowered to select as many as he thought he could manage. It is a magnificent court, enriched with the delicate and prankish work peculiar to Moorish ornamentation, and embellished with no less than fifty-two marble columns. By direction of the guide we sat down where old Abdul-Azis used to sit when making his selection, and pondered. My companion was married, and what his thoughts were I do not presume to divine. I am still spared to myself, and my thoughts, I must honestly confess, had rather a wistful leaning towards "the good old times."

We next saw the bed-chamber of Charles V., and the seraglio of the Moorish potentates, and many other apartments interesting from their historical associations and beautifully adorned with arabesques and tracery-work and Arabic inscriptions worked in mosaic. Underneath, in the cellar as it were, is the old bathing-tub—a most commodious affair—in which the Infidel, and after them the Christian, ladies were wont to perform their ablutions. Here the lady Mary de Padilla used to bathe, and it is stated that our old friend Don Pedro and his gang would be on hand to see the operation, and that it was held to be a piece of high gallantry to take a drink of the wash-water; and it is further stated that on one occasion one of this honorable body declined to partake to the scandal and indignation of all the beholders, but was accounted excusable when he assigned as his reason that "if the sauce should prove good he might want a taste of the bird."

The gardens attached to the Alcazar are not the least beautiful portion of it. Under the walks are subterranean fountains made to play through the crevices of the bricks in a multitude of little streams. The aforesaid Pedro was accustomed to beguile his lady visitors into these walks and then turn on the water—a most joyful and right royal amusement. The gardener set the fountains at work for our better understanding of the *modus operandi*, and we were satisfied that it must have been glorious fun.

One of the places which a stranger in Seville who falls under the yoke of a guide is required to see is the so-called House of Pilate. One of the progenitors of the Duke of Medina Celi, returning from the Holy Land, conceived the idea of constructing a fac-simile of the house occupied by Pilate when governor of Judea, and this is the fruit of the conception. It may be said to be neutral in politics and religion,—being built after the Jewish plan and in the Moorish style; and the Pagan, Mohammedan, and Christian faiths are all represented in the filling-in of the design. It is not a poor-looking edifice, however, by any means, but, on the contrary, is in portions, at least, very elegant and beautiful. It is well supplied with marble columns, crosses, mosaic and tracery-work, with busts of Roman emperors and statues of heathen goddesses. How much it resembles its prototype is a question for the archæologists, but, at any rate, it presents a duplicate of everything of which the record makes mention as pertaining to the original. The Judgment Hall of Pilate is reproduced, and also the Pillar of Flagellation. Even the cock identified with Peter has his counterpart. This bird appears in the semblance of a rooster, urbane and sociable in mien, in a coop, looking down from on high through slats. At one time the counterfeit presentment of Peter himself was seen sitting by the stove cosily warming his fingers; but some sacrilegious relic-hunter coming this way tweaked the apostle's nose out of his face and made off with it. This was the beginning of a long series of nasal spoliations. No sooner was a new nose stuck on than it was pulled off, and this so continually recurred that at last the custodian, feeling that he was no longer able to supply the demand, removed Peter altogether from the scene.

Perhaps the most attractive of all the sights of Seville to many persons are the paintings of the illustrious Spanish masters which abound there. They are to be found almost everywhere. The Cathedral has plenty of them, and the other churches are well supplied. Their head-quarters, however, is the Museum. This institution is a sort of omnium gatherum of art. In the yard and passages is a woful lot of trash, consisting of old heads, arms, legs, feet, toes, and scraps and chunks of stone carcasses of all sorts, excavated from the ruins of Italica near the city. In the basement is the glorious company of apostles, saints, and martyrs, gouged, chopped, and whittled out of wood; and up-stairs are the pictures. Things were in something of a jumble when we visited it, in consequence of alterations going on, which gave the show an unsatisfactory complexion. La Caridad, which is part church part hospital, contains some famous paintings. Indeed, a connoisseur has a continual feast spread before him in Seville, on which he may batten for weeks. Now, as for me, be it understood, I have an eye for a house, or a sign, or a lady's cheek, when artistically painted, but in the walks of art higher than these I humbly acknowledge my unworthiness to tread. I shall not, therefore, point out the excellences nor criticise the defects of the Murillos and the rest which were presented for my inspection. The guide was a connoisseur and took us to see every one of them, dilating awfully on all of their good points; and to show him that Richmond, Virginia, could produce appreciative artists I chimed in with him, and with my mind dazed by trying to comprehend his elucidation of the *frio*, and the *calido*, and the *vaporoso* styles, I leered and squinched my eyes at them, and (Heaven forgive me for the prevarication!) exclaimed "exquisite!" "charming!" "beau-u-utiful!" and, having done all this solely for the credit of my dear home, I grew athirst, and an hungered, and aweary, and agape, and yearned for the red bricks and the green window-shutters, and the blue-and-black smalt, and the chalk-balls and rouge-pot, which were all in all of art to me.

But the most thrilling sensations of any I experienced in this glorious city were derived from the Government Tobacco Factory. Here I saw snuff made by machinery, whose patent-right claim the heirs of Noah could successfully maintain in any court of justice, and worked by jackass-power; and it was good snuff, too, competent to educe a vigorous and wholesome sneeze, as I did prove. But it was not this that thrilled me. What thrilled me was to have the eyes of five thousand female cigar-makers concentred in one fell swoop upon me. This is the number employed here. Not satisfied with looking, they winked and blinked most diabolically. Protected by the shield of bachelorhood, under which I have safely progressed for a number of years too tedious to mention, I deemed that I could confront them without a ruffle across my peaceful breast; but on trying it—good gracious! I blushed till my nose looked like one great and glorious grog-blossom, and I cleared out after I had seen not half enough, and yet a hundred times too much. Who can resist the Andalusian beauties? with skins whose hues vary between that of law-calf and peach-peelings, though richer and more luscious looking than either; hair, dark and glossy as a tar bucket; eyes, than which the most artistically polished pair of boots is less black and shiny; ankles, symmetrical as ten-pins; and feet too soft and tiny to dint a hole in the mud. But let me pause before I transcend the sober limits which befit my character as a grave and philosophic traveler. The stern fact is that the cigars the goddesses of the factory make are of a sort the smoking of which would infect a whole neighborhood with the asthma.

Around the corner from La Caridad—but whether it be this corner or that, or whether it is this side of it or the other, at this distance of time I misremember, but somewhere about there, at all events—the stranger's attention will be arrested by a blood-stained block erected in the street. Upon this spot has many a sanguinary deed been done, for here take place the public executions of hogs. The victim is drawn to the block, his head laid upon it, and his throat cut from ear to ear with neatness and dispatch. Turning away from the sickening spectacle, the wayfarer will very probably encounter other victims, robust and rotund with fatness, slowly waddling to the slaughter.

The wave of republicanism that rose when Isabella fell and went surging through Andalusia swept over Seville with its other cities; but I saw or heard of nothing special that marked its progress save that sundry places were baptized into the fellowship of freedom by the transforming of names, and that the boys of the town took advantage of the public commotion to invade the Plaza of Liberty (the New Plaza of the day before) and completely ravage it of the sacred oranges of the municipality nurtured therein.

Among all the impressions made upon our minds during our excursion to this fair city none touched us more than those derived from a sight of the ruins of Italica. Ruins became common enough with us before we closed our European career, and most of them outstripped these immeasurably in all the essentials of your good and proper ruins; but these had the inestimable quality of novelty. We had never beheld any of these sublime wrecks of time before, and the first contemplation of them solemnized us to the point of profound and thoughtful moralizing. We drove across the bridge over the Guadalquivir through the suburb of Triana, on the opposite side, which is the residence of the Gypsies and other riffraff, and then for about four miles along the banks of the river till we reached a spot where nothing was to be seen—this being Italica. Yes, nothing of what was once a magnificent and important city, the birthplace of no less than three Roman emperors. It was very mournful —mournful thus to look and see nothing. But leaving our carriage, and floundering on foot over great lumps of clay, we presently saw something. It was the ruined amphitheatre that has been partially excavated, and this, save some trivial scraps of the city walls, is all that remains of Italica.

We found a warrior there on guard, who was wonderfully familiar with every part of the structure and knew the exact purpose to which each nook and cranny in it was applied. There were also a man and his wife who dwelt in a hut hard by, and by virtue of domicile assumed the function of guides, knowing nothing about it— though they were either too honest or too inexpert to allow this deficiency to delude us. The amphitheatre is two hundred and ninety-one feet long and two hundred and four wide. Much of it is still buried, but they continue to dig away at it—a little leisurely, perhaps; but in time the bottom of it will be reached, though for some months past, I believe, the operations have been seriously impeded, either by the death or the impressment into the army of the mule employed in the work. What has been unearthed is in a fair state of preservation, and we were pleased to have pointed out to us by the military man the dens for the wild beasts, the gladiators' green-room, the platform for the dignitaries of the land, the vestal virgins' private boxes, and the seats for poor folks.

The scene seemed very desolate and melancholy now as viewed by us from the places graced by our illustrious predecessors, and it appeared more desolate and melancholy the more we looked at it; so presently we rose and repaired to the hut of the self-styled guide, where there were mementos of the ruins for sale. These mementos were chiefly coins and teeth of vestal virgins and lions. The tariff of prices was uniform, being five cents per specimen. We purchased a couple of beautiful vestal virgins' teeth—that is, beautiful teeth of vestal virgins—sworn to as such by the vender,—though it is but fair to state that his wife had lost several of her own proper stock of dental organs, and there is very little doubt that she would gladly have pulled every one of them out for five cents apiece. We also secured some old Roman coins, which there is every reason to suppose were struck in Paris as long ago as the latter part of the reign of the Emperor Napoleon III. Also some lions' teeth, of whose genuineness there can be no doubt whatever; since it is absolutely certain they were not human, and must therefore necessarily have been those of some beast—unless, indeed, they belonged to a fish. Carefully depositing these inestimable relics in our waistcoat pockets, we re-entered our carriage and returned to Seville, assailed by various vagabond beggars and passing several squads of polite and well-bred rustics at work in the fields, who cheered us most heartily and graciously as we rode by.

Not the least grateful characteristic of Seville to us was its climate, which at that time of year during the day was as balmy as heart could wish. At night, however, it was cool. We wanted a fire, and were furnished with a pile of ashes in a brazier—an arrangement about as cheery to behold as any other ash-bank, but which has the property of giving out such heat as it is blessed withal apparently forever at the rate of seven cents a brazierful. It is true the hotel had a room with a fireplace in it, but the provoking fellow who occupied this apartment remained in the establishment as long as we did; and after a vain attempt to have him turned out, we sat down with what satisfaction we might to our contemplation of the lemon which was stuck in the midst of the ashes to sweeten the deadly exhalations arising therefrom. Authorities generally concur in encomiums upon the climate of Seville in the latter part of winter and in the spring, and if the few days I spent there may serve as a criterion, I can heartily indorse all that is said in its favor. As the city is, in addition, by far the most interesting in the south of Spain, teeming with the grand, the beautiful, and the picturesque in art for the entertainment of the sober-sided married folks, and with the loveliest productions of Nature for the soothing of us single ones, it affords to the invalid one of the most pleasant places of residence during the season specified with which I am acquainted.

CHAPTER VIII.

How we retrace our Steps to Cadiz and go thence to Malaga—How we put up at the Fonda de la Alameda and make awful Discoveries of what is in the Pot—A general Description of Malaga, with the Incidents of our Stay there—How we go from Malaga to Granada and get Experience of Travel by Diligence.

BEFORE daybreak of the fourth day of our sojourn in Seville we caused ourselves to be reboxed under the superintendence of the hotel corps and drawn to the railroad station; and, mightily refreshed and encouraged by the glimpse we had obtained of the glories of that most admirable city, glided majestically back into Cadiz, where we were welcomed with unspeakable joy by the whole household of the Fonda de America, and by none more joyfully than the fleas which it inherit:

"'Tis sweet to know there is an eye will mark
Our coming, and look brighter when we come."

Here we tarried a couple of days, making ready for our farther pilgrimaging, and delayed by the uncertainty of mood and movement indigenous to the nautical men of these parts.

On the afternoon of the first of March we were enabled to embark on a comfortable little steamer which had touched at Cadiz on her way from Liverpool to Malaga; and for the latter city we departed, only one hour later than the advertised time. A Spanish war-vessel set sail simultaneously with us, laden with troops, who were now just entering upon the long and weary road that stretched across the Atlantic to Cuba—and the grave. The receding shores looked very beautiful, but the wind was too fresh to make a prolonged contemplation of them from the deck agreeable, and we went below, where the fund of entertainment contained in the one other passenger was soon exhausted, and, the state-room accommodations being excellent, we disrobed and retired to our slumbers. We jogged along comfortably all night, and before sunrise next morning were in the harbor of Malaga.

We were delayed some time after anchoring waiting for the proper officers to board us, and in the mean while, as is the manner in the Mediterranean ports, sundry boats came forth to us. While waiting for the lazy rascals to come to our deliverance, certain of the boatmen leapt on deck, and, pouncing on our trunks, began to drag them off with might and main. All our prayers and curses availing nothing to check them, we applied to the captain, who most chivalrously entered the lists in our behalf, and after some pretty stiff fighting achieved the victory and saved our plunder. As soon as the officers had manumitted us we and our effects were stuffed into one of the boats and borne to the custom-house. By the functionaries thereof—and, as I am persuaded, though I did not obtain opinion of counsel in the matter, in contravention of the laws regulating commerce between the cities of the realm—our baggage was subjected to rigid inspection. Our case of medicinal juices especially excited violent suspicions. The top of it was split off, and the dozen quart vials which it contained being accurately counted by the authorities, they were pleased to express the doubt whether our sanitary condition was of a sort to require so much and so strong medicine; but, in the mean time, the commissioner of the Fonda de la Alameda had appeared upon the scene, and on his assurance of our unparalleled feebleness the case and the rest of the baggage was allowed to pass. In recognition of his services we could do no less than patronize the house he had the honor to represent, and thither he conducted us, it being close at hand.

The Fonda de la Alameda is not an overgood inn. The attendance, as far as the female department extends, is unexceptionable,—the chambermaids being wonderfully nimble of foot and dexterous of hand; the male servitors are, however, something stupid and slumberous. It has a reading-room furnished with papers which are pretty fresh to one who has not communicated with the outer world for a month. Its chairs are lamentably weak in the back and legs. To two of them befell fracture and disarticulation in the struggle to do their office by me, albeit I am one of the lightest of weights and the most circumspect of sedentaries. The bill of fare is heterogeneous in material and cookery, and among its items— *horribile dictu!*—is cat-flesh. With the waiters the English synonym of this viand is "hare." But let no man be deceived by this delusive dish as I was. My companion beholding me partaking of it copiously was the first who suggested doubts. His suspicions were confirmed by an exceeding grave and reverend English gentleman, who had anxiously investigated the subject in his own interest, and who announced his intention of quitting the country at once and forever. The felinity of the meat was put beyond peradventure by a lady of singular intelligence and acumen with whom I subsequently conferred at Gibraltar, who herself had not long before been a guest of this house, and who was unimpeachable authority on the anatomy of the animals from being an enthusiastic cat-fancier of long standing. Can such things be?

In the reminiscences of mine youth this town was ever a place of sweet memory as the fountain and origin of the Malaga grapes and raisins on which I battened in those blithesome days. But the inspection of it has added but few pleasing visions to gild the recollections of my later years. There is nothing in it particularly interesting. The best things pertaining to it—the grapes and raisins above mentioned—are sent out of it, and we get them in our country as good as, and even better than, they can be had in their native land. Its Cathedral makes no impression upon one who has just seen that at Seville. When viewed afar off, the exterior of this edifice makes a fair enough show, but the interior is commonplace. On the east side of the city is a lofty hill, surrounded by the remains of a Moorish fortress of historical interest. It is the Gibralfaro,—memorable in the siege of Malaga by King Ferdinand, when that potentate captured the city and did an admirable piece of commercial strategy in disposing of the inhabitants to themselves,—whereby he not only realized a handsome profit on the transaction itself, but was able to get back all the merchandise into the bargain,—as is pleasantly related in Fray Antonio Agapida his chronicle. Designing to inspect these remains I girded up my loins and marched up the hill till I reached a point where a warrior, towering on a pinnacle of the old castle, in the most urbane manner offered me the alternative of stopping where I was or of being shot. I elected to stop, and contented myself with gazing upon the panorama spread out before me. It was very beautiful. The city lay like a map at my feet, encircled by hills and washed by the Mediterranean, whose bright expanse, so blue and so placid, stretched far away.

The situation of Malaga is peculiarly fine. Its circle of hills protects it from noxious winds, so that it is regarded as perhaps the best residence in point of climate for invalids in the south of Europe. The general estimate of it in this respect is, I am disposed to believe, correct; though our own experience was far from confirming it; for we had during the latter days of our stay there (about the middle of March) a good deal of cloudy, windy, and cold weather, which made us cuddle the fire with marked affection.

It is a pity that Malaga has so little besides its climate to recommend it. It shows more tendency to business than any city I saw in Spain, donkeys moving hither and thither pretty constantly. It is, however, an old-looking place, and full of beggars; the streets are narrow and twisted; the houses are sombrous in appearance; and, to my mind, it is not a cheerful city. Worst of all, the female population is in pulchritude considerably below the Sevillanas, who are my standard of loveliness and grace,— but, let me hasten to say here that this quality is notoriously a mere matter of individual taste, and that by some critics the Malaga ladies are held to be the type of Spanish beauty. There is nothing to be seen calculated to enliven a sick man, who can do little better than lounge about the Alameda, where he can, at any rate, obtain as much exercise as his constitution will bear by combating with or flying from the vast army of tatterdemalions who charge down upon him from every quarter. To one whose physical organization is of a sort that assimilates him to the chameleon sufficiently to qualify him for living on air, no place could be found more salubrious; for here he will find this staple abundant, sweet, and wholesome; and if, in addition, his digestion competes with that of the ostrich, and, above all, if he has that superlative frame of spirit which I can describe only as *don't-care-a-damativeness*, this is the spot of all others where he can let his life ebb pleasantly away.

Being myself a person the very reverse of the hypothetical being whom I have just drawn, I grew weary of Malaga some time before I left it. It was my habit to kill as much of the morning as I could in bed, and then to saunter forth in the desperate hope of seeing something to sharpen my appetite for breakfast. Before venturing beyond the portals of the hotel it was, however, always necessary to reconnoitre carefully for beggars, who, you might be sure, were lying perdu somewhere about, waiting to waylay you.

After breakfast, in company with my fellow-traveler, I generally adjourned to the Alameda, which was in immediate proximity to the hotel, where we would take a seat on the back of a bench, and from this advantageous position strive with the beggars. It was as much as a man's fortune was worth to yield to charitable impulses now, for the eyes of the whole fraternity, visible and invisible, were upon him, and the bestowal of half a cent upon one was the signal for a general advance of the whole column in irresistible force. In the end we would be driven off, and would fall back to the hotel, where we read the Bible and waited for dinner. I finished up the day by a prolonged prowl about town.

In the course of my diurnal and nocturnal wanderings I traversed every inch of Malaga, reducing myself to the extremity of a renewal of shoes, and being marvelously ill requited for the expenditure of leather. One night I encountered a large bare-headed procession, equipped with lanterns and sacred implements, preceded by a bell ringing dolorously. It was on its way to administer the last rites of the church to a dying man. As it passed all the people knelt in the street, and a great many signals were made to me to conform with the usage. Innumerable bloody noses and black eyes have come on occasions of this kind from the obstinacy of stiff-kneed Protestants. I declined to kneel, but compromised by taking off my hat, and the procession passed me by without maltreating me in any way,—a sad proof, I fear, of the decay of religion in Spain.

The only thing of interest I met with in my morning walks was the market, which was held partly in a building situated on the border of the River Guadalmedina, and partly in the adjacent space, and also in the bed of the river itself,—which is a remarkable stream, in that it possesses banks, and bridges, and a channel, and all other appurtenances of a river, save and except only water, not one drop of which did it have. For its credit, however, I must state that it is said not to be always thus, but that at certain seasons it rolls a most portentous and disastrous current through the city. Business is exceedingly vivacious in this market, all kinds of commodities being for sale there, especially myriads of oranges; and the hubbub is terrific.

The rag-tag-and-bobtail citizens of Malaga are eminent lovers of liberty,—none more so. They pant for freedom, and are ready to strike a blow in her behalf in season and out of season. As a consequence, they had vigorously opposed the imputed monarchism of the central government, and two or three months previous to our arrival had raised the standard of revolt against it. The government pounced down upon them with promptness and energy. Our unhappy landlord was sorely afflicted in those evil times. The national forces who had invaded Malaga, unfamiliar with its localities, could not be made to realize that his hotel was a hotel. They looked on it as either a nest for insurgents, or else bound to become one, and so anticipated their adversaries by taking possession of it themselves. It was a woful thing they did, for they were no sooner safely within its portals than they captured and sacked our landlord's larder,—ruthlessly devouring all his eggs, and grapes, and cakes, and cat's-meat, drinking all his wine, sucking all his oranges, and cracking every nut on the premises,—all of which terrified the landlord to the point of flight. In addition, they ravaged his chambers, and dragging out the beds stuck them in the windows for barricades, from behind which they peppered away at any foot-passenger who had the presumption to come in sight.

The public mind was still excited while I was there, feverishly expecting something to turn up. One night, as I was poking and smoking pensively along one of the streets, a gun of preternatural loudness was fired somewhere near by. The street was full of people, who at once stampeded in every direction. At home I should have first endeavored to ascertain the cause of alarm and then run; but it has always been held a wise maxim to do in Rome as Romans do, and as the people manifestly thought that another rebellion had commenced, and it was certain that they were better judges of their own affairs than I was, I followed their example, and gathering up my pipe and old umbrella, traveled. Several of us made for the sanctuary of a church in the vicinity, trusting for protection to the well-known reverence for holy things which adorns the reprobates of these countries.

Here the women fell upon their knees and the men waited for developments; but nothing occurring, I speedily sallied forth again to investigate the matter. As well as I could understand it a man had been killed, but how or why neither I nor anybody else could determine.

As we were within a day's journey of the renowned city of Granada, we concluded to mitigate the monotony of Malaga by packing up our carpet-bags and making a diversion thitherward. The route as far as Loja is by diligence, and, as the company's one vehicle is somewhat over-patronized, it is necessary to procure tickets betimes. We procured ours the day before the one on which we set out early, and spent the intervening time very agreeably in puzzling over the comprehensive rules and conditions with which these documents are indorsed. These rules and conditions are to the following purport: The company held itself responsible for the safe transport of baggage in every particular, except when it was lost, stolen, or damaged, but would on no account hold itself liable for the mashing of hat-boxes or capsizing of the vehicle. It bound itself to convey passengers straight through to the railroad station at Loja, without fail, if nothing occurred to prevent. In the event of a breakdown it was intimated very gently that the passengers would save time and trouble by picking up their duds and traveling, as the company considered, in such case, that it had discharged its duty to the best of its ability, and the journey for that trip was at an end.

There were one Irish and two Scotch gentlemen who designed making the same journey; and in their company and under the domination of the above rules and conditions we started at six o'clock in the morning in the company's diligence. This vehicle is a species of concentrated omnibus, though hardly as comfortable, with all sorts of nettings and pockets for the bestowal of small baggage, and studded within and without with places for passengers, and possessing its congener's capacity for always holding one more. My companion and myself had inside places, I upon the rod of the brake, which passed under the cushion of the seat, and stowed in with us were several greasy and dirty foreigners, natives of Spain, who smoked horrible tobacco continually and grieved our spirits sorely in divers ways. The fellow-traveler next to me was one of the most somnolent individuals I ever journeyed with, and, using me for a bed, he slept all over me, and bored me almost out of my life with his elbows, besides startling me with the almost palpable certainty that he was transforming my garments into a kind of zoological garden or entomological museum. Before I got rid of him my back was one solid crick from top to bottom. Along with him I was mightily pestered by the brake, whereby, whenever the machinery was put in operation, I was lifted up and presently suddenly dropped, to my serious discomposure. We had to carry food and water with us, and I earnestly recommend all who propose to go on a similar journey to take, in addition, some chloride of lime, a strengthening plaster, and a pot of mercurial ointment.

Among the corps of officials required to run the machine is a functionary whose province it is to chastise the team, and under his efficient efforts we whirled through Malaga gloriously, the smaller parcels on the roof of the diligence flying behind us merrily, though by the eternal vigilance and despairing yells of their owners most of them were rescued. The road led up mountain-sides, winding round and round, and frequently passing by the edge of dangerous precipices. The country presented an aspect of hill and dale, and sterile crag and fertile slope. Here and there were to be seen cork-trees and olive-trees. Every now and then, as we ascended to some commanding height, Malaga would burst into view, far below us, embosomed within its circle of hills, and bathed by the blue and placid Mediterranean, forming a beautiful and striking picture. As we advanced we presently caught occasional glimpses of the lofty peaks of the far-off Sierra Nevada covered with snow. I do not remember that we passed through more than one village, and that was dreadfully decayed and poverty-stricken, though the sight of habitations scattered among the hills was frequent.

Our chastiser was an excellent officer. The diligence was drawn by relays of mules, eight in number, which were kept well warmed up to their work by incessant thrashing while they were going, besides being soundly wolloped before they started, by way, doubtless, of an antepast, as well as receiving a thorough correction after they had stopped, in order to keep their memories green against the next time their services were to be required. The stages were long and the way so difficult that no creature not endued with everlasting life would be able to withstand the pulling, and tugging, and lambasting incident to the journey. At four o'clock we reached Loja, which is planted down in a valley on the banks of the river Genil. In days that are gone Loja was a city well-to-do, but it is a hard-looking one enough now. It is saturated with beggars of a violent temperament, and in rankness of flavor it outranks any place I ever smelt.

At the station we lunched, and loitered for an hour waiting for the locomotive to be greased, and watered, and fired up. Our Irish and Scotch friends, all of whom were English to the backbone, and ourselves took a compartment together, and off we went slowly and smoothly. The Britishmen were in a terrible swivet the whole way, for the road was known to pass somewhere near the farm presented by the Spanish government to the Duke of Wellington, and they were insane to see this memento of His Grace. In their extremity they appealed to us to help them fix the locality, and for pity's sake we made two or three surmises; but, as we never knew till that moment that the duke owned land in these parts, we were not quite sure that we were resolving them their question aright. In two hours' time all speculation on the subject was cut short by our arrival at the famous city of Granada.

10*

CHAPTER IX.

Granada—Of the Hotel de Washington Irving, and the Landlord of that Hostel and his all-accomplished Son-in-Law —Of the Alhambra—Of the Generalife.

THE genius of Washington Irving has thrown over this region a charm so great that few are capable of appreciating its magnitude until a personal inspection enables them to make a discrimination between the romance and the reality. The Granadians are vastly indebted to him, and in grateful commemoration of his services they have called a hotel by his name,—an honor which I hold to be not a little enhanced by the difficulties in which the pronunciation of his name, and especially of his Christian name, involves a Spanish tongue. To the Hotel de Washington Irving our Scotch friends had telegraphed from Malaga, directing apartments to be reserved for the party, and, accordingly, as soon as the cars stopped we were accosted in excellent English by an attaché of the hotel, the son-in-law of the proprietor thereof, who dragged us out of the coach, incarcerated us in the hotel box, and gathered up the baggage. Our fellow-travelers, journeying as do the Anglicans, of course had at least four times as many packages as there was occasion for, and so one piece was left behind—a truly indispensable india-rubber overcoat, the property of the elder of the Scotch gentlemen, which he would not have taken anything in the world for, and which he never got back any more. In blissful belief that all was right, we started off in the box, and jogged along for an interminable period up hills, and seeing nothing, because it was dark when we arrived, till we stopped at the hotel door.

The landlord of the Hotel de Washington Irving, believing that he is justified in taking his ease in his own inn, does nothing except make out the bills and pocket the proceeds—not even exhibiting himself to his guests,

—but leaves all the work to the son-in-law above specified. This invaluable son-in-law was a clever fellow, being in a manner a jack-at-all-trades; and, having lived for a time in New Orleans, conducted the establishment rather after the American than the European fashion,—that is to say, he laid more stress on the boarding than the lodging of his patrons. And, indeed, let me say just here, this distinction between the two modes of keeping a hotel is well marked. In our country the traveler is deposited in a room supplied with only the bare necessaries of a chamber, but, at the same time, he is gorged with feasts of fat things. In Europe, on the other hand, he is ensconced in apartments redundantly furnished with gorgeous curtains, sumptuous carpets, rugs, sofas, lounges, rocking-chairs, marble-top tables, an eight-day clock of the chastest pattern and with visible brass works, articles of ormolu and virtu, a piano, and a harp of a thousand strings. The landlord does not deem it possible that the human heart can desire anything beyond this, and consequently the question of diet is thrust down into a very subordinate place indeed. As an exemplification—though I have been a frequent guest of the St. Nicholas, of New York, I have never had a room there furnished materially better than the worst in which I lodged while in Spain; but neither in London, nor in Paris either, did I find a table that deserved to be named in comparison with that of the St. Nicholas.

An American, therefore, will be disposed to consider the Washington Irving of Granada a very fair hotel. Under the tendency to wool-gathering which is promoted by seclusion, however, the landlord is betrayed into something of diffuseness in keeping his accounts; thus, we found ourselves charged with telegrams which we had neither sent nor received, and for the transportation of baggage which we had left at Malaga. In the bills, too, the guests are rated *per capita* for the dining-room fire,—the rate being for each person one hundred per cent. on the gross value of the fuel; though, as we ascertained by actual trial, the landlord will strike this charge off rather than be whipped. The waiter, moreover, had a way when you asked him for bread of hurling a pone of it at you across the table. With the exception of these trifling shortcomings, it is good enough. It has a very neat garden attached to it, well adapted for a lunching-place, and possesses the crowning advantage of being situated in the Alhambra grounds; so that I recommend it, and the more cordially because of the great consideration shown me by the landlady in spanking her baby for refusing to kiss me.

There were but few strangers in Granada at this period. We found that we had done a work of supererogation in ordering rooms to be reserved, for we constituted the Washington Irving's entire register of guests, save one gentleman who had long before taken up his abode there permanently. The Hotel of the Seven Floors across the street was utterly desolate, with not a patron on any of its floors. Three or four new ones came to our establishment during the week, but our rival got only one solitary couple the whole time. This so encouraged them, however, that in their exultation they must needs cast reflections upon and belittle us by digging up all the rocks on their side of the street and relaying them. But, confound them! we matched them by excavating a ditch on our side to carry off the water,—which was a much more useful piece of work than theirs.

The glory of Granada is, of course, the world-renowned Alhambra; and to it we repaired at the earliest opportunity,—our landlord's talented son-in-law officiating as guide. For association's sake we would fain have employed in this capacity "José Jiminez, son of Mateo Jiminez, Guide of Washington Yrving," as set forth on his card, who could be found any time of day sunning himself before our door; but it was impossible for us to put ourselves in suitable communication with him, for he spoke no English, and his French being uttered identically as if it were Spanish, the one was as unintelligible to us as the other. José was better dressed than Mateo appears to have been, but despite his good clothes there was an air of the ragamuffin about him that showed him to be a legitimate descendant of his historic sire. He, however, had the luck to chaperon one of our party, the Irish gentleman, who being able to devote but one day to the sights, and, having arrived on Saturday night, made his visit to the Alhambra on Sunday,—though by special permission, for the authorities of Granada are uncommonly pious, and do not allow the place to be shown on other than week-days, except on emergencies. As we had more time at our command we employed the Sabbath in usurping José's station in the sunshine, and deferred our visit till Monday.

Accordingly on Monday morning we set out in company with our two Scotch fellow-travelers. The elder of these was a most amiable and excellent old gentleman, and an archæologist, natural philosopher, singer of comic songs, and theological controversialist,—in every one of which departments he excelled, and in all of which he was an enthusiast. He was a man with an exquisite sense of humor, and it was delightful to hear him tell how at Malaga, when he asked for a *wafer*, the waiter brought him an *egg*,—egg being *huevo* in Spanish, and pronounced astonishingly like wafer; at the relation of which fact he would become filled with rapture, and I, and all others who heard it, could not refrain from rejoicing with him. He bore about with him a barometer, a thermometer, a compass, an almanac, and a host of similar appliances; and guide-books, and maps, and authorities without number. On the present occasion he took along various volumes pertinent to the subject,—all of which he insisted upon studying and consulting at every step, to the unadulterated disgust of our guide, the all-knowing son-in-law, who found his statements controverted and corrected continually. It was his wont at home to edify the children of his Sunday-school with lectures, and, as Spain was to be the subject of some of these discourses on his return, he felt it to be his bounden duty to gather every possible fact for their enrichment; and to this end not a rat-hole would he pass without minute investigation of its origin, its history, and especially its relation to the Moorish domination. In addition, the old gentleman had a capital eye for the picturesque, and one of his great aims was to get what he called a *pong-de-view*,—from which, when he got one, he would inspect the scene with rapture so lengthened that it almost ran our guide distracted with the fidgets. It was this consummate perception of the beautiful that led him on the first Sunday afternoon of our stay in Granada to summon us all in the utmost haste from the basement of the hotel to the top. We thought that the house was on fire, but it turned out that he wished us to share with him the pleasure of seeing the reflection of the sunlight on the snowy tops of the Sierra Nevada. It was a most gratifying spectacle, but obtained by my poor companion at an expense of wind he could ill afford to disburse.

To those who would read of the Alhambra in its romantic relations I must commend the glowing pages of Irving. To me a great part of the interest of the visit to it sprang from awakened reminiscences of thoughts and feelings excited by the perusal of his descriptions long before, and I must confess that but for the spell he had put upon me I should not have been greatly affected by what I saw. It has changed materially even since his day. Squalor and decay have effaced beauties of which he speaks, and the fountains whose drops then fell tinkling in their marble basins have ceased to play. On the other hand, some of its original beauties long vanished have of late been restored, though I know not but that this diminishes in a measure rather than enhances the charm. But such is the magic of genius that the insubstantial images that he created arose and usurped the place of realities, and I beheld the Alhambra with his eyes, not with my own. Indeed, the most interesting spot of all to me was the room occupied by this man of genius and geniality, and in clamoring to see it I displayed no less insanity than was exhibited by my fellow-travelers in their efforts to obtain a peep at the estate of the Iron Duke. To those, then, who wish for the romance of these crumbling halls I heartily commend the pictures of my friend Washington Irving—I can truly call him my friend. I am but a plain matter-of-fact man myself, with but little poetry in my soul and none at all in my pen, and my account must be dressed in very common linsey-woolsey prose. My chivalric and love-sick readers had better, therefore, skip ahead, and leave the prosy old creatures to go with me for the present.

The Alhambra derives its name from the reddish hue of the earth of which it is constructed, the word signifying "red house." As is generally known, it was both a palace and a fortress for the Moorish monarchs, and in their day the space encompassed by its walls was sufficiently capacious to accommodate forty thousand troops. It is situated on the summit of a large hill, rising high above the town of Granada, which spreads about its base. A great part of this hill is thickly planted with elm-trees—too thickly, indeed, for them to thrive—which were presented by the Duke of Wellington as an offset to the gift of his estate; and amongst them run two or three avenues leading to the city. The nightingales, for which these groves are notorious, had gone off somewhere to spend the winter and we were deprived of the pleasure of their society. Time, and Charles V., and the French, and whitewash, have dealt upon the Alhambra's pride till it is wellnigh destroyed. Erected and adorned at an expenditure of money so enormous that it was believed that only the devil could supply such sums, it would now hardly tempt a man of our practical country to speculate in it as old brick.

The usual entrance is by the Gate of Judgment, a massive square tower, which is entered under an immense arch of the horseshoe shape peculiar to Moorish architecture. On the keystone of this arch is sculptured a great outstretched hand, and over an inner arch just within the tower there is also sculptured a great key; and it is stated—and I believe that all who have examined the subject admit the reasonableness of the statement—that when the hand shall grasp the key the whole concern will go to smash. At this gate in ancient days the justices of the peace for this magisterial district were wont to hold their court. Ascending the stairway of the tower we came upon a wide open space, like a small parade-ground, to which is applied the name of the Place of Cisterns.

This place derives its appellation from the vast tanks beneath it hewn out of the rock. The water is drawn from them through the medium of a well, and has a most enviable reputation. There is a kind of bar established at the well for the sale of the fluid to thirsty visitors, and while ranged before it our Scotch friend read us a tremendously full account of the cisterns and all thereto pertaining, compiled from the numerous authorities he had along, which the barkeeper listened to with much complacency and which moved us to patronize him. The water is very good—a little weak, but cool.

Full before us stood the uncompleted palace commenced by the Emperor Charles V. Despite the fact that certain recent events in my own country had made me somewhat dubious of republican principles, I was very nearly reconverted to my original faith when I saw that this embodiment of monarchy had destroyed an enormous portion of the beautiful palace of the Moors to make way for his abortion—a pile begun with most arrogant promise and ending ignominiously in the middle of its career; a ruin unable to elicit the veneration which is a ruin's right and due. It was his purpose to outdo the Moorish kings on their own dunghill, and it is impossible to estimate the ravage the wretched man would have wrought but for the merciful interposition of a party of earthquakes that came and scared him off the premises. Most visitors contemptuously leave this shell of a palace to be inspected last, as we did now. It is a square structure, much the greater part of which is monopolized by a central circular court surrounded by columns, which would, doubtless, have appeared very grand when finished, though by its size it makes the rest of the building seem deficient in that comfortable roominess which we look for in the abode of magnates. The court has justly been likened to a bull-ring, and, indeed, has been used in that capacity very satisfactorily. Close by this palace is the door by which you enter into the palace of the Alhambra.

The Alhambra was built by different potentates at different times, and none of its architects seem to have troubled themselves about the general effect; being decidedly more solicitous for the beauty of parts than for the symmetry of the whole. Hence the plan is an irregular jumble; the various portions being placed not where they would be most appropriate, but where they would dovetail most snugly with the rest of the structure.

The first thing to be done on entering is to surrender canes, old cotton umbrellas, and all other offensive weapons at the behest of the custodian of the pile, who dogs your steps incessantly till your exit, to provide against an outbreak of the spirit of pilfering which is so apt to possess the mind in a place like this. You are then ushered into the Court of the Myrtles, or, as it is otherwise termed, the Alberca, from an enormous oblong pool, which is its most prominent feature. This pool is full of goldfish, and its sides are bordered with neatly-kept myrtles. It was used as the place for doing the family washing—not of the clothes, perhaps, but of the person. The court is adorned with elegant windows and arches, and with marble pillars sustaining galleries. Upon the walls is frequently repeated the inscription to be found plentifully in other parts of the Alhambra, "There is no Conqueror but God,"—the motto of the pious old Ibn-l-Ahmar, the projector of the palace. From the crystal bosom of the pool is reflected brilliantly the Tower of Comares, which rises boldly at the northern end.

It is well known that Mohammedans have always looked upon murder as a very common everyday piece of business, deserving of very little consideration as to why, when, or where it is done. They make no bones in cutting off a man's head in their parlor, or bedroom, or dining-room,—anywhere that happens to be convenient,—it is all the same to them. As a result of this trait there is probably not an apartment or court in the Alhambra where there has not been at least one taking-off, while in most of them numbers have been slaughtered. Authenticated history records many an instance of the sort, and tradition teems with them. The Court of the Myrtles has had its share.

Embracing all the lower portion of the Tower of Comares is the celebrated Hall of Ambassadors, which was, as its name denotes, the audience-chamber of the kings of Granada. It is a large and lofty apartment, and splendidly adorned. It walls are covered with inscriptions, devices, and escutcheons, and its vaulted ceiling, made of white and blue and gold inlaid-work blended into circles and crowns and stars, is a marvel of elaborate workmanship. On either side of the entrance is a niche in the wall. These are seen at the entrances of other apartments of the Alhambra, and were intended, say some, as places of reception for the slippers of visitors,—for the followers of the Prophet, seeing that the removal of their headgear would be a job tantamount to the unswathing of a small mummy, sagaciously uncover the feet as a mark of respect instead of the head, as we Christians do; others say, however, that these recesses were meant to contain water-jars by day and lamps by night. The hall overlooks the little river Darro, flowing at a great distance below the walls of the tower, and the scene embraces a portion of the city and the vega, forming a lovely picture. From one of its windows Boabdil, the last of the kings of Granada, was let down in a basket when a child by his mother to save him from the wrath of old Muley, his father. There is another window, in a small room leading to the Royal Chapel, from which he was also let down at the same time and under the same circumstances. We leaned out of both of them, by which simple expedient we freed our minds of some annoying doubts as to having seen the right one.

By the narrow, winding, and dark and difficult stairway we ascended to the top of the tower, and from its crumbling pinnacles, at the risk of our necks, gathered some moss as a souvenir. From this point the view is one to please the eye and touch the imagination of the most insensitive. All the lovely vega of Granada was before us, green and fertile, girdled by mountains, and dotted over with villages,—almost every spot of which is linked with some historic story or romantic legend. At its farthest bound was seen the low and dreary hill which bears the mournful name of "The Last Sigh of the Moor," where poor Boabdil took his parting-look at home, and in the centre of it is the town of Santa Fé, which sprang all at once into existence during the siege of Granada, and from which Columbus made the first step on the way that led him to a new world. From amongst the hills close by arose the white palace of the Generalife, while to enhance the charm appeared the so-called rivers Darro and Genil,—streams of surpassing fame in the songs and tales and sober histories of all this region, but which, without exaggeration, would, if concentrated into one, not be equivalent to the least pretentious of our creeks; and whose contemplation fills an American bosom with amazement at the audacity of their sponsors in thus misapplying the honorable appellation of river, and with unfeigned commiseration of themselves for the false position they have been made to assume before the world. But most beautiful of all that was to be seen were the snow-covered peaks of the Sierra Nevada, so clear and pure and brilliant that they seemed almost at hand, and giving a glory to the scenery impossible to be described.

From the Court of the Myrtles we enter the Court of the Lions. This is the most noted portion of the Alhambra. Here we indeed see what the Moors were capable of accomplishing. This court derives its name from the twelve marble lions which sustain a large and handsome alabaster fountain in the centre of it. The fountain is constructed of two basins, a lower one twelve-sided and nearly ten feet in diameter and two feet in depth, which is surmounted by a smaller one not quite four feet in width by one and a third in depth. The border of the lower basin is inscribed with some verses from the pen of the poet-laureate,—a writer whose productions are marked by an admirable simplicity of sentiment amounting almost to fatuousness, but withal somewhat turgid in style and muddy in diction. The fountain is no longer allowed to play, except on special occasions, from fear that the dampness may accelerate the progress of decay. The lions are dwarfish in stature, with villainous-bad countenances, and altogether are scraggy-looking specimens of the plastic art. In one of the guide-books of our Scotch friend they were furthermore described as being "barbecued,"—a term which, notwithstanding his profound conversance with art-nomenclature, mystified him exceedingly. It is truly a judicious injunction which bids us to regard them not from an artistic point of view, but simply as heraldic effigies. An interesting question has been raised as to who sculptured these lions, seeing that their religion interdicted the Moors from representing living beings. It is probable, I think, that the Mohammedans did as Christians do in the face of such difficulties,—that is, they availed themselves of the services of the less scrupulous children of Satan.

Mere verbal description would fail to give an adequate idea of this famous court. It is wonderfully elegant in conception and in execution. There are within it no less than one hundred and twenty-four marble columns, of light and tasteful workmanship, and the arches connecting them are of a most delicate pattern worked in filigree, —very frail to look upon, indeed, yet which have withstood the tooth of time for centuries. Mosaic devices are seen everywhere, and the walls are blazoned with Arabic inscriptions, elaborately and neatly done in beautiful stucco-work. One of these inscriptions is worthy of especial note from the kindly encouragement it holds forth, being in words to this effect: "Be not, O thou, scared at these lions; they aren't sure-enough lions." The extent of the roofless court, the glaring white of its ornaments, the solemn group of figures circling the fountain, and the absence of any sign of the habitation of man, contribute to give the place a desolate and spectral air of solitude, which greatly augments the impressiveness of the scene.

The Court of the Lions was one of the favorite slaughtering-places of the lords of the Alhambra. The Muley before mentioned here beheaded all the children of his sultana Ayeshah, the mother of Boabdil, the blood of the little ones mingling with the waters of the fountain,— Boabdil himself, with his usual bad luck, escaping.

On one side of the court is the Hall of the Abencerrages, noticeable for its fine stalactite roof, but especially for being the reputed scene of the butchery of the gallant chieftains from whom it takes its name. The marble floor and the fountain in the centre of it exhibit some broad, dingy splotches, which are said to be marks of the blood of the murdered men; but they are due, no doubt, to a no more ghastly cause than the oxidation of iron contained in the marble. By some authorities the fountain in the Court of the Lions is asserted to be the locality where the slaughter was done. On this point a most dreadful dispute arose between our Scotch friend and the landlord's son-in-law,—the former relying for his facts on his guide-books, and the latter for his on his omniscience. It were difficult for me to say with which of the champions the weight of probability rested, inasmuch as the argument had not been concluded when we left Granada. Wherever it was done, however, the wretched Boabdil has been given the credit of it, though it has now come to be acknowledged that in this, as in several other villainies, he, like Nero and some others of evil name and reputation, has been vilely calumniated.

Opposite to the Hall of the Abencerrages is that of the Two Sisters,—so named from two large and similar slabs of marble in its pavement. This hall is exquisitely beautiful, and is especially famous for its magnificent roof, in whose construction there enter upwards of five thousand pieces. It was one of the private apartments of the ladies of the harem, and for their refreshment the walls were profusely inscribed with lackadaisy sentiments and awfully love-sick verses.

At each extremity of the Court of the Lions is an elegant pavilion, and through the upper one we enter the Hall of Justice, where the Moorish cabinet held its sessions and the king dealt out the peculiar quality of justice current in those days. The calumniators of the much-enduring Boabdil locate here the performance of another of his atrocities, for here, say they, he arraigned and tried his innocent queen on the charge of infidelity. In another part of the palace is a sort of cage with an iron grating, apparently intended for the incarceration of some unfortunate individual, and this has been astutely seized upon by the calumniators to confirm their story, for, according to them, this cage was the prison of the queen. It appears, however, to be established that what shreds of facts there are to hang the tale upon pertain not to the history of Boabdil, but to that of his persecuting old father, while the cage, it is likely, was constructed for the confinement of poor Crazy Jane, the wife of Philip I., during her paroxysms of insanity.

The Hall of Justice in its ornamentation fully maintains the delicacy and beauty characteristic of the other apartments, and in some respects excels any of them. But the most striking objects in this hall are several paintings done on skins and nailed to the domes. They are certainly not overwhelming for their grandeur, or beauty, or correctness, or for any other admirable quality of the limner's art; but their interest is great from the wide field of conjecture they open as to what in the world they are intended to represent, seeing that they are a conglomeration of Moors, ladies looking out of windows, knights, boars, chess-boards, dogs, and birds of surpassing strangeness and feather, and as to who executed them, seeing that the Moors themselves were altogether too sanctimonious to commit the damning crime of picture-making. In one of the recesses of the hall is placed a large and beautiful porcelain vase, finished in white, blue, and gold enamel. It is inscribed with the words "Eternal Salvation,"—a marvelously happy label when we consider that it was found filled with gold. Besides the vase, there are here a couple of common old tombstones, the property of two royal defuncts, and a second-hand sarcophagus.

The portions of the Alhambra which I have now described are those that are most celebrated and interesting. There are other parts of it, however, that deserve a passing notice ; among these the bath-rooms are worthy of especial mention from their elegance and completeness. As the ornamentation has recently been restored to almost its original perfection, we are able to form something like an adequate idea of the luxurious style in which their proprietors washed themselves. In the bath-rooms proper are large bathing-tubs for the old folks, and small ones for the youngsters. The room for repose was particularly comfortable, being furnished with places for couches, on which the bathers could rest and be lulled by music from the band perched in a gallery above. The architectural arrangements of this saloon are remarkably delicate and showy, consistng of a series of columns, arches, galleries, and windows, which I can liken only to such fancy-gilt caskets as the fashionable confectioners of Brobdingnag would use to incase their French candies in for the little ones at Christmas. Other places of interest are the Royal Chapel, principally interesting from its sombre ugliness; and the garden of Lindaraja, which is a little patch of ground in an odd corner, economized by planting it with shrubs and flowers.

The Alhambra was formerly surrounded by a wall which was topped by a great number of towers. Many of these are now nothing but ruins. As they offered numerous and excellent *pongs-de-view*, in company with our Scotch friend I clambered up all that afforded a foothold, and was rewarded by many a lovely prospect. In these investigations we had to rely upon our own acumen, for the landlord's son-in-law, completely sickened with the pragmatical incredulity with which his expositions had hitherto been met, contented himself with merely putting us on the track, and, taking a seat on a rock, left us to come by what results we might. This was, however, a matter of trivial moment to our friend, for, among his other appurtenances, he was provided with a little opera-glass, in whose superb mechanism entered no less than twenty lenses, the performance of which rivaled that of my own double-barreled monocular, whose other eye, it may be recollected, had been knocked out in Cuba; and in the enlarged and enlightened views furnished by this instrument he reveled with the amplest satisfaction.

The interior of most of these towers was adorned in the delicate and elegant style of the apartments in the body of the Alhambra, for they were used as residences by the scions of Moorish royalty; but as they were likewise designed to be defenses, their exterior is plain, substantial, square in form, and devoid of windows. The absence of the latter, besides the protection it afforded from arrows, brickbats, and bullets, subserved another extremely useful purpose, for the poor Moors amongst the divers afflictions and tribulations with which they were beset, were most mortally afraid of the Evil Eye, and would cheerfully block up every hole to shut out its glances,— especially from the womankind, who, as might have been inferred from the inherent tenderness of the sex, stood in pre-eminent awe of the malign influence, while their natural curiosity made them particularly liable to get in the range of it.

In alluding to the towers of the Alhambra it behooves that I should make express mention of the Torre de la Vela, for about this one there yet lingers some of the necromantic influence which once was rife through all the place. It resembles the other towers in its general aspect, but its peculiarity is that it is surmounted by a large bell. On the great festival day celebrated every year in commemoration of the surrender of Granada, the damsels for miles around bundle hither in hot haste, and ring the bell with untiring alacrity and zeal; and this they do because it possesses the seven-times blessed virtue of guaranteeing the ringer a husband or his equivalent before the close of the year.

Efforts are being made to restore the Alhambra to its former splendor. But in spite of restorations, never again can the Alhambra be made the glorious pile it was. What Charles V. and the French have wrought upon it is past all architectural surgery, for their mode of dealing with it was of the knock-down and blow-up schools. By Irving and others the French have been much commended for the care they took in preserving it during their occupation. But, unfortunately, these exemplary conservators were not permitted to remain there forever. Their attachment to it appears to have been very firm; so firm, in fact, that when they tore themselves away, they tore a vast portion of the structure away, too. Besides demolishing several of the towers they would have annihilated the palace itself, but that a magnanimous soul was found who had the courage to withdraw the match connected with the mine they had prepared. Some folks there are who think their proceedings in this regard savor strongly of vandalism, but I am happy to believe that no American familiar with the sanctifying power of "military necessity," has had the hypocrisy to condemn them.

Not much behind these two potent practitioners of the obliterative arts were the pious Christians who took it from those who reared it and delighted to adorn it; for in their most holy horror of the infidel inscriptions and heathenish abominations of all sorts that made its walls hideous to a champion of the true faith, they mixed their whitewash as thick as mortar and laid it on apparently with a trowel, so that frequently it can be removed only by means of a pickaxe—an instrument something clumsy for the delicate manipulation required. Its towers, and other portions of it, have long been the abode of a class of persons whose mode of livelihood the most persevering researches of travelers have never hitherto been able to discover, and where they have set up their staffs they have soiled, and smoked, and injured the place beyond redemption.

It may please some of the readers of Irving's "Tales of the Alhambra" to know that the little Dolores so frequently mentioned therein ultimately married her cousin to whom she was engaged, and is now blessed, as the saying is, with sundry children. They do not live at the Alhambra now but in a neighboring village, where the said cousin officiates as pedagogue. These facts came to me from the omniscient son-in-law. In prosecuting my inquiries I also learned that my friend Irving was an awful splutterer of the Spanish language,—a discovery that tickled me mightily, for, though it might not be supposed, yet it is nevertheless true that even in my well-ordered bosom there is a whiff of that spirit of envy in which the rest of my wretched fellow-creatures are steeped to the ears.

At a moderate distance from the Alhambra on the side of an eminence stands the Generalife, which was a kind of summer-house whither the Moorish monarchs repaired to hold their feasts and revelries. The sheen with which it glitters from afar is found upon entering it to be an optical delusion, for it has been put in too good a state of repair to have retained a great many of its former characteristics. It has a very handsome garden set off with yew-trees clipped after a very fanciful fashion and with many old-time cypresses, to one of which our attention was specially directed by the lady custodian of the place as the Cypress of the Sultana, of which and whom *on dit* —what the reader can readily imagine. There is also in the building a picture-gallery claiming to contain portraits of various Christian kings and heroes, as well as of the notorious Boabdil himself,—of all of which it suffices to say that the execution might be forgiven could the authenticity be guaranteed. But the chief attraction is the mirador attached to it, which merits especial notice for affording, in the judgment of our Scotch friend, the most glorious *pong-de-view* of any we obtained. From the mirador we were turned out upon the adjacent hills, the nearest of which is that known as the Silla del Moro,— the chair of the Moor,—where Boabdil on one occasion sat all night waiting for the ending of a row down town. We clambered up all the other ridges in the vicinity, which in the cold and rainy weather of the time looked dull and desolate, possessing no interest except as *pongs* for seekers after the picturesque.

CHAPTER X.

Of what other Things are to be seen in Granada, especially the Cathedral and the Carthusian Convent—Of the sociable and edifying Nature of our Indoor Life there—How we returned to Malaga, with the unpropitious Circumstances of the Journey, and how we were comforted on the Way.

HAVING duteously "done" everything in our neighborhood we prepared to descend from the heights and make a progress through the town. To this end the indefatigable son-in-law hitched up the hotel box or omnibus for our accommodation, rammed us in, and put us through.

Direful is the change that has fallen upon Granada since the glorious days of its Moorish lords. It is like enough that its streets are not more crooked now than they were then, and it is hardly possible that future ages can intensify their present crookedness, but the life and bustle which then animated them are gone; indeed, from the excitement our vehicle created as it bounced over them and the universal staring we evoked it seemed that its

citizens were famishing for the want of something to stir
them up. The Bibarrambla, so famous as the whilom
meeting-place for pleasure, for business, and for fighting,
has degenerated into a poor, plain plaza with scarce more
relish of romance about it than any brickyard. Whether
the enormous rivers have degraded *per se* or dried up along
with the prosperity of the town, I do not feel competent
to determine, but they are not what I had taken them
for. The Darro goes mumbling through a valley a world
too wide for it more in the manner of a city drain than
of a respectable and well-to-do river, while the classic
Genil, or Jenil, or Xenil—it boots not in which of these
fashions it be spelled so it be pronounced Haneel—is
prostituted to a convocation-place for washerwomen, and
its illustrious waters are polluted with dirty clothes.
Upon the whole city there rests an air of decay and ugliness and sombreness peculiarly striking and disheartening to the sojourner who recalls the fact that it was once
so lovely and desirable as to lead the enraptured Moors
to believe that it was directly under Paradise.

The first place to which the son-in-law bore us was the
Cathedral, which we found wedged in among a mass of
profane shops and dwelling-houses. The interior of this
edifice is really very noble and imposing. Its cupola or
dome has a particularly fine effect from its height and
the tastefulness of its ornamentation, and is made more
striking by a curious twist which the architect, by a combination of mechanical devices and ocular delusions, has
contrived to make seemingly exist in a part of its circle.
There are fifteen chapels, variously adorned, within the
church. The chapel containing the high altar is extremely rich and beautiful. The church has a profusion
of paintings, many of which are highly venerated by
those versed in such things, a great number of them
having been executed by Alonzo Cano. Among these
art-treasures those that most attracted my unskilled
fancy were the portraits of Ferdinand and Isabella and
Adam and Eve, all vouched for as authentic likenesses
taken from life. Prominently displayed in various quarters of the sanctuary I observed notices—which are,
however, relics of the past—sternly prohibiting all men

from talking with any woman within its precincts,—an idea which might possibly work some good if applied to our congregations.

Passing through a stately door we entered the royal chapel, the most interesting portion of the Cathedral, for here lie Ferdinand and Isabella, the conquerors of this land,—as an inscription in the chapel tells,—who brought it back to our faith,—the inscription goes on to say,—who acquired the Canary Isles and Indies, as well as the cities of Oran, Tripoli, and Bugia; who crushed heresy, expelled the Moors and Jews from these realms, reformed religion—and died; the queen, November 26, 1504; the king, January 23, 1516. With them rest poor Crazy Jane, their daughter, and her husband Philip, whom she loved with such an appalling love. To commemorate them are two mausoleums, wrought of alabaster with exquisite skill and beauty and taste. On one of these magnificent monuments lie extended the effigies of Ferdinand and Isabella side by side, and on the other those of Philip and Jane. Both are elaborately sculptured with allegorical figures, emblems, and ornaments appropriate in design and delicately executed. The bodies are in plain coffins deposited in the vault below, and Philip's coffin, it is said, is the one that his poor demented wife was wont to bear about with her for love of him.

In this chapel are kept sundry relics of the sovereigns. There is a sword of Ferdinand's, and a sceptre and a crown and a mass-book belonging to the queen, together with a chasuble weighty with gold embroidery worked upon it by her own hands, and which our Scotch friend tried on with much satisfaction. The decorations of the altar possess a special interest, for amongst them are representations which give a valuable insight into the fashions of the times of the Conquest. And here is perpetrated another slanderous assault upon Boabdil, truly surnamed the Unlucky. Surely, one would think he had been sufficiently vexed by the two Muleys, by his father Muley, and by his uncle Muley, and by evil tongues, to stay the further uplifting of the hand of man against him. But not so. After blighting him in fortune and in name they have at last struck a deadly blow at his personal appearance, for here is a representation of the surrender of Granada, scooped and gouged and chopped out of wood, in which the miserable monarch is figured with a visage which would have justified his harem in the eyes of men and devils in withdrawing from him in a body. Such depicturing as this can only be regarded as a mean outrage on the defenseless, and the advantage they have taken of him is rendered all the more glaring by the fact that his religion forbidding the graving of images cut him off from retaliating in kind.

Having fructified us fully with the Cathedral, the son-in-law repacked us in the omnibus and took us away out of town to the Carthusian Convent, in former days the abode of certain monks of that order, but now depopulated. But though solitary it is not desolate; on the contrary, it contains a variety of well-kept objects worthy to be seen, for its legitimate occupants seem to have been a community of geniuses, gifted with skill in divers arts, which they exercised for the glory of the saints and the adorning of their holy habitation.

We were first treated to some of the handiwork of the brother who was blessed with the gift of painting. This genius has adorned one extremity of an apartment with columns and arches hardly to be distinguished from solid marble; and on the wall of the old refectory he has painted the representation of a wooden cross so naturally as to delude the eye effectually,—nay, the astute birds of the air themselves have actually been deceived by it, and have flown into the room and become terribly flustered to find that it yielded no rest to their feet. This is art,—and, above all, it is that style of art with which I do not scruple to claim a substantial acquaintance; wherefore it is no empty compliment when I award to the artist my hearty word of approval and commendation for his imposing work. The versatile brother has, however, essayed in another walk,—and one that is, by some other critics, considered to be of a higher order than the one to which my own tastes incline,—namely, that of historical painting. He has executed a great number of pieces in which, as one whose paramount object is to instruct should do, he has entirely subordinated the esthetic to the practical by depicting plain matter-of-fact representations of the hanging, drawing, and quartering of his fellow-creatures, their crucifixion, their roasting, the sawing off of their limbs, and other villainies perpetrated upon them; whereby it is his design to keep in everlasting remembrance the persecutions inflicted upon the Catholics by the Protestants. It may possibly be imagined with what relish a pillar of the Kirk of Scotland, an expounder in the General Assembly, an adept in the shorter and the longer Catechism, and an earnest student of Fox's Book of Martyrs would partake of such a feast as this. Our Scotch friend turned his nose high up as we passed by the long series with which the walls are covered, pronouncing them to be hideous daubs in manner and popish fables in matter. For my part, though they savored powerfully of the dissecting-room and charnel-house, I was monstrously pleased with them, for I am a man of extraordinary fairness of mind, ever glad to hear and see the other side of a question. It has been brought to my knowledge occasionally, for some years back, that the Catholics were wont to deal dreadfully by the Protestants, and it was now quite comforting to find that they had been paid back in their own coin; so that when I left the Convent it was with a feeling of sorrow for the frailty of all human flesh, and charity towards both of the great sects, and a determination to trust neither as far as I could sling a bull by the tail. This same brother has also bequeathed us several specimens of his powers in another phase of the historical walk, consisting of passages in the life of St. Bruno, the founder of the order of Carthusians. In execution they partake of many of the plain matter-of-fact characteristics of the persecution series, and, as to the verity of the scenes depicted, I must confess that even my tolerant credulity was somewhat strained. Thus, it was at variance with my ideas of physiology and pathology that a thoroughly dead man should be able to talk, even though his remarks were words in season; and yet it was so represented on the canvas, and other anomalous incidents besides. Our Scotch friend summarily thrust them in the same category with the others, utterly abjuring faith in any of the paintings except the marble columns and the wooden cross.

Our attention was next directed to the work of that brother whose gift was carpentry and cabinet-making. His talent was exercised chiefly in the manufacture of doors, and there is no gainsaying his ability. Nothing can be neater and more beautiful than the manner in which he has blended silver, and ebony, and tortoise-shell, and mother-of-pearl. Passing through his doors, we entered the church, to whose adornment every brother who had any sort of gift whatever has contributed, and which is resplendent with rich marbles and precious stones. The sacristy adjoining is a complete phantasmagoria, being lined and profusely decorated with variegated marble, in which the veins form all sorts of images. In one place I observed a profile of Louis Philippe, which, to the best of my recollection of him as seen on an occasional five-franc piece in the days of metallic currency, was strikingly like. There were also cats running up and rats running down, a number of men of note, beasts, birds, and fishes, and women, in great variety. It must be owned, however, that it requires something of the clairvoyant faculty to see these things clearly, and where several persons are contemplating the same object there is pretty sure to be a confusedness of vision with some of them and a contrariety of judgment as to what the configuration most resembles.

This finished the sights of the Carthusian Convent, and the Carthusian Convent finished the sights of Granada which the son-in-law thought worthy of our attention,— excepting the spot where Boabdil surrendered the keys of Granada. This is a place comparatively solitary, where stands a small and time-worn structure, originally a mosque, and now called the Chapel of San Sebastian. On the front of it is a tablet recording the fact of the surrender and identifying this as the scene of the impressive event.

We had made arrangements for excursions into the vega, but the beautiful weather with which we had been favored on our arrival gave place to a series of cold, rainy, and snowy days, compelling us to abandon our plans. During this rough spell we had perforce to remain in the house a great part of the time, where each one occupied himself according to his bent,—I fertilizing my mind by reading the Madrid newspapers, my companion jarring up his torpid circulation by shivering, and our old Scotch friend laboring for the enlightenment of his benighted Sunday-school scholars by arranging notes for his lectures. All met at dinner, which was served at six o'clock, and remained together in the dining-room till bedtime. The social communion thus brought about was the most agreeable feature of our stay at Granada. Then would meet with us the gentleman of whom I have before made casual mention as a permanent inmate of the Hotel de Washington Irving. He was an English artist, possessing a great store of miscellaneous information, profoundly versed in Egyptian antiquities and other kinds of lore which one can acquire satisfactorily only by traveling. In his studio, to which he had the kindness to admit us, were a number of gems of art in the shape of paintings, vases, coins, fragments of mummy, and other like curiosities, which the tasteful traveler picks up in his wanderings. Our Scotch friend, it must be remembered, had also journeyed into the land of Egypt, and claimed to be no less skilled in the learning of the Egyptians than the artist, and I know not when I have been more wholesomely edified than while listening to their vivacious disputes concerning the hieroglyphics, in which were elaborately discussed the era and interpretation of these symbols, and their relation to Biblical statements. In prosecuting these questions many other topics of exceedingly abstruse interest would be hit upon,—as The Causes of Things, The How-Be-It, The Why-Be-It, and The Wherefore-Be-it, The Was, The Is, and The To-Be,— such matters as it is not given unto any man of our laggard land to understand till he have been illuminated by the light of The Hub. For a day or two there were some other American guests at the hotel, and when perplexed with hieroglyphics and metaphysics, I would turn to them and refresh myself with that blessed solace and comfort of our nation—the talking of politics. Now and then, too, our Scotch friend would fill up an interval with an admirable comic song, of unexceptionable gravity and de-

corum, and always conveying some useful moral lesson;
being every way worthy of the répertoire of an elder of
the kirk. As we had the inexpressible good fortune to be
unencumbered with any of the softer sex, our ideas and
words flowed freely, and under the influence of the Val-
depeñas wine they sometimes assumed a phase of downright levity, which would shock and scandalize our good
Scotch friend not a little. Frequently, on these occasions,
would be with us the brother-in-law of the son-in-law,—
a most apt and ingenuous youth, worthy of relationship
with that paragon,—who served at table in the capacity
of assistant-waiter, auditor, and interlocutor. He picked
up many scraps of wisdom in this way, and in return, it
was to him we were indebted for the knowledge of that
inestimable charm against persecution by beggars, which
consists in saying, "*Perdone usted por amor de Dios,
hermano,*"—"Excuse me, my brother, for the love of
God,"—which, as is well known, no really deserving
beggar can withstand, and which would have been of
incalculable service to us could we have framed to pronounce it right.

The bad weather disheartened and discommoded us
very much. Our Scotch friend's barometer had fallen in
sympathy, and, as it remained most doggedly down, we
concluded to return to Malaga. We would fain have had
him return with us; but he was bent on seeing the sun set,
which it had not done to our knowledge for lo these many
days, and, as there was no prospect of its ever visibly setting again, we were obliged to bid him adieu, with little
chance of renewing our pleasant association. The provident son-in-law put us up a straw bag of provisions,
gave us a bottle of water, ordered up the vehiculary box,
deposited us in it, commended us to God, and ordered
the driver to take us off.

We reached the station at Loja about nine o'clock, and
speedily transferred our straw bag, our bottle, and ourselves into the diligence for Antequera, but providentially
discovered our mistake in time to get into that for Malaga.
We had great hopes for awhile of having the vehicle all
to ourselves, but in the town there boarded us a lady and
a child, and two gentlemen, as we would call them in our

country, though they would hardly answer to that designation in their own. It was a dreadful day, corresponding in all respects to the kind known in Virginia as "a real March day." There were great blasts of cold wind, with occasional violent bursts of rain, hail, and snow, making a dismal scene outside the diligence. At some of the more elevated points of the route we passed through snow three or four inches deep, and the wild crags and tortuous valleys, under the influence of the winter storm, looked bleak and cheerless to the last degree.

But while all was dreary without we nestled together within, and contrived to be comparatively comfortable. Our lady passenger was a fat, lively, and easy soul, full of loving kindness towards her male fellow-creatures. Her two countrymen became acquainted with her instantaneously. One of them was of a somnolent frame of mind, more inclined to seek solace from intrinsic than extrinsic sources, and so he slumbered and slept; but the other, more social in his temperament, planted himself by the lady's side, and soon made himself so agreeable that he was offered a share of her shawl, which he did not hesitate to accept, and was in other respects placed upon a footing of the most delightful intimacy by this amiable woman. She was, indeed, a most affable and complaisant creature. Even I, grave, severe, and unapproachable, as is generally admitted, was beguiled by her into sweet converse, and found myself actually engaged in the unwonted occupation of edulcorating sentiments for her titillation. It is true that we did not have a common language; but the gentleman by her side, who spoke French, was so exceptionally self-abnegating as to volunteer as interpreter, and I have every reason to believe that he faithfully preserved all the original sweetness of our remarks. In response to an inquiry, I told her I was from the United States,—which fact did not impress her as forcibly as it should have done, because of her belief that that country was in England— a land with which she was reasonably familiar. On the other hand, however, she was powerfully struck, and, indeed, bewildered by the discrepancy in time between America and Spain as exhibited by my watch, which was set to Richmond time, and eagerly demanded how could such things be. Upon this I did as erstwhile did that Smith whose name was John, when in the hands of Indians panting after astronomical truth. I drew forth my watch, and by "that jewel instructed her concerning the roundness of the earth, and how the sun did chase the night round about the earth continually,"—whereat she marveled greatly.

We dined off and on during the whole day, sharing our respective supplies with each other. The two gentlemen had provided nothing, relying trustfully upon Providence, which befriended them signally, for our excellent lady companion had brought a basket stowed to overflowing with succulent meats and dainty fruits and cakes, of which they partook ravenously. As for ourselves, when we came to investigate our portly straw bag, we found that the usually cautious son-in-law had committed the singular oversight of packing it with all bread and no meat. Under these circumstances we felt that we could not equitably partake of the good lady's hospitality; but she fed us with rich morsels from her own fair hands, and would take no denial; in return for which we could only water all hands out of our bottle, which was, however, considered to be a full equivalent.

Among the commendable traits for which this worthy lady was conspicuous, was charity to the poor. She dealt out half cents with a profuse hand among the beggars which beset us along the way. She gave away all she had, and then mourned because she had no more to give to the new applicants. One persistent petitioner grieved her especially. He followed us for miles, trotting through the snow and sleet with an energy which, if exercised in any other calling, would have secured him an independent fortune, being now and then left far behind as we galloped down into a valley, but always catching up with us as we toiled up a hill. His solicitations were made in a tone of heart-rending dolor which no representations, or expostulations, or threats could silence for a moment. Even the never-failing "Excuse me, my brother," etc., failed totally. The good lady's soul was becoming sorely distressed. In this extremity we bethought ourselves of knocking him down with our bread-bag, which we did accordingly. It utterly demolished him, and the examination of its contents afforded him interest sufficient to divert his attention from us permanently.

At length through the misty air we descried the Mediterranean and Malaga far below us We rumbled on for a long time after this, and the shades of night had settled upon the bleak earth by the time we reached the city. We dashed through the streets with great fuss and furore to the office of the diligence, where the passengers rapidly diverged,—the lady and gentlemen speeding to some unknown places, or place, and we repairing to our original apartments in the Hotel de la Alameda.*

CHAPTER XI.

Of the Steamer Jackal, and of our Voyage in her to the Rock of Gibraltar—Of Gibraltar and its Features, Military and Civil.

IT was our purpose to retrace our steps to some extent by going to Gibraltar, and having no wish to linger in Malaga, we immediately set about investigating the modes of egress. They proved to be very precarious. A steamer from somewhere bound for Gibraltar was momentarily expected to enter the harbor, but she never did it in our time. Another steamer, then in port, was advertised as certain to sail thither each morning, but she invariably postponed her departure to the next day. In this manner we were kept in a vexatious fidget for three days,

---

* From statements in "Search after Sunbeams," by the Hon. S. S. Cox, whose visit to Granada was subsequent to mine, I perceive that the extraordinary son-in-law, of whom mention is made in this and the preceding chapter, has added another feather to his cap by assuming command of the Granada militia.

waiting for one vessel that was coming, but didn't come, and for another that was going, but wouldn't go.

At the end of the three days, however, the hotel commissioner, on whom we depended in our troubles, brought us a positive assurance that the advertised steamer would inevitably venture forth next morning beyond the peradventure of a doubt. He also gave us the encouraging information that this steamer was a most noble and commodious specimen of naval architecture, and, further, that by his interest with the captain he had induced that functionary to do us the honor of placing his own cabin at our entire disposal. Accordingly, we rose betimes on the appointed day, pretermitting an early breakfast in deference to the representation of the commissioner that all the luxuries of the season were to be obtained on board, rewarded the said commissioner munificently for his care of us, took boat in fine spirits, and were soon alongside.

As we stepped on the deck of the steamer, and viewed the scene, our hearts grew heavy within us. Her name was Jackal, and she was the most minute craft I ever knew to have the temerity to navigate the high seas. The passengers' cabin was a little box containing hardly more space than was necessary to stow away our overcoats and carpet-bags. The captain's cabin, reported by the commissioner to be assigned to us,—though the report was not confirmed,—was a cavity in which a landsman would die in less than an hour, the entrance into which was effected by tumbling in, and the exit by crawling out on the back. Into this tiny vessel passengers, by no means of a select order, were gathering in crowds, for the long interval that had elapsed since the last departure had caused a great accumulation of them; and I have no doubt that it was with a view to this accumulation that the Jackal had lingered. These people seemed to be emigrating permanently, judging from the heterogeneous mass of baggage they were taking with them. It encumbered the whole ship, and it was absolutely appalling to contemplate the loss of old bedsteads, old chests, and old lumber, that must accrue in case of shipwreck. As many of the ladies as could cram into the coop below got in it, and there they stuck as tight as wax. As for the men, they deposited themselves where and how they could.

At seven o'clock we began to weigh anchor,—in which operation, however, we were suddenly brought to a stand-still by finding the contrivance foul. The cheery pull of the mariners now rapidly degenerated into a disheartening tug,—the resistance was too great for them, and they were obliged to send forth a wail for succor to the passengers. These responded promptly,—conspicuous among whom was a tall Moor in full national rig of dirt-colored turban and night-gown, who tucked up his petticoat and went right in, straining for life, and out-jerking the Christians all hollow. All kinds of mechanical dodges were brought to bear in aid of the work, but at last it was only by the desperate resort of cutting the cable with a cold-chisel that deliverance was obtained. These manipulations consumed an hour, at the end of which time we made a *bona fide* start,—the old thing wobbling gloriously from top-heaviness. As the captain did not suspect that he had more load already than he ought to have, he took a sloop in tow,—as he would have unhesitatingly done by a hundred more had the opportunity offered. Indeed, all nautical business in these waters is carried on with a view not to special but general accommodation; commanders being perfectly willing to depart from their course, or retrace it, or linger, or stop for any length of time on the way, if any one wishes it, and will pay reasonably for it. Persons, therefore, who have occasion to voyage over these seas must bear these facts in mind, and prepare themselves in accordance therewith.

In the mean while we took counsel with the steward, cabin-boy, and cook,—all of which personages were consolidated into a dirty little youth,—hoping that at least the statements of the commissioner relative to the sumptuousness of the fare might in some degree be verified. We found, however, that the dirty little youth also filled the position of common seaman, and could by no means attend to us till the ship was fairly under way. When this was accomplished, he set about preparing our repast, in which he showed great aptitude, getting it ready in a jiffy, and setting it forth in the captain's cavern, where we tumbled into it. It comprised bread and cheese and no meat, but, in lieu thereof, fried eggs impregnated to the core with garlic. A more abominable mess, not even excepting the assafœtida mixture of the Pharmacopœia, I never saw; in fact, the only edibles in the range of my experience comparable therewith were certain eggs whereon I once banqueted in Minnesota, on which a skunk had incubated the preceding night. We bolted a little of it down our throats as a matter of duty to our stomachs, when finding that if we escaped strangulation by the breakfast we were sure of suffocation by the cabin, we rose from table, got on our backs, and crawled to the upper air.

By this time we were well out of the harbor to where the sea was a little rough, and the Jackal began to ramp and rear mercilessly. The natural consequences followed. Sea-sickness was developed and rapidly spread. It broke out first among the females in the passengers' coop, and, as they neither would nor could get out, some appalling scenes ensued among that densely-packed community. The deck-passengers likewise suffered severely. The tall Moor became infected, but he loomed up patient under the affliction, supported by the resignation engendered by his accursed creed. He was evidently satisfied that there is but one God and Mohammed is the prophet of God, and let her rip. I myself was by no means scathless; indeed, on no voyage was I ever less so. Though pre-eminently a much-enduring man, the garlicky eggs had unmanned me and my resolution palled. The scrupulous regard for appearances, however, that ever actuates me nerved me to put forth all my self-control, and I made no visible sign of yielding; but had nobody been looking I would assuredly have given up and allowed the tyrant to do its worst.

The prudent captain skirted the shore closely all the way; and truly it presented a goodly scene as we wended slowly past. It rises green and fertile from the sea, culminating inland in mountain-peaks, many of them clad in snow—the range continuing almost to Gibraltar. Every now and then a village comes in to fill up the picture,

and an abundance of detached houses scattered everywhere spreads animation over the whole landscape.
Right ahead towers the great rock of Gibraltar itself,
visible long before we near it. The time from Malaga
does not usually exceed six or seven hours, but, encumbered by the sloop in tow, we were yet some distance off
when the evening began to close in. Aware that no
earthly power could get us within the gates of the town
after sunset, it was with great anxiety that we meditated
upon the possibility of having to spend the night on the
Jackal. On reaching the rock we had to almost circum-
navigate it, and our little steamer seemed to shrink to
nothingness as she grazed its tremendous sides rising
steep and inaccessible far above us. A dingy vegetation
covers it, looking like the moss on an old weatherbeaten
cow-house, and at its base are several groups of buildings, seeming no bigger than baby-houses by the contrast. We rounded Europa Point, passed batteries innumerable, and then anchored in the bay before the town.

The abominable mode of landing by boats prevails
here likewise, and our anchor dropped amidst a great
flock of them. The boatmen were the most rapacious
monsters we encountered anywhere. Without a moment's notice they seized our baggage, and we had to
rise like men and defend it. A regular battle was joined;
but we, having right and sticks and umbrellas on our
side, were crowned with a precarious victory. During
the unstable truce they gave us pointedly to understand
that we should have no peace till we definitely fixed on
one of them. This ravenousness was explained by a
musty old veteran amongst them as due to the circumstance that "there were too few bones for so many dogs."
Charmed by the pregnant wisdom of the mouldy sage,
we straightway selected him, and, there being honor
amongst thieves, the others yielded us as his exclusive
prey.

On attaining the shore we were forthwith reminded
that we had passed out of the pale of civil liberty and
were in the dread limbo of martial law. We were halted
before a tribunal outside the gates and made to give an
account of ourselves, after which we were furnished with

a pass which secured us entrance into the town. But from an absolutely groundless terror that we might use our medicine-chest for the demoralization of the troops they temporarily confiscated it—an intolerable outrage, which, however, the priceless wisdom we had accumulated in the Confederate War enabled us partially to circumvent, for we contrived to smuggle in a goodly vial of medicament. As we were passing through the streets on our way to the hotel a flash of light glimmered and then a roar came booming from the heights above. It was the evening gun, and we felicitated ourselves on being happily in the town; for they are strict constructionists here, and would feel no delicacy in slamming their gates in the face of the most illustrious foreigner were he a minute behind the appointed time.

We put up at the Club-house Hotel—an establishment which confronts the town-hall, the tobacco auction, and the market, and which is in high favor with the military. Owing to the European proclivity of foisting upon one man space enough to accommodate a whole family, the hotel had become overstocked, and we had to take quarters in an adjoining building—and at the very summit of it. As there were two of us, they felt that we could not be adequately lodged in less than three rooms, and this was the number we were put into, which were sumptuously furnished with the customary lounges, pictures, bijouterie, etc., and a clock hamstrung, but made of the purest brass. To serve us we had two maids—one a very old maid, a grandmother in fact; and the other a very young maid; the former speaking no English, and the latter speaking excellent English, but strictly in the line of duty; for I was amazed after hearing her fluent discourse on wash-basins, beds, etc., to find that on not another topic could she be brought to any understanding. In order, however, to avail ourselves of their services we had to resort to devices. One was to go out on the landing and dance a breakdown with stick and umbrella; another was to poke our heads out of window and bawl without remorse or dread; but the most certain was to go down-stairs, catch a maid, if we could, and fetch her up. Hard by us was an important post at which a sentinel was kept stationed after dark, who suffered nothing whatever to pass his beat without obtaining his permission,—which was, however, always granted, and in the tone of a funeral dirge. As wayfarers by this road were rather frequent, the singing of such staves as "Pass soldier—and all's well," "Pass donkey—and all's well," was common—whereby our sleep was relieved of much of its monotony.

Our sustenance was taken in the hotel proper, where the *table-d'hôte* was set for dinner at seven o'clock. In the preparation and conduct of the meal English customs were intended to be followed, but I perceived no striking difference from the Spanish fashion except a religious withholding of wine unless it were paid for extra. At the dinner-table the military patrons appeared in great glory, and, with the boldness proper to their calling, were ever pressing manfully to the front in the conversation. Vast quantities of valuable observations were being continually fired off by them heterogeneously amongst the plates and dishes, which if they shed no great light made a very satisfactory noise.

As seen from the hotel the rock towers grandly to the skies, as well it may, being fourteen hundred and thirty feet in height. It is three miles in length, and of a shape which has been likened to that of a lion, and the observer will readily admit that the comparison is well sustained. Nestling at its base and clinging to its sides is the town, which is not large nor by any means bewitching in appearance, though it has a busy look about it. A good deal seems to be done in Barbarian tea-trays and trinketry, and smuggling is a most thriving branch of industry. The houses are severely plain in architectural style and finish, and the streets are narrow and disposed to run in polygons, many of them bearing names of direful augury suggestive of war. Donkeys abound, and the mode of vehicular locomotion is by Irish jaunting-cars and other outlandish contrivances. Beggars are few, and the women are pretty.

The town is inhabited by a mixture of English, Spaniards, and Moors, who give an interesting variety to its scenes by their peculiarities; and it is enlivened by the constant passage of bodies of the military, making it a perfect paradise for the boys, who can follow the warriors around from morning till night. It is pleasing to the eye to see these fine-looking red-coated soldiers, some of them clad in pantaloons of black cloth, and some of them in pantaloons ostensibly of rag-carpeting (though in reality they may be of a kind of Scotch plaid), while the ear is no less interested in hearing the clatter of kettle-drums, the shrill whistle of fifes, and the mortal groaning of bagpipes. At evening gunfire a grand combination of all these musical appliances is wont to go over the town to notify all concerned that it is getting dark, with an effect which is electrical upon one not used to it. One of the favorite evening hymns of the band, if not the "Rogue's March," was something of appalling likeness to it, and another was that great and good Yankee melody of "Tramp, Tramp," which, I may mention by the way, I heard in almost every European town I entered.

This immense rock stands solitary and alone, being surrounded on all sides by the sea, except at its northern extremity, where it abruptly terminates in a junction with the broad plain called "the neutral ground," which connects it with the Spanish territory. Both parties have a line of sentry-boxes on their respective borders of the neutral ground where they mount guard with the solemnity and circumspection due to a state of war, though they are very lenient to non-combatant passengers, especially if they be smugglers. The English have all this place undermined, so that they can blow up invaders who might have the audacity to approach in this direction; and if the blowing up should fail to stop them, they have contrivances for flooding it, so as to drown them into the bargain. But, indeed, an army competent to mount this face of the rock, or any other, for that matter, must be an army of acrobats. If there be one part naturally more vulnerable to assault than another it is the western side, where the town is situated; but wo betide him who should hence be tempted to assail it; for art has rectified any shortcomings of nature, and this is now as impregnable as any other portion. In fact, all around and over the rock are fortifications of different kinds, many of them at points palpably unassailable, and although the place is already absolutely proof against any assault, they are still erecting additional works of the most elaborate and costly character.

Having surfeited my sight with the works on the outside, I prepared to inspect those made within the bowels of the rock, as well as to ascend to the summit for the sake of the prospect. In order to do these things, the regulations require that a permit must be obtained from some military functionary or other. As the permit is never refused, this requirement is clearly a case of red tapestry, inflicting bother without commensurate advantage; and as it involves a waste of time, which is sinful, I concluded to have nothing to do with it, but to trust to my pleasing countenance and engaging manner to get me through. Accordingly, I set forth with great spirit, and, after climbing awhile, found myself entangled in somebody's yard, hard by an interesting-looking old castle, which has come down from the days of the primitive Moors. The proprietor of the yard and his wife soon sallied out of their dwelling to see who it was that was trying to pick their locks and break down their gates and doors. I demanded of them to show me out of there and direct me in the right track, which they did with much suavity and kindness. I was greatly pleased with their deportment, and paused for some time in order to commune with them, when we discussed the relations subsisting between the United States and England, agreeing in the judiciousness of fomenting peace and good will between these two great peoples. Setting forth again, I had climbed a little higher, when, somewhat to my dismay, I fell in with a guard, who halted me and asked for my pass. I told him I had not thought it necessary, and so had not got one. I spoke with a doubting heart, but simultaneously drew upon him one of my most wide-extending and seductive grins. The event confirmed my belief in the irresistibility of my charms. Said the guard, in his most complaisant tones, "It is absolutely necessary to have a pass, but not to have one makes no difference in the world." By this time my visage was mantled all over with grins inexpressibly winning; and this operated on him so that he straightway hunted up a gunner, and, putting me under his charge, ordered him to show me everything.

Accordingly, under the care of the gunner, I penetrated into the interior of the rock and beheld its wonders. It is a surprising example of what man can accomplish by the expenditure of labor and money, and here the expenditure of both has been enormous. The rock, from near the base to the top, is tunneled into a series of passages, and at intervals is excavated into spacious chambers, in the walls of which numerous embrasures are pierced, through which peer out the voracious snouts of ugly, snaky-looking cannons. The magazines for ammunition, and the other arrangements proper to a fortress, are all upon the most judicious plan; so that it is one of the safest and most commodious places for fighting purposes imaginable,—the defenders having nothing to apprehend except being smothered in their own smoke or run crazy by their own noise, or possibly of getting a crack on the cranium from a flake of the wall, which seems rather crumbly, and looks as if tolerable-sized chunks might be jarred down by the concussion of firing, though I was informed by the gunner that nothing of the sort ever occurred. There is decidedly more work bestowed hereabouts than there is any need for; but this may be partly due to the fact that, during the great siege that begun in 1779 and lasted over three years, the occupants being at ease and feeling the want of something to do, turned to excavating, and a great deal of the tunneling and chambering now to be seen is the result of their industry.

Parting with the gunner, who kicked up from the road a great piece of bombshell, a relic of the three years' siege, and presented it to me as a token of regard, I proceeded to toil up to the very summit of the rock. The way thither is long and with abrupt turns, passing frequently along the edge of declivities; and, being formed of rough fragments of stone, involves considerable wear and tear of the muscular system and entails death and destruction upon shoe-leather. Persons who study economy in these particulars, in making the ascent are wont to invoke the aid of donkeys; and in coming down I encountered a party of my fellow-guests of the hotel thus circumstanced, who, as they were law-abiding people, had craved passes of the authorities, whereby they had been kept waiting all the morning, and a very imposing spectacle they presented on donkey-back. The topmost pinnacle of the rock is occupied as a signal station, and beer is for sale on the premises. Here are all the appliances for signaling,—guns, masts, flags, and telescopes; and two or three observers, with their eyes forever on the strain. These observers appear to be somewhat selfish and unsocial, treating their visitors rather cavalierly, and conducting themselves in a manner which is not seemly towards people who have come so far to see them. They did not pray me to be seated, nor insist upon my taking a look through their telescopes, nor even speak to me; in short, I inferred that they did not desire the pleasure of my company; for these reasons, therefore, I reclined against the ramparts, drew forth my spy-glass, and stayed a long time with them. From this lofty height the view is one of the grandest in the world, embracing vast portions of Africa and Spain, the Mediterranean Sea, and the Atlantic Ocean. Below me lay the town of Gibraltar, spread upon the side of the rock with its bay dotted over with vessels, all made wonderfully diminutive by the distance. Before me was Algeciras, and sweeping to the right extended a vast expanse of hill and plain, with here and there a Spanish town, and bounded by far-off ranges of sierras. To the left I could catch a glimpse of the African coast, but obscured by the misty weather that day prevailing; while behind me rolled a great waste of waters, made gloomy and portentous by a hazy shroud, into which now and then a wandering ship would penetrate, become enwrapped, and disappear.

To a contemplative mind, such as mine becomes when I have no one to talk to, a scene like this affords food for prolonged reflection, and I was slow to shut my spy-glass upon it. But the winds blow rudely round this bare and lofty ridge, and it behooved me not to linger unduly. In the descent I collided with another guard; but having now happily accomplished my purpose, I felt that it was

scarcely worth while to waste my sweetness upon him.
In response to his inquiry about my pass, therefore, I
simply stated that I saw no sense or reason in such
things, and so had lent no countenance to the custom ;
at the same time, however, I favored him with a semi-
smile to let him see I bore no malice to him personally.
He was a much more rigid constructionist than his predecessor, and believed firmly in the salutary power of
passes, and gave me reasons for the faith that was in
him ; but, seeing that I was moving off of his premises
as fast as I could, he consented to overlook the grave
error I had committed and allow me to go on unmo-
lested.

The military authorities, while concentrating their best
energies upon the fortification of their stronghold, have
yet directed some of their efforts towards its adornment.
They have laid out an alameda, or public square, with
flowers and shrubbery, and pyramids of balls, and a monument or two, and have done it very handsomely. They
have made of it a pleasant place wherein to lounge or sit
and dream over the mysterious sea that stretches before
it, or to watch the skillful evolutions of the troops upon
the spacious drill-ground adjoining. The citizens glory
in the alameda and patrol it pertinaciously, for of other
recreation there seems to be but little. Yet there is not
a total dearth of amusement even in this iron town. I
saw bills posted announcing that there would be a public
execution of a drama, whose name I forget, by the officers
of her Majesty's Somethingth for the edification of the
people,—and God save the Queen prayed her Majesty's
Somethingth. There was also a fair running in full blast
for the benefit of the poor. The bond of fellowship that
connects me with this worthy class induced me to attend
to see what they were doing for us. I found the fair
to be identical with the church fairs of our land, where
the sanctuary is filled with lovely beings lying, cheating,
and committing highway robbery in every quarter. Here,
however, they had the grace to notify the victims by pla-
card that whatever they got their hands on they kept,—
no change being given on any pretense whatever. I was
drawn into the vortex by a seductive creature, who lisped

just enough English to make her irresistible. Under the baleful influence of her enchantments I expended forty cents in a bunch of weeds, which I bestowed upon her for her adorning, and then took to gambling, at which I was crowned with so much success as to win a very chaste collocation of chicken feathers; but, as the distribution of booty was not to take place till I should have quit the country, I did grant and confirm my right in this also unto the tempter, to have and to hold the said collocation of chicken feathers, unto the said tempter, her heirs and assigns forever.

When the military features of Gibraltar have been sufficiently studied and the novelty of the alameda has been worn off, a great vacuum is left to daunt the sojourner's mind. To replenish it as far as might be, I betook myself to the market, whose propinquity to the hotel made it a very convenient loafing-place, where I spent many hours contemplating the phases of life there exhibited. Here are sold old iron, cracked crockery, wormy books, and garments of the deceased; and as the purchasers are of many nations, ranks, and conditions of men, women, and children, the picture, while it may not enrapture the weary spectator, will possibly keep him from perishing utterly before he is able to get away from the rock. Here, too, on certain days is held the tobacco auction,—a great business being done in Gibraltar in the smuggling of this commodity,—and as part of the auctioneer's "once, twice, three" and "going, gone" is rendered in English and part in Spanish, the effect upon the casual listener is quite pleasing.

The climate of Gibraltar is amongst the worst in Southern Europe,—a circumstance largely due to the fact that the town is swept by the noxious wind called the Levanter. Hence an invalid would do well to make but a short visit, even supposing that anybody having power to get away would make a long one. But, indeed, there are no inducements tending to a prolonged stay. It is a spot that possesses no abiding interest for any but those who relish the pomp and circumstance of glorious war,—for which, after the shoving up to the front I not long ago had from my Southern brethren and the chasing back to the rear I got from the fierce men of the North, I, for one, am free to confess that I have no great stomach. As no immediate opportunity for leaving it offered itself to us we had perforce to remain some days more than we intended, and we suffered not a little from the surfeit.

CHAPTER XII.

How we extended our Observations into Heathenesse, and of the strange Things we there saw.

THE shores of Africa spreading beyond the Straits offer a tantalizing sight to the traveler tarrying at Gibraltar, luring him irresistibly to cross the narrow waters that roll between. For us, especially, that country was of absorbing interest from the vast influence it has exercised in shaping the destinies of our own people. We yielded to our feelings and went over; and it is a source of never-ending rejoicing and thanksgiving that we have been permitted to enter the fatherland of the new order of statesmen appointed to regenerate the South.

The point at which we proposed to make our descent was Tangier, in Morocco, about thirty miles from Gibraltar. Accordingly, one Sunday morning, in company with sundry other temporary residents of Gibraltar, we took passage in a steamer small in size but great in name, being entitled "The Belgian Lion." It was our purpose, having no wish to journey unnecessarily on the Sabbath, to have made the voyage on another steamer advertised all over town as sure to go to Tangier on the day before; but this craft had received more advantageous overtures, and with characteristic duplicity had stolen off to Cadiz in the night. The Belgian Lion waited long beyond the appointed time, so as to afford any waverers there might be on shore ample opportunity to make up their minds to go, and at last reluctantly started.

When we had got well under way, the passengers,

with one accord, as germane to the day, fell into discourse concerning religious topics. Nothing begets argument more surely than religion—except politics; and in nothing does argument advantage controversialists so little; for I have observed that the only unequivocal conviction ever attained is that each disputant is convinced that the other is a fool. Between two of our passengers an argument of this nature burst out, embracing in its scope faith, works, and being born again,— and sugared through and through with sweet morsels of instruction dripping with nourishment for the listeners. But at its most succulent and nutritive part, to our great loss, it was most unhappily concluded by one of the disputants getting irremediably sea-sick just as he was on the point of establishing beyond all doubt or cavil that his views were correct,—a conclusion still more infelicitous in that it afforded his opponent plausible ground for claiming a great victory. Allowing the victor time to digest his self-satisfaction I then entered into conversation with him myself, judiciously changing the theme. I found him to be a gentleman of parts and observation, who had traveled much and been on terms of intimacy with some of the distinguished men of the earth. Of these worthies he gave me many interesting particulars. He spoke, among others, of Sir Samuel Baker, whose accounts of achievements in the subjugation of wild beasts I had perused with feelings of the most respectful wonder, and he informed me that by the citizens of Ceylon, who knew Sir Samuel well, and were conversant with his attainments in gunnery, he was esteemed to be more dexterous with the long-bow than with any other weapon.

The European and African coasts were both in sight during the whole passage,—the latter presenting a monotonous aspect of low hills clothed in a sickly green. The waters of the Mediterranean pressing through the narrow straits are rapid and turbulent in their flow, and as it was somewhat windy on this occasion the Belgian Lion grew very rampant, prostrating most of the voyagers. In about four hours and a half we turned into the bay of Tangier and beheld the town rising before us. From the sea Tangier presents a very imposing appearance, though the full measure of the imposition will not be realized till the beholder gets on shore. As we approached a multitude of boats came off loaded with Arabs eager to take us to the land. These persons were uncomely exceedingly to look upon, and the squalls and squeaks and blubberings, which are the elements of their vernacular, to hear were most grievous. We fell into the power of a fat, squabby, yellow Moor, with a face which looked for all the world as if it had been peppered with peas during a raid on a watermelon-patch, who beat us and several others down into a boat already overflowing with the superabundant crew which navigates these crafts. And now before we started a terrible outbreak occurred, occasioned by the discovery of a surreptitious boatman, whom the rashness of insatiable greed had impelled to interpolate himself amongst the legitimate navigators in the hope that he might peradventure obtain the twentieth part of a cent out of the earnings, even at the sacrifice of his hide and tallow. Such screams as arose when this enormity was brought to light are altogether inconceivable. All hands fell to swearing and blubbering dreadfully, and fastening upon the impostor set to work with might and main to throw him overboard. As these proceedings gave an indubitable earnest of the swamping of the boat the matter became personal to every soul in it, and every soul in it at once became implicated in the controversy, bellowing forth his sentiments with all the emphasis of the language which nature had endued him withal. In the mean time the false one, being of a thin and wormy corporature, had intertwisted himself so with the seats of the boat that he could not be extracted; wherefore the true men at last were contented to simply subject him to pressure by standing on him, and then laid their course for shore.

While still some distance from the landing-place we reached a point where our bottom dragged, beyond which boats are unable to go, and where it was necessary to take to manback. A large fragment of the population of Tangier was out riotously demanding to be employed in this capacity. Almost before I knew it a little Arab pulled my legs around his neck and ran away with me.

Being equipped with an overcoat, a carpet-bag, a cane, and my companion's big black vial of medicament, and, furthermore, being so suddenly hoisted up, I was rather top-heavy. My Arab steed soon began to stumble awfully, and for awhile I thought I was doomed. I yelled " Gee hup !" and " Wope sar !" and he squealed and seemed to intimate that I was choking him to death, but at last, glory be to Allah! we floundered safely to land. Our peppered-visaged guide, who hitherto had had as much as he could do in bawling and swearing and throwing people overboard, here resumed control of us; and working us dexterously through the custom-house soon had us in the Royal Victoria Hotel, where he introduced us to Mr. Martin, the landlord—a real, simon-pure African, as pure as any in our cornfields. We shook Mr. Martin's hands most warmly, and were by him heartily welcomed to Africa, and straightway furnished with lunch—at which repast we consumed Mr. Martin's whole supply of sardines, comprising three-fourths of a box. After this we went forth to inspect the city.

Tangier is one of the few spots at which the worthy old empire of Morocco suffers itself to come in contact with the defilements of the outside world. For two hundred years or so the Portuguese had violent hold of it, and it figures somewhat in the military history of England during the times of Charles II. Its inhabitants are reputed to number something like ten thousand; and some of those inexplicable biases of mind which at times so strangely influence human actions have led about four hundred Europeans to become an element in its population. It is one of the great consular stations of the earth, almost every nation big and little having a representative here; but what except a desire of showing its enterprise could induce any country to inflict such an appointment on an unoffending citizen, or what except a monomania for office-holding could induce any citizen to accept it, is hard to divine.

Heaven has clearly abandoned Tangier, and the Genius of Lethargy has taken it body and soul. It consists of a mass of whitewashed, amorphous houses jumbled together, the bare sight of which is sufficient to narcotize a man from America; and amongst them winds a horrible maze of narrow, miserably paved, breakneck streets. Communication with Europe has impressed the magistracy with the advantages to be derived from attention to public hygiene; and, indeed, they profited so greatly by the examples in this particular set before them as at one time to have almost annihilated the town by the establishment of an interminable quarantine. It is, natural, therefore, that they should have organized a Board of Health and Sanitary Police; and I was pleased to see the organization, consisting of a big man and a little donkey with a pair of panniers over his back, trying to clean the thoroughfares,—though, as I looked around, my mind misgave me that the municipal authorities had undertaken a task to which their abilities were not commensurate. As viewed from some of the eminences in the vicinity the place has quite a picturesque appearance, but it bears close inspection as ill as can well be imagined.

The amount of business done here is almost imperceptible. They do some trading with Gibraltar in oranges, chickens, and cattle; but they do it at their leisure. The inhabitants are exquisitely lazy, although they are generally a tall, muscular set of fellows, abundantly capable of work if they were made to do it; but they are not pleasing to look upon, by reason of their dress, which is of the semblance of a shroud, giving them a hideous likeness to a community of ghosts,—though, fortunately for the nerves of the beholder, the illusion is mitigated by the color of the vestments, which is far indeed from the spotless white which is a *sine qua non* with a genuine ghost. The women keep their faces covered; nevertheless, they are not averse from giving a Christian gentleman a glimpse of their charms when it can be safely done. I was vouchsafed two or three glimpses of the sort, and I do emphatically assert that if the "mugs" which I beheld were fair samples of Moorish beauty, it is a work of supererogation in the ladies of Morocco to cover their countenances from *my* gaze.

Under the superintending care of the guide we were mounted on donkeys, forming a cortége which would have caused all true friends of ours to hang their heads in shame and sorrow could they have seen us, and trotted in the most remorseless manner all through and all around the town. These unfortunate animals are maintained by the heathen to be hired to Christian visitors, and are surmounted with big bags of rags for saddles, on which the rider sits in any way he can best endure, seeing that there are no stirrups; while they are spurred by their owners into sudden bursts of speed by sticks, kicks, and yells of direful portent. To say nothing of the perils of nose-bleed and tooth-break imminent in this mode of equitation, the comfort of it is immensurably below that of being tossed in a blanket,—to which it bears some resemblance. We procured our donkeys from the congregation in the market-place,—a dirty space on the outskirts of the town. It was market-day, but the market-men had sold out, and we saw little more than a crowd of the ghostly denizens, who were squealing vociferously in their native tongue, together with the assembly of donkeys, and a quantity of scraps and remnants of straw and trash of a heterogeneous description. We, however, here had the unspeakable pleasure of beholding a camel,—a beast richly entitled to "take the knife" from his fellow-creatures, but any strictures upon whose personal appearance I withhold in consideration of his generally recognized services to society. We were shown the wonderful docility with which he would kneel when bidden to do so; and, after his brains had been almost beaten out, and he had been knocked down with sticks, the docile manner in which he got upon his knees was marvelous indeed.

The guide profiting by the temporary absence of the Belgian consul, in the first place, took occasion to break into the town residence of that officer, and to throw it open for our inspection. There is no concealment with these worthy Mussulmans; when they begin to exhibit anything they keep steadily on to the last scrap. Consequently we were religiously shown everything in this mansion,—even to the last week's linen that His Excellency had shucked off that morning, and the basin of dirty water in which he had last washed himself. We, however, saw other things of more interest. The interior of the house is handsomely finished in the Moorish style, and is filled with guns, pistols, swords, knives, and saddles—curious articles of Moorish workmanship—many of them being presents from the Commander of the Faithful of Morocco. The front room, on the lower floor, is elegantly furnished, this being the antechamber to the apartments of the horses, to which access is had by a door on one side. In these apartments, at that time, there abode one steed,—also a donation from the Commander of the Faithful.

From here the guide took us to a friend of his who kept shop in a jungle about twenty twists off, in the hope that we might purchase some of his morocco shoes, tea-trays, coral-work, brass ear-rings and nose-drops, and jimcracks. But not seeing the advantage of giving from five to ten times the Richmond quotations of this merchandise we could effectuate no trade, and set out for the suburban gardens of the Spanish minister. These are situated a mile or so from the town, and get their appellation of gardens rather through courtesy than desert; but though dreary and dead looking, they contrast most favorably with the barren and withered country surrounding them. The minister himself was absent somewhere, but our conscientious guide rested not till he had hunted him up and forced him to welcome us. He was a polite and pleasant gentleman, and invited us into his house, from which was a fine prospect of the rock of Gibraltar and the European coast. After an agreeable conversation, embracing French politics and a consideration of the sharply-defined boundary between civilization and barbarism which could be traced at Tangier, we returned to town; and by this time the St. Vitus's dance having broken out amongst us, as a consequence of the donkey ride, we were constrained to forego further sight-seeing for the day, and got back to the hotel.

There is a deadly hostility subsisting between the guides of Tangier, and they are ever on the watch for each other's patrons, whom they bushwhack and bear away without the least regard to professional etiquette. For the rest of the day, therefore, we were subjected to the most assiduous scrutiny by our legitimate guide, who confronted us at every turn. Much was he relieved when, at night, I consented to accompany him to see the nocturnal sights. The chief of these was a Moorish coffeehouse. This superb establishment comprehended the whole of a dungeon on an upper floor, the approach to which was as dark as Erebus and as crooked as the ways of sin. Following the guide closely I stumbled along till I entered the dungeon, wherein several Tangerine hardcrabs were squatting on matting, smoking tobacco poisoned with Indian hemp, in very minute pipes. I squatted with them and called for coffee for the crowd, which was served by a perfectly black darky in a perfectly white shroud, who appeared and disappeared solemnly, uttering no word, and forming a dreadfully chilling apparition to be gliding about a house of merriment. The place was made additionally funereal by the mode of illumination, which was by means of a tumbler of oil with a taper-wick floating upon it, and hung by a string from the ceiling. Its festive character was sustained, however, by a vase of nice flowers standing upon the floor, and a kind of two-stringed banjo, on which one of the hard-crabs would execute a love ditty, while the rest accompanied in tones of heart-shattering dolefulness. A more wo-begone-looking set of roisterers than these crabs I never rejoiced with. In the lulls of the amorous dirges they were wont to refresh their dirty noses with a terrific sniff of the flowers, and I noted that every now and then a crab would be attacked with a sort of frenzy of the fingers, in which he seemed to be tearing himself to pieces,—an excitement which I was able clearly to trace to its true source when on departing (a procedure not unduly delayed) I found myself loaded to the gunwale with fleas. A hideous rumbling of sepulchral laughter arose as I turned my back upon the gay scene,—attributable, according to the interpretation given me by a foreign resident of Tangier, to the Moslem estimate of the Christian philosopher whose hungering after wisdom leads him into such dens to satisfy it.

In further prosecution of sight-seeing the guide took me through darkness and tortuosities, and up acclivities and down declivities ineffable, to inspect what he said was a French hotel. Truly it may have been such, but on walking into an inner apartment I fell all over into a fearful fluster at beholding a gentleman with his arm around a lady's waist. Observing my agitation, the guide endeavored to allay it by explaining that the couple were married. And truly this may have been so, too,—though I must confess that my conception of the relations of the conjugal state would not lead me to form such a diagnosis from such a symptom; but my virtue was so much alarmed that I was unable to digest the explanation, plausible as it was. I therefore cut my visit short, staying not longer than an hour or so, by which time I was so bristly with morality that the corrupter was abashed, and took me back to the tavern, where I devoted myself till bedtime to Mr. Martin.

The Royal Victoria Hotel is commodiously situated in an alley over a battery of cannon, and with a tan-yard on one side from which a savor of animals returning unto dust ascends for ever and ever. It is a decent, well-kept establishment, much better than could be expected in such a town, and I cordially recommend it to the patronage of the traveling public. The table is good, and I remember that among the viands was hare,—of the quality of which, however, I cannot testify, having acquired a disrelish for the lesser quadrupeds at Malaga. The Madeira is superior to that of the Club-house across the Straits. Breakfast is served at half-past nine and dinner at six, and Mr. Martin, having in his day had considerable nautical experience, is scrupulous in setting his clock to true Tangier time,—taking Gibraltar as his meridian; though, with all deference to his skill, I cannot avoid the surmise that he has made some slight miscalculation in the longitude; for by his reckoning Tangier time is some sixty minutes behind that of Gibraltar, while no other observer, as far as I am aware, rates it at more than two, —a difference of some import to a hungry man. Mr. Martin himself is as black as the ace of spades, but a remarkably well-educated and gentlemanly man, nevertheless,—having once been steward on a British man-of-war, —and speaks English perfectly and with the genuine accent and intonation. Thus said he, "Relly, 'pon honar,

I carn't for me life" do certain things, while he likewise referred feelingly to the narsty weather of the parst week. About him and obsequiously obedient to his nod were male and female white servants, whom at times he stirred up sharply. As an antetype and prefiguration of what we of the South may be coming to I studied Mr. Martin and his establishment with a curious eye.

In the course of my conversations with Mr. Martin I was let very fully into the state of his feelings and opinions concerning matters in Tangier. It was his conviction that it was not the blarsted place commonly supposed, but with much that was tolerable and even desirable to one who was well broken into its customs. His chief objection to it was that the firing of salutes from the battery under his windows had at various times occasioned the smash of one hundred pounds sterling worth of his glarss. "Don't the government reimburse you for the damage?" I asked. "A-heh-heh!" laughed Mr. Martin, with that soft, amiable kind of laugh with which many good-natured people are wont to precede a remark in order to put themselves on pleasant terms with the listener, and which was the usual prelude to all of Mr. Martin's observations,—"R-r-raimbarse! oh, my deyar sar, not at arll—not at *arll*, my deyar sar!—Aheh, heh! I larf, but, 'pon me soul, relly it is no larfing matter. On one arccasion, sar, at one discharge they shattared arll the windars on one side of me house, and while I was r-r-rushing to secuar the othars they fired again and damalished, heh, heh! arll the rest, sar. I was paid nothing at arll for that, sar. The fact is relly, these people nevar pay for anything of the kind. It was va-a-ry savear upon me, I do assure you—varstly so, varstly." And Mr. Martin went on to state that repeated losses in glarss being followed by a prolonged enforcement of quarantine in the port during the last cholera epidemic at one time brought about such embarrassment in his affairs as almost to drive him to suspend. He put a higher estimate upon the general character of his fellow-citizens than any mere sojourner could possibly feel himself warranted in forming. According to him they were not so deadly bad, but had some good points,—

though I do not recollect that he mentioned any of these
specifically, except that when they washed themselves
and put on their clean clothes, which things were done
on certain festival days occurring off and on during the
twelvemonth, they looked pretty fresh and decent. One
of these washing and cleaning days was to be the day
after the morrow—on which occasion, also, Mr. Martin's
windows were again to be put upon their mettle by the
battery down below.

My intercourse with Mr. Martin pleased and profited
me greatly, and by way of reciprocation, when at night
he expressed an earnest longing to be thoroughly informed on the American question, I gladly undertook
to enlighten him. Commencing with the discovery of
America, I gradually brought the subject down to the
time of my exodus from the country, and was proceeding
to add a supplementary account drawn from the newspapers I had read while in Europe, when the profound
attention with which he listened to me becoming somewhat suspicious I observed him more narrowly, and
found that I had talked Mr. Martin fast asleep. In my
natural feeling at this discovery I rapidly drew my
remarks to a conclusion, using both hands to draw with.
An English gentleman—he that was crowned with victory in the religious conflict on the Belgian Lion—was
sitting on the bench beside me, listening and sipping a
jorum of grog with unspeakable complacency; and in
the energy of my movements the knob of my elbow
impinged against his goblet, projecting it to the floor
with a vehemence which dumfoundered him, nonplused
me, and woke Mr. Martin up.

On the ensuing morning my companion coming down
first was at once pounced upon by our vigilant guide and
marched off, and I descending soon after was waylaid by
one Hammed, or Mohammed, who cunningly seized the
opportunity afforded by the absence of my natural pro-
tector to make me his prey. By way of decoy he
invited me to breakfast, knowing that this was a bait
that could not be resisted. He was an ancient Arab,
venerable and sneaky, with a voice like that of a crow in
the last stages of clergyman's sore-throat. On accom-

panying him to his house, into which we entered only after a vast deal of croaking at the outer gate, he did me a very rare honor, indeed,—he introduced me to his wife. She was a plump and comely yellow lady, who bustled about pretty much as other men's wives do. He had a colored servant-maid,—the identical counterpart of our colored so-called maids,—whom he dispatched under the bed, whence she extracted a stool, a tea-tray, and the establishment's best china cups. The latter were set forth on the stool, which served as a table, close to which we adjusted ourselves by squatting on mats and tucking in our legs,—as is the *ton* among the true believers; and Mrs. Mohammed proceeding to make coffee we soon had breakfast, which was simply coffee and cold biscuits, but enriched by a large slice of nice warm bread, buttered and presented to me by my hostess's own fair hands. It was a grave and solemn feast, for besides the inherent dignity with which my entertainer partook of sustenance, the amount of Arabic and English reciprocally possessed was altogether inadequate to the maintenance of connected discourse. The greater part of the conversation, indeed, was that which was carried on between the master and the maid; and I noticed an unmistakable mark of the maid's identity with the great American sisterhood in her disposition to "jaw back."

On expressing myself as sufficiently plenished with biscuits and coffee, Mohammed led me from the banqueting hall to inspect the arrangements of the house; and thinking, as do his countrymen in general, that the curiosity of a Frank is of that cormorant kind that can batten on anything, he was especially assiduous in showing me his son's bedroom. It bore a striking resemblance to the bachelors' bedrooms in our own highly-favored land. The bed was kicked and tumbled into chaos, a cast-off garment lay here and there on the floor, and a rope stretched across the apartment sustained divers trousers and specimens of old clothes. It had a little dungeon-window, through which the happy parent directed my most particular attention in order to contemplate the sweet and inspiring prospect that every morning gladdened the bachelor's orbs. I looked, and beheld the wall of a portion of the premises, eye-scorching with whitewash, and hung with culinary vessels basking in the sun.

Having bestowed a fitting measure of commendation on all I had seen, and made due acknowledgment for my hospitable entertainment, I was departing when Mrs. Mohammed came running up and presented me as a token of esteem, or, maybe, of affection,—who knows?—with a large ring-shaped chunk of bread. This chunk, I may mention, I took with me to Gibraltar, and lugged it through the streets of the town as I journeyed to my hotel,—doubtless much to the astonishment of the citizens of that place, who, of course, could not divine the tender memories circling round it. As the hospitality of the Arabs is proverbial, it may be thought vainglorious in me to make a display of the reception I met with from this household, but Mohammed having brought in a bill of sixty cents for the entertainment to which he invited me, it has rather too strong a hold upon my feelings to be altogether suppressed.

On leaving, it was my purpose to return to the Royal Victoria, but the crafty heathen circumvented me by a dazzling parade of the marvelous sights it was in his power to show. I yielded to his wiles and we began the rounds. The first morsel he introduced me to was a bake-house,—the novelty of which consisted mainly in all the bakers being as black from top to toe as soot and dirt could make them, in contradistinction to the bakers of the other quarters of the globe, among whom the color of flour is wont to predominate. From here we wended our way to the Basha's palace and jail,—a highly whitewashed structure; but which part was the palace and which the jail was not altogether clear to me, for the guide knew not enough English to specify them accurately, and their visible differences were not sufficiently marked to render the discrimination certain.

Mohammed next took me to the abode of the principal Jew of Tangier. The unfortunate man was at the time in company with some little boys engaged in religious exercises,—reciting prayers from a book in full song, which he maintained in the intervals of communion with us; and evidently would fain have had us depart in peace and leave him to his devotions. It would be a pretty thing, however, if true believers must square their conduct in accordance with the wishes of Jews. Mohammed insisted upon going in, and in we went; and once in I was treated with unexceptionable courtesy by the master, who conversed with me and asked numerous questions in French, and sang with undiminished unction while I was replying. Mohammed made straight for the grand saloon on the upper floor, into which he marched me without ceremony, pointing out its glories,—which were, doubtless, the town talk of Tangier, though they would scarcely have made a sensation anywhere else. He was proceeding, in obedience to custom, to carry me to the bed-chambers, the pantry, the kitchen, the wash-house, and so on,—to which the miserable Israelite was able to oppose no valid objection, but I felt sorry for the man, and refusing to countenance any further outrage upon him left him to pray for the dawn of a better day.

I cannot sufficiently admire the patience and courtesy of the people of Tangier in submitting to intrusions of this kind. They would hardly be tolerated by a civilized community. I certainly feel safe in strenuously discouraging such course towards my fellow-citizens of Richmond, where it would infallibly and speedily eventuate in the fracture of one or more bones of the invader.

From the rich Jew's house Mohammed led me to the Synagogue, into which he penetrated with his accustomed straightforwardness and independence. The building displays considerable taste and richness in its interior decoration, and may be considered an ornament to Tangier; but it is situated in the midst of surroundings imperiously demanding the attention of the sanitary police; and that morning was brimful of an odor not of frankincense, nor of myrrh, nor of spices of a sweet savor, but of something which in our own country would be combated to the death with chloride of lime and carbolic acid.

In the synagogue, and in the other places we had visited, my purse was depleted of a little of its nutriment under the advice and management of Mohammed; but a

closer inspection of his method of operating now led me
to suspect that he was swindling me. This was a horrible suspicion, which I would not have entertained unjustly of so reverend-looking a person for the world; but
as I could not by any effort prevent it from rising in my
mind whenever I looked at him, my veneration for him
forced me to the conviction that it was better we should
part, and I therefore bade him set my face hotelwards.
He accompanied me thither, and on the way informed
me that our regular guide was a "blaggard," and almost
suffocated himself in trying to make me comprehend that
if I deemed him a man of any value whatever in his day
and generation, there was no way of preventing his sudden cutting-off in the midst of his usefulness but by most
carefully avoiding to tell the blaggard that he had been
with me. I promised that no indiscretion of mine should
imperil him, but what was his consternation, on turning
the corner by the hotel, to behold the blaggard himself
looming frightfully fat and yellow before him! At this
apparition his sneakiness became condensed and concentrated intensely, and he rendered himself imperceptible
of a sudden, before my eyes, and without my knowing
what had become of him. The blaggard rushed up to
reclaim me, and after rebuking me as much in sorrow as
in anger for venturing out of the pale of his guardianship, proceeded to draw an awful portrait of Mohammed,
whom he pronounced a blaggard in turn; and, as he had
a better knack at English than the other, he was vastly
more specific, elaborate, and effective as a depicturer of
character.

We should have been well pleased to make some excursions into the country adjacent to Tangier, but we
could have gone only a little way before entering a region
where the heathen rage; requiring the adoption of troublesome precautions lest the adventurer should be devoured of them. We should likewise have been extremely gratified to see the citizens washed and dressed,
and Mr. Martin's windows put to the proof, but the Belgian Lion was about to return to Gibraltar, and we did
not feel justified in risking the contingency of another
opportunity to get away. We, therefore, called for our

bill and made ready to go. In the act of preparing this document, Mr. Martin, as he sat at his desk with his writing implements before him, certainly afforded an impressive spectacle—though I am bound to admit that he operated somewhat slowly, but this may have been due to the unwieldiness of his pen,—for it was a remarkably prolonged, plethoric, and plumous instrument —as well as, in some degree, to his mode of holding it,— which was as if it were a mortar-pestle. Accounts are rendered in Tangier as seems preferable to the creditor, either in reals of vellon or reals of plate,—two very different affairs,—a system very obfuscating to a plain-minded traveler, who conceives that one real is the same as any other real, but which is of incalculable utility to landlords, who can make their charges in one kind, and effect the settlement of them in the other. I am far from insinuating that Mr. Martin turned this duplicity of the currency to his advantage, although it is true that we could not precisely follow his calculations till he had explained this peculiarity to us.

Having finished with Mr. Martin, our guide took us under his wings once more, and wobbled off with us to the water-side. As it would be yet some time before the departure of the Belgian Lion, we ensconced ourselves within the purlieus of the custom-house, and watched the scenes enacted there. The little inclosure presented quite an animated picture for Tangier, for the captain of the Belgian Lion was taking in freight, and was stirring the porters into unwonted activity. A grave, white-robed, pie-crust-complexioned Moorish gentleman, who, I suppose, was the collector of the port, was seated in the midst, profoundly passive and listless,—the embodiment of quiet meditation. Amongst the crowd there continually permeated hither and thither another official, also a Moorish gentleman, tall and finely built, but with a countenance of ink dashed with ashes, who bore a whip in his hand, and made the little Arabs shrink as he walked through them. His function seemed to be to see that the State took no detriment from violations of the revenue laws, and he was exceeding zealous in the discharge of his duty. An offender in this particular was caught while we were sitting there. He was one of the little Arabs, and being seized by the tall functionary was first shaken as is a rat by a terrier, and then violently hustled to the bar of justice, which was erected in an adjacent room. Upon examination being proved to be entirely innocent, he was honorably discharged by being kicked unmercifully off of the premises. Shortly after this happy adjudication the guide had us horsed, deposited in a boat, and taken aboard the Belgian Lion, which in a little while was curveting towards Gibraltar, with six or seven passengers leaning over her sides, peering into the depths of the deep with faces pallid and mouths agape.

In closing the account of my adventures in Heathenesse, it is meet that I should say something further of our guide, forasmuch as he besought of me and was promised recommendation amongst my fellow-unbelievers. Of his personal appearance I have already spoken: of his fatness, of his shortness, of his thickness, of his yellowness, and of his indented countenance. His voice was less that of a Christian man than of a bullfrog, though with less ring in the croak. For his apparel he had a kind of bolster wrapped round his cranium, and his body was clad in a simple garment, which, if what I have heard and read concerning these matters is to be depended upon, must have been closely analogous to those vestments in which the gentler sex are enrobed when they retire for the night. Upon the inner or skin surface of this garment he had some kind of contrivance for holding his purse, in which it was secured after a fashion so complex that to insert or withdraw it required such procedures as under our decorous municipal regulations would subject him to arrest and fine. His legs were bare, and he had on his feet a pair of brilliant red morocco slippers of about number twenty. He was an apostate from the faith in some degree, being a partaker of wine with relish. He spoke English with an execrable fluency, begot of self-sufficiency, and claimed to comprehend all tongues. As a guide he was worthy of all praise, being truly indefatigable, dragging his ward everywhere, and omitting no sight how trite and marrowless soever. He was a powerful reviler, pounder on the ribs, and breaker of the backs of his fellow-citizens—an invaluable trait in this land, where the natives would soon worry an unprotected stranger to death. He inherited all the skill in numbers for which the Arabians of old were so distinguished, and could work out a more comprehensive result from fewer data than any other mathematician I ever saw. We had taken with us to Tangier resources ample, as we thought, to meet all expenses; but, when we came to settle with him, he figured up a total which took every solitary cent that both of us could rake and scrape to liquidate it,—nay, we went away in his debt. It irks me sorely that I cannot give his name; but, as I was never able to pronounce it, I could not fix it in my memory; and although he committed it to writing on a fragment of paper, I have not met with any one who can read it with surety. It appears to be Cxqgmktw; and, in concluding my recommendation, I can do no better than to advise all inquirers to ask for him under this appellation.

CHAPTER XIII.

Of what Manner of Men the Spaniards are, and a Political Prelection concerning the Reconstruction of Spain.

WE now prepared to go Italy. We were, however, kept a wearisome time at Gibraltar waiting for some means of getting to Naples, which was our objective point. At last one day there came into the harbor one of the Peninsular and Oriental line of steamers, the Syria, bound for Alexandria, but which touched at Malta; and as we could see no satisfactory prospect of a more direct transit, we concluded to take our chance by this roundabout way.

In bidding adieu to Spain it will not be inappropriate to make a few general observations concerning the country and the people. None of my European reminiscences are more pleasant to revive than those connected with my sojourn there, and it is a source of regret that the state of my companion's health compelled us to restrict our experience to but a limited portion of it. It is a land full of interest, every way worthy of a visit from the traveler, and the interest is enhanced by the fact that it is out of the ordinary track of tourists from America, by which it is invested with more of novelty than will be found in those portions of Europe commonly embraced in a scheme of travel, whose characteristics have been familiarized into tameness by innumerable descriptions. Visitants from the nations nearer at hand are, however, sufficiently numerous, and, unfortunately, from the cause above stated, our travels were confined to those well-trodden paths where frequent intercourse with foreigners has awakened a disposition to make things conform to their tastes and usages, it being to the interest of the people to conciliate them. This disposition is especially marked with respect to the English, who cannot live anywhere except in English style, and do not hesitate to indignantly denounce any deviation from it, no matter in what part of the world they find it. Practically in Spain an American is the same as an Englishman. The Spaniards do not thoroughly comprehend the difference, and so both are put in one category and regarded alike. The consequence is that in the large cities and towns the hotels, from which the ordinary traveler must necessarily draw most of his ideas of Spanish domestic life, have become bastardized to such a degree as to deprive them of many of the national peculiarities. To understand Spain properly, therefore, one must penetrate to the less frequented portions of the country,—an enterprise of some labor, but one which, I am convinced, would furnish a rich and delightful field to the observant traveler.

In my estimation the men of Spain, as a class, are not a fine-looking race. They are short in stature, and have a bilious and puny look. The contrast between them and their old enemies, the Moors, in appearance is very marked, and it is a matter of some surprise how those tall, stalwart Infidels were so completely demolished by these little Christians. Though their countenances are not over-handsome, they have a cast of mournfulness which conciliates, and this, together with a soberness of demeanor, renders a Spaniard a man of presence. I found the people uniformly dignified, courteous, and well-behaved. The chief defects I noted in their character were an extravagant notion of the power of endurance of dumb creatures, a strong proclivity for putting off till to-morrow what can be done to-day, and an invincible disposition to pass counterfeit money on foreigners. We suffered grievously from the operation of this last propensity. The quantity of brass dollars and pewter quarters that we contrived to accumulate during our sojourn amongst them was truly disheartening, especially when it is considered that they could never be passed back on any of the natives; for when a Spaniard receives a coin he rings it, and weighs it, and bites it, with such savage determination to elicit its true character that nothing but the most unimpeachable metal can stand the ordeal.

With the Spaniards—as is the case with all the continental nations, indeed—courtesy is an inherent trait. Its mode of manifestation is very unlike that of the French —being extremely grave and stately, but without coldness; while theirs is highly gymnastical. When a Spaniard does you a favor you are inspired with an internal sentiment of heartfelt liking for him. When a Frenchman does the same you are excited by sympathy into an external exhibition of acrobatic feats in recognition of it. How vastly different in this matter of politeness are both of these peoples from the English and from us! In the narrow streets of a Spanish town you may saunter listlessly along and never fear being run over and trodden down by your more diligent fellow-pedestrians, but wo betide you under similar circumstances in the commodious thoroughfares of London or New York,—where little short of a miracle could save you from being jammed to jelly or ground to powder. How great the contrast, too, in the mode of considering that trying calamity which befalls at times the most staid and majestic of our fellowmen—the blowing off of the hat in the public highways! Who of our kindred and tongue who has ever been visited by this sore trial, as he agonized in the struggle for re-possession, but has felt his heart sink within his bowels to hear the hideous rout of the ignoble populace in riotous jubilation over his misfortune; to know that he can expect no sympathy or aid in his dire strait; nay, to be assured that, if so be it Heaven prosper him, his success will bring deep regret to the bosom of every beholder! When an affliction of this sort overtakes one in Spain it creates no less stir, and the people also participate in the scene; but their part is that of philanthropists. The hue-and-cry is raised; the whole community join in pursuit; nimble feet and cunning hands are in the work; and in a little while the bereaved sufferer is transported from misery to ecstasy,—for he has his truant vestment clamped with both hands upon his head.

In the general estimation the standard of morality in Spain is thought not to rate very high. From my observation I infer that the innate virtue of the Spanish people is about equivalent to our own, though it really seems to be vastly less—peradventure from the fact that they do not appreciate the excellences of hypocrisy as highly as we do. They gamble a little,—nay, a good deal,—in fact, dreadfully. But they are not seen vociferously drunk, as are the Anglo-Saxons—even if it be true, as some have surmised, that they must needs be constantly semi-drunk from the incessant use of wine. Indeed, so marked is this contrast that "as drunk as an Englishman" is the common expression of opprobrium passed upon a brother who has been so abnormally weak as to be beguiled among the traps and pitfalls of alcohol. They do not pad the streets of nights terrifying all good people in their beds with squawks unearthly; nor do they drive everybody in the neighborhood distracted by the so-called singing of songs when they possess not the fitting afflatus, and the malmanipulation of instruments they know no touch of; neither do they essay unseemly liberties with a man from the country, or behold with contempt a foreigner sojourning in their midst.

Living in Spain is cheap—to Spaniards. All the food necessary for their comfortable nourishment is an orange, which they take from the first convenient tree; and a clove of garlic—which any one will readily give to a needy compatriot. These constitute one day's ration—abundant and wholesome. Eligible lodging can be procured anywhere out of doors they may think fit to drop at. For clothing a pair of pantaloons is almost indispensable; but no additional garment is needed other than a cloak, which forms an unexceptionable substitute for shirt, vest, and coat. A due appreciation of these facts will serve to elucidate in some measure that great mystery which is continually obtruding itself upon the mind of the traveler in Spain—how it is that so many people contrive to live with so few visible means of support.

The use of wine is one of the ingrained characteristics. Everybody drinks it who can get it. Babes and sucklings are brought up on it. The children at table have their allowance, and if backward to take it are urged up, even to the resort to gagging, by their affectionate parents,—forming a sight which would make the eyeballs of an apostle of temperance pop with horror, and his soul burst in sunder with presages of wo. Garlic, the great national condiment, is being abandoned at the hotels,—which places are kept more for the robbery of Englishmen and Americans than for the accommodation of the natives, and it being found that the former do not admire any such flavoring. Even the formerly inevitable *olla podrida* is not usually forthcoming in these latter days, except by special request. In fact, as far as they know how, the landlords endeavor to make their bill of fare conform to the English palate, and the result is that it is generally *sui generis*. During all our stay amongst Spaniards, almost the only characteristic Spanish meals we partook of were those on board the steamer Guipuzcoa.

I have already in preceding chapters spoken of the Spanish ladies, and paid my meed of praise to their charms. One circumstance that greatly enhances their attractiveness is the exceeding sweetness of their native language. No language to my mind equals it in beauty and softness. It exacts a peculiar delicately prolonged undulation of the voice and gentleness of intonation, quite incompatible with any but tender sentiments,—so that a crabbed and ill-tempered person cannot speak it aright; and it seems strange how it is possible to quarrel in it. It is as unlike as can be to our harsh tongue,—in which an opprobrious epithet can mostly be recognized by the mere sound of it; while in Spanish the coarsest vituperation comes forth so round and smooth that a foreigner might well mistake it for the most elegant compliment. *Scoúndrel, hog,* and *jackass* sound rough and bitter, but *picaro, puerco,* and *borrico* are very pleasant to the ear indeed. Perhaps one reason why the Spaniards are so prone to resort to the unmistakable arguments of knife and gun is that their words do so provokingly distort and obtund the due expression of their wrath. This sweetness of speech, combined with voluptuous beauty of person and perfect grace of movement, makes the women of Spain the most fascinating creatures extant, and it needs but the minimum of combustibility to get set afire and totally burnt up by them.

Good reader!—while providing thee with dainty bits picked up here and there in my wanderings, for thy gratification, I feel that I would be but illy acquitting myself of my duty by thee were I to withhold the precious nourishing morsels gathered with patient care that make to thine increase. Rather than be lacking in this, I hold it were better I should cast aside my pen as an idle recreant thing. Wherefore, since it may, perchance, one day come within the scope of thine intent to journey into this witching land, I cannot let thee go till I have administered to thee somewhat of admonition,—and see thou that thou takest heed to mine admonishment, for it is wholesome. Mark, then!—Before thou settest forth from these our shores, get thee to the hymeneal altar and make there the appointed vows; or, if thou beest one who hath aforetime done this, I pray thee renew them, and with an immovable purpose of mind to keep and perform them. Thus, peradventure, it may fare well with thee in thy pilgrimage: otherwise,—wo be unto thee,—except, indeed, thou hast that rare discreetness that ariseth only out of profound conversance with philosophy; such as he that here uttereth this wise counsel claimeth to be gifted withal,—and yet, know to thy warning, that even he, though beclad with his panoply, was ofttimes himself in marvelous great peril, and at the last did but hardly escape.

Visiting Spain, as I did, at what has been hailed as a period of transition from the bigotry and backwardness of past times to the liberality and progressiveness that characterize the mode of thought and action of the present era, it may be expected of me to say something of the political condition of the country; and, therefore, I will offer a few observations upon this subject. But, indeed, I was, and am, thoroughly sick of politics in all its phases, and took but little heed of the political affairs of any country I entered, which, after all, were no concern of mine, and hence I can advance nothing very profound on this topic, but profess to present only such views as would be likely to be deduced from what would come under the notice of the most careless observer. At that time the process of reconstruction inaugurated by the expulsion of Queen Isabella was still operating, but with no great marks of progress. If it were not retrograding, it at least had come to something like a stand-still. The northern portions of Spain were madly monarchical, and the southern were more madly republican. The latter, in their frenzy, had endeavored to establish their principles by force; but they were completely foiled in their attempt, and now remained thoroughly subjugated, but waiting and longing for the flimsiest semblance of an opportunity to renew it. Both schisms appeared to unite in abhorrence of the exiled queen; no one had anything to say in her behalf, and outrageously coarse caricatures of her were in circulation, over which the people gloated. To this point reconstruction, as far as it came within the scope of my comprehension, had arrived, and there it stuck.

And yet to me the reconstruction of Spain seems to be a matter sufficiently plain, or, rather, perhaps I should say, one huge step towards it is so. It is to throw the chimera of a republic to the dogs. There is but one race of people on the earth which holds anything that approximates to the true theory of republican government, and that race has shown itself abundantly deficient in the practice. The essence, or, at any rate, an absolute essential of this form of government seems to so humble a political philosopher as I am to be the acquiescence of the minority in the decisions of the majority, coupled with a recognition on the part of the majority of the rights of the minority. This idea is unknown to the Spaniard. He is a strenuous believer in unanimity of sentiment, and he resorts to strenuous means to secure it—even to the extermination of the dissentient. Seeing how difficult it is to remove rooted opinions by mere process of reasoning, he cuts them out of the recusant's breast with a knife, or blows them out of his head with a gun. The majority and the minority are alike in this particular,—the one will not submit to numbers, and the other grants nothing as a right. Hence, whenever they have had the opportunity to fight among themselves, they have always joyfully availed themselves of it. With such opportunities as the formation of a republic on the American *ante bellum* system would afford them, we might almost certainly predict a state of anarchy such as constantly prevails in the Spanish so-called republic of Mexico.

To have a successful republican government the people themselves must be republicanized; not with that hideous hypothetical republicanism which inculcates the omniscience and omnipotence of the mob, but with that true practical republicanism which restricts participation in public affairs to those who are fit to exercise it; which not merely proclaims, but also practices, toleration in politics as well as religion, and which admits that minorities have rights that majorities are bound to respect. In this sense the Spanish people are far from republicanization. No one who is not influenced more by blind zeal for republican institutions than by a correct knowledge of the Spanish character can wish to see the inauguration of a republic amongst them at this time. The Anglo-Saxon species of the tree of liberty is an indigenous plant whose culture is understood only by Americans and Englishmen. Even under their careful and skillful training it has at times borne bitter fruit. It does not thrive out of its native soil, and when transplanted it at first rapidly degenerates, and then it dies.

The past history of the Spanish people abundantly corroborates this estimate of their capacity for self-government. They have even begged to be enslaved. This was the case when Ferdinand VII., who had been deprived of his crown by Napoleon, was restored to sovereignty. At that time the country possessed a highly liberal constitution, framed by the Cortes, which they insisted that the king should respect. But the people almost unanimously insisted, on the other hand, that he should disregard the Cortes, and overwhelmed him with the most urgent petitions and memorials clamorously entreating him to declare null and void all enactments savoring of liberality, and to reign as an absolute monarch. Nay, when the king yielded to these pressing supplications of his loving subjects, which he did most graciously, the very troops dispatched by the Cortes to enforce the democratical view of the question, instead of fighting Ferdinand, welcomed him with acclamations of "Long live our absolute king!" Such a spirit as this is not of a kind to bring forth or cherish true republicanism.

It is interesting to remark in this connection that this same Ferdinand, who for reasons of state was excessively anxious to have an heir, after many discouraging failures, was at length happily enabled, by a little well-timed assistance from a strenuous friend of the family, to become the father of that victim of the capricious resurrection of liberal ideas—the present exiled Isabella.

But I have not formed my estimate of Spanish fitness for freedom from history alone. I was mostly in that part of Spain which was largely republican in sentiment, and I conversed with many republicans. I found almost invariably that their republicanism was of that bigoted, bloody sort which holds that the life of a monarchist should be made to expiate his opinions. The reader probably remembers the hotel commissioner at Cadiz, who was the first champion of freedom with whom I had the satisfaction of communing, and who told me at the very outset of our acquaintance that he had recently slain two monarchists with his own hands, and, while chuckling over the agreeable reminiscence, expressed great hopes of such a turning-up of public affairs as would shortly enable him to let slip the wind of several more. He is not an isolated instance, but the type of a class. If, therefore, the true end of a government be to promote the prosperity of a people, only a strong form of it—strong even to concentration—appears capable of accomplishing this object for Spain.

Some sweeping reforms have of late been promulgated, but these are not in every case as efficacious as they seem to be upon the face. Thus religious toleration, which has been hailed as so vast a step in the line of progress, has yet to fight its way against a great and active opposition, especially on the part of the female population, whose minds are tarred through and through with bigotry, and who have already threatened to tear down heretical churches with their own tender claws. The men alone, if it were in human nature for them to set at naught the influence of the other sex, would be tolerably easy to deal with,—for they have no great amount of religion of any sort to obtrude in the way. There seems to be substantial ground for believing that Roman Catholicism, while it is spreading outside of its long-established bounds, is decaying within them. This was my conclusion from what I observed in Italy as well as in Spain. But Protestantism has no great reason to be elated at this, for its creed has made no lodgment in the strongholds from which its antagonist is being ousted. So far as Catholicism has retired, Infidelity has usurped its place. Nevertheless, as much religion as the men have retained, which is hardly more than what is necessary to be married and buried by, is Roman Catholic in its spirit. They have no desire to see Protestantism flourish, and where there was any sort of contest or rivalship between the two their sympathy and aid would be thrown unequivocally and zealously on the side of the faith of their fathers and the womankind.

The mode in which the Revolution was conducted—a marvel of quiet change, the like of which in Spain is not within the remembrance of the oldest historian—led many observers of the times to believe that a radical modification of the character of the people had taken place, and gave a hopeful augury of future prosperity. Some lowering clouds have risen in the skies since then, making men doubtful and anxious, but nothing so far has occurred to occasion despair. But smooth as was the revolutionary movement, it was not absolutely free from the grinding and scraping which is almost inseparable from the operation of such gigantic and portentous machinery; and as usual there were individuals who had to suffer for the good of the community. Some of these sufferings were detailed to me, with no great show of resignation, by those who were called upon to make the sacrifice. A band of patriotic ragamuffins that sprang up near Seville made themselves especially conspicuous for their zeal in behalf of their unhappy country. With a shriek for freedom that appalled all that heard it, they made a rush for the railroad and forced the officials to prepare a train and give them transportation somewhere —their object being to go forth as apostles of liberty and raise the country. When the country was raised, and the people had hurried off to the scene of expected action, the apostles went to work and stole everything they had left behind them. A landlord who, after having had the honor of entertaining this company of patriots, had the sordid illiberality to make out a bill against them, received a rebuke that chastened and purified him mightily, by being arrested, tried by drum-head court-martial as a self-convicted enemy of popular rights, and sentenced to be shot to death with rusty nails; and it was with difficulty that he got his sentence commuted to confiscation of all his edibles.

There is no doubt that in Spain, and throughout civilized Europe, American ideas are now exercising a tremendous influence. It is a momentous question whether this influence is for weal or for wo; and one not to be answered by the flippant tongues of those of our countrymen who are forever blazoning and boasting over it. I am sorry to be constrained to think myself that it is not working for present good. But it is not needful for me to enlarge upon the topic. My chief reason for this opinion I have indicated in the preceding remarks—the inability of the people to assimilate our ideas. They swallow them readily enough, it is true, but they are not able to digest them; as a consequence they are cramped and made colicky by them—as is shown by their occasional spasmodic uprisings, and the gassy, crude, and insubstantial manifestoes eructed from time to time by their acknowledged leaders. Ultimately, however, I hope and believe that, perfected through suffering, they will attain to that light in these matters which we can honestly claim to possess—and may they make a discreeter use of it than we have. In the mean time, upon poor, proud, misused, glorious old Spain I lay my benison, and heartily wish her prosperity and happiness.

CHAPTER XIV.

Of our pleasant Voyaging from Gibraltar to Malta—Reflections on the Character of the English People—How I displayed and magnified our Country's Greatness in the Belles-Lettres—How we reached the City of Valetta, with various Matters to its Disparagement.

AT Gibraltar we made acquaintance with an English commercial traveler bound as we were to Malta. In fact, his representations had a large share in fixing our decision definitely upon this route, with which previous voyages had made him familiar. He was a clever gentleman, and a man who had had losses—having become separated from an immense bulk of baggage during a recent expedition to Seville. All his efforts to recover it had failed hitherto, but now that he was on the point of cutting clean loose from the country and apparently abandoning all hope, he contrived by his cleverness to make his prospects loom up brighter than ever they had done before,—for he made the settlement of his pretty large hotel-bill contingent upon the restoration of his property; so that the landlord became vastly interested in its fate, and promised, no doubt with the utmost sincerity, to exhaust every means to reclaim it. It is only your abnormally complaisant landlord that can be manipulated in this manner, and only your abnormally clever man that can so manipulate him.

In company, then, with the commercial traveler we passed without the gates, sued for and obtained our sequestrated medicine-chest, and embarked in one of the harbor boats to be taken to the steamer Syria. In spite of his terrible losses, what with valises and satchels and boxes our friend had still as much baggage left as both of us, and it would have been a miracle if more of it were not fated to be lost yet. Indeed, on this very trip his umbrella was seen for the last time. It is amazing, it is disheartening, it is deplorable that one Englishman cannot travel about the earth without lugging along as much lumber as would serve for a dozen. But — I say nothing — let them go on. We had fresh reason for execrating this intermediary mode of getting from the shore to the ship; for the Syria was far out, the water was exceedingly rough, and the boat plunged about so frantically that we began to think we would have to swim part of the way. Our boatmen were, however, men of skill and strength, and pulled us safely through the yawning perils that beset us.

Having finished coaling, about five o'clock in the afternoon we up anchor and left. This steamer was the best I ever traveled in. She was an unusually large sidewheeler, finely fitted, and with plenty of space. Her staterooms were none of your wretched, cheerless cribs, in which a man feels like a buzzard in a cage ; but commodious, spacious apartments, with scope enough actually for the full play of a rocking-chair ; where one felt comfortable and at home. She was kept scrupulously neat and clean, the most lavish and minute attention being directed to securing this condition, — even to the following up of the hawkers and spitters by an assiduous youth, who paraded behind them with a large mop and kept an eagle-eye upon the workings of their mouths. The discipline aboard was complete, everything being done with the system and regularity of a war-vessel, and her officers were thorough gentlemen, with all of the heartiness and none of the coarseness of the sailor character. The fare was abundant, well cooked, and well served. Eating or drinking was going on continually. We had in regular and rapid sequence breakfast, lunch, dinner, tea, and grog,—each sufficiently substantial to furnish forth an ordinate stomach for a day; while every facility was afforded for the satisfying of such as became an hungered between-times. To crown all, there were no extra charges for anything; wines, liquors, ale, beer, porter, "arf-'n-'arf," and soda-water being furnished *ad libitum* gratis. Truly this was a most delectable and greatly-to-be-desired craft to voyage in, and methinks I would freely go to the world's end therein.

We had no great number of passengers. Almost all of them were on the way to India. Amongst them were several ladies and some children,—these being tended by Hindoo nurses, who were the first of this species of my fellow-creatures that I had ever had the pleasure of beholding. From as minute an examination as was practicable for me to make I rated them ethnologically as the type of the ideal Darky, highly improved and fully reconstructed, to which he is to attain as soon as the Millennium gets well under way. But though not numerous, our passengers were of an approved quality, being exceeding cheerful, agreeable, and social. One of our chiefest pastimes was the propounding of conundrums to one another,—in which admirable divertisement the English people seem greatly to delight ; and there were some amongst us who were blessed with an excellent gift at it,—among whom the captain himself cut a conspicuous figure. Of nights whist was much played, and besides we spent a goodly portion of our time in edifying conversation. Some of the passengers were young men going to join the army in India, and being enthusiastic in their profession they never tired of hearing of my eventful campaigns as a surgeon in our war,—of my moving accidents, as well as hair-breadth 'scapes while at rest behind trees, from falling branches; and I was able to enhance their military knowledge greatly with the rich fruits of my experience. With the generous ardor of youth they took a great fancy to my commander, General Lee, and were assiduous in plying me with questions about him. I informed them that our conscientious manner of discharging the duties pertaining to our respective spheres of usefulness so engrossed our time and attention as to preclude us from cultivating that intimacy that I desired to see subsisting between us; but that, nevertheless, I had once had the honor of conversing with the general; and having told them this they would not let me rest till I had given them full particulars of the conversation. I told them that it was early on the morning following the unsatisfactory fight at Boonsboro'. I had been marching all night and now sat on my horse, worn and weary, in a cornfield, suffering the exhausted animal to nibble at the ears. Near me was the general seated in an ambulance, thoughtfully scanning the field on which two days after was joined the great battle of Sharpsburg. Under these circumstances occurred the conversation, which I distinctly remembered and could give word for word. It was as follows:

General Lee to me.—" Take that horse outer that corn there!"

I to General Lee.—" Yesur."

I hope no one will do me the injustice to suppose that I reproduce this colloquy here from any vainglorious desire of vaunting abroad any notice that may chance to be bestowed upon me by the great men of the earth. Such is not my motive. It is to the honor of the general himself that I record it,—to show how tender was that regard for the interests of non-combatants which would not allow a perishing horse—good rebel and stanch follower of his though he was—to take a mouthful of sustenance belonging to an unbelligerent enemy.

With some of the elder and graver of the passengers I held discourse on literature; and this, while profitable, was also entertaining; for nothing delights me more than to soberly commune with them who take pleasure in this topic. I found that they were perfectly familiar with some of our own most noted prose-writers—by name; though of our poets they did not seem to be quite as well informed; and heartily grieved was I that I could not greatly enlighten them on this point. In response to their expression of surprise that our civil war had given birth to no sublime effort of the muse, I suggested that experience showed that great crises were pregnant rather with exalted deeds than with brilliant thoughts; and that trivial circumstances had been the occasion of more real poetry than those of vastly more importance. Nevertheless, I asserted with emphasis that we had great poets in our land. I myself, let it be understood, am lacking in the poetic taste. For a man of my nice discernment, well-balanced mind, and comprehensive intellect, I do think that the want of appreciation for poetry with which I am cursed is absolutely inexplicable. As a consequence of this deficiency I was dreadfully pressed when asked to sustain my assertion by specimens from the works of our masters. Fortunately, I happened to remember an admirable lyric composed by one who is very near and dear to me, and who, in my estimation, is as good as the best of our poets or any other man; and this I commended to their notice. In introducing it I laid stress upon it as illustrative of my thesis—that lesser events more thoroughly arouse the true poetic nixus than do the greater—since this effort was inspired by the epidemic of garroting, whose rapid spread a few years ago alarmed the whole country; against which scourge it was directed as a counterblast; and in evidence of the tremendous influence it had exerted I stated that at the present time that horrid practice was almost subverted. I went on to remark that if there were any example in the whole compass of English poetry fit to be compared with it it was doubtless Coleridge's "Rime of the Ancient Mariner,"— which, I admitted, had some likeness to it; though the most bigoted admirer of that very passable production must be bound to confess that the resemblance is purely superficial. With this prelude I proceeded to recite it, rendering it with exquisite modulation of voice and unsurpassable impressiveness of gesture. The effect upon my auditors was most marked. They listened to it in an ecstasy of silence more eloquent than speech, and at the close were entirely at a loss for words in which to express their admiration of it.

As I have the best of reasons for believing that the author's own countrymen are themselves ignorant (more shame on them for it!) of his contribution to the national garland, I insert it here that they may have the opportunity of committing it to memory:

THE RIME OF THE THREE GARROTERES.

It was a Shaggy-Whiskered Man,
    The fiercest one of Three—
That stopped a vagrant Citizen:
    "Now, wherefore stopp'st thou Me?"

Upspoke the Shaggy-Whiskered Man,
    "Right speedily thou'lt see."
"Be not thou, Sir, a Garrotere?"—
    The fierce man said, "I be."

At hearing this the Citizen
    Did quake like Anything;
And felt as when in Hawk's talons
    Doth feel the Gone Gosling.

Then round about his shrinking form
    Did gather these Three Men:
Now Heaven—no other help is nigh—
    Defend this Citizen!

His Hair did bristle up on end;
    He wist not what to do;
His Brain whirled round, and in a trice
    His Body whirled round, too.

Away he sped and cried aloud,
    "Haste, Watchman, to mine aid!"
The Three uprose, and after him
    Full manfully they made.

Anon he felt their fingers meet
    About his Jugulare:
"Thou suffocatest Me!" he cried—
    "I yield, Sir Garrotere."

Then did they vilely mash his Nose;
    And black, also, his Eye,
And did in divers ways entreat
    Him most despitefully.

They took from him all that he had;
    Then bade him to depart;
And each one graciously did give
    A kick to help him start.

This Citizen did ail somewhat;
  Withal was Rheumatic;
The which to ease he had that Night
  Obtained a Specific.

This Sovereign Balm they do concoct
  By steeping in Whiskie
The fruit that groweth on the plant
  Ycleped the Pokeberrie.

A quart Bottelle of this they took
  From that sick Citizen;
Forsooth, they wot it not to be
  Rheumatic Medicine.

Nay, they did deem it right Whiskie
  From Foreign Parts, most choice;
And, much puft up at their good hap,
  Did mightily Rejoice.

Straightway they drew the stopple out,
  And lustily did bouse;
And so did these Three Garroteres
  Most gloriously Carouse.

Be warned, my Friend, and think, ere thou
  Dost Whiskie Bottelle ope:
'Tis the true Box of Pandora,—
  Save that it hath not Hope.

All of a sudden One did gasp,
  "Lo! I feel fit to Die!"
Eftsoons The Others answered him
  With, "So do I;"—"and I."

Then spoke The Shaggy-Whiskered Man:
  "Did note how that Stuff burned?—
Great Grief! If we ain't all Pisonned,
  I wish I may be Derned!"

At this dread speech a Sore Dismay
  Did fall on these Three Men;
And now They trembled full as much
  As erst did Citizen.

And lo! The Shaggy-Whiskered Man—
  The fiercest of The Three—
Fell down and shrieked in wild panic,
  "Have Mercy, Lord, on Me!"

But the Discreetest One did say,
  "Let us be making tracks,
And get us where some Doctor-man
  May pump out our stomachs."

>   Quick hied they to an Hospital,
>   And called the Doctor-man;
>   And showing him the dread Bottelle,
>   Their Woful Tale began.
>
>   "I prithee hold," cried Doctor-man,
>   "How gat ye this Bottelle?—
>   Methinks, Fair Sirs, it is mine own,—
>   It hath mine own Labelle.
>
>   "I' faith, it readeth,—'Tinctura
>   Baccæ Phytolaccæ.
>   S.—Gutt. xx cum paululo
>   Aquæ, ter in die.'
>
>   "This Matter must be looked into.—
>   Bid Chief Cook Fyshe attend!"
>   Anon up from his pots and pans,
>   The Chief Cook did ascend.
>
>   "Speak, Chief Cook!" saith the Doctor-man;
>   "Dost know who be These Men?"—
>   Good lack!—What see The Garroteres?—
>   Hah!—'Tis the Citizen!!
>
>   "Exult, my soul! sing Jubilee!"—
>   Loud shrieked the glad Chief Cook,—
>   "For in Captivity be They
>   That stole my pocket-book!"
>
>   "By Saint Brimstone!" sware Doctor-man,
>   "I do withhold my skill,
>   Till on these losel Knaves the Watch
>   Their Function do fulfil.
>
>   "Go, hie thee hence, good Chief Cook Fyshe,
>   And summon the Police.
>   When These be safely housed in Cage,
>   I will do mine Office."
>
>   So said, so done. What need that I
>   Should say what more befell?—
>   Suffice it that They did Atone:—
>   So ends this Chronicelle.

The intimate relations I established with my fellow-passengers afforded the means of giving me quite a fair insight into the character of the English nation. I found them to be eaters of tremendous pith and power, and drinkers in full proportion. Despite the rapid recurrence of the meals, they gathered in solid phalanx, fresh and vigorous, at every one, fell undauntedly upon it, and annihilated it with ease,—as, there is every reason to believe, they could have done by as many more. It has been supposed that the Americans are no laggards in imbibition,—and the supposition is certainly well grounded,—but it appears to me that we have scarcely overtaken the Britons in this direction. They love good substantial liquors, being particularly prone to brandy, just as they like good substantial food of flesh of cows, and bulls, and oxen. That deep-rooted American custom which requires every man who orders a drink at a bar to invite all beholders to partake with him does not seem to greatly obtain amongst them. They opine that whoever wishes refreshment will ask for it, and should of right bear all expenses incurred,—a not wholly irrational view, and one that might, if adopted in our land, save many hospitable and philanthropic topers from the poor-house. They are greatly more wicked than we; for while we will play whist ofttimes for its own sake alone, they will have nothing to do with it on any consideration short of sixpence a rubber. Neither do they detest dancing and the drama, and if a novel be interesting they shudder not a whit at the sin of reading it. They, however, abhor slavery utterly; nor did I meet with an Englishman who cared to conceal his dislike of it in conversing with me, who was born and bred in its midst and might have owned slaves had she I adored linked her fortune (of some thirty or forty) with mine.

My association with these gentlemen was likewise the instrumentality of my happy conversion to the belief that the traditional reserve and surliness of the English traveler is something of a myth,—and I find that other Americans have been forced by their experience to come to the same conclusion. Much have the wandering sons of Albion been rated on this score; but as far as my knowledge of them extends I am constrained to lift up my voice and testify in their behalf. Not merely in respect of those I met on board the Syria, but wherever else I encountered them, I always found the English as courteous, communicative, and social as any other travelers. It is very true I never thrust my acquaintance upon them, cross-questioned them, nor sought to establish confidence by interrogatory guessing. Had I pursued this plan it is not impossible that I would have to join in the general estimate of their outrageous grumness, unsociability, and impracticableness. As it was, our acquaintance was made readily by the quiet process of simple association, and it was uniformly cordial and pleasant; for as I said nothing to awaken their prejudices, they were alike forbearing towards mine. One of their most glaring traits, which protrudes a fraction too obtrusively at times, is a tremendous estimate of the grandeur of their land and people,—which they steadfastly believe and will maintain to the death to be the greatest and most excellent in all the earth; and, beshrew me!—having myself had a glimpse of their country—if I am not become extremely tolerant of their opinion in these matters. Among the most plausible accusations that I have heard laid upon them are that they seize on the most comfortable apartments in hotels and try to get the best of everything at table. These are indeed grave charges, which are not to be gainsaid or defended, and can be palliated only by considering that the same thing under the same circumstances is done by poor frail humanity universally.

Let not my fellow-countrymen attribute any apology I may make for our hereditary foes, or such commendation as I bestow upon them, to any taint of that state of denationalization into which certain of our too highly sublimated citizens fall when they chance to come within the atmosphere of European society and manners. Believe me, no one ever adventured forth from our shores and came back less soiled with this disfiguring tarnish. In all my wanderings I breathed no whiff of the air of courts and communed with none of the nobility or gentry,—unless, forsooth, the consummate hypocrisy, which is well known in our country to be a not unlikely outgrowth of monarchism, led my associates to deceive me concerning their social status; for they comported themselves as mere common gentlemen—and hence was preserved from their contaminating influences. I returned loving my own land, its people, its institutions, and its customs better than those of any other,—nay, loving its very defects better than their excellences. I prefer our stupendous, awe-inspiring locomotives and convenient, cosy, supple-jack cars to the portable saw-mills and hackney-coaches that run so glibly along the European railways. To my taste the sumptuous fare of our hotels is more to be desired than the sumptuous furniture of theirs; and my bowels languished and yearned within me for bacon, and greens, and corn-bread amidst beef, and biscuits, and gizzards, and livers, and intestines of the fowls of the air, and the earth, and the water, though daintily baked in little paste-board boxes. My palate was not debauched by any of their ways. For the augmenting of the succulency of my sustenance at the matutinal repast my choice still is coffee rather than wine; and when I am cut off from fellowship with my brethren of the Noah's Flood division of Sons of Temperance, of which it is my proud privilege to boast myself a most unworthy member, I shall take to whisky in lieu of 'arf-'n-'arf. Upon my ears, "tote," and "nigger," and " can't," and " laff," and " eether," and " neether," and such like modes of my vernacular fall with a dump more natural than " carry," and " negrow," and " carn't," and " larf," and " eyether," and " nyether." And yet, with all these American likings and prejudices, I was not made so stone-blind as not to see that in some important matters Europe is as far ahead of us in reality as in others we surpass her apparently.

After the first day we were in sight of land pretty much all the time, and the monotonous sea-view was relieved by the gleam of many a sail. The obliging captain pointed out to us the coast of Algeria, made somewhat noticeable by mountain ranges in the interior, and called our especial attention to the site of Carthage as we went steaming past it.

"Assyria, Greece, Rome, Carthage, what are they?"

Yes, what is Carthage?—and where? The captain strenuously and untiringly projected his index-finger toward the Lybian depths before us, and said, " There !" And I gazed earnestly—gazed and saw nothing. But I cogitated powerfully and deeply, for, though I had no basis for my reveries much more substantial than when I would turn my face to the west, and, peering over the ocean, dream of home, it sufficed for busy thought, and on it she marshaled forth the memories and visions of the past. The great city is utterly blotted out and its place is desolate.

On the raw and cloudy morning of the fourth day we were running by Gozo, a bleak and hilly island not far from Malta, and soon the city of Valetta came into view. As we steamed along the Maltese coast, an indentation was pointed out as the veritable scene of St. Paul's shipwreck. We were not near enough to obtain a satisfactory sight of it; however, I gazed in that direction with all the faith I could rake together, but I was grievously pestered with doubts nevertheless. By twelve o'clock we were safely housed in the harbor of Valetta. This harbor is a very fine one, resembling that of Havana, having a narrow entrance, and is rendered impregnable by a series of immense thick stone fortifications. As seen from the water the city presents a very picturesque appearance. The amiable officers of the Syria now bade us a kind adieu, in which our fellow-voyagers joined; and we embarked in a boat along with our friend who had lost all his baggage and went ashore. On the way we were incessantly besieged by certain amphibious youths of Malta who make a livelihood by diving after sixpences, which they beguile persons of aquatic tastes into dropping into the water.

We landed at the foot of a declivity, where the commissioner of the Imperial Hotel was lying in ambush, and clamped us on the spot. By his command we ascended a weary flight of stone steps, and then wended our way over sundry precipices till in time we stood beneath the Imperial dome, where we were greeted with the disheartening intelligence that the house was full. Hard by, however, was the Inglaterra, to which we straightway repaired, and here we procured accommodations. This hostelry is a spacious labyrinth, in which it is not easy for an unskilled person to make much headway without a map. It seems to be well managed, except that the purveyor appears to be deficient in the calculative faculty, inasmuch as an awful pause occurred in the middle of every meal, arising from the untimely consumption of all the edibles on the table, and the consequent necessity of waiting for them to be duplicated in the kitchen.

We had scarcely taken possession of our apartment before we were waited on by a citizen bearing a chest filled with that species of lace which is manufactured on this island, and which I understand is in high repute with the vainer sex. He was terribly persistent in his efforts to induce us to purchase some of his goods; and when we represented the malignancy of the custom-house people as an insuperable bar, he grew extremely fertile in expedients for counteracting the machinations of those worthies; but, as we were barbarously ignorant of the value of the commodity, and, of a truth, little anxious for an increase in any such knowledge, all of his eloquence failed to do more than make us yawn abominably. Having at last persuaded him to depart from us, we put ourselves under the guidance of him of the lost baggage, who took us to a cigar-store kept by an acquaintance of his, where we fell a-smoking and discussed the local news.

While refreshing ourselves in this manner in the cigar-store, there came to us, first, a fan-merchant, who bore an armful of his wares, made of paper gaudily painted with Maltese crosses and other cabalistic figures. He was instantly followed by a seller of shawls. Then came maidens bearing bunches of wild, not to say ferocious, flowers; then dealers in dogs; and, lo, presently reappeared our indomitable lace-man, who undespairingly had tracked us up. *Pari passu* with him came a mortal rival of his, another lace-man. Interspersed among them was an innumerable company of guides, ravenous to show us the wonders of Valetta. In an evil moment we patronized the fan-merchant. The encouragement that this circumstance afforded to the rest was tremendous, and the consequent onslaught upon us was terrible. Only by the most unflinching determination did we escape utter ravage.

The city of Valetta is one of the most up-and-down places on record. Its thoroughfares are a series of inclined planes, diversified with flights of steps, which disconcert and balk thick-winded people completely. It is indispensable that these unfortunates should do their peregrinations on wheels, and for their accommodation there are numerous oddly-contrived vehicles—though it is requisite that he who makes use of them should be a man of nerve; for, independently of the great risk of being tossed out on the stones by the outrageous jolting, the constantly recurring incitements to run away offered to the animals by the steep descents, and the exceeding imminency of a fatal catastrophe in such an event, cause the passenger to feel pretty sure that he is rushing into eternity. The buildings resemble those of the Spanish cities, being furnished with balconies to the windows, and appear tall and stately, and withal gloomy by reason of the narrowness of the streets. It is a dingy-looking town, but rendered lively by the crowd of do-nothings prowling about seeking prey, and by the military and their music which is dealt out in a perfect diarrhœa of melody. A distressing dash of melancholy is, however, infused through the air by the ringing of the church-bells, whose awfully lugubrious notes were pealing forth with scarce an intermission day and night, till they almost turned our brains by the heaviness of heart they engendered.

While poking about the outskirts I stumbled upon a British warrior off duty, and fell into a long conversation with him,—its length being vastly augmented by the circumstance that the English veteran knew not the English tongue. From him I gathered an immense fund of information concerning the military features of the island —whereof I understood not ten words; but presently, upon mentioning St. John's Cathedral, he kindly offered to pilot me thither.

The church of St. John is one of the most notable relics of the old Knights of Malta. The British warrior conducted me to it, but I had barely got within its shadow before a legion of guides snatched me away from him. I made what opposition I could, but it was entirely futile, for they chaperoned me through it whether or no. I did not profit greatly by their assistance. Their language was almost incomprehensible, and the multiplicity of expounders rendered everything obscure by reason of the shedding of overmuch light. Now it was that I had cause to rejoice that I had perfected myself in the knowledge of the Latin by conversation with the padre of the Guipuzcoa, for the fluency thus acquired enabled me to extract much valuable information from the various inscriptions, which I perused with what seemed to me to be a tolerably near approximation to their true intent and meaning; though, really, I would have been pleased to have had a dictionary and grammar with me. In my judgment this church is not the extraordinary object that it has been represented to be. It is adorned with the usual variety of sculptures and paintings, but it has a faded and neglected look about it, not resembling the mellowing effect of time, which is not prepossessing. It is a charnel-house for the bones of the old knights, and the most striking portion of it is the pavement, which is almost made up of sepulchral slabs engraved with obituary notices in their honor.

> "The knights are dust,
> And their good swords are rust,
> Their souls are with the saints, we trust."

I was dragged and shoved down by my persecutors into a dungeon below, and made to stare at the tombs of certain illustrious dignitaries of the order,—of whom a circumstantial account was given me in Arabico-Italian, but I will not detain my narrative by repeating it.

The Palace of the Grand Master, which is now occupied by the governor of the island, contains some specimens of armor and tapestry said to be worth seeing; but as all its entrances were vigilantly guarded by the very flower of the guides, and I am a man of peace and no upholsterer, I forbore to make any attempt to penetrate within it.

At night I lighted my pipe and strolled forth to contemplate the city in its nocturnal aspect. In wandering through one of the streets the sound of boisterous revelry proceeding from a tenement that I passed smote upon my ears. The funereal clangor of the bells, my conflicts with the guides, and the desperate struggles I had been compelled to make to preserve myself from the purchase of cats and dogs, had affected my nerves; carking despondency was eating me up, and to lighten my weight of woe I bethought me to enter this place of merriment. It was a very unpretentious establishment, patronized almost altogether by soldiers, who were collected there in pretty large force, and seemed to be enjoying themselves very much. One of the most prominent figures was a personage in a red coat, with his hat off, of great grumness of visage, who sat on a bench with his arms crossed over his breast, executing a comic song in a distressingly cracked-pot voice, with the precision and fixedness of purpose of a leader of the church psalmody. I thought it was one of the worst songs ever composed; not so the songster, however, who insisted upon its merits being fairly investigated; for being constantly disturbed by the noise of dancing and talking, he was as constantly breaking off in the middle of a line to exclaim in a tone of highly indignant remonstrance, "'Ishe, carn't you? and 'arken to me sing!" Nay, so determined was he that his ode should be rightly appreciated that whenever he reached the end of it he instantaneously began at the beginning again.

I took a seat on a bench opposite to that occupied by the melodist, and hearkened to his warbling with the most respectful consideration, being, I believe, the only person in the room who had sufficient regard for the claims of etiquette to do so. While thus engaged one of the company, a burly, rough-looking individual, approached me, and remarking that he perceived I was of foreign parts, invited me to partake of a glass of porter. Finding upon minute inquiry that nothing stronger was sold here, I concluded that the place was to all intents and purposes a temperance house, and so very cheerfully partook—knowing full well that I would be sustained therein by a unanimous vote of the Noah's Flood division. To one who studied human nature in Malta simply from its outcroppings, an invitation of this sort under these circumstances might readily be suspected to be a delusion and a snare. It was not so, however, in this case. My entertainer had not drugged my liquor, he did not pick my pocket, nor did he garrote me on the street; on the contrary, after extending his hospitality, he had little more to do with me, and even excused himself from taking a reciprocal glass. Surely this was a Maltese in whom there was no guile, and I gladly put the incident on record to show that even after a sojourn in Valetta it is not well to absolutely abandon faith in our fellow-man.

At the seventh repetition of the song or thereabouts it began to pall somewhat upon me, and thinking I had listened to it sufficiently to satisfy the requirements of politeness, and my melancholy still oppressing me, I concluded to rise and endeavor to kick off the incubus,—in other words, I proposed to participate in the dancing. But at this moment the hour struck beyond which it is not lawful for military men to be out of their quarters. In the twinkling of an eye an utter change overspread the scene. The lips of the minstrel became hermetically sealed and the joints of the dancers became stiff, and before I could well realize it I was almost alone. The interest of the place was now gone, and I wandered forth again, continuing till I reached the seashore, where I planted myself in a bastion, and putting my hands in my pockets gazed ruefully upon the waters, attuning my sombre fancies with the solemn dirge sung by the awful image of the vast unknown whose dread bosom palpitated before me.

When I had sufficiently tasted of the luxury of woe at this spot I turned to go back to the hotel. It was a very dreary, lonely place, such as none but a sentimental person would care to linger at after dark. Immediately upon quitting the bastion I espied a sinister-looking individual dodging in the shadows, directly in my path. "By'r Lady," said I, "I am surely to be garroted. But," I continued, "thanks to a beneficent Providence, there is nothing to be squeezed out of me but my breath—which is itself no more than a vapor and idle wind. Howbeit, since, methinks, I am endued with some poor skill in surgical anatomy, in such case I shall put it to the proof with this pocket-knife; if, please heaven, its infirmities— seeing that it has lost the spring of its back—do not enforce it to shut up untimely at the pinch." With these encouraging reflections I marched on.

A melancholy man ofttimes becomes unwontedly bold through mere indifference to fate, and I now felt tremendously valiant from this cause. Upon coming up to the skulker I stopped promptly and glared at him most undauntedly. He at once came to my side, simultaneously bursting into a torrent of Arabico-Italian, and we went along together—my responses to his observations, whatever they may have been, being extremely short, sharp, and decisive. Whether his intents were wicked or charitable I could not accurately ascertain. I acted on the assumption that they were of the former class, and being one of those who deem it wrong to put temptation in a man's way, I gave him none whatever; on the contrary, if he designed to assault me he must have perceived that I rather discouraged the attempt, for I kept him well in the field of vision, and in the most advantageous position for the ready performance of the operation of tracheotomy till we reached the frequented portion of the city. He continued with me even into the hotel, where he spoke me a speech, which I supposed was a parting benediction, and, receiving it as such, was going to my room, when so violent a paroxysm of words seized him as made the landlord hurry forward to interpret. By this help I made the astounding discovery that he was having the inconceivable effrontery to claim salvage for bringing me back safely to the hotel! Upon this I had a mind to cut his throat anyhow, but pacified myself by denouncing him as a highway robber and midnight assassin.

I lay in bed meditating with a thankful heart upon my more or less complete deliverance from the lace-men, the fan-men, the flower-girls, the guides, and the sellers of dogs and cats. Before morning I had reason to be especially grateful for the restraining grace that had enabled me to resist the enticements spread around the latter animals; for, believe me that however different Maltese cats may be in physical conformation, in manners and customs they are identical with the cats of our own kindred and tongue,—as was made clear to me by the evidence of apparently no fewer than one thousand of them, who had gathered together on the housetop to make love and war. Rising above the din of battle ever and anon came a soul-withering clang from the church steeples; and thus lulled the livelong night by caterwauling and bell-ringing we sank and rose in rapid alternation to and from repose.

The first thing in the morning the enemy renewed their assaults. While making our toilet our original indomitable lace-merchant charged the door, took it by storm, and had effected a lodgment in the chamber before we could take any measures for defense. Close upon his rear followed others, less bold but equally rapacious compatriots of his, bent upon sharing the fruits of his daring. Some terrific skirmishing ensued, and in the end we got them out—maintaining the entirety of our pocketbooks; but it was truly a narrow escape.

Such things as these made our sojourn in Valetta a time of bitterness to us, and for peace' sake we fled to Citta Vecchia,—a little town about six miles distant,—where we hid ourselves from the eyes of men in the catacombs. On returning to the city we hurried to our apartment and locked the door, venturing no more into the streets till we set forth for the steamer *en route* for Naples.

The climate of Malta is highly commended by sundry authorities for its salubrity. I stayed there too short a time to form any opinion of its quality from personal observation. From my knowledge of Valetta I cannot advise any person short-of-puff to take up his abode there, and gentlemen of a fractious frame of mind had better go somewhere else.

CHAPTER XV.

Of the ominous Bark wherein we set sail for Italy, and of a very distressful Accident that happened to me, and of the unrighteous Accusations made against me therein — Of our Transshipment into another Bark, and the fresh Tribulations engendered thereby— how we sped triumphantly past Scylla and Charybdis and got safely to Naples—With brief Descriptions of the Places we saw on our Way.

THE steamer in which we escaped from Malta bore the portentous name of Scylla. She was a little English-built propeller, strong and well furnished, as English builders generally make their ships, but maltreated, as they are very apt to be when they fall into the hands of Italians. The chief defect in her construction was excessive smallness of the staterooms. Ours was situated at the tip-end of the saloon, and was the smallest in the lot; moreover, its door did not open outwardly, but inwardly, upon the adjoining stateroom, through which it was necessary to pass in making our exits and our entrances, and which was held and possessed by a fat, old, and irascible Englishman. There were a great many passengers on board, which caused us to be uncomfortably crowded, and likewise occasioned a distressing panic to arise at the announcement of every meal, because it must needs be the inevitable lot of some one or more to bide his time for the second table.

We started propitiously with a smooth sea, though two or three of our companions contrived to get seasick. The company did not fraternize very well. There was a feeling of distrust and animosity amongst us in consequence of being packed too closely together; and accordingly we sat and glowered at one another till it became dark enough to justify us in going to bed, and then retired in high dudgeon and supreme contempt.

The wretchedly diminutive size of my stateroom caused me a great deal of trouble in making my adjustments for the night, for I did not know what to do with my clothes and portable baggage. I arranged things at last, however, by rolling all up in a lump together and sticking it under the pillow, leaving out my umbrella, which I put to bed by my side and lay with all night. Soon after depositing myself in my berth, war broke out between me and a nation of hardy and unconquerable fleas, whose homes I had invaded, which was waged with scarce an interval of peace till daybreak. About two o'clock in the morning, just after a terrible struggle, in which I had slain one of the enemy, in looking through the port-hole a most beautiful vision refreshed my eye. It was the city of Syracuse, which we were approaching, basking in the moonbeams. It looked like a gossamer city under the influence of the soft, benignant light, forming a picture of indescribable sweetness. Little did I think while soothing my soul with this delightful scene that our guardian angel, the man at the wheel, was fast asleep. Nevertheless, so it was, and but that the officer of the watch providentially woke up in time to rouse him, some of us would, peradventure, have been rendered rather damp and mouldy, for the harbor of Syracuse is not one readily entered with the eyes shut.

Surely this ship was built in the eclipse and rigged with curses dark. In rolling over next morning my orbs beheld a spectacle that made me fairly gasp with dismay. In the wild battlings of the night I had overlaid my umbrella, and, to my inconsolable sorrow, crushed the handle off. Poor, dear, old cotton umbrella! It had been my companion in all my wanderings—from amongst the barbarians of Minnesota to these amongst whom its usefulness had been curtailed. Its handle, in the opinion of the most sagacious zoologists who had examined it, was designed to represent a *Cynocephalus*, or dog's head, and was carved in the simple, massive style peculiar to Egyptian art, which chastely indicates rather than clearly bodies forth the ideal of the sculptor. It was unique,— no other dog's head I have ever seen bearing comparison with it,—and was the crowning, and, indeed, the only glory of the umbrella; for the rest of it, both in structure and fabric, was somewhat commonplace, its spine being bent, and its ribs bowed with age and hardship, and its integument having the ashy pallor of anæmia. With the loss of the dog's head the implement lost all that redeemed it, and thenceforward became a byword and a reproach among all nations that I afterwards visited.

The upgetting of the company in the morning was attended with a great commotion, arising from the simultaneous calls upon the steward for water for ablution, none of this element being to be found in the stateroom tin pitchers. Our fat, old, and irascible neighbor contributed abundantly to the clamor. So did I, and opened the door between us to give freer vent to my voice. He was out of bed, and filled the room as he sat on a stool making his toilet, and smoked with hotness engendered by cramped quarters and tight boots. As I opened the inner door the steward opened the outer, which thereby was caused to impress a very palpable pat upon that huge segment of his carcass which protruded over the hinder edge of the stool. Straightway, with vehemence, he turned upon me. "Wot are you a bumpin' of me for?" says he. "I'm not a bumpin' of you," says I. "You *are*," says he; "carn't I feel? If you'd a told me you wanted to go through, I'd a got out of your way, sir." "I don't want to go through," says I, "and I haven't bumped you; it was the steward." "If you've got patience enough to wait one minute," says he, "I'll be dressed and leave, and then you won't have to bump me any more, sir." "I haven't bumped you at all," says I; "it was the steward, I tell you!" "I have no doubt of it, sir, no doubt of it," says he; "but still I ask you to please not to do it again, anyhow." As it was bootless to argue the point any further, I closed the door and waited for him to finish. In the mean time the steward gave him another pat, which he had the perverse audacity to lay to my charge also; but this accusation I indignantly refused to repel.

On going upon deck, there was Syracuse before me, looking by no means like the fairy city I had seen through the port-hole in the night. I had risen too late to go ashore, for we were already on the point of setting out again, and hence saw no more of the place than was to be seen from the vessel. Thus viewed there was nothing peculiarly striking about it, but the picture was not an uninteresting one for all that; for it was backed by the great volcano Etna, whose mighty bulk rose in the distance till its peak became mantled in the clouds, which, as they from time to time were blown aside, revealed it covered with fields of snow and emitting huge whiffs of smoke. I would have been glad to tarry for awhile at Syracuse for Archimedes' sake and for its other associations, of which it has its share; and this, indeed, is wellnigh all it has to commend it to the traveler, for it is now fallen very low from its old-time pinnacle of opulence and power.

Leaving Syracuse, we sailed along the fertile Sicilian coast, the constant sight of habitations amongst the hills brightening the landscape, and snow-crowned and smoking Etna always in the scene, till mid-day, when we stopped at Catania. This is a town of some seventy-five or eighty thousand inhabitants, situated at the base of the volcano, which towers grandly behind it, and by which it has time and again been treated with great harshness. Besides having been well drenched with the offscourings of the ill-tempered mountain, it has repeatedly been thoroughly shaken up by earthquakes. It is likewise a favorite resting-place for pestilences on their travels. The cholera took off seven thousand of its people at one sweep,—a circumstance which should go far towards weakening the confidence which some entertain in the potency of sulphur fumigations against this malady. Encompassed thus with manifold and mortal perils, the citizens of Catania have grown to be uncommonly pious—so I judge from the fact that there are a hundred and eight churches in the city; and at the same time they have exhibited that admirable trait which makes the best of a bad thing by building their houses of the very lava that was intended for their sarcophaguses. From the harbor, which is a very unreliable one, the city presents a picturesque appearance, which is enhanced by the numerous church-towers and the long row of arches pertaining to the railroad which they have at last got through to Messina.

We remained here four tiresome hours and then went forth again, still sailing close to the pleasant shores of the island. When night came on, a brilliant mass of lights resting upon the waters to our right indicated the town of Reggio, which sticks out like a corn upon the toe of Italy. We were now in the narrow Strait of Messina which parts the island from the mainland, and at nine o'clock were at Messina itself. It required a great deal of patient manipulation to get our craft safely into the harbor, which is a most excellent one and perfectly protected from the fury of the sea, being so secure, in fact, as to be dangerous; for an unwary ship may readily run her nose into some of the defenses, especially if entering at night. We, however, had the man at the wheel bawled at till he was wide awake, and then put in direct communication with our commander astraddle of the bowsprit by means of a line of mariners. There was also a branch line connecting with the engineer. By dint of these measures after alternately going forward a little and backward a little more, we ultimately got into the great basin within, and there dropped anchor.

The Scylla had now attained her goal, for she connected with another steamer here which plied to Naples, and to which we were notified that we must transship ourselves. Excepting the microscopic staterooms, the somnolency of the pilot, the struggle for sustenance, the ravening greed of the fleas, the internecine propensities of the passengers, the baseless accusation of bumping, the ruin of my umbrella, and two or three other trivial discomforts, my voyage on the Scylla had been as pleasant as heart could wish, and I was prepared to leave her with the most favorable impressions; but when I was overhauled and charged by the head-waiter with an attempt to abscond without paying for a bottle of their commonest wine, she fell in my opinion mightily. I had risen after having for the second time contributed liberally of my slender substance to the necessities of their fleas, had packed up, and embarked in a boat for the other steamer, when the head-waiter arrested me and preferred his accusation. The thing was preposterous and bore the marks of its enormity upon its face. Had it been a bottle of whisky or brandy involved in the question, I am free to confess that the waiter might have had some tolerable ground to stand upon, and I should have felt some disposition to debate the case on its merits; but to suppose that a man of my feeble constitution would do violence to his nature by purchasing, still more by paying for such weak, paltry stuff as wine, was so ridiculous that I laughed him to very scorn, and simply bade him, and the boatman simultaneously, to be off.

The new steamer was the Milano, yet smaller than the Scylla but more commodiously arranged, though by no means exceptionally comfortable. A great influx of fresh passengers occurring, so augmented our numbers as to overstrain the resources of the vessel to such an extent as to throw us into a state of painful uncertainty about obtaining quarters; for the commander was a man of gallantry, and ordained that the ladies should have their pick and choice of the staterooms before the claims of any gentleman should be considered; but as through-passengers were next in favor we in the end procured accommodations. Having come to something like a satisfactory understanding on this point, I took boat and went ashore to make observation of the city.

Messina is beautifully situated at the base of ranges of hills and upon their sides, and is environed with lovely scenery. It is a large city, containing a population of upwards of one hundred thousand. It has broad streets and is well built, its houses being tall and fine looking, and set off with balconied windows. It appears to be a thriving commercial place with an energetic people, whom I was pleased to note, both male and female, briskly poling about town, manfully attending to business in spite of the showers of rain that were falling. The large amount of shipping that flecked the harbor was an additional and unmistakable evidence of its prosperity. Like Catania it has been severely jarred by the earthquakes, and the one of 1783 jarred it near about down, but it has since arisen in full-fledged triumph from the rubbish.

My inspection of Messina was a somewhat hurried one, for my acquaintance with the Italian language was not sufficiently thorough to enable me to obtain from the captain of the Milano an exact knowledge of the time

18

when he purposed to depart, and this day being the critical First of April, I was loth to offer him any temptation to perpetrate the capital joke of leaving me adrift on the island of Sicily with no money in my pocket,— wherefore I deemed it judicious to hasten on board again; by which was occasioned to me the loss of sundry edifying spectacles. Above all, I deplore my inability to have visited the Cathedral, where, as I am assured, are deposited an autograph letter of the Virgin Mary's to the towns-people of Messina inclosing a lock of her hair, an arm originally appertaining to the Apostle Paul, and Mary Magdalen's own proper skull,—things full worthy of attentive observation, and which no intelligent traveler would willingly fail to see.

On returning aboard I found the ship in great commotion. Another influx of passengers had poured in and a death-struggle was prevailing for quarters. If we had been packed on the Scylla, we were rammed and jammed on the Milano. The ladies, as might have been easily predicted, had exercised to the full the privilege accorded them by the gallant captain of prime choice of staterooms, and every woman had chosen a whole one for herself; in which she was now enacting something akin to the rôle of the dog in the manger, strenuously declining to share it with any one of her own sex, and proposing no compromise on any one of ours. This state of affairs occasioned such an amount of jawing and capering and fermentation as to cause the intervention of the governing powers, who, under the operation of the martial-law, which is the normal rule on shipboard, shoved the passengers into the staterooms whether or no till they were filled to overflowing, and then gave the rest of the company unlimited authority to bestow themselves upon the tables or wherever they could.

About two o'clock in the afternoon, while the crowd was still wriggling and seething like a cupful of fishing-worms, we weighed anchor and struck out for Naples. In no great while we had reached the mouth of the Strait, infamous by reason of Scylla and Charybdis,—the former being, or having been, a rock on the Italian side, and the latter a whirlpool confronting it on that of Sicily.

As all know, this was a spot of direful terror to the seafaring men of former days.

There are good reasons for the belief that the portentous descriptions of the classic writers are not altogether poetical extravagances, and that at one time the passage presented formidable difficulties to the mariner. If so, the scene has, however, greatly changed. The strait certainly looks wide enough for all practical purposes, and there is no extraordinary commotion of the waters. Nothing at all of Scylla in any shape or form did I discover, nobody on board knowing where to look for her, and Charybdis has degenerated into a plain sea-beach, whereon reposes in desolate majesty an assemblage of fishermen's huts. Having steam-power we shot through without swerving one jot or tittle from our course; but I likewise observed common sail-boats pursuing their way with an equanimity of soul inconsistent with the close proximity of peril. All the classic terrors of the spot are gone. It is stated that its regeneration was effected by the revolutionary energy of the great earthquake of 1783, which tore the whirlpool up by the roots and scattered its fragments to the winds and waves.

Turning our backs upon the abased and impotent Scylla and Charybdis, we beheld before us as we entered the open sea the lofty peak of Stromboli, famed for being a volcano forever burning, in which glory it is nearly or quite alone. It is an island belonging to the Lipari cluster,—a group composed of small dabs of lava and pumice and sand that have at different periods been spit up or vomited out of the bowels of old mother earth,—and shoots up three thousand feet, rising from the waters like some tremendous tapering pillar. It forms an extremely striking object, and we longed greatly to see its fires; but though we were still sufficiently near to it when night came on black enough to set off even a faint light to advantage, its summit was hidden in impenetrable clouds and we saw nothing of this interesting phenomenon.

The sea roughened considerably as we got farther out,— a timely and grateful dispensation, whereby my companion and myself and some few other veterans of the deep were mercifully delivered from a pressure upon the dinner-table that would otherwise have been overwhelming. As night approached, the wind freshened a great deal, the sea rose still higher, and the weather looked positively ugly. In casting about for some one to commune with, I came across an American who, though resident in England, had kept himself unspotted from its heresies. Worked up by the leaven which operates in every American bosom, we instantaneously commenced to talk politics. He was the hardest-headed man I ever encountered, and the least amenable to the reception of truth ; for though I never argued clearer or more cogently in my life, it was absolutely impossible to convince him that my views on slavery and secession were right and his wrong. Despairing of ever opening his eyes to the true light, I gave him over to darkness and turned to a solemn middle-aged English gentleman who, sitting hard by with his chin in his hand, had been contemplating us every now and then with a rebuking scowl upon his countenance. He was a most doleful figure, and the first attempt at conversation showed that his soul was troubled to its depths by apprehensions of imminent shipwreck. His scowl was the manifestation of his amazement and indignation that any one should be so thoughtless and foolhardy as to discuss politics in such a crisis as was then upon us. I started various topics, but he invariably and immediately got back to the deadly peril we were in, which he contrived to connect with the theme of discourse with an ingenious appropriateness which was extremely creditable to his constructive faculty. "If the ship founders out here," said he, using good logic, "she will go down; then what will become of us?" "We shall be drowned," said I, with all the confidence of one who feels that he is asserting an assured fact. But he, too, was prejudiced and sterile, and was bettered by this perfectly plain statement of the case no whit more than had been my political antagonist under similar circumstances. I then endeavored to comfort him by declaring that there was not the least danger, and that I had myself, in my limited experience, come safely through incomparably worse weather than this. But he was non-comfortable. "Yes," returned he, "so have I come through worse than this. It was worse from Dover to Cally—[the Channel is always the criterion and exemplar in maritime affairs with your inchoate English traveler]—but that's no reason we shouldn't founder now. A pitcher—[he said "jug," but I translate into our dialect]—a pitcher that goes many times to the well will be broken at last—and the more times it goes the nearer it is to the last one. I believe I have gone once too many." "It may be so, indeed," said I; "the best way, therefore, will be to go to bed and sleep till the time for action arrives, when you will awake refreshed and strengthened for a good swim. Have you a berth?" "No, I haven't," said he, sharply, "and I don't want one. I do not propose to sleep to-night. I wish to meet the event in full possession of my faculties." There was nothing more of consolation and hope that I could think of to offer, and I left him furbishing up his prayers. Meanwhile, those of the passengers who had berths to go to went to them, and the rest coiled themselves away in any place they could find to hold them; and everything being now very dull and gloomy I turned in, too.

I rose early next morning, and going upon deck found that we were sailing in the glorious bay of Naples, but whose beauties were sadly obscured by the fog and drizzle of a wretchedly disagreeable day. We could, however, see Vesuvius, by whose base we passed, looming through the mists, his sides dank with vapors and reeking with hazy-looking smoke. Proceeding, the city revealed itself, gradually growing more and more distinct and imposing, till presently we were amongst a multitude of vessels packed together in almost solid mass, in whose midst we dropped anchor. Straightway boats came off to the steamer and bore us and our possessions ashore in a quiet and gentlemanly manner quite alien from the style of disembarkation prevailing in these seas. Before quitting the Milano I took leave of my foreboding English friend, whom the surety of land had intensely revived in spite of a sleepless night and rainy morning, wishing him prosperous gales across the Channel, whose perils he must needs again encounter before reaching home,—which wish he received very benignantly, especially when, bethinking myself, I struck out "gales" and inserted "breezes" in the aspiration. As for our individual selves, my companion and I on landing were taken in charge by a bloaty-complexioned, decayed man, smelling furiously of old and defunct drunks, who pronounced himself to be a hotel-commissioner. He escorted us into the custom-house, had us scrutinized,—which was done with a superficiality worthy of all laudation,—and in ten minutes we were made free of Naples

CHAPTER XVI.

How we had difficulty in setting up our Staff in Naples, and of the place where it was finally set up—Of Naples in its out-of-door Aspects.

UNDER the superintendence of the man of ancient drunks, we rode through long streets and by many a stately structure till we reached the Hotel d'Angleterre, which was the one we proposed to patronize. That establishment was chock-full. We went to another, and that was full, too. We went to still another, and that was full, too, excepting an apartment in the cock loft, which was offered but declined with thanks, on account of insufficiency of wind to climb up to it. We began to get a little troubled in mind at these unexpected difficulties; but next tried the Hotel of America, formerly the Hotel of the Britannic Isles,—the change of name, let me by no means forget to state, being made out of compliment to our own great people—a change which, while it must be excessively humiliating to our old puffed-up enemy, should be to us no less a cause for national exultation. Here they had two vacant rooms, and, as our commissioner now dolorously notified us that he was at about the end of his list, we were constrained to deposit ourselves under its roof—*right* under its roof, in fact, for the rooms were in the very uttermost top of the house, forming a very trying abode for my sick companion, who, when up, could never venture down save for the gravest reason, and when down could never go up except as a finality for that day's proceedings. The admirable American device of elevators has not been introduced into European hotels as yet; nor will any thoughtful man censure this backwardness in the march of improvement when he considers that the charge for apartments falls in proportion as they rise in the air, and how preposterous it would therefore be to offer any facilities or inducement for going aloft.

We tugged up to our quarters, whither our baggage followed immediately, — the commissioner lending his valuable co-operation in the transportation. His sides, scorched and corroded by alcohol, palpitated like jelly under the effort, and in his pantings the chamber became surcharged with pestilent vapors from the mouldering relics of innumerable toddies whose spirits had utterly departed. It was with more than usual willingness that we gave him his fee, knowing full well that it would be forthwith applied to the kindling of a new and more fragrant flame.

Notwithstanding that national feeling would lead me to extol any establishment bearing the cherished name of America, I do not find myself able to subordinate facts to patriotism sufficiently to tell more than the truth about this one, and therefore I am constrained to say that I have been in better. At the same time it is but fair to add that I suspect there are worse. It is very possible that it may be as good as any in Naples. It is situated on the street, or place, or whatever it is, called the Chiatamone, and confronts the sea. In point of bulk it is a very grand affair, and its parts are connected together by mysterious and solemn passages, narrow and dubious, and built seemingly in the walls. Its outlook commands an extensive prospect of salt-water and an unexceptionable view of a drill-ground, which is right before its front door, where every morning the military taught themselves to harmonize their movements with cabalistic blasts of the bugle, to the scandal and disgust of peaceable people. Its accommodations and charges do not quadrate even approximately. The establishment took the entire day to cook its dinner, which was served at half-past six o'clock, and achieved a splendid failure after all. At this meal each dish was set swinging round the circle, each guest helping himself if thereto minded and anything was left by the time it got to him, so that there was no absolute need for speech; but at breakfast, where you ordered what you wished *viva voce*, that man who spoke nothing but English was in jeopardy of famine; for albeit this was an American hotel, our tongue was but ill comprehended by its men of function. When fried ham and eggs, or such like matters, were requested of the attendant, his mode was to demand a consultation with his professional brethren, and the staff being got together around us we were subjected to a searching examination, when, by combining their wisdom, they generally managed to make out about as accurate a diagnosis of the case as is commonly got at in consultations.

In some particulars Naples presents a marked alteration from the city as pictured by ancient travelers of ten and twenty years ago. The Lazzaroni, in the description of whom they were wont to grow so fervid, are wellnigh passed away,—having perished either by process of natural decay, or by the strangling grip of King Victor Emmanuel. No perfectly well-defined specimen of this once numerous and strongly characterized class came under my observation. The dirt, too, against which so many and vociferous howls of execration have been sounded, had, when I saw the city, disappeared; but whether to attribute its absence to the enlightened administration of the potentate, or to the cleansing properties of the rain which had been washing out the place almost every day for some weeks, is more than I know. Suffice it to say, that when I was there it was not dirty at all. But, notwithstanding these deprivations, there is still enough within it and around it to distinguish it and to embalm it in the memory of the visitor.

Every one who has been to Naples speaks in terms of glowing admiration of its bay,—except certain men of Gotham jealous for the honor of their own bay. Its beauty has become proverbial. Few persons gaze upon the works of nature with more calmness and dignity than I, or are less disposed to form an exaggerated estimate of their charms, but in this instance my sentiments are in consonance with those of the herd. Surely it is a beautiful bay. But how could it be anything else where there is a broad expanse of blue and limpid water, cut off from the sea by picturesque islands, and inclosed by circling shores moulded by the hand of Nature into sunny heights and verdant slopes and embellished by man with all his art; having a great and magnificent city rising gloriously out of its waves; while to crown the scene there towers a mighty mountain smoking continually? The dullest imagination must kindle somewhat at the picture it presents. Not a little of its artificial beauty, it appears to me, is derived from the peculiar style of architecture of the houses that sprinkle its borders, which harmonizes admirably with the other features. Let the New Yorkers copy this in their villas and they will make a notable stride in their rivalry. Their bay, speaking dispassionately and candidly, is not, I think, at this present time quite as good to look at as that of Naples,—but they might make it better than that. They have water in profusion, and they need only a little alteration of contour, the transplanting of an island or two, some shoveling up and shaking down of dirt, a volcano, etc. etc. etc., to enable them to bear away the palm.

Naples has nearly five hundred thousand inhabitants, being in point of population much the most important city in Italy. Amongst such a mass of humanity there must needs be a vast amount of stir and bustle, and hence it has an extremely animated appearance,—quite shocking to one who has been taught to mourn over the land as effete and sunk in sloth. In some of the principal streets what with the rush of pedestrians and the whirl of vehicles I could easily believe myself to be in Broadway, of which I was continually reminded by the resplendent shops, whose windows were filled with enticing articles set off with all the inveigling environments in which the cunning Manhattanese are such adepts. To enjoy these goodly sights to which I was irresistibly drawn I polished my nose to the slickness of an onion against the glass, counting as dross the reproach of being a man from the country. The number of mathematical and philosophical instruments thus displayed speaks well for the progress of science in these parts, and horology is so far advanced that nearly every watchmaker manufactures his own time, keeping a chronometer, jerking it out in presence of the public to show them that his time is of another guess sort to that of any of his competitors. Sellers of jimcracks, unmatchable practitioners in the indigenous mystery of improvising, are stationed at the corners, and in your progress you jostle against republicans and sinners, and scribes and pharisees. The sinners are very pertinacious, having an exceeding sharp eye for a foreigner, whom they fasten upon almost immovably and strive to beguile into devious ways. If current tales say true—and no doubt they do—these rank amongst the chief of sinners. I was spotted by them instanter, and though it should seem that my appearance ought to have acted as a salutary check upon them—for I will be bound a more demure and virtuous-looking person they never set eyes on in all their experience—still they bedeviled me much. The scribes are an institution of the place. They have not as yet become sufficiently enlightened in this country to tax people for the education of other people's children, and consequently the knowledge of the chirographic art is not as widely disseminated as we find it elsewhere. Hence it is that a goodly part of the population are wont to employ amanuenses in the transaction of business in which writing is required, and the demand for talent of this description has given rise to a distinct profession. The great bulk of its patronage is derived from those afflicted with love,—a propensity to scribbling being one of the pathognomonic signs of this variety of monomania. The scribes I encountered were all men of age and discreetness, as is fit in those who are to perform functions of delicacy. They received the tender whisperings, moulding them into shape and spicing them with tropes, and figures, and sentiments, and then charging an envelope with the mixture, dispatched the amatory bombshell on its destructive mission.

The traveler of delicate feeling will be flattered soon after entering Naples by receiving a posy—of no great dimensions, it is true, monochromatic very likely, and inodorous or rankish almost certainly—from the fair hands of a damsel who is one of many who appoint themselves to do this courtesy to strangers; and if he accept it with a becoming acknowledgment—that is, with a reciprocal present of half a franc—he may confidently count upon a continual repetition of this tasteful attention. He will be flattered,—but really with very little reason, for the damsels are by no means fastidious in selecting the beneficiaries of their floral favors. Even I was chosen, and presented by them with scarce less than a scuttleful of the little bouquets by actual measurement. One of the girls, especially, of about forty or forty-one years of age, not perhaps faultlessly beautiful,—though of her features it were difficult to form a perfectly accurate conception unless she had been first tooled with a scraper,—seemed to be mightily smitten with me; waylaying me every morning and evening, and sticking a posy into my buttonhole whether I would or no. Anxious not to introduce any sordid element into our purely sentimental communion I forbore to make any pecuniary recognition of her affection, excusing myself with the plea of no small-change and with promises for "to-morrow"—the *manaña* of the Spaniards, in the use of which I had perfected myself during my residence amongst them. I had every hope in this way of tiding myself safely through and out of the city,—and had done so even to getting into the carriage at the hotel door *en route* for the railroad station, when she overhauled me. She bounced in upon me, jerked that morning's posy out of my button-hole, and both in action and speech proceeded in a way to hurt my feelings greatly. Travelers having any character to lose—I had none myself, traveling incognito in Europe—do well to put their feet down firmly at the first onset of the flower-maidens, seeing how hard it is to touch pitch and not be defiled.

Naples is one of the musical centres of the earth. Its denizens are gifted with an inimitable aptitude for untangling the mightiest mysteries of the gamut, and are capable of mastering any instrument that can be devised. The shops pour forth a flood of melody, and the streets are bathed in it by tuneful choirs perambulating them night and day with guitars and harps and fiddles. The national instrument, which the Italian exiles have made so familiar to us, the hand-organ, of course abounds, and, truly, they are right crafty in playing on it, and nowhere have I heard it made to discourse more bile-stirring notes. The monkey attachment appears to be an innovation upon the original simplicity of the instrument adopted in our country to suit the more material character of American taste, since I do not remember to have observed this appendage anywhere in Naples. Invention has not, however, been idle here, and I noticed particularly an improved organ that was much in vogue,—the improvement consisting of the addition of a pair of wheels, which served as an admirable substitute for the old neck-strap in common use, and vastly lightened the labor of transporting the apparatus from place to place. In its improved form it was operated by two men, one shoving the machine along and the other grinding out the music. One of this class of instruments was rolled up and brought to anchor in front of our hotel regularly every morning, where it remained till breakfast was thoroughly accomplished, banging out its appointed cycle of fantasias in one long, unbroken chain of repetitions.

Upon our dull ears the harmonies of the organ fall unappreciated, but they readily attune themselves to the cultivated auricular appurtenances of the Neapolitans. When a musician implants his box before the door of a citizen of Naples, he lets him play on undisquieted till he plays himself out; not seeking to cajole him away, nor to drive him off by revilings, or by setting the dog on him, or by bestowing red-hot cents into his hand; nor yet bribing him in any manner, as we are wont to do, and thus unwittingly aid in perpetuating the already too abased condition of musical science in our country.

I was not prepared for the paucity of beggars I encountered. From what I had read I expected to find the place made almost impervious by them. I saw very few indeed. Whether they had died of starvation, or seen the error of their way and turned rich, or what had become of them, I could not clearly ascertain. I strongly suspect King Victor Emmanuel has had some hand in the matter, for he is a sagacious monarch, skilled in the modes of driving poverty out of sight—which is the approved plan of dealing with it when it is impracticable to drive it out of existence. Certain small boys were by far the worst of the importunates that I fell in with. These sought to awaken my charitable impulses by making themselves extremely agreeable or disagreeable—I could not positively determine which they intended—through the medium of gymnastic exercises performed in my presence and on my behalf. However they meant it, I was scandalized beyond measure by it; for what could be more humiliating than for a gentleman dignified and sanctified almost to primness to be preceded in his progress along the public streets by a boy walking on his hands, or, with a ferocious shout, whirling over and over before him like a hoop? This I endured, and without chance of remedy; for all my attempts to kick the persecutor failed completely by reason of his superior agility,—while the failure signally increased the contempt which his proceedings were bringing down upon me from all beholders.

But while the beggars have dwindled away, the ecclesiastics hold their own manfully; and this in spite of the fact that Emmanuel, being on bad terms with the Pope, never misses an opportunity of snubbing them. A unique assortment of these personages is to be met with on the street—some with no hats on their heads, some with no hair thereon; some wearing cowls, and some having hats of commodious crown and far-stretching brim, like those worn in Spain, but unlike those with the brim spread out and wriggled into a variety of rather dandyish cocks and twists. Some of them look supremely sleek and gentlemanly, and others, barefooted and abominably dirty, have the mien and port of sacred vagabonds or holy loafers. One of their chief functions appears to be to attend at funerals, upon which their presence with tapers and crucifixes and sacred utensils confers great *eclat*. An additional solemnity is given to these melancholy celebrations by an array of mourners clothed from head to foot in a sort of meal-bags, with ghastly yellow-bordered apertures near the top for eye-holes—at whose appearance the dumfoundered beholder from a far country knows not whether to laugh or weep.

In this connection I may mention a hideous mode of burial perpetrated upon such defuncts as in their lifetime had not amassed enough of this world's gear to forefend it. They have a cemetery which contains three hundred and sixty-six pits, one for each day in the common year and a supernumerary one for bissextile or leap-year; and one of these pits is opened every evening, into which that day's swath of the Great Reaper is slung heterogeneously and then shut in till the recurrence of the anniversary, when it is scraped up and shaken down to make room for the new batch. What with Ku-Klux for the funeral cortége and such sepulture as dog-catchers give to dogs, it is a fearful thing to die in Naples. To provide against the last-named horror, the inhabitants have hit upon the device of clubbing together in burial societies, each society owning its own tomb, in which every member in good standing who pays his monthly dues regularly is entitled to accommodations.

Not only is it very unsatisfactory to the deceased himself to die in this town, but in certain cases the event is apt to result in considerable bother to his surviving friends. It is a prevalent belief in Naples that consumption is an infectious disease, and there are no stancher professors of this faith than the hotel-keepers. If, therefore, a guest with this malady succumbs to their mephitic vapors, indigestible provender, and Alpine stairways, and dies under their roof, it is in their judgment necessary that his chamber should be torn to pieces, fumigated, and reconstructed—due charge for all which is wont to be incorporated in the bill. Upon this matter dreadful disputes have arisen between them and the heirs, administrators, and assigns. It must not be supposed, however, that when the disinfection has been paid for, the landlords invariably act in accordance with their judgment and have it done. The imperfection of human nature forbids us to entertain the supposition, for if their pathological views are sound, the purification of the apartment must unprofitably retard the robbery of the next occupant. My professional brethren of the city, I am pleased to record, do not hold this heretical doctrine concerning consumption, but discourage it—possibly, somewhat to their detriment; wherein our most noble order contrasts gloriously with our deadly enemies the lawyers, who, I am informed, have contrived to segregate to themselves nearly all the real estate in Naples by dint of the ingenious incubating and wire-drawing of lawsuits.

While there can be no difference of opinion as to the beauty of Naples when seen from a distance, a person of a critical taste might easily discover great blemishes on a nearer inspection. It will strike the ordinary traveler, however, as a very pleasing city. Its houses are generally lofty, which of itself suffices to give them an imposing appearance, though at the same time it imparts something of gloom to the less animated portions of the town. It is a compactly-built city, not large enough to hold the people that are in it, many of whom, it is said, reside out-of-doors, never sleeping in a room except when in jail. The streets, which are above thirteen hundred in number, are for the most part narrow. Some of them are decidedly zigzag in their course, and when followed up will suddenly split into a bi- or trifurcation,—a circumstance which may lead a plain, straightforward newcomer into grievous straits. Some of them, again, are so precipitous as to require steps for their ascent, and some of this class I found to be outrageously delusive, for on mounting them in the laborious prosecution of the researches which give such a value to this volume, I occasionally found myself brought to a stand-still in somebody's stable-yard or poultry-preserves, and at a great loss how to account for my presence to the inquiring proprietors. On the other hand, however, a few of the streets are very spacious and full of life, as I have described, and that known as the Toledo, which is the principal thoroughfare of the city, for activity and variety of scene will compare well with any street in Europe. For so large a place Naples is very deficient in public squares, there being but one of any consequence. This is the Villa Reale or Royal Gardens, a narrow space stretching along the seaside for about a mile. It is laid out very neatly into walks, and planted with evergreen trees and shrubbery, and is adorned with a great number of copies of celebrated pieces of ancient statuary. It has also two little temples, containing respectively a bust of Virgil and of Tasso, and now holds on the spot formerly occupied by the Farnese Bull a statue of Vico—a distinguished Neapolitan who, having fractured his skull, was set to thinking, and became a great philosopher. It is furnished with refreshment-saloons, and in my time its attractions were augmented by the presence of a flock of artificial birds, at which sportsmen were allowed to shoot with a popgun at a reasonable price per crack. It is a place high in the regard both of citizens and strangers, for here the indolent can loll refreshed by the sight of pleasant prospects, while the stroller finds it one of the most delightful promenades.

CHAPTER XVII.

Naples within-doors.

So far we have confined our observation to the out-of-door aspects of Naples: let us now go within-doors for awhile. And here we are met by the fact that there are no great number of doors whose entrance will repay us for the trouble of going to them, for the objects of interest in the city itself are very few, though it must be added that among them are some of the most remarkable in the world.

Of the palaces I shall say nothing, having seen nothing but their outsides,—nor of the three hundred and forty churches did I see any that deserve a particular description. Closely akin to churches are charitable institutions; with which, to its honor be it said, Naples is liberally supplied. They might be made to furnish many profitable lessons were I at leisure to inculcate them—among the rest to exemplify most lucidly the retroactive blessings of almsgiving; for it is currently reported that their worthy managers have in many instances waxed rich in dispensing their charities. Few of my readers, I believe, are sufficiently philanthropic to tolerate a description of these institutions; nevertheless, nothing shall induce me to omit the mention of one which surely was founded in the golden age, and whose counterpart I fear we shall never see in our land till the millennial dawn. It is a hospital, surpassingly magnanimous in its scope and objects, where they not merely receive the unfortunate and take care of them, but *pay their debts* in addition! Such a fact as this deserves to be widely promulgated among our countrymen, that they may ponder upon it while they are ignorantly proclaiming the fogyism of Europe. Thus it may happen that they may humbly confess their error and—Heaven speed the time!—may imitate the example.

Of the jails great complaint is made by those who have resided therein. The accommodations are described as very ordinary indeed, and the authorities are denounced for their disregard of the welfare of the body-carcerate, whose numbers, already very large and rapidly increasing, it is contended should entitle them to greater consideration. In the days of that old villain King Bomba and his line, these places became horrible dungeons, where he who dared to breathe a word or a sigh for liberty was shut in, and manacled, and watched unceasingly, and prohibited from conversation, and denied the consolation of books and newspapers (in *their* case not even a Bible or prayer-book was allowed), and weighed down with all the indignities and cruelties with which tyrants vainly hope to degrade and crush out the champions of the sacred cause of freedom. Fearful and overtrue tales are told of atrocities inflicted on these unfortunate men. Their poor bruised and insulted bodies indeed perished into dust, but their unquenched spirits passed triumphant through the prison walls and moved among the people, doing their holy mission; and this day the remnant of the race of their tormentors, beaten from their seat, mope like owls in Rome, objects of scorn and abhorrence to every manly soul in Christendom.

Few persons who visit Naples fail to go to the theatre of San Carlo to witness the Italian opera. I happen to be one of the few. This is a humiliating confession, and it is manifestly incumbent upon me to state why this was so.

In the first place, then, I find it insufferably difficult to comprehend a language that I do not understand, and Italian is not one particle more intelligible to me when sung than when said. Secondly, I had no fine clothes of my own to display to the public, while I am apathetic even to downright stolidity to the sight of them on other people. This reason will of itself, doubtless, amply suffice to excuse me; since these two circumstances are the great, paramount, and controlling motives that determine us Americans in our patronage of the opera in our own country; but, in addition to this, I was assured by acquaintances who did go to San Carlo that they were given entirely too much for the worth of their money; for the performance began a little while after sunset and ended no great while before sunrise, so that they were constrained to lose a vast portion of it—there being no provision for sleeping, and it being considered bad *ton* to be gaping eight or ten hours on a stretch.

But in fact almost the only in-door sights in Naples of real interest are to be found in its Museum, and for these it must be confessed that it stands alone; for among them are the relics from the dead and buried and exhumed cities of Pompeii and Herculaneum. Besides this distinctive feature, the Museum has a respectable stock of the staple articles of European museums—choice paintings, ancient crockery-ware (of which a redundancy is in existence), and antique statues, some of which are seemly and symmetrical in appearance, and others *torsos*,—as chunks of sculptured rock sans head, sans arms, sans legs, sans everything, are euphemistically designated by the connoisseurs; some of these last being tastefully rehabilitated with the heads and appurtenances formerly belonging to other torsos. Amongst its statuary are two works of especial celebrity—the Farnese Bull and the Farnese Hercules. The former illustrates the mythic story of Dirce and Antiope, vividly showing how Dirce, for beguiling Antiope's husband, got herself tied to the horns of a wild bull, and is an enduring warning to the all-potent sex how they go about fascinating us weaker vessels. Antiope and her whole family are represented participating in the performance—all except Lycus, her lord, who, husband and manlike, kept shady, and left poor Dirce to bear the brunt,—and from the figures about the base of the piece it appears that sundry small animals graced the occasion with their presence. The Hercules bodies forth, in massive proportions, that hard-working character resting on his club after a big job, and is an admirable representation of a strong man exhausted with fatigue. His legs are new, his original pair having given out.

This Museum possesses the finest collection of bronze statuary and sculpture in existence. A peculiar supernatural air is given to some of the busts and statues of this material by glass or silver eyes, which contrast awfully with their black visages. It is also rich in mosaics, the floors of several of its apartments being formed of specimens of this kind of work brought hither from houses in Pompeii and Herculaneum. Of course it has a collection of Egyptian curiosities, for this is a *sine qua non* with all museums. The specimens of glass and crockery-ware include decanters, tumblers, pie-plates, sepulchral urns, etc. etc., and amongst them are a number of those votive figures by which the pious invalids of old were wont to manifest their gratitude for recovery. To this collection one worthy has contributed his photograph in baked mud, which exhibits his countenance liberally sprinkled with grog-blossoms, or some other cutaneous eruption. Here, too, are included several of that skillfully contrived kind of money-box which allows the money to go in and then holds it irrecoverably, one of them being the property of a penny-wise-and-pound-foolish man of Pompeii, who, instead of spending his money generously, withdrew it from the channels of trade, and hid it away in this receptacle, at the end losing the use of it forever, and bequeathing to future generations a solemn testimony against laying up treasures in this world. The numismatic collection embraces some forty thousand coins and medals of ancient dates, as well as some of modern periods—and a Peruvian mummy.

One department of the Museum is devoted to old inscriptions. Amidst a great deal of rather recondite matter here spread out something occasionally appears that can be grasped by the common mind. Thus, there is a most excellent stone almanac, being a square block calculated for the meridian of Rome, and giving the names of the months, the number of days therein, the length of the days and nights, the signs of the zodiac and the sun's place therein, the times for sacrificing to the Penates, and other festivals of the Church, the period for sowing and reaping grain, pulling fodder, and gathering apples, together with other information of transcendent interest to country people,—and, in short, needing only predictions of the weather, days auspicious for venesection and hog-killing, times of meeting of the county courts, and some jokes and receipts for making good cheap pies, to entitle it to rank with the best almanacs of the present era. We also see amongst these inscriptions certain placards of astonishing resemblance to some which we occasionally observe at home; for they appeal to the people to rally to the polls and avert impending destruction from the country by voting for Servius Tommus, Spurius Diccus, and Gassius Harrius. A couple of the Public Documents of the days of yore are likewise preserved here in the shape of bronze plates recording the enactments confirming the right and title of Bacchus and Minerva to certain parts and parcels of the public lands, from the use and benefit whereof the said Bacchus and Minerva had been unlawfully restrained by the withinmentioned parties, against the peace and dignity of the commonwealth. Along with these enactments are others concerning the taking of the census, the distribution of bread, and the making of roads,—these latter, inasmuch as they involve the interests of the government, being published in plain vernacular Latin, while the former, affecting only the rights of private individuals, are very properly set down in abstruse, outlandish Greek.

Some of the articles I have mentioned were obtained from Pompeii and Herculaneum, but many of them from other places. There are, however, collections comprising specimens exclusively from the buried cities, and these are the most unique and interesting portions of the Museum, for they enable us almost to participate in the everyday life of twenty centuries ago. It is an impressive sight to see these exhumed relics from the grave of a long dead and forgotten city, the meanest of which affords so much for fancy to sport with, and for thought to ponder on. Who can help asking himself where now is the fair being to whom belonged that finger-bone with the golden ring upon it? or forbear to picture in youth and loveliness her whose skeleton arm lies eloquently mute before him, clasped with its silver bracelet? And how fares it with Q. Cranius, baker, who, himself blotted utterly from the earth, has left behind him a loaf of his bread stamped with his name, carbonized to charcoal, it is true, but shapely and symmetrical as on that memorable day when he turned his back upon his bake-house forever? And the paint-seller whose stock in trade has been transshipped thither—what of him? But most rueful spectacle of all to me was a pill-tile and spatula, the mortal remains of a brother of mine, who, while busied in the merciful work of pill-making, had to take to his heels, and, it is greatly to be feared, lost all his practice.

The objects of this class are numerous, and every one tells us something of old-time modes and customs; and a great deal of the feeling of wonder that overspreads us as we gaze upon them, I find from careful analysis, is due to the discovery we are thus enabled to make that these ancient people were eating and drinking and sleeping and breathing beings astonishingly like ourselves. Many of the articles are of a kind quick to perish or be injured, as nuts, and fruits, and eggs, yet they are well preserved and very fresh looking, having suffered more during the few years they have been unearthed than in the whole eighteen centuries they lay buried in the ashes of Vesuvius. Among the curious objects must be mentioned a sun-dial of the rather uncommon shape of a shoulder of bacon, and something which has been surmised to be a lens for reading,—which is important if true, for the modern world has long mourned over the misty state in which the elderly portion of the ancients were condemned to wander for the want of spectacles. Lady visitors to the Museum are generally more struck with the collection of jewels and gems than with anything else, and I have seen the sweet creatures moping and mowing over them for a long time. The collection embraces ear-rings, finger-rings, chains, and a variety of such ensnaring gear, bespeaking the sad fact that in every age the female sex is one and immutable. There are several cases containing cameos and intaglios representing various ancient worthies and mythological subjects, and amongst them are some pieces made ready for the engraver, but from which his hand was stayed. Many of these specimens of jewelry are tasteful in design and elegant in execution. In this department is to be seen what some esteem to be the most precious object in the Museum, being a shallow onyx cup eight inches in diameter, which is said to be worth a million dollars. Upon its bottom is depicted a visage surmounted by a crop of hair like a hurrah's nest, which is reputed, and no doubt truly, to be designed for a Medusa's head, while within is sculptured a set of figures the interpretation of whose intent and meaning has bred terrible tornadoes amongst contending antiquaries.

A further inspection of these memorials of the past might well make us pause in our ranting boasts about the inventive genius of our age. It may seem incredible, but the proof is here before us, that, in the lapse of nineteen hundred years, we have not been able to advance a step in the construction of hammers and nails, or pokers and pickaxes, and other things of prime utility. Here I saw pots and skillets differing scarcely perceptibly from the utensils in use at this very day in the preparation of bacon and greens and corn-bread by the highly enlightened people of the State of Virginia. There are very many other articles of household and kitchen furniture on exhibition which are not essentially different from ours. Thimbles, hair-pins, combs, and fish-hooks are shown not to be modern inventions. Cow-bells, it appears, were rung by means of clappers even in those early times. In their day and generation the people of Pompeii were called upon to suffer as we in ours under the dispensation of flutes, and were besides afflicted with a strange kind of clarionet, the touch of which we are mercifully permitted not to know. They had scales and weights resembling those still in use, and they were sagacious enough to adopt our custom of having an inspector of weights and measures, as we learn from one of the implements which bears the certificate of that functionary avouching its accuracy. They possessed no contemptible knowledge of some departments of physics, being, for example, as conversant with the laws governing the operation of gravity practically as was Sir Isaac Newton theoretically —as witness their loaded dice. Some of their mechanical adaptations, however, exhibit unnecessary complexity; thus their stocks—whereby I intend not the attire so denominated for the neck, but gear for the legs—was unduly cumbersome, lacking the simplicity which the progress of art in our day has impressed upon the instrument. Indeed, it is possible I should not have divined the purpose of the clumsy piece of ironmongery but for the obliging assistance of a picture-seller at my elbow. But, though unshapely in construction, the apparatus was all that could be desired in the paramount quality of security, as appears from the four skeletons it had kept clamped for eighteen centuries. Finally, in pursuing our investigations, we find that the resources of humanity, whose cultivation is so creditable to any people, were not altogether neglected by the Pompeians. The kindly consolations of surgery were within their reach, and from the array of knives and other invaluable chirurgical appliances that have come down to us, we are warranted in drawing the gratifying inference that the method of relieving our suffering fellow-creatures by cutting them open and sawing them up was understood and practiced before Christianity had spread its beneficent light over the world.

One of the discoveries at Herculaneum, which promised a great deal, has so far turned out to be very barren. In making excavations in the buried city, the workmen opened a room in one of the houses which contained a great number of black dumpy lumps of something that were taken to be pieces of charcoal. The regular manner in which they were laid, however, suggested that they might be something more valuable, and upon examination this was found to be the case. The workmen had hit upon the study of some great Herculanean genius, and these black lumps were his books. They were made of the leaves of the papyrus and rolled up, as was the style of the period, but had become so glued together by the influences to which they had been subjected as to present almost insuperable obstacles in the way of unrolling them. To accomplish this object various mechanical and chemical devices were resorted to unsuccessfully; but at length a machine was invented which, though slow and imperfect in its operation, does the work passably well. Upon unrolling them they were found to be long sheets of the papyrus, varying from eight to sixteen inches in width, written in columns between three and four inches wide, separated by about the distance of an inch, each column containing from twenty to forty lines. The ink with which they were written was of a sort soluble in water, and consequently easily washed away, a circumstance offering one of the chief difficulties in unrolling them by any of the more obvious methods. Between seventeen and eighteen hundred of these papyri have been collected, of which some five hundred have been unrolled and deciphered. I perused some of them that were spread out for inspection, and was utterly nonplused thereby. They had the appearance of broad, jet-black, quadrangular patches, with ragged borders, and here and there a bit plugged out of the midst. They were in Greek characters, capital letters being used exclusively, some of which were more catacornered and mystical even than those of the orthodox shape, so as in some instances, in fact, to be unrecognizable; and the characters were collocated in a way that was far less satisfactory to the reader than the writer, who wrote straight along, unhampered by the trammels of punctuation, or breaks between words and sentences, or any other of the conventionalities of chirography which so bother and impede modern penmen. In the thorough carbonization of the mass, the letters had become almost indistinguishable from the surface on which they were inscribed, and it was only at particular angles of the light that I could discover them at all.

What I gathered in my researches amongst the papyri was, as I have intimated, not much; but there are those with more patience and erudition than I can claim who have devoted their lives and energies to the study of them, and been rewarded with great success. By these martyrs we are told that they are almost altogether upon such themes as dull fools suppose to be hard and crabbed, embracing such perpetual feasts of nectared sweets as prelections on Virtue, and Vice, and Rhetoric, together with antibilious treatises on the divine philosophy of Epicurus; wherefore we are authorized to conclude that the sage, their possessor, was a philosopher filled with wholesome admonition and wise reproof, an admirable companion for young people, and to the general public an excellent substitute for opium.

The Pompeians seem to have been not near so cultivated a people as their companions in disaster, the Herculaneans,—nothing whatever indicative of a taste for literature having been discovered in their city except a cast in ashes of a scrap of papyrus, and it is a fact of melancholy significance that this is a portion of a law-paper.

The bibliophilist will be pleased to visit the National Library, which is in the Museum building. It contains about two hundred thousand printed works and four thousand manuscripts, some of both classes being very rare and valuable. Emblazoned upon the floor will be seen a long and gorgeous line of rams, and bulls, and crabs, and scorpions, and other objects more recondite, which the beholder will gaze at with awe and wonder till he recruits himself with sufficient of his astronomical lore to identify them as the signs of the zodiac. From observation and reflection I infer that this brilliant affair is some kind of a sun-dial. The Library likewise possesses an echo of good quality, which the excellent librarian takes the greatest delight in evoking by clapping two big volumes together, for the edification of the visitor.

CHAPTER XVIII.

Of sundry noted Places in the Neighborhood of Naples—The Tomb of Virgil—The Lake Agnano—The Grotto of the Dog—The Solfatara—Monte Nuovo—The Grotto of the Sibyl—The Lake Avernus, and the Town of Baiæ,—together with Contributions towards the Biography of a certain ardent Follower of Science.

The visitor to Naples will find more that is worthy of his attention outside of the city than in—and surely there can be but few places in the world with surroundings of such great and varied interest. Here the lover of the picturesque can batten on the beauties of the land and sea, and the student of Nature watch her at her secret work in the caverns of the earth; while on every hand the thoughtful mind meets with some memorial that lulls it into pensive meditation on the past.

Just at the western termination of the city, upon a height that overlooks the sea, stands the reputed tomb of Virgil. It was on a Sunday that I made my pilgrimage to it. Like the ashes of some other great men I have heard of, those of the Mantuan bard have become the vehicle for turning an honest penny—the pilgrim who comes to sigh over them being estopped at the foot of the hill by a stanch gate, whose key I found was in the custody of a classic blacksmith hard by, and who never opened the portal under ten cents. I sought the janitor in his fiery den, where, undeterred by the sanctity of the day, he was hammering with all his soul upon a piece of red-hot iron, and surrounded with aiders and abettors in his sin,—and speedily negotiated an entrance. Following a subordinate detached to conduct me, I penetrated the inclosure and began the ascent. The way led up a long and fatiguing flight of stone steps, passing through such poetic scenery as vines and weeds and cabbage-patches, until it attained the summit of the eminence, where it descended into a little glen, in which, secluded and almost hidden, was the tomb. It is a square vault, built of a crumbly kind of stone, and overgrown with ivy. The interior is about fifteen feet in length and the same in width, having two windows and one entrance, with a level floor of sand. Upon the sides within are ten little niches intended for the reception of urns. It is a very humble and unimpressive sepulchre.

Virgil and I had not been friends in youth; but, as has been beautifully asked, "Who can look down upon the grave even of an enemy and not feel a compunctious throb that he should ever have warred with the poor handful of earth that lies mouldering before him?" In later years, when acquaintance with him was no longer forced, I sought him out voluntarily, and then obtained a juster idea of his merits, finding him all elegance and sweetness. I was, therefore, prepared to venerate this spot as the resting-place of one whom, estrangement reconciled, I had come to love as a gentle minister to my happiness; but here the sad fact presented itself that there was no certainty that the poet's bones lay anywhere near me. There was a tombstone, it is true, affirming it,—but who can believe a tombstone?

The case is very doubtful, to say the least of it. Virgil himself directed that his remains should be interred at Naples, and there is no reason to question that the injunction was obeyed; but there are no means of identifying with exactness the spot where they were laid; for no writer who lived sufficiently near the poet's time to make his statements trustworthy records it, and the original memorials have utterly perished long ago. Tradition has fixed upon the glen on the height by the seashore, and the choice has been confirmed by apocryphal passages in certain authors and by an adroit construction and application of the words of certain others—methods of approved use in settling classical topography everywhere. Many illustrious men have stood here reverently in full faith, and, again, many have stood here reverently, too, perhaps, but full of skepticism,—so that, at any rate, it is become hallowed ground. The pilgrim believer in the infallibility of the latest authority will be delighted to find the spot certified by a monumental slab erected at so recent a date as 1840, and its evidence is made almost unimpeachable by the fact that the inscription upon it was written by Virgil's own hand:

> "Mantua me genuit; Calabri rapuere; tenet nunc Parthenope. Cecini pascua, rura, duces."

The inclement weather, with which we were greatly troubled, prevented us from doing ourselves full justice by the environs of Naples. We did our best with them, however. One of our most interesting excursions was along the western shore of the bay as far as Baiæ. We devoted a day to this, hiring a vehicle and a guide, and starting early in the morning, in company with two other gentlemen—an Irishman and a Scotchman. Passing the tomb of Virgil we came immediately to the Grotto of Posilipo—a tunnel cut hundreds of years ago through the hilly range that shuts in the city on the west.

Issuing from the grotto and proceeding for about two miles through pleasant scenes, we reached the Lake Agnano. This is the crater of a volcano whose fires have been supplanted by water. I saw nothing remarkable about it, nor does it possess any trait that exalts it above one of our full-sized mill-ponds, except that it utters forth a quantity of vapors pestiferous and odoriferous with sulphuretted hydrogen. On the shore is a sort of lime-kiln with compartments, into which the wretched victims of gout and rheumatism are thrust to be kiln-dried by the great whiffs of sulphur vapor that in this infernal region burst out of the earth in blasts hot from Tartarus. I entered the kiln to inspect it professionally and found that it felt very warm and smelt very nasty; also, that when I put my foot down firmly there came forth just such a sound as if I had trod on the head of a drum; and a heaviness of feeling overcoming me all at once, I came out.

But the great object of interest at this lake is the celebrated Grotta del Cane, which obtains its appellation from the circumstance that dogs are caused to taste of the pains of death therein for the instruction of the philosophic visitor. This is an excavation in the side of a hill large enough to permit three or four persons to stand in it, and with the bottom of it sunk a foot or so below the level of the ground outside. In the cavity thus formed the deadly carbonic acid gas collects from crevices in the cavern, from which it is continually issuing, its great weight causing it to accumulate in a stratum high enough to reach to about the knee; all the gas above that height diffusing readily into the outer air through the door; so that one can stand in the grotto with impunity, while to lie down in it would be attended with marvelous difficulty in getting up again. A dirty, clay-colored scientist conducts a course of edifying experiments here designed to elucidate the physical and chemical properties of this remarkable exhalation—fee for the entire course twenty cents. We observed under his skillful manipulation how that a turpentine torch in full blaze was by simply depressing it towards the bottom of the cavity instantaneously quenched as effectually as if it had been dipped into a tub of water, while the surface of the invisible gas was clearly defined to us by the lighter smoke that floated in masses upon it. Our guide was a valuable co-operator with the scientist in his elucidations. He directed our attention specially to the odor of the gas, which he bade us note was distinctly that of champagne, and taking off his tall and capacious beaver dipped up a hatful and passed it round for our examination. I inserted my nose deep into the hat and took several prolonged sniffs. The smell was unquestionably well marked, but it seemed to me scarcely that of champagne—it was, I thought, rather that of rancid hair-grease with a predominant savor of oil of bergamot.

But by far the most conclusive and satisfactory of the experimental demonstrations was that with the dog. The one employed on this occasion was of small dimensions and cadaverous complexion, with a hide besprinkled with dingy splotches resembling patches of a very mean quality of wet brown paper—all due, doubtless, to a concoction of his humors brought about by his unwholesome mode of life. He, however, was cheerful and even vivacious in spirits, coming up readily at the heels of his learned master with his tail a-wag and a canine grin on his countenance. Indeed, it is confidently asserted by those who have looked deeply into the matter that the dog takes a morbid delight in dying; for, be it understood, that in these performances—

> "Non omnis moritur; multaque pars sui
> Vitat Libitinam"—

the dog does not altogether die, a goodly part of him survives, inasmuch as the operator takes heed to snatch him out of the jaws of death ere he has utterly given up the ghost; wherefore he presently becomes fond of reveling in this champagne gas and willingly repeats it,—as a veteran toper duplicates his sprees, reckless of the horrors of the sobering stage. Our dog was cast into the depths of the cavern, where for a minute or two he kicked up uproariously and then lay dead drunk. At this point he was hauled out and dumped neck and heels upon the grass outside, where he fell into a series of drunken fits, presenting an awful warning. Little by little consciousness returned and reason regained her throne, but all the time we stayed at the grotto he retained a look of deep despondency, seeming sore sick at heart and stomach and full of unavailing remorse.

I was myself more particularly interested in this striking experiment from having been at one time the trusted colaborer of the celebrated vivisectionist Dr. Brown-Séquard, with whom I was associated in the capacity of dog-decoyer and cat-catcher. In the days when this learned savant was professor of physiology in the Medical College of Virginia and I co-operated with him, hecatombs of animals were sacrificed on the altars of science erected in his lecture-room and in the dissecting-room,—for he taught physiology not in the way which is universal in this country, by precept, but by example. To provide materials for his purposes, the students were granted roving commissions, with instructions to permeate the highways and byways of the city and ascend to the housetops for dogs and cats,—these being subjects of special quest with my able coadjutor,— at the same time being enjoined to disregard no form of animal life however unpromising, all being grist that came to my able coadjutor's physiological mill. The students entered into these pursuits with an assiduity that gave the most cheering evidence of their zeal for learning and the most flattering auguries of their future attainments in knowledge. All over town they could be heard whistling up recruits, and scarce one ever came to lecture without some trustful canine quadruped pattering at his heels.

A result of their ardor in this direction was the speedy raising of something like a panic in the city over the constantly-recurring "mysterious disappearance" of dogs, some of them among the best known and most respected in the community; but owing to the judicious manner of their taking off their fate has never been known even to this day. The seductive whistles to command their presence, the indignant calls, the frantic bawls, have long since ceased to echo through the yard and back alley; the shoes that bore their anxious friends up and down in inquiry through all the neighborhood have years ago mouldered into dust upon the ash-bank; the advertisements offering recompense for their discovery lie among the forgotten literature of the past; the wonderment of where on earth they can be in Gracious Goodness' name once so rife upon the tongue has now died utterly away; the very remembrance of most of them has in the lapse of time perished from out the memory of man:—but—murder will out! and the awful disclosures of which I am now unburdening my conscience tell all the dread secret. Amid the burst of grief that these revelations must needs revive, let me, stricken friends of theirs! let me conjure you to take of consolation from the sweet recollection that they did not die in vain; and that, though they themselves are gone, their contributions to physiology are enduring.

Cats as well as dogs came in profusion, with ducks, and geese, and pigeons, terrapins and fish, and game in season. Coons and 'possums—or, as they are denominated by precisians, raccoons and opossums—appeared at intervals, and, being a Virginia production hitherto unknown to my able coadjutor, elicited his profound attention, affording him much food for grave reflection and useful research. Guinea-pigs were scarce, their cultivation having never enlisted the energies of our people to any great extent. Owing to their peculiar adaptability for purposes of science they were absolutely indispensable to him, it being impossible for him to live in a country where there were no guinea-pigs. For this reason he became an exceedingly valuable citizen, for through his countenance the growth of guinea-pigs received an impetus which enlarged the crop many hundredfold, and thus proportionately augmented the material prosperity of the commonwealth.

To accommodate the animals, the cellar of the college building was turned into a menagerie, where the dogs, cats, terrapins and all, were comfortably quartered; and where they lived together as a sort of happy family, eating one another up at every opportunity. Never was heard such a to-do as they made there. Internecine feuds prevailed,—not a day passed that did not witness one or more assassinations amongst them. Their wailings ascended continually by day, and at night the acutest theologian could not have diagnosed their outcries from the howlings of the damned. The building got an evil fame and reputation with the public,—being supposed to be infested with spirits, and from the very worst quarters of Tartarus.

From the cellar as occasion required they were transferred to the dissecting-room for the private investigations of my able coadjutor, or to the lecture-room for his public demonstrations. Those of them who were performing tours of duty in the cause of science,—that is, those with broken backs, slit wizens, tied-up interiors, and so on, were allowed to mess in the dissecting-room, and were treated with special consideration,—as is proper for such as are bearing the heat and burden of actual service. From here by facile descent they ultimately reached the lecture-room, and it is impossible to overrate the assistance they rendered in this phase of their usefulness. Nothing can be imagined more calculated to set forth the excellency and dignity of science than the sight of my able coadjutor equipped with a box of knives and a bottle of strychnine, with a dog unsuspicious of the future sitting before him upon the table regarding the assembled disciples with a cast of the utmost complacency and good-fellowship in his frank honest muzzle; with a battered terrapin lying quite unconcerned on his right hand, and a goose abashed and distrustful of the company standing on his left;—and with a ruined coon in one corner and a demolished cat in another,—and then to hear him begin with the established exordium,—" Zhonteel-man, I zall now poozeed too devil-up ze zoobzyake;"—and then to note how speedily and how completely he did devil it up.

Certainly there was no malevolence in the case of Professor Séquard and myself,—the animals suffered not for the idle gratification but for the substantial benefit of their fellow-men. And an immeasurable advance have they imparted to physiological knowledge; for amongst other things, our experiments have settled conclusively the great facts that a dog with his stomach kept empty emaciates rapidly; that a chicken with his head twisted off is thrown into convulsions; that a guinea-pig when his skull is pounded upon will wink; that a terrapin with his back hammered in moves his hind legs when his tail is pinched; and that to resuscitate a 'possum professing death it is only necessary to cut his throat,—facts which while they might possibly be inferred by *a priori* reasoning, can manifestly be irrefragably established only by actual experiment; and whose importance is sufficient to justify us in disregarding as maudlin those sentiments of humanity which some affect in dealing with this subject. In deference to sentimental clamors we, indeed, occasionally resorted to chloroform to dull the sensibilities of the martyrs, but we found it an undesirable complication of the case; for, besides that in numerous instances the production of yells was the very point to be demonstrated, the animals exhibited an incorrigible proneness to die from the effects of the anæsthetic,—ofttimes clandestinely in the midst of an operation, which fact would not become known till everything was artistically completed, when its discovery would draw forth unseemly jubilation from the students, and occasion great chagrin to my able coadjutor who deemed he was manipulating with a live dog and not a dead one. Moreover, *Ars longa, vita brevis*,

—art is long but life is short;—and we were extremely unwilling to waste time from researches of value and importance to attend to a matter merely æsthetical and in no wise subsidiary to the success of our experiments.

My able coadjutor was by no means a cruel or heartless man. I have seen him again and again while carefully dissecting a dog pause, and, though he always had a great press of business of this kind on his hands, steal a moment to pat the patient benignly on the head and say to him such kindly words of encouragement as " Poo faylow !" and " Nice dug." He would even whistle and talk French to him. American animals, indeed, were great favorites with him, much above those of Europe ; and he always spoke in the highest terms of their noble power of endurance under affliction, which enabled them to survive a degree of comminution fatal to their transatlantic brethren. He was in a manner forced to illustrate his subject by vivisections, not having sufficient fluency in English to present his views with clearness by mere verbal statements. At the same time he was one of that high order of teachers who assume that the novice can know nothing at all till it has been demonstrated to him. Hence, when he enunciated that a dog with one ear off has but one ear on, he drew forth his scalpel and proved it right there by *experimentum crucis*, trimming away all scraps and fragments with rigid scrupulosity to obviate objections on the score of fractions. Or when he stated that the gastric juice was sour, it was his wont to enforce the assertion by poking his finger into a hole in a dog's stomach and tasting it, at the same time passing a tumbler containing some of it round amongst the students to afford them an opportunity of verifying the statement for themselves. I may mention in this connection that the physiology of digestion was one of his special objects of study. To facilitate investigations in this department of research we always had a number of prepared dogs on hand, keeping them in stock, with holes in their stomachs. From these apertures my able coadjutor would all day long be milking gastric juice, and inserting into them pieces of bread and meat, which he would soon rake out again to submit to minute examination. Another variety of our stock-dogs was those whose pharyngeal apparatus had been tampered with for the elucidation of the remarkable fact that under these conditions they might hollo but could not swallow.. This variety, likewise, commanded the special attention of my able coadjutor, and generally at lectures one of them would be ushered into the amphitheatre and set upon the sacrificial table with a plate of succulent victual before him, when it would be both interesting and instructive in the highest degree to see him ravenously take morsel after morsel into his mouth, not one of which for his soul could he get down his throat, till his jaws would be fit to split asunder with the accumulation; and then it would be no less interesting and instructive to hear his long and reiterated howls in bitterness and vexation of spirit at the unaccountable impotency of his efforts. And here, to show how little amenable was my able coadjutor to any charge of inhumanity in his proceedings, I need merely observe that pitying their inability to take sustenance by the natural channel, it was his custom to convert this class of martyrs into the order before mentioned by humanely cutting a hole into their stomachs, through which he nourished them artificially by introducing and raking out food in the manner already alluded to.

In spite of my able coadjutor's tenderness towards his subjects, some of them made occasionally but an ill requital of it. I have seen dogs, the fearfulness and wonderfulness of whose make he was demonstrating and eulogizing before the class, ungratefully rise up from under the knife and bite him. The coons and 'possums had at various times demeaned themselves so discreditably as to breed considerable estrangement between him and them; and the ill-advised conduct of a certain cat so embittered him that at last he closed the door of the college cellar against the whole race forever. The cat in question my able coadjutor was galvanizing, passing a current of electricity through her from stem to stern, to show, if my memory serves me, that electricity would go from stem to stern of a cat—myself holding her tail to steady her nerves. In the very crisis of the experiment she so far forgot what was expected of her as an exponent of science and what was due to my able coadjutor as an expounder thereof as to pull her tail out of my hands and jump upon the very summit of my able coadjutor's cranium, where she attempted to sustain herself by her claws. As she might have known, had she reflected for a moment, her weight was too great to be supported in this way. When she found herself slipping down, she put forth all her strength to save herself, clawing into every available spot on my able coadjutor's visage and striving desperately to hang on. Under such a strain as this the fragile structure of my able coadjutor's visage gave way at every point, and when, losing her last hold, she fell to the floor, she left it a perfect wreck and ruin behind her, completely guttered from top to bottom. It is impossible to describe the tumult this scene occasioned in the amphitheatre. The disciples rose as one man and pursued the recusant, and, capturing her, held her forcibly to her duty till her breath was galvanized out of her body—my able coadjutor turning the crank of his engine to the very uttermost of his ability.

A conclusive proof that my able coadjutor in his career of slaughter was actuated solely by a thirst for wisdom is furnished by the fact that he spared not his own carcass in the search for it. One instance will suffice. At one time, becoming sorely troubled in mind concerning certain points connected with the cutaneous transpiration, or sweat, as it is commonly termed, in order to get light upon the subject, he bedaubed himself from head to foot with water-proof varnish, and sitting down, note-book in hand, proceeded to record the phenomena as they arose. Among the first things he noted was that he was beginning to die, and this would also have been the last but that some one, accidentally entering his slaughter-pen, found him stretched. He was in a desperate fix, for the varnish was of the primest quality, made after his own receipt, and stuck closer than a brother; and it was only by the most assiduous scraping, and rasping, and sand-papering that my able coadjutor was saved to publish the invaluable results of this admirable experiment.

To crown and set off his humanity, my able coadjutor was distinguished by the possession of the strictest probity and honor, never permitting one of his crop of dogs to be diverted from the strictly scientific sphere of his duty. It would at times occur that among the additions we were constantly making to the menagerie in the cellar there would be a dog of birth and breeding—a pointer, perhaps—which some student, with a taste for the sports of the field, would wish to appropriate to himself by the substitution of another quadruped, as well suited to the purposes of science, but of lower degree. An application of this purport made to my able coadjutor invariably astonished him, such an appropriation of another's property being, as he politely but unequivocally remarked, no less than stealing, while his consent to it would be simply a connivance with robbery—a crime from which his feelings instinctively revolted; and then, with singular acuteness of reasoning, would my able coadjutor proceed to show that the taking of a man's dog to be anatomized for the good of all mankind, so far from being censurable, was made, by the end in view, to smack of the highest philanthropy, while to purloin him to hunt with for the individual's mere selfish gratification was reprehensible to the last degree, constituting the purloiner that most despicable of men — a dog-thief.

I have been led unconsciously to say far more concerning Professor Séquard than I at first intended. Nevertheless, I will let it stand, knowing how highly prized are reminiscences of great men when from unimpeachable sources—and Professor Séquard is truly a great man, standing in the foremost rank of living physiologists.

Leaving the Grotta del Cane we repaired to Pozzuoli, a small decayed town lying comatose upon the shores of the bay, redeemed somewhat by the possession of the remains of the temple of Jupiter Serapis—a relic which is the pride and joy of the geologists. This being disposed of, the journey was resumed, and presently we reached the foot of a hill, at which the driver commanded us to alight, declaring that he could aid us no further, but that to get at the top we must shift for ourselves. There was a rough and rather long and wearisome road leading thither, over which we padded till we came to a gate. Entering this, after satisfying the porter, we found ourselves in a large and irregularly-shaped, flat-bottomed basin, whose sides were formed by a circle of hills. This was the Solfatara. It is the crater of a volcano which, as far as is certainly known, never indulged in but one eruption, and that was between six and seven hundred years ago, since which time it has comported itself with demureness. Its innate fieriness of spirit, however, manifests itself to some extent in one corner, where there is a cavern from which come roaring forth great clouds of steam mingled with sulphuretted hydrogen and other abominable vapors. From this corner are raked masses of sulphur beautifully crystallized. In one part of the crater we were shown a thrilling experiment. It seems clear that the ground here is nothing more than a crust of earth covering an awful chasm below, and there is a man on the premises who makes his living by raising an enormous rock above his head and letting it fall upon the crust, in order to elicit the hollow sound natural under the circumstances for the entertainment of visitors, who remunerate him for the intense gratification such an exploit must needs afford. It is a portentous sound that is thus brought forth, awaking strange feelings in the auditor's breast, and causing him to tread with circumspection lest he break through. A tolerably deep hole has been already worn in the ground by this constant pounding upon it. One of these days, if the man continues at it, he will pound clean through, and the spectacle then will be truly sublime. We paid him half a franc speedily, and being pressed for time left in some haste.

Among other things to its discredit, it is believed that this Solfatara is an aider and abettor of Vesuvius, being in communication and sympathy with that truculent old mountain, for it has been noticed that when the latter is from any cause impeded in the discharge of its venom the former falls a-grumbling, and the cavern in the corner and sundry smoke-holes scattered about it fume much more vigorously than common.

From my inspection of this whole region made on this day's excursion, as well as from my subsequent examination of the Vesuvian district, I am thoroughly convinced that Naples is no place for a man who loves peace and quiet and is conservative in feeling to abide at; and inasmuch as I forbore to pay my addresses to any Havana heiress on account of the uncertainty of slave property there, so here I felt constrained to withhold my affections from any landed Neapolitan signorina on account of the ruinous fluctuations to which real estate in this section must be exposed.

Our next stage was to the so-called Grotto of the Sibyl, on the way to which we were again ordered to alight by the driver—this time out of his kindly regard for our necks—while making a very precipitous descent by a road on whose smooth stones his horses, after performing prodigies of terpsichorean skill, fell for dead and required the whole party to set them up again. Before reaching this precipice we passed by Monte Nuovo, another geological curiosity, being a mountain a mile and a half in circumference and four hundred and forty feet in height, which was mostly formed in one night. It occupies the site of a little town which in those days was a great resort for invalids, who repaired thither for the benefit of its warm springs. During the month of September, 1538, all this region was pestered with violent and constantly-recurring earthquakes, which the inhabitants bore with the philosophy that is born of familiarity; but on the evening of the 29th the invalids in the town were completely upset by seeing it split in two. From the chasm thus formed there thundered forth for thirty-six hours ashes, pumice-stones, and great blocks of lava, in quantity sufficient to form this mountain. It continued in quiet labor for about a week, with occasional strong throes, at the end of which time it was seized with a paroxysm of puerperal mania and began to throw stones promiscuously about with great fury, knocking several persons in the head who had intrusively come there to see how the thing was done. This was its expiring effort, and it has never rallied since.

Propping up our prostrate horses, we were enabled to proceed, and soon arrived at the Grotto of the Sibyl. It derives its appellation from being the reputed residence of her of Cumæ, who attended the pious Æneas when he adventured down below,—though, in sooth, it is but a plain tunnel through a hill, like the Grotto of Posilipo, made many centuries since the days of the Sibyl as a highway to facilitate travel. It is as dark as Egypt and the way is very uneven, so that to penetrate it satisfactorily it is necessary to have lights and discreetness. Our guide preceded us on foot, bearing the torches, and we followed slowly and cautiously in the carriage. I cannot say that I was overmuch charmed by the trip. The tunnel is a long one, and our way of going through it made it seem ten times longer. It is also very low in places, with a decidedly shaky look about it, and an occasional big chip scraped from the roof by the top of my head descending into my lap evoked some awful doubts. It is said that the Jaws of Hell, *Fauces Orci*, are somewhere about there, but we did not see them, nor, indeed, anything else but a few air-shafts pierced through the incumbent hill. Such holes as this offer few attractions to a man of my kidney, and it was with pleasure that, after being bounced about in the darkness, besprinkled with dust and dirt, and kept under the shadow of death for the required time, I at last beheld the gate of Hell gleaming before me in the shape of the Lake Avernus.

When I was a good little boy at school, poring over the classic poets with the assiduity which befits the student of such inestimable lore, reading about Avernus, mayhap with a hope, but certainly with no prospect, of one day seeing it, the idea I formed of it was strikingly at variance with the scene which now presented itself. Instead of a lonely, drear, and noisome pool, lightless and lurid among sombre forests, I beheld a cheerful little sheet of water, where merrisome wavelets, flashing in the sunshine, were dancing pleasantly before the unobstructed gaze, while upon its banks common, sociable mortals were at work. It is said to be a mile and a half in circumference, but it did not appear to be even so large as that to me. The spirit of utilitarianism, which prevailed in the era of Augustus as in our own, has dealt a fatal blow upon this reverend spot; for Agrippa, son-in-law of the emperor, and a great advocate of internal improvements of those days, not having the fear of the infernal gods before his eyes, conceived the sordid idea of making the lake useful instead of terrible by converting it into a sort of naval station. His scheme was to connect Avernus with the neighboring Lucrine Lake,—then a well-to-do and flourishing body of water, high in the public estimation for its wealth of oysters, but now a swamp in very moderate circumstances,—and through this with the sea, so that the two lakes might form a secure harbor for the Roman navy. He carried out his plan ruthlessly. He cut canals, occasioning a marked shrinkage of Avernus; chopped down the Cimmerian woods, by which act the venerable miasms were deprived of their time-honored abodes, and ruined the place generally. All of his elaborate works have since been reduced to chaos by the commotions terminating in the formation of Monte Nuovo, which at the same time threw the greater portion of the Lucrine overboard into the bay of Baiæ. Any hope of the resuscitation of the poetic glories of Avernus is futile, for the thrice-baleful hand of the modern engineer is even now upon it. However we classicists may mourn over the desecration of the spot, I record as a fact, which must be consolatory to some of my readers, that this renowned outlet from the nether regions now possesses the inestimable advantages of railroad communication. The construction of this much-needed improvement evinces the practical spirit of the age,—though, to prevent disappointment, it is well for me to add that connection has not yet been completed with the ferry-boat; so that for the present the use of the road is restricted to the transportation of stone along the banks.

We now drove along the shore of the magnificent bay of Baiæ, of which Horace declares that no other in the world excels it. In proceeding we saw on the hillsides and occasionally under the water the remains of splendid structures, which formed part of ancient Baiæ itself, and presently halted before an antique, cross-roads kind of tavern, which forms modern Baiæ. What a fall is here! Once it was full of people and palaces, for Baiæ was the great watering-place in the palmier days of the Roman empire, brimming with wealth and luxury and dissipation, the gigantic antetype of our springs, where the First Families resorted,—the old gentlemen to talk politics, and the young squirts to eat oysters and get drunk, and to which, to quote the mildly-worded statement of the record, the ladies came Penelopes, and from which they departed Helens. According to all accounts, it must have been a dreadful place. It is impossible to imagine any place worse, indeed, as the most charitable constructionist must at once acknowledge when told that a lawyer was actually constrained to apologize to the court for having accepted as a client a man who had been there (*vide* case of Commonwealth *vs.* Marcus Cœlins,—Marcus T. Cicero for the defense). It was a favorite place with many of the great men of antiquity. Cicero was overfond of it; and Cæsar, Pompey, Sylla, Domitian, and other persons of quality had villas there. So, too, had the exemplary Cato of Utica, who was so virtuous that he could not abide the sight of a man in his shirt-tail; and the wise and grave Seneca's thunderbolts against it were the result of personal observation, if not of experience. The monster Nero ofttimes hied thither; but the worst man, in my professional opinion, who ever set foot in it was Publius Ælius Hadrian,—the "Vital spark of heavenly flame" man,—a Roman emperor, who starved himself to death there, leaving directions for the publication of the unheard-of calumny that the doctors had done it.

Of this gay gathering-place almost all that can now be made out are three dilapidated structures, each having had originally a circular chamber and a vaulted roof, in two of which these peculiarities are still well preserved. These structures are called temples and are assigned to Venus, Mercury, and actually to Diana; but there are evidences about them by which they are identified as being in reality connected with baths, probably appurtenances of the luxurious villas that once stood here.

While we were standing in one of the chambers solemnly ruminating upon its departed glories, suddenly there burst upon us in one terrible irruption all the women in the neighborhood, bearing in their hands lutes and timbrels, or, as we denominate such instruments in our country, banjoes and tambourines. Instantly, with a great whoop, they surrounded us and let fly their music, accompanying it with huge squalls of vocal melody and stupendous drawings-in and strikings-out by way of dancing, —the racket being intensified a hundredfold by the bellowings and rebellowings arising from the catacoustic properties of the hollow roof. We were given to understand that they were doing the Tarentella, the national dance, which essays to represent the gyrations of those who have lost their wits by the bite of the tarantula while undergoing medical treatment, music being the approved remedy in such cases for the restoration of their senses; and truly the performance was just what we might reasonably expect from lunatics at a crisis, being executed as they would do the can-can in Bedlam. Knowing that such an exhibition as this could not possibly be afforded gratis, and, not desiring it at any price, we broke through the lines and fled. With an awful crash of lute and timbrel, the tarentellians made after us, but we escaped, all except our Irish companion, who, being a gentleman of a sedate port and carriage, declined to break into a gallop with the rest of us; and on looking back we saw him completely environed. But he was stricken in years as well as sedate, and so had come to lose that regard for the sex which is so marked a feature in the character of his countrymen; therefore he simply stuck up his nose at an angle of forty-five with the perpendicular, and recklessly and heedlessly penetrated the cohort of fair mendicants.

We retreated into the cross-roads tavern of the place, and proceeded to refresh ourselves. The landlord furnished us with a very nice collation. Among the items were the illustrious oysters of these waters. These oysters, so bepraised by the sages of antiquity, certainly greatly excel ours in delicacy—of proportions; being about one-tenth the size of a good fat Virginia oyster. Their shells are thin and smooth with a fine play of rainbow-hues on the inside, and the meat is decidedly palatable, and, when dressed with vinegar, has an agreeable relish of verdigris. If their present small dimensions and great price be not the result of modern degeneracy, it was a serious matter to indulge in an oyster-supper in the olden time. We also had excellent Bologna sausage, made, if I apprehend aright, at the Grotta del Cane; while to wash the solids down we were served with a bottle of wine,—none of your old, stale stuff that has been kept on hand for months or perhaps years, as we sometimes find it, but new and fresh from the vine. Its greatest recommendation, however, was that it was the classic Falernian,—so we were positively assured by the landlord, and as none of our party were sufficiently skilled in Falernian to advance an opinion of our own, we of course were not guilty of the presumptuous folly of disbelieving him. It will please my countrymen who delight in the lyrics of Horace to know that they can obtain an exact conception of the true Falernian by swigging a can of new cider.

When our repast was all eaten up, we went out-of-doors and sat on a log to digest it, where we gave audience to all the boys and girls of Baiæ, who waited upon us with petitions for small change. While this business was still unfinished, we arose and got us back into our carriage, returning to Naples along the seashore, after having spent a remarkably interesting day.

CHAPTER XIX.

Containing the Character of Pliny the Elder, and an Account of the City of Pompeii, Past and Present.

ABOUT twelve miles from Naples lies the silent and solemn city of Pompeii. It presents one of the most impressive scenes to be witnessed in all the world, inspiring strange and almost awful emotions in the mind of the traveler wandering among its solitudes. To describe it topographically is sufficiently easy, but to body forth in apt and fitting language the thoughts that the theme suggests is altogether impossible. As for me, I shall not even attempt it, but in dealing with the subject confine myself to my usual poor, plain style, eschewing erudition and sentimentality, and sticking to simple matter of fact as much as in me lies.

Pompeii was overwhelmed on August 24, A.D. 79, by showers of ashes accompanying an eruption of Mount Vesuvius, which occurred at that time. Sixteen years before it came near going down under the operation of an earthquake which engulfed six hundred sheep and ran several citizens crazy,—as Seneca circumstantially records. The eruption which finally destroyed it is minutely described by Pliny the Younger, who saw it. His uncle, old Pliny, also saw it; and I may be doing a service to some of my readers who have an itching for looking into things by recalling to their minds what he saw, how he saw it, and what came of his seeing it.

This old man was an extraordinary person. He rose before other people went to bed, and himself frequently never went to bed at all. When he took his meals, instead of eating he read; and when he took his bath, instead of washing himself he read also. When he was so broken down that he could no longer hold his book before his eyes, he made somebody read to him. It made no difference to him what the book was, for it was a maxim of his that no book can be so bad as not to have some good in it. When he was not reading he was writing, and when his fingers became so cramped that they refused to wriggle, he ordered up an amanuensis. He never went out of the house without his note-book, and took down every bird, beast, and fish, stratum of brick-bats, ash-formation, and bilge-water current that he set eyes on. What it was impossible for him to find out by his individual researches he got from anybody that he thought ought to know, and hence consulted much with the country-people and sea-faring men, whose accounts of natural phenomena he carefully recorded. By proceeding in this manner he accumulated an awful amount of inestimable facts, coming at last to be steeped to the very eyebrows in wisdom, and knowing more or less of everything.

One day while on duty with the Roman fleet at Misenum—for he was a great office-holder as well as man of science—he espied a good-sized cloud of vapor shaped like a pine-tree issuing from some mountain on shore. A common man in such a neighborhood seeing such a sight would have jumped at the conclusion that it portended a dangerous outbreak of Vesuvius and run away. Not so this uncommon man. Nothing short of close and minute ocular inspection could satisfy the rigid requirements of his practical mind. This thing must be looked into, said he; and gathering up his note-book he ordered a vessel to take him on the expedition. His nephew, young Pliny, was at that time a student of his, and the old man wishing to afford him every opportunity of improving himself in knowledge, kindly invited him to go along. This youth subsequently became extremely erudite himself, and even at this early age showed that he was rather wiser than his uncle, for on the present occasion he declined the offer with thanks,—ingeniously alleging that he wished to do some studying,—a plea than which none upon earth could have been more satisfactory to the old man. Pliny the Elder accordingly put off alone, courageously poking about in places into which his crew begged him for Heaven's sake not to venture. But like any man of supereminent talent he had a proper contempt of these illiterate ignoramuses, and heartily despising their fears pushed along till he reached a point where even his strong and sappy head began to crack and bake under the hot ashes and big rocks that came down upon it by the cart-load. And now for a moment he had a mind to shut up his note-book and go back, especially as the land seemed to be turning inside out and the sea to be flowing away, and probably he would have done so had not the unlettered ass of a pilot strenuously urged it upon him. As it was, however, the intrepid old philosopher concluded to make the best of his way to the house of Pomponianus, a friend of his residing at Stabiæ. "Fortune favors the brave," screamed he, though the event proved him to have been something too credulous in this aphorism, for he was suffocated that self-same night.

He appears to have maintained his philosophical equanimity to the last, for on reaching Pomponianus's premises he very coolly lay down and went fast asleep, which no one else dared to do, and was getting very comfortably blocked in and buried alive by the stones which were constantly falling around the entrance to his chamber, when his friends ventured to wake him up. A crisis being thought to have now arrived, a council of war was held to determine what was best to be done, old Pliny assisting. It was resolved to take to the fields—a resolution which, says Pliny the Younger point-blank, the council was scared into—" except my uncle," says he, "who embraced it upon cool and deliberate consideration." And here his uncle was peremptorily obliged by the force of circumstances to sacrifice somewhat of the dignity of mien characteristic of the sage, for he had to surmount his head with a pillow tied thereupon to save it from being staved in by the descending stones. Thus arrayed he proceeded with the rest to the seashore, where he lay down again—being, it should seem, in these stirring times, most remarkably sleepy for a man commonly so wide awake. A great burst of sulphurous vapor compelled him to rise immediately, and at that moment he died. So ended Pliny the Elder—a martyr to science, say we men—a victim to curiosity, will say the women.

Pliny the Younger, the discreet, despite his sagacious prudence became entangled in the eruption after all,— and was monstrously flustered thereby. He has bequeathed to us a graphic description of his tribulations on the occasion.

Pompeii was a fussy, third-rate town, eternally in a row and forever at law. Especially were there innumerable squabbles between the citizens and the military stationed there; and on one occasion a regular knock-down-and-drag-out fight occurred at the circus, in which they effectually fanned out certain windy fellows from Nuceria —another fussy little town hard by. Of course, with such worthies, this fight led to a lawsuit. The Pompeians lost their case and were sentenced very severely,—no less, indeed, than by the forfeiture of their right to go to the circus for ten years. It was while waiting to have their disabilities removed that the earthquake happened that killed the sheep. It was a walled city. The walls, which were surmounted by towers, were very thick and substantial, and have been ascertained to be about two miles in extent, inclosing an area estimated to contain a hundred and sixty acres. In spite of its boisterousness it must have had peculiar attractions as a residence, for we know that it was a favorite rusticating-place with many of the ancient dignitaries. In one respect it must have been the most delightfully unique of all towns,—for there were no poor trash in it—so we infer, at least, from the fact that all the houses yet unearthed manifestly belonged to well-to-do people. There is some ground, too, for surmising that there were no sick folks there, else we ought to find their skeletons lying around— unless, indeed, we suppose they were miraculously healed by the stress of circumstances surrounding them, as I have known rheumatics and paralytics to be by the house providentially catching fire. What a place was this to live in! nobody bedridden, and with no poor kin. Alas, that this paragon of cities should have been blotted from the earth!

It appears to be established by the small number of skeletons discovered that almost all of the inhabitants of Pompeii were able to save themselves; and, though their contemporary neighbors may reasonably have lamented that such a fractious and impracticable set should have been turned loose to leaven other communities, few of the present generation have attained to that lofty pitch of righteousness which entitles them to carp at the circumstance. When things had become settled again, some of the people returned and started a new town on top of the old one, but the eruption of Vesuvius, which occurred in 472, destroyed this also. No attempt was made to resuscitate it after this, and in process of time the very site of Pompeii was forgotten. It is true that the wall of the great theatre stuck out prominently above ground to keep the place in remembrance, but the country is so full of ruins that nobody bothers his head about any particular one. It is also true that Fontana, the engineer, running a subterranean aqueduct in 1592 went plumb through the town, knocking down the buildings and columns that stood in his way; but he was a man of business, who went straight along without troubling himself with extraneous speculations. Thus it was till 1748, when a man in digging a well chanced to break through into a chamber containing such an array of statues and curious objects that it was impossible to ignore the place any longer. Cupidity as well as curiosity being now excited, excavations were begun and have been prosecuted to the present time. The work does not pay very well, however, pecuniarily, and hence has been carried on in a miserably desultory manner—sometimes for a month or two, sometimes for a day or two, but more frequently for no time at all. So far, one hundred and twenty-two years from its discovery, about two-fifths of the city has been dug out; and taking this as the basis of calculation and estimating one-horse power as thirty-three thousand pounds raised one foot in a minute, and an Italian power as one hundred and fifty pounds falling flat on the grass in an instant, I find, unless I have inadvertently omitted some essential element in the figuration, that the entire city will be uncovered one of these days. As long as Victor Emmanuel lasts tolerably steady progress may be expected, for he is a sovereign of liberal and enlightened views in these matters, being in marked contrast with the Bourbon dynasty that preceded him.

We were lucky enough to secure a pleasant, sunshiny day for our visit to Pompeii. The railroad to Salerno passes close to the buried city, and it was by this route that we went to it,—though many persons for unknown reasons prefer to drive there through dust and ashes in a carriage. As we knew we should have to do a great deal of walking, and were doubtful about the hotel accommodations thereabouts, we took the precaution to provide ourselves with lunch, which we carried in a bottle. The trip occupied about an hour, leading us for most of the way along the pleasant shores of the bay and through many suburban towns and villages. Pompeii is not exhibited gratis, but has a ticket-office at the entrance, the price of admission being forty cents—children half price. As fast as the patrons procure their tickets they are collected into parties of five or six and handed over to a guide, of whom there are thirty employed by the government, and who—blessings on the government therefor!—are obliged to do their duty and get nothing for it, being turned out of office if they accept of any recompense from visitors. At the outset we were hopelessly cast down by being assigned to a guide who spoke only Italian, but by a dexterous manœuvre we were after awhile so fortunate as to transship ourselves to the care of another one more gifted in tongues. Said this able archæologist to us on coming under his wing, "I speak anyting here—Ruman in Rum, and in Napelis I speak Macaroni." At this merry conceit he opened his ponderous and marvelous jaws and grinned from ear to ear, and we ourselves cracked an audible smile,—as we did forty times over again during the day, at the least; for it was the most valued observation in all his répertoire of good things, which he repeated at every opportunity, and as he was a clever fellow we felt it incumbent upon us to laugh every time. The party we were now thrown with consisted of a family of ladies and gentlemen from Sweden, and they bothered us amazingly, for they were very perverse and hard-headed, and there was no bond of union between us—especially not between us and the ladies, to whom we were obliged to defer by virtue of their sex; wherefore, I make bold to declare that, in my humble judgment, with all reverence for my female fellow-creatures, they are mighty poor company on a sentimental journey.

There is almost nothing to indicate the presence of the city till the gate is entered, when it bursts suddenly upon the view in an extended and startling vista. The first glimpse I obtained of it reminded me irresistibly of the "burnt district" at Richmond after the evacuation, to which its roofless houses and bare walls gave it a striking resemblance, the most noticeable difference being the absence of rubbish. It has a very lonely, solemn, and awe-inspiring look about it, which is not materially dissipated by the sight of the groups of visitors wandering amid the ruins, or a horse and cart slowly bearing away a load of excavated dirt. An imaginative person might here easily convert himself into a profound moralist or else a melancholy loon by sitting off in a corner and giving rein to thought.

Our guide gallantly relieved the ladies of a great stock of surplus dry-goods,—at the same time by his courteous anxiety to see ourselves unencumbered, forcing us to permit him to carry our bottle of lunch,—and led us on.

The city has been pretty thoroughly sacked by the powers in authority over it, almost everything movable having been taken away, and it was a remark of incessant iteration with the guide, as we entered the houses, that here used to be such a thing but that it was now in the Museum at Napelis. It was laid out with considerable regularity, the streets generally crossing at right angles, though most of them are very narrow, not exceeding eleven feet in width. They are paved with blocks of lava, and it is a striking sight to note how this has been cut into by carriage wheels, some of the ruts being astonishingly deep. Frequently they are provided with high-pitched stepping-stones leading across them to keep the feet of dainty pedestrians out of the mud in rainy weather. Every now and then we meet with a well surrounded with a stone curb, on which are plainly to be seen the chafings made by the ropes in drawing up buckets. There are also specimens of a sort of town-pump, consisting of a stone basin on the side of which is sculptured a face, from whose mouth, in the times when the water-works were in repair, issued a stream of the blessed element. Ah, me! how many jolly old souls of Pompeii after an all-night frolic have cooled their overheated coppers at these fountains! They have actually rubbed and burnt away goodly segments of the cheeks of these stone faces by the pressure of their glowing gills.

The houses of Pompeii were for the most part of small size and not more than two stories high. What windows they had were monopolized by the rooms on the upper floors, and some of them boasted the luxury of panes of glass. Wherever the area of the premises was sufficiently spacious to allow it, an inner court was included in the architectural plan, and around this were ranged the various apartments for the use of the family. In the decoration of the rooms mosaic work entered abundantly. Paintings, too, were much affected, many of which are still to be seen looking very fresh, though the subjects are frequently of a kind that would hardly be selected to adorn the parlors of our highly delicate age and country.

The citizens of Pompeii were largely employed in keeping shop. Some of the first people of the place, the upper ten themselves, were implicated in this vulgar mode of getting a living. And they were not ashamed of it, as appears from the fact that their palatial residences and their grimy shops were under the same roof; and they were not above soliciting a share of the patronage of the public by written notices tantamount to "Best Superfine Flour," "No. 1 Tar," "Family Groceries cheap for Cash," "Lime & Hay for sale here," etc. From the evidences they have left behind, it seems that their modes of doing business were pretty much like those in vogue with us, and many of their callings were such as are still assiduously pursued. Among the establishments have been clearly identified bakehouses, blacksmith-shops, soap-factories, doctors' offices, taverns, and numerous others, including, of course, bar-rooms, and some places much worse. Over the doors of some of these were inscribed the names of the proprietors, though many were furnished with signs more comprehensible to the great bulk of the community. Thus, the academy where was taught the manly art of self-defense was designated by a representation of two men waging battle; and Professor Somebody's Classical and Collegiate Institute was pleasantly made known to the Pompeian youth by a hieroglyph showing the Professor in the act of the endermic application of knowledge to one young gentleman horsed on another young gentleman's back. Certain institutions which amongst us flourish the best the less they are known, sticking to the symbolical system, announced themselves with such naked protrusiveness that to accommodate modern ideas it has been found necessary to take down the signs,—though some still remain and can be seen on the streets, being cut in the stone of the pavements.

The worthy shopkeepers of Pompeii were annoyed with some of those petty encroachments upon their comfort which so rile ours at the present day. Occasionally we behold a house whose wall is made terrible by the depicture of a pair of tremendous snakes overlapping one another. This was intended as a direful warning to whom it might concern to commit no nuisance there. And at one place this plain, pertinent, and impertinent notice to gentlemen of leisure is stuck up,—" No place for loungers: clear out, loafer!" (*Otiosis locus hic non est, discede morator.*)

There is not a spot in Pompeii but what possesses a share of interest for the visitor. A detailed account of everything to be seen would, however, weary the reader, and I shall, therefore, mention only a few of the more striking objects. It would require many visits to give the city such an examination as it deserves. We were there several hours and saw but a portion of it, and much of that, owing to the discordant elements in our party, very cursorily. The Forum was the first place of prominence we were taken to. It is a spacious quadrangle adorned with numerous columns and with pedestals for statues, and is surrounded by temples and public buildings for various purposes. Its most interesting features are those that indicate the sudden knocking-off from work of the stone-cutters, who at the time of the eruption were engaged in repairing and improving it. We see this in the unfinished columns and the rough blocks of marble lying about, which are just as they were left by the artisans when they put up their tools eighteen hundred years ago, expecting, doubtless, the gods willing, to recommence work in a week or two, at the furthest.

Leaving the Forum we visited a multitude of houses, including those of such dignitaries of the city as Caius Sallust and Marcus Lucretius, many of them still giving ample evidence that their proprietors were persons of taste and means. In the prosecution of these inquiries, while moving along one of the streets, all at once the guide beguiled the party into a little dungeon of a room with nothing in it, and then called the gentlemen out, one by one, ordering each man forth with as much precision as if he were detailing us to be shot, while the attempt of the ladies to follow was summarily and unceremoniously squelched. Wondering greatly at this proceeding, we saw him draw forth a key and unlock the door of an adjoining house, into which he commanded us to enter. Merciful Diana! what place was this? The pictures on the walls answered the question quick as a flash. It was no place for such decent and virtuous gentlemen as we were to be in, and, accordingly, after examining every nook and corner thoroughly, we instantly withdrew. It was a very small and incommodious apartment, having an awfully hard stone bed and pillow on one side. This, too, was apparently no place for loafers; for at the foot of the steps leading up-stairs was erected a sort of pulpit, in which, I opine, the boss-lady sat, and admitted no one till he had paid for his ticket. If this surmise is correct, we did some things better in Pompeii than, as I understand, we do them here. Blushing with conscious innocence, we rejoined the ladies and went ahead.

Two theatres have been dug up at Pompeii, showing that the drama was appreciated there. The citizens also had the benefit of the elevating influences of gladiatorial and wild-beast combats, being provided with an amphitheatre capable of seating ten thousand persons. They were refreshing themselves with an exhibition at this place when the eruption broke out; and it is owing to this circumstance, indeed, that so few of them perished; for all hands being assembled at this comparatively distant spot, and finding it impossible to return to their homes, they had simply to all run away together, with the advantages of nothing to encumber them and plenty of elbow-room. Let this fact be duly noted to the credit of the much-abused sports of the arena. I have heard good people, logical and sagacious thinkers, when denouncing the practice of dancing, declare that they required no other proof of its awful wickedness than that Herodias danced John the Baptist's head off. Can they possibly shut their eyes to the saving efficacy of a dog-fight when they see that on one occasion a somewhat similar performance was the means of preserving ten thousand lives?

The Pompeians were blessed with baths excelling those that any modern city can boast. They also enjoyed the privilege of a good court-house and secure jail, and a branch of that odious institution, the custom-house, was established in their midst. Such satisfaction as can be derived from the presence of soldiers was likewise vouchsafed them. I have already made a slight reference to the belligerent relations subsisting between the citizens and their defenders. In the destruction of the city, the military suffered heavily, no less than sixty-three skeletons having been discovered in their barracks. Had these been Confederate troops, I am prepared to prove that the whole detachment would have got off without the loss of a man—such is the superiority of our system. But, unlike our independent-spirited veterans, a Roman warrior when assigned to a post subordinated his ideas of what ought to be done to those of his commander, and so there he stuck, through thick and thin, till further orders.

We finished our inspection of Pompeii at the suburban villa which has been assigned to Diomedes for the inconsequential reason that the family burying-ground of this individual happens to be across the street from it. It is but a short distance without the city, cheerfully situated in the midst of a graveyard, where tombs line both sides of the highway, and, barring the undesirable company of the defuncts, must have been a delightful spot for rustication. It had all the modern improvements of those days, and commanded a view of the bay as well as the tombstones, and was just the place which a man fond of ruralizing, and who was not to be intimidated by ghosts, would like to see in the possession of his particular friend. It had a cellar containing good store of wine. In this cellar were found the skeletons of eighteen persons, who, it is presumed from the gold ornaments upon their necks and arms, were nearly all females. Amongst them were two children, upon whose skulls when discovered there was still some hair. We saw upon the wall the imprint of the bodies of some of these poor creatures where they had cowered against it in their last agony.

One day the workmen, while excavating in the city, happened to strike their implements through into a hollow space in the midst of the ashes. Sig. Fiorelli, the supervisor of the works, surmising that this cavity was the mould of a human body left by the decay of the flesh, was led to the ingenious expedient of filling it with liquid plaster of Paris. His surmise proved to be correct, and the result was that he in this way secured casts of four bodies. These are kept at Pompeii and form the strangest and most impressive sights there. The plaster has copied all the peculiarities of the originals very faithfully—their features, their clothing, the rings on their fingers, everything. The bones are incased in the plaster, portions of them being visible where they have failed to be covered by it. One of these unfortunates was a man, two were women, and one a girl about fifteen years of age. The girl and one of the women were found very near to each other, and are supposed to have been a mother and daughter. The casts of the females have a swollen appearance, the consequence of the distention of the bodies by gases evolved in decomposition occurring while the ashes around them were still wet and yielding. In their despair the women had put their hands before their eyes to shut out the horrid vision of death; but the man, it seems, faced it courageously, for he was found lying upon his back, though the marks of contortion about him would indicate that he died in convulsions. The cavities corresponding to the bodies were not on the level of the street, but nearly fifteen feet above it, whence it is inferred that these persons had remained in the house till the matters ejected by the volcano had obtained a considerable depth when they issued from the upper windows and tried to escape, but were overwhelmed by the showers of ashes and water, which, mingling into a semi-fluid mass, formed a mould around them.

In consequence of having to do a vast deal of tramping hither and thither to make our observations, it at length fell out that our flesh failed us, and we would fain have recruited it with a morsel or so of lunch. But, wo was us! on applying for it to our bottle-holder, the guide, to our dismay we found he had drunk it all up. We had at the first, thinking him a man of frugal taste, given him authority to refresh himself with it when so minded, and, forsooth, had been measurably tickled at noting how deftly he could stand with his abdomen confronting his auditors, and, crooking his face full to the rear, contrive to take in his drink and give out his elucidations simultaneously, after which he would stop the vent of the bottle with his thumb, having lost the cork—purposely, I have time and again imagined—at the very beginning. It was with considerable chagrin at our lack of the faculty of judgment that we realized how egregiously we had miscalculated his sucking power. By some mysterious means his brother guides got information that we had opened a temporary bar-room in the old city (but not till all the liquor was gone), in consequence of which we beheld them at every corner, dodging, and winking, and blinking in a fashion that spoke volumes for the dispiriting character of the place. In our difficulty we betook ourselves to the Hotel Diomede, the modern hotel of the town, where we procured a very satisfactory repast, being entertained meanwhile by an exceeding strange-looking guitarist, withal a desperate poor player, of whose strains we could obtain no surcease even by threatening to cast a loaf of bread at his instrument.

CHAPTER XX.

How we journeyed to the Eternal City, and of our Besetments and Contentions and Strivings by the Way, and how hard it was to make good our Lodgment therein.

OF the climate of Naples I shall briefly remark that as far as I became conversant with it there is nothing commendable about it. Indeed, all that its best friends have ventured to offer in its behalf is that it is not quite as bad as the malevolent have represented it. The weather was either rainy or cloudy, and frequently very chilly and disheartening, for most of the time we were there, and it had been the same, we were told, for weeks before. The hotel had fireplaces as a fundamental feature in its construction, with andirons ready set for an emergency,—a bad sign, indicating that cold was felt and feared there, and which shows the invalid he has not entirely evaded the rigors of winter by going thither. We consumed many baskets of wood during our sojourn, not one chip of which escaped record in the bill, where they made a most ghastly item, for wood is an intensely precious commodity in these *blasé* countries. As the result of my experience, I recommend the consumptive especially to tarry but a little while in sunny Italy in the winter season.

Having completed our allotted period in Naples, we embarked for Rome. We went to the railroad station early, finished up the harassing details connected with the baggage, and broke into the train while it was yet moving itself into position at the platform,—for both of us being incorrigible expectorators, my companion on account of his cough, and myself by reason of tobacco-chewing, we earnestly desired to procure places in the coach near the windows, where we could indulge our vices in ease and comfort, and were willing to risk our legs and necks in order to do it. We succeeded perfectly in our object, no one competing with us, and were sitting praying for the train to speed away when a supereminently hard-favored, bald-headed, paunchy little man, astonishingly self-asserting and consequential, walked into the coach, and taking off his hat and putting his foot down firmly, proceeded to deliver an address to us. He seemed to plume himself most of all on his bald head, which was rugose and dinted as well as hairless, looking as if it had been soaked in a lime-vat; while to magnify his importance yet more, he had enveloped himself in a big, long, invisiblo-visible black-green coat, reaching almost to his heels, deposited a pair of spectacles with seven-by-nine glasses before his eyes, and turned out a woolly, manure-colored beard. To this imposing figure we listened with all the respect and consideration which utterances from such a source must inevitably command. We *thought* the little man asked us to get out and give way to his party of friends, eight in number, just a compartment full, who wanted to journey sociably all together to Rome; but we were miserably deficient in languages, and do what we might could not possibly understand him well enough to appreciate the reasons he suggested why we should leave the coach and hunt up new places to accommodate his friends. He lavished a vast amount of majesty of mien and argumentum ad hominem upon us to enable us to see the point, but we couldn't see it. Perceiving that we were dull of comprehension, he proceeded to elucidate his meaning by practical demonstrations, setting about removing our carpet-bags from their receptacles. Unfortunately we misconstrued this, regarding it as an invasion of our rights, and thereupon we put ourselves in a posture of defense, with a dash of offense in the posture. At this piece of effrontery on our part he grew amazed. He appeared to think we were demented, and shutting out from our gaze the splendors of his glorious old punkin of a cranium under his hat, and puffing out his invisible-visible black-green coat till all its wrinkles were obliterated by the accumulation of his dignity, he stalked out of the coach.

The party was duly informed, no doubt, of our indisposition to be awed out of the coach, for presently another gentleman, whose method was the *suaviter in modo*, entered and addressed us. He was a most soft and sweet-spoken gentleman, and, moreover, knew a word of English—the word he knew being "ladies." This one English word he used copiously, to give pith and point to the body of his argument in Italian, his aim being to make us comprehend that we would be obliging the fair sex by turning ourselves adrift with our carpet-bags to agonize for new quarters. Now, inasmuch as my companion was married and I am absolutely free from any hopes of such a condition, it will not seem strange that we could understand him no better than his stupendous little predecessor. The ultimate result of the whole negotiation was that the party was sundered into fragments, each individual having to take his or her chances,—as, alas! too frequently happens in traveling through this vale of tears. Five of them packed themselves in with us, one of them a lady, and along with them came the redoubtable fugleman, head, specs, beard, coat, and all,—and counting him as two people, our coach now had its full complement. They turned up their noses at us and we turned up our mouths at them, and in these harmonious relations towards each other we set out for an all-day journey together.

In this country of Italy the railroad people are not such bigoted adherents to the schedule as we find them in ours. On the present occasion we started full half an hour after the appointed time. They, however, interfere most unreasonably with the liberty of the subject. Under our free institutions a man traveling on a railroad has a perfect right to drop down between the cars, get run over, or get left, and no one ever thinks of molesting or hindering him in the accomplishment of these things; but in Italy and other despotic countries of Europe you are bolted in your coach and not permitted to issue forth even when the train stops, except it be at such places as the officials in their wisdom have allotted A cordon of the functionaries are around you all the time, watching your every movement. You could not get yourself left behind or massacred even with malice aforethought, and if, asserting your manhood, you burst out, the hue-and-cry is raised instantly, and you are hustled back peremptorily.

We passed continually in sight of the Apennines, many of whose peaks were clad with snow. The country through which we journeyed was most of it fertile and well cultivated, and with a frequent succession of small towns. As we proceeded, the animosity existing between us and our traveling companions gradually died out, and in time we became as sociable as people unable to communicate with each other can well be—always excepting the important little man. He sat to himself, or when he moved about moved in a circle of his own. He kept his hat off the whole time to give the grisly glories of his head full scope, and seemed to have an abiding assurance that we would be petrified presently. At every station the original proposition to leave the coach was renewed to us, and in every case as at first was declined from lack of comprehension. In process of time we attained the limits of Victor Emmanuel's dominions, and here we were stopped to have our passports examined. King Victor seems to fash his brains more about people who are quitting his territories than about those who are coming into them. When we entered Naples, passports were not mentioned to us once. Thrown off my guard by this show of liberality, I had contemptuously slung my cursed document into my trunk among pieces of old bricks, ruins of temples, and other trash, and there it was now at this critical juncture, irrecoverably locked up in the baggage-car. It is no joke to be without a passport in a country whose government is so assinine as to require you to have one; and as the inspector came nearer and nearer to our coach I poked my head out of the window to see what sort of a place this was as a temporary residence. But the inspector was a worthy old superficial incompetent soul, who examined our papers in a lump, so that I was able by judicious dodging and superabundant fussiness to satisfy him that he had seen mine as plain as a pikestaff.

I was quite delighted when we got away from this ill-boding place, and was still sniggering most complacently over the clever manner in which I had deluded the old gump, when the train stopped again. An investigation into the reason of this caused my mouth suddenly to pucker in the reverse direction. We had now come within the jurisdiction of the Woman of Babylon, so called, and before going farther must submit to another inspection of passports, and endure an examination of baggage in addition. A functionary of the Woman's aforesaid, most formidable in mien by reason that he was surmounted by a cocked hat and was incased in buttons and belts and other military toggery from top to toe, came to our coach. Every one showed his papers but me. There was no hoodwinking this lynx-eyed inquisitor. "Monsieur," said he to me, "passyporter." "Monsieur," returned I, "I haven't got it,"—simultaneously adjusting myself to that state of easy repose which marks the man conscious of rectitude when appearances are against him. The functionary was a miserably poor physiognomist, and misinterpreted my composed aspect to mean an insolent braving of his authority, and, accordingly, waxed very hot on the spot. "Monsieur," shouted he, "passyporter, *passyporter*, PASSYPORTER!" "Monsieur," said I, "do you speak French?" "No-r-r," said he, with fury; "passyporter." I therefore confined myself to English, and explained the matter minutely and carefully, going over it several times, so that I thought it must needs be plain to the dullest comprehension. He did not understand it one particle, however, and grew yet more clamorous for the passport; whereupon I lay me back in dignity in the coach, declined to waste further discourse upon him, and bade him go to Babylon, or some equivalent exterranean limbo. By this time he was convinced that I was a most desperate and dangerous republican and pestilent heretic, bent upon the annihilation of the pontificate, and so brought the affair to a summary settlement by ordering up one of his janizaries and delivering me over to his custody.

A great deal of time was now wasted in transporting the baggage on the backs of porters from the cars to the building where it was to be examined. During this tedious process I sauntered about under guard, impatiently waiting for my trunk to appear. At length it was brought in among the very last entries. It was speedily opened, and the first thing I did was to extract the accursed paper and project it into the nose and eyes of the functionary, who had drawn near and was standing in judgment over me. The document was unimpeachable. There it was, indorsed and sanctified by the Great American Eagle in water-mark, and describing my head as average, face ordinary, and features common,— all of which even a blind man would be obliged to admit accorded with my physiognomical characteristics to a notch. At this triumphant vindication of my integrity the functionary was amazed and nonplused, and had no other resource than to wreak unmanly vengeance on the contents of my trunk, which he raked up root and branch. It was the worst overhauling I received in all my travels, but my possessions, without exception, miraculously escaped his malice. With his conception of my warlike purposes of course he demanded if I had pistols. This question, which was never propounded to my companion, was put to me regularly at every examination of baggage, —making me, albeit I felt in my heart that I was a most tame and well-disposed person, to flatter myself that I did show a most martial and terror-striking presence. The present demand was met with the accustomed response, and as my coat-tail was not looked into I was not disarmed.

Meanwhile a most momentous scene was enacting outside. On going forth, after disposing of the passport and baggage imbroglio, to seek my companion, I found him standing before a coach shaking his fists in excessive wrath. At the window loomed our old enemy the little man, rampant with his hat off. There he stood intrenched, having as an additional barrier against our entrance bribed the guard to lock the door; and now warned and defied us in the Italian language, which was of all the multifarious tongues wherewith we had been tormented the one in which we were the most helplessly deficient. To be thus forcibly excluded from the coach which was ours by pre-emptive right when suasion had failed to remove us, was intolerable. The guard passing at the time I stopped him, and, explaining the state of the case in French, demanded to be reinstated in our places. He replied that he could understand no such French as I spoke, and went on. This iniquitous slur on my lingual acquirements augmented my choler one hundred per cent. The usurper thinking to strike terror into our souls shook his sun-dried and weather-stained cranium at us with extreme viciousness. Struck by his appearance I contemplated him critically. He was certainly a mighty ugly man. There was no reason that I could see why he and the gorilla might not have their photographs printed from the same negative. His seven-by-nine spectacles glared and his manure-colored beard bristled. But he could not terrify me, for I was within a fraction or two of being as bald as he was; and my companion had been fighting so long with the King of Terrors that it was hard to scare him by any means. Now, except me, my companion was the peaceablest person that ever was, but when you raised us you raised Tartarus. At the then present time we were raised, and under cover of a tremendous fusillade of English in response to the enemy's Italian, we stormed the coach. Slinging our overcoats, canes, umbrella, carpet-bags, and medicine-bottle through the window, we squeezed in immediately after them, the usurper giving ground before our impetuous advance, and were straightway in undisputed possession.

My companion did not cease hostilities for the great victory, but fell upon the baffled and defeated usurper with his tongue and gave him an awful scoring. "Do you know what I'd do with you if I had you in America?" asked my companion of the usurper, at the same time flourishing his fist about his visage. The usurper did not appear to know, and posing himself comfortably away in a corner evinced no desire to be enlightened; wherefore my companion informed him gratuitously. "I'd choke you," said my companion with raucous emphasis. This question and the answer thereto he reiterated again and again for a long time, even after the train had resumed its journey,—nay, till the usurper had fallen fast asleep in his corner and snored. The strength of wind displayed by my companion in his gymnastical and elocutionary efforts on this occasion was more than I had supposed him possessed of, and gave me hopes that his lungs had been measurably invigorated by travel.

Now it came to pass when we had become composed somewhat and began to look around the coach, we found from certain marks that we were not in the compartment originally occupied by us, but in some other to which we could justly lay no pre-emptive claim,—in fact, that we ourselves and not the little man were the usurpers!—a most astounding and grievous discovery. It was an impressive lesson against rash conclusions. Alas, how often, and sometimes how fatally, do we err in this way! I should have been warned by the instance of old Mrs. Adkison, a chronic and consistent patient of mine, who, it may be, has made shipwreck of her salvation from this cause by too hastily rejecting with wrath and scorn the awakening and convicting tract entitled "Why Will You Die?" presented to her by a worthy colporteur. She uses "hair restorer," and conceived the tract to be an impudent intermeddling with her private concerns.

Since, however, we had made good our footing in the coach by the valor of our arms we did not condescend to make any apology or reparation, but retained our places by right of conquest.

After a long and weary detention at this wretched spot, we sped away and were no more molested. As the day declined, we entered that desolate, depopulated, and unwholesome region known as the Campagna, which presented a most dreary aspect in the gray light of the evening. Drawing near to Rome, some of the passengers were vouchsafed a misty view of the illumination of St. Peter's,—an imposing spectacle which is annually exhibited, wind and weather permitting, on Easter Sunday. These contingent circumstances had, however, not been propitious the present season, and consequently the Sovereign Pontiff had postponed the exhibition, which by right should have taken place on the second Sunday night preceding, to last Sunday night; and then, for like cause, had postponed it again to next Sunday night,—to wit, to-morrow night. We were cognizant of this alteration in the time of the performance, and as we should then be in the city had indulged great hopes of witnessing it, but His Holiness, now justly distrustful of the meteorological indications, by virtue of the plenary powers with which he was invested had antedated the show twenty-four hours, and lighted up this Saturday night, to our great disappointment.

The Eternal City has no suburbs, and we were in it before we knew it. It was about eleven o'clock at night when we arrived. We debarked from the train, and in doubt and perplexity scuffled on our way till we stumbled upon the omnibus pertaining to the Hotel d'Angleterre, in which we secured passage,—being assured by the man in charge in response to repeated inquiries that we could readily find accommodations at the said Hotel d'Angleterre. The American custom of checking baggage is pooh-poohed in Europe—for no other reason, I verily believe, than from a complacent conceit that we young upstarts can't teach such old doty folks as they anything about traveling. As a consequence a man must trust to his individual eyes and feet and hands, and to Providence, to preserve his trunk, and scrutinizingly note every one of its transmigrations and tergiversations, to his great vexation and tribulation. By the miserable system in vogue here we were on the present occasion subjected to surpassing trouble. All of the baggage was first extracted from the train and thrown higgledy-piggledy into a room where no one was allowed to enter till the slow operation was completed, when a general rush was permitted, and everybody got what he could of his property. My companion undertook to engineer this part of the business while I stayed in the omnibus to maintain our position there, and by dint of unstinted expenditure of breath and small-change upon the surrounding depot-loafers, in the fullness of time contrived to extricate our trunks from the general chaos. Out of a whole omnibus-load of passengers we were the only ones who accomplished this feat, the rest in despair concluding to abandon their baggage to its fate till the morrow.

The omnibus had tarried an inordinate time to give every passenger a chance for his possessions, but now by unanimous consent we set out for the hotel. On arriving there what was our indignation against the omnibus man when we were told by the Secretary—or whatever the person in authority was—that he had but one room left, and that one the worst in the house! We besought him to consider the gravity of this circumstance and to reconsider its announcement, but he could by no means be brought to do it; in fact, the more we humbled ourselves the more he exalted himself, until at last he came to regard us as no better than burglars, and as good as ordered us out of the house. By vote the only room was allowed to a lady of the party in deference to the fact that she was a woman, while the rest of us by supplication procured the use of the omnibus to seek quarters among the neighboring hotels.

Accordingly, we sought and sought—but all in vain. The city was overflowing with people who had come to witness the pageants incident to the celebration of the fiftieth anniversary of Pius the Ninth's induction into the priesthood, and not a room was to be had anywhere. In the prosecution of the search, the occupants of the omnibus had been dropped and lost here and there, and finally, when all hope was fled, my companion and myself returned alone to the Hotel d'Angleterre, where we reported our utter failure to the Secretary and bemoaned to him our desolate state. This exalted man spoke English well and replied to us with promptness and fluency.

The Secretary (indignantly).—" We carn't let our omnibus"—[or stage, or coach, or chariot,—for, truly, I do misremember the identical appellation he bestowed upon his vehicle,—but, anyhow, said he]—" We carn't let it haul you people about town all night—and won't."

We (deprecatingly).—"' Have mercy, sir, on us poor forlorn travelers, houseless and belated."

The Secretary (pie-crustily).—" Sharn't do it—go somewhere else. [*To the omnibus man, decisively.*] Take them people to the Hotel de Rome, drop 'em out there, and bring the omnibus back here."

We (to one another).—" Od darn his old hide of him !"

In Murray's Handbook the Hotel d'Angleterre is the subject of unqualified eulogy, and the Secretary is especially commended for his obliging disposition. Now, I do not complain of the fact that they gave us no rooms when they had none to give. I cheerfully forgive them for this, but I decidedly object to the manner in which it was done, which was wantonly curt and insolent. Had they not been quite so full, unquestionably they would have welcomed us with distinguished consideration; which leads me to infer that they can't stand prosperity, and to advise that they be brought to an endurable condition by a measurable withholding of the public patronage.

In striking contrast was the behavior of the person in charge of the Hotel de Rome. His house was full, too, and he could not furnish us with a room, but he generously offered to relieve us of the incubus of our trunks, which were become a source of unutterable anxiety to us, and to our great deliverance piled them away in his back-yard, where we found them next morning neither ruined by bad weather nor opened by any unauthorized party. Moreover, he hunted up for us a man who had lodgings for hire, and did sundry good offices for us without fee or reward, so that I heartily recommend him to travelers as a Christian Secretary and his hotel as a Christian hostelry.

Following the man with lodgings for hire we traversed some dark and unknown region and were presently ushered into a kind of dungeon, where we were caused to grope our way up a flight of dismal stone steps to a chamber above. Here a candle was lighted with much ado, and by its rays we beheld a dreary apartment whose principal piece of furniture was a mammoth bedstead, whereon we beheld reposing a most exceeding uncomely man, with a feather bed on top of him for covering and a nightcap adjusted to his head by swathing. It became necessary now for me to furbish up my entire stock of French, for we were about to essay in that tongue the extremely intricate business of determining the price of the lodgings. Talleyrand, who spoke French himself, has remarked that the design of language is to conceal our thoughts,—and from my experience I can in the main testify to the judiciousness of the observation. In the complex chaffering that now ensued between the landlord and me, neither more than half comprehended what the other was driving at. It is my custom, as it is that of most persons not habituated to the use of outlandish tongues, when forced to speak in other than my vernacular, to involuntarily interlard my discourse with fragments from any other language with which I may chance to be conversant in order to eke out the meaning. It thus happened that when I resorted to French in Europe—and Heaven knows I did it never from any vanity of scholarship, but only from the direst necessity —it was usually much diversified with Spanish and English; and I did ofttimes conceive, and was to a degree puffed up by the conception, that the Europeans hearing me speak three languages must needs esteem me to be a man of uncommon erudition,—especially as I spoke all three simultaneously, and far more especially, unless they differ widely from the rest of our wonder-worshiping species, because ordinarily I made all three great mysteries unto them. Slowly and painfully the landlord brought me to understand his ultimatum, which was that we could have the dungeon and the big bedstead for three dollars a day,—provided we pledged ourselves to remain for a week; or, if preferred, we could have them for one night for twenty-one dollars. We brought him quickly and readily to understand that we declined the proposition by taking up our carpet-bags, medicine-bottle, etc., and stumbling and tumbling out of the place. The wretch in the nightcap during the conference composedly lay in bed looking and listening, sagaciously retaining possession till the question was decided, and the fact that we should have had to occupy his place was a weighty reason with us for not acceding to the landlord's terms.

We stood in the street and took a calm review of the prospect. The result was that we became wellnigh panic-struck. It was after midnight. We had had nothing to eat since breakfast and our maws were empty and our souls famished within us. Not knowing what to do we returned to the Hotel de Rome, and there providentially found another hirer of lodgings. As the case was now desperate we determined with ourselves to take these lodgings for the night, no matter what sort they might be, and to ask no questions, but to struggle over the price on the morrow when we would have daylight in our favor. Accordingly, we were again led forth for a short distance and up another flight of stone steps, but this time into quite a cheerful and well-ordered room, carpeted, and adorned with family portraits done by photography, and, judging from their numbers, comprising the whole race and kindred to the remotest generation.

We took seats and waited till the preparations for our induction could be completed. Never were we treated with greater consideration and respect. On our behalf a lady was hauled out of bed and caused to make it over again for our reception. Tables and chairs and other things were dragged in quantities into the bed-chamber for our comfort, and when we asked for a drink of water all hands dropped whatever they were doing on the spot and rushed to bring it to us in a body. Such marks of courtesy and regard gave us a most favorable impression of our quarters, though our enthusiasm was sobered down in some measure by misgivings as to their market value; nevertheless, we adhered to our original determination, asked no questions, but went to bed with the universal benison pouring in loud acclaim upon our heads, and waited till the morrow.

By our judicious silence we got the landlord at an advantage, and next morning were able to negotiate with him on very satisfactory terms. We retained these lodgings during our stay in Rome, taking our meals at a restaurant, and were very well pleased with them. Our apartments comprised a bed-chamber containing a big bedstead identical with the one of the dungeon before mentioned, and like it equipped with a feather bed by way of quilt, while the portrait gallery was assigned to us for our parlor. A delectable little maiden ministered to us with unexceptionable care, never failing to refresh us every morning with a vase of nice flowers. We depended on her for egress and ingress, for the door at the top of the steps was kept always fastened by a recondite kind of lock whose mysteries we never fully mastered. The good girl in the kindness of her heart spoke French to us, though, in sooth, her knowledge of the language was limited to "*Bon jour, monsieur.*" These words, however, she uttered to us continually, at our outgoings and incomings, at our uprisings and downsittings, in season and out of season,—in short, whenever and whereever she set eyes on us.

Almost the sole complaint we could reasonably make against these lodgings was due to the fleas, which were allowed, not to say encouraged, to colonize therein,—and really they were somewhat annoying to us. In the bed alone there was, I am certain, not one less than a full Roman legion of them. My last care every night before retiring was to take off my under-clothing, turn it inside out, and shake it with inconceivable fury. This operation was faithfully repeated three times before daybreak, with much floundering, and rearing, and tearing, and moaning in the intervals, and again performed as the preliminary of my morning toilet. In spite, however, of my most strenuous exertions to get rid of them, I was kept in a rack of misery more or less all the time, and was reduced to such straits that I could spare but one hand to eat with, having to reserve the other for the purpose of scratching. How the Roman people can endure such torments as these is hard to comprehend. Possibly their indifference is due to the fortitude they may inherit from their invincible forefathers—probably it is due to the impenetrability of the quasi-stucco in which their hides are usually incased.

CHAPTER XXI.

How we strove to do our Duty by the manifold Sights to be seen at Rome, and of the Expert whose aid we invoked—Containing also an Exposition of the Science and Art of Topography as applied there, with Descriptions of some of the principal Churches, and Notes on the Vatican.

MY first day in Rome, which was the Sabbath, was a very melancholy one. The labors and privations of the preceding day and night had fagged me; my spirits were weighed down; I saw nothing in anything; but was eminently atrabilious and blue-devilish. There was little in the general aspect of the city to ameliorate this frame of mind, for it is, in my judgment, an excessively sombre and disheartening place, and the pervading gloom was augmented by the closing of the shops in deference to the sanctity of the day,—a tribute of respect to which we could not, of course, object in the capital of the Christian world, but which we had not seen paid for now a long time, and, in truth, did not anticipate.

After getting breakfast at a neighboring restaurant and having our trunks transported to our lodgings, we sauntered forth listlessly, not knowing what to do with ourselves, and presently espying some kind of a column towering before us made towards it. It was situated in a spacious square called the Piazza del Popolo and proved to be an Egyptian obelisk which had been reared thousands of years ago to adorn the Temple of the Sun at Heliopolis, but brought to Rome by the Emperor Augustus. After sufficiently studying the hieroglyphics with which it is pictured we were moved to fall into a throng of people who were hurrying past us as if they were tending to some point of great attraction, and, accordingly, following the crowd through a gateway at one side of the square and so out of the city they ultimately led us to a church—the English Protestant—to our great disgust; for we were not in a frame for the reception of the Word. We therefore retraced our steps to the piazza, and from there we gradually worked our way to the top of the Pincian Hill hard by. This hill is appropriately laid out as a promenade, and is a favorite place of resort for pedestrian and equestrian idlers. From it is to be seen a magnificent panorama, and here we spent a great part of the day, contemplating the city as it lay before us and the citizens as they lounged around us.

We had come to Rome fully alive to the momentous duties that would devolve upon us as sight-seers, and fully determined to discharge them. We felt that we were in a city brimful of moving memories, where every pebble was classical, and where the wind could not blow without disturbing the dust of empires. We knew that our anxious friends at home relied upon us to see everything that any of our predecessors had ever seen or professed to have seen, and that if we failed in any particular, on our return we should be chided, and pitied, and despised. That we should not be found derelict, therefore, we made it our first business on Monday morning to hire a guide and a two-horse carriage. This guide was a stout and elderly personage, with gloves and a stove-pipe hat, and a visage tanned and hard as whit-leather. He was the staidest of men, a mortal hater of all jests and idle sayings, with an unbounded conception of the dignity of his office, and of remarkable independence—being ready to wash his hands of us at a moment's notice. He delivered his oracles jejunely and with method, brooking no interruption, but repressing such questions as in his judgment were out of order by gentle but firm flappings with his open hand and an injunction to wait with patience till that point should be attained in its proper sequence. He was but ill versed in the English tongue, which he confounded ofttimes with the French, and it was only when we were about to part with him that we considered ourselves qualified to interpret his discourse. He called Augustus, Owgoostooz; Caius Cestius, Caiooz Chestiooz; and Claudius, Cloud ; and when at any time pressed to give more particulars, would frequently quietly decline and refer us to Murray's Handbook. Under thraldom body and soul to this sage, we sallied forth to explore the city, riding unweariedly all day for a week, stopping only to eat. We were but human, and it is possible that after all our efforts we may not have accomplished the work thoroughly, but this I can aver, we did it conscientiously, and for conscience' sake did many times endure boring to the last extremity.

The Goth, the Christian, Time, War, Flood, and Fire, have dealt upon the seven-hill'd city's pride so relentlessly as to put effectually at fault any common man who should attempt to trace the void and say, "Here was, or is." Nevertheless, there have been undaunted spirits who have valorously faced every difficulty and mapped it out as it was in the days of the Cæsars,—nay, as it was in the days of Romulus. They have accomplished this result, in a great measure, by boldly assigning some well-known name to a certain uncertain locality as a starting-point, and, this being established, deducing the position of other localities from it through the medium of incidental allusions in the works of ancient authors. In this way the locations of a multitude of places are indubitably fixed—subject, however, to be revised by some succeeding antiquarian, at whose dictum they are all changed and indubitably fixed over again. For instance—Sig. Roriborialli conjecturing that a certain wreck was the Temple of Jupiter Nitroglycerans, and there being no survivors of the period of the Empire to contradict him, sets it down so as a fact known and admitted of all men. Now, Seneca says plainly, in his treatise *De Pulsante circa Urbem*, that the Baths of the Jimcronian Venus were "*plura vestigia*"—a few steps—from here; which identifies the load of rubbish confronting it three yards off as the said Baths beyond all dispute. Moreover, from a passage in Horace's elegiac *Ad Sassiges* it appears that Cæsar's Circus Maximus Caninus, or dog-opera, was over against (*exadversum*) the Baths. This clearly settles the character of the hoary and crumbling pile of bricks that lies behind them. By inferences of this sort Sig. Roriborialli has identified numberless other temples, and baths, and arches, and places of renown, and thousands of cultivated travelers from every clime coming to the Eternal City have reverently gazed upon and sighed over scenes which but for the erudition and research of this accomplished archæologist must have sunk into utter oblivion. Having finished his labors Sig. Roriborialli, satisfied that he has contributed to the measure of his ability to the great cause of Truth, dies triumphant and goes to his reward. But since Roriborialli's time other light has been shed upon the subject. Other erudite and researchful archæologists, each one more erudite and researchful than his predecessor, have arisen, down to the period of Pochinozi, who by means of the improved methods of reasoning invented in our day has entirely wiped out Sig. Roriborialli's very base-line. This distinguished investigator has proved conclusively by certain inscriptions on the walls and by the careful collation of passages that the temple so long believed to be of Jupiter Nitroglycerans is in reality of Cloacina. This, of course, upsets every one of Sig. Roriborialli's deductions and necessitates an out-and-out reconstruction of his map. In corroboration of Sig. Pochinozi's views, Zwoschlager, the profound German Latinist, expresses the opinion that the phrase translated "a *few* steps" may mean *many*,—*sc.* three miles instead of three yards,*—and that the term *exadversum* may be as justly rendered "before" as "behind." But, above all, his accuracy is incontestably assured by the fact that he is the very latest authority on the subject. Having identified the temple, his next step has been to form a series of deductions of his own, which he has done with surprising skill, whereby he has been enabled to rename all of Roriborialli's places ; and no one who knows anything of his ability can any more doubt of the fixedness and finality of his nomenclature than of the egregious credulity of those persons who doubted not the same thing of the nomenclature of the old-timey Roriborialli. In my descriptions I shall adhere to Sig. Pochinozi implicitly.

It is a difficult matter to give within restricted limits a satisfactory view of a city which in its various aspects

---

* As somewhat pertinent to this point, *cf.* the memorable controversy concerning the signification of the words *pluribus verbis* in the oration of Cicero for Marcellus.

has afforded material for hundreds of volumes without exhausting the subject. To describe everything that was shown me would be simply an outrage upon any but a mouldy archæological reader, and I shall therefore confine myself to a matter-of-fact description of some of the more prominent objects of interest without aspiring to seem learned or original,—and, above all, to the best of my ability stifling those reflections on the transitory nature of earthly things and soliloquies on the Past with which most writers on Rome feel constrained to get bemaudled. When I was there I was too full of fleas to be reflective; but though my cuticle is no more irritated and I can now sentimentalize in peace, it is not consistent with the reputation, which I have no scruple in forestalling for myself of being the most trustworthy of didactic travelers, that I should pass off my own manufacture for nature's genuine article,—no, not even though, as I verily believe, the most accomplished expert could not distinguish between them. In undertaking to give some account of the city, I find that it is difficult, too, to know where to begin. In leading us around, our guide adopted a plan of his own too complex to be understood by us, and too digressive to be followed in description. On the whole, I think the simplest and best way will be to consult my own convenience.

Let us, in the first place, consider the churches. The number of these is legion, or, at any rate, is much above three hundred, and more are in process of erection. One of the most important of the Pope's spiritual functions is the building and repairing of churches, and I visited several of them in which scaffolding and mortar-beds formed prominent features of the interior scene. Among such a multitude of structures designed for the same special purpose, there must necessarily often occur a near approach to uniformity of style and decoration, and one must be a devoted church-goer who does not soon tire of them. The renowned St. Peter's, of course, leads the list. Every one who has seen this stupendous pile has remarked upon the false conception of its dimensions as a whole and in detail which is formed at first sight. Whether the illusion is to be attributed, as is commonly asserted, to the harmonious proportion of all the parts, or to some other cause, I fully concur in the general opinion that it exists, and that nothing short of physical demonstration can dispel it. It is surprising how completely one is set back who presumptuously thinking to take a saint by the hand, finds when he has approached that he can barely reach his Worship's toe; or, when he would pat the little leg of a baby cherub, perceives it suddenly swell under his touch into a full-grown seraphic calf.

From the façade of the building there branches out at each extremity a majestic colonnade formed by four rows of columns, extending forwards in a semicircular sweep, and numbering altogether two hundred and eighty-four. Nearly two hundred statues of saints look down from the entablature which surmounts these columns. The effect of the colonnade is admirable, such as befits the entrance of a temple. The space inclosed by these semicircles is embellished with two fine fountains, while from its centre rises one of those Egyptian obelisks which the Roman emperors were so wont to bring over for the adornment of the city.

On entering the church our attention is directed to a line of stars set in the pavement at different distances from each other; these are signs of vanity designed to vaunt the excess of St. Peter's over other vast fanes, both of Christendom and Heathendom. Thus, according to the data appended to the stars, this church is two hundred and fifty-three feet longer than St. Sophia of the infidel Turk; while it is ninety-three feet and a half longer than St. Paul's of London, the masterpiece of us Protestants,—being itself six hundred and thirteen feet and a half long. I saw no comparison made with the Cathedral of Seville, and on expressing my surprise thereat was coolly informed by the guide that they had never heard in Rome of any such structure. As I have said, we do not realize its magnitude at once. We glance about without being awed,—in fact, almost without being impressed,—and deem it to be only a fair-sized pile, till in making some examination we discover how grossly we have deceived ourselves, and then its vastness and grandeur break upon us.

Passing along the nave, after many steps we presently stand beneath the great dome. Panegyric has been exhausted in attempting to describe the sublimity of this marvelous work. It gives but the skeleton of a conception of it to say that it is a hundred and thirty-nine feet in diameter, and that the altitude from the pavement to its summit is four hundred and five feet. The vault is adorned with gilded stucco ornaments and mosaics, bold and exaggerated in execution in order that they may be defined at that great height, but softened into beauty by the distance. Around its base is inscribed in letters six feet long that passage of Scripture on which the Catholic Church so greatly relies for its exaltation of the apostle Peter: *Tu es Petrus, et super hanc petram ædificabo ecclesiam meam, et tibi dabo claves regni cœlorum.* But the dome as seen from the interior, vast as it is, is but an inner shell, for surrounding it is another dome a hundred and ninety-five feet and a half in diameter, and between the two runs a stairway by which an ascent may be made to the ball and cross that crown the whole. Four enormous piers, two hundred and fifty-three feet in circumference, sustain this " Pantheon in the air." Beneath the dome rises grandly the baldachin, or canopy of the high altar, composed largely of bronze which, in obedience to a proclivity that we have frequent occasion to deplore in Rome, was ruthlessly torn from the Pantheon; and beneath the high altar, which is plain for so grand a temple, and in the subterranean church, is the *sanctum sanctorum*—the tomb reverenced as that of St. Peter. In front of the high altar is a large open crypt surrounded by a marble balustrade, in which is placed an imposing statue of Pius VI. in the attitude of prayer before the tomb.

There are a multitude of chapels in St. Peter's, and these are especially worthy of attention as displaying one of the most interesting features connected with the church,—the reproduction of celebrated paintings in mosaic. There are very few paintings proper in St. Peter's, but nearly every chapel is adorned with one or more of these mosaic copies, which, regarded merely in their mechanical aspect, are beautiful and wonderful.

There is also a great array of sepulchral monuments, exhibiting this sombre sort of sculpture of various degrees of merit and under a diversity of designs,—some of them fantastical, some hyperbolical, and a few natural. They are erected principally to the memory of departed Popes, though other parties whose claim to be commemorated herein is not altogether unimpeachable have contrived to get their monuments smuggled in amongst the number. In obedience to the undying perversity of political opinions we have here, on a memorial to the last of the royal race of Stuarts, the Pretender, as his opponents stigmatize him, dignified by the title of James III., and his sons styled kings of England by implication; while in the church below, where they lie buried, all three are assigned the sceptre under the explicit titles of James III., Charles III., and Henry IX.

One of the prime objects of attraction in St. Peter's is that far-famed bronze statue which good Catholics so adore. These say that it is the similitude of the saint himself, and a most precious work wrought by holy hands in early Christian times; but their enemies will have it that it is no more nor less than Jupiter, the heathen, unchivalrously discrowned and transfigured, and made to personate his mighty rival and subduer. But be he St. Peter or St. Jupiter, there he sits black and rusty on a marble chair, with his foot stuck well to the front and, with all respect be it spoken, of a decidedly unchristian, ungainly, and unprepossessing presence. Notwithstanding, however, that his appearance is so against him he is regarded with the utmost veneration, and the faithful deem it a paramount duty on entering the church to press their foreheads against his foot and kiss the toe that presents itself so complacently to their lips. It is said that he has been kissed stump-toed by centuries of osculation; but the crowd pressing around him was so large that I was unable to verify the statement. Most of those whom I saw making the salutation were priests; and I was scandalized by observing the unseemly efforts these holy men made to squeeze in before each other. A young priest, I noticed, over-sensible of his unworthiness, was outflanked more than a dozen times by his self-righteous and more obtrusive brethren.

Owing to the interposition of certain red-tape restrictions we were prevented from carrying out that part of the programme which requires the visitor to descend into the damps of the charnel-house below and ascend to the giddy summit of the dome above,— whereby we escaped being poisoned by sepulchral vapors in the one, and being hurled down in apoplexy from the other. Seats were being erected and other preparations going on in the body of the church for the reception of the Œcumenical Council which had been summoned to convene here; and I am not surprised to learn since that several who came to the convocation and sat all day in this barn of a place, listening to and talking Latin in the depth of winter, have yielded up the ghost.

St. Peter's stands on the right bank of the Tiber, amidst a jumble of other buildings. The usual approach to it takes us by the Castle of St. Angelo,—whilom the Tomb of Hadrian, now the Pope's earthly tower of strength,—whose cannon, however, are almost exclusively used to bellow forth his glory and honor and to assist in operating the somewhat complex machinery of the Catholic ritual. As we cross the river, if we turn our heads and look down the stream, we shall see one of the most impressive sights that Rome can show,—the melancholy relics of the bridge called the Triumphal, the prescribed pathway over which her heroes marched in glorious procession into the city.

I do not intend to enlarge on the churches, but I must say a few words about St. Paul's without-the-city, which is, I think, the most pleasing church I ever entered. It is the successor of one of the oldest Christian temples in the world, which after standing for nearly fifteen hundred years was almost utterly consumed by fire in 1823. Though there is much to be done to it yet, it is sufficiently near completion to give the visitor an adequate idea of the character and scope of its design. No place of worship I have seen can compare with it for elegant splendor combined with majestic simplicity. It exhibits one of the rare instances in ecclesiastical architecture where a profusion of material has been tastefully wrought up. Instead of lavishing his resources on details, the architect has concentrated them on the erection of a noble colonnade of eighty Corinthian columns, each of a single piece of granite, with marble capitals, arranged in four rows extending the length of the edifice between the nave and aisles; and no one who has not beheld it can conceive the grandeur of this simple plan. The baldachin over the high altar, itself a magnificent work, is sustained by four columns of alabaster, each of which is also a single piece, fraternally presented to Pope Gregory XVI. by that chivalric old heathen man, Mehemet Ali, Viceroy of Egypt. A striking characteristic of this church is the extensive series of portraits of the Popes done in mosaic, which is intended to include all of them, beginning with St. Peter and running on *in secula seculorum*.

With all its magnificence it is likely that this church will never have a flourishing congregation, for, in the first place, it is entirely out of town,—so that none but the very pious are going to journey so far to attend divine service; and in the second place, those who go are extremely apt to be struck down in the flower of their piety by the chills which make the neighborhood accursed.

I must at least mention the church of St. Agnes without-the-city,—worthy to be visited as the best representative of the ancient churches now left at Rome, and especially memorable as the scene where a mighty miracle was wrought in this our day. It appears that Pope Pius IX. being by some chance hereabouts one afternoon in the year of grace 1854 was invited within by the brethren who tabernacle here to partake of some refreshment. While at meat with divers dignitaries of high degree in the ecclesiastical, civil, and military services, all unconscious of what was coming, or rather going,—lo, the floor broke down and the Sovereign Pontiff, the dignitaries of degree, the holy brotherhood in waiting, the crockery and the victuals, all slid into the cellar together. And now, behold the miracle! St. Peter descending interposed, and leaving the rest of the assembly to shift for themselves clamped his worthy successor; and, albeit he is of a portly make, let him down as gently as two hundredweight of feathers on the soft carcasses of those below,— so that, while sundry of his festal companions were sorely bewildered, becrippled, and begreased, His Holiness was scarcely soiled. All these particulars are matters of record, for they are preserved in an admirable fresco painted on the wall in commemoration of the event, which faithfully represents the table upsetting and the dishes and contents slipping off, while the dignitaries are rearing and kicking, perfectly demoralized,—one in especial being seen making furiously for a window grated too closely to let out a cat,—the whole forming a most thrilling picture, on which I gazed in rapture, for I am not insensitive to humorous subjects seasonably presented. St. Peter looms powerfully in the fresco amid the wreck of household and kitchen furniture,—though our guide, who was a witness of the catastrophe, does not remember seeing him, unless, indeed, that *gendarme* whom he saw hauling Pius out of the ruins was the apostle in disguise. Be this as it may, however, Pius himself, who is naturally the best judge in the matter, is satisfied that a special miracle was performed in behalf of his corporal salvation, and in grateful recollection of it he has repaired and adorned the edifice, and having in particular confirmed and immovably established the flooring goes thither every year to offer up thanksgiving for the great deliverance. But while he thus unequivocally shows his own estimate of the affair it is but just to add that I have heard that the dignitaries whose heads were cracked and shins barked do not think it was so mighty much of a miracle after all.

The basilica of the Lateran is one of the most famous churches of Rome, but I will only say of it that I there saw the identical well of the Woman of Samaria, dug up and brought over by some pious hand,—or, at any rate, they show the marble curb of it; and also a table marking the height of Christ, being six feet high. Connected with this church is the celebrated *Scala Santa*, or sacred stairway, belonging originally, they say, to Pilate's house, and by which the Saviour descended from the judgment-hall. No foot is allowed to tread these steps, but whoever wishes to ascend must do so on his knees. It is deemed a potent means of grace to do this, and at all times there can be seen several penitents making their way to the top in this fashion, presenting a curious, an uncouth, yea, a humiliating spectacle—*i.e.* to us Protestants, stiff-kneed and incredulous generation that we are. I perceived one prayerful old man, a "poor child of Doubt and Death, whose hope was built on reeds," with the rheumatism, or some other impediment in his joints, desperately toiling on, triumphing the more abundantly for the difficulties that clogged his progress, and working an amount of damage to his articular structures that a whole dozen of opodeldoc would scarce undo. The attrition of innumerable knee-pans long ago threatened to utterly grind away the original marble of the steps, and they were planked over to save them,—since which time three suits of plank have been rubbed out.

Let us leave the churches and next turn our attention to the Vatican. But who is long-winded enough to fully describe this, and who is long-suffering enough to read the description? How can I be expected to recount all I saw in four thousand four hundred and twenty-two rooms?—not, indeed, that I really entered that many, but that is the number in the Vatican, and we went into enough of them to come out dazed and mystified beyond recapitulation. Let it suffice to say that we gazed upon myriads of paintings—though what they were I do not remember, except that I know from the accounts of my predecessors that many of them are great masterpieces of art which once seen can never be forgotten; also, an incalculable quantity of feet, legs, arms, and hands of statues, and even whole ones, whose execution it may be lawful for the present race of sculptors to hope to imitate but is madness to aspire to rival, and which haunt the memory like some beatific vision—though what they were like has almost slipped my recollection. We saw, moreover, a vast accumulation of very indifferent-looking pieces of stone called Roman antiquities, the scrapings of old graveyards and such places which the unhallowed hands of resurrectionists have rooted up and carted hither from the last resting-places of those ancient defuncts who were so unfortunate as to have been put away in something of style. Furthermore, we were trotted through an immense and most precious library of some forty thousand books and twenty-four thousand manuscripts in Turkish, Coptic, Chinese, Sclavonic, etc., not one of which we were allowed to read. Would that I had the memory of an ostrich that I might be able to relate, and my reader the ears of an ass that he might be able to take in, but a thousandth part of the wonders that are here displayed! But, alas! almost the only thing I distinctly remember is the sight I obtained of the rare and costly gifts bestowed upon the Holy Father by the kings and princes who in these patricidal times remain dutiful sons of the Church,— or, let me more correctly say, my attempt to get a sight of them, for my remembrance of the treasures themselves is likewise miserably misty.

The kingly offerings were kept in an apartment to themselves, where they lay in state, only a limited number of persons being allowed to behold them at the same time, and an obdurate janitor standing at the door to admit the spectators in turn. This apartment became a point of special attraction, and a large crowd collected there, a goodly part of it, you may be sure, being constituted of the justly denominated soft sex, who, as every man secretly believes,—and they can't intimidate me into suppressing the fact,—will suffer themselves to be compressed till they are solidified for a glimpse at a piece of jim-crackery. Naturally, under these circumstances, there was a good deal of pressure, and not a little counter-pressure. As for me, I maintained strictly an armed neutrality, making no aggressions whatever, but being content with holding my own.

While thus comporting myself in a most placable, inoffensive manner, of a sudden a great surge vibrated through the assembly, whereby a little Italian gentleman, standing with a lady directly in front of me, was goaded into a frenzy, and, falling straightway into a paroxysm of maniacal convulsions, began kicking up behind and before, and especially butting backwards into me individually with surpassing venomousness. No candid person, I am certain, would see anything but the merest dictate of self-protection in the upraising of my leg and the projecting forth of my foot in the manner of a cow-catcher,— an expedient which I adopted, and which checked up the little Italian gentleman with the most gratifying thoroughness.

No candid person would condemn this proceeding,— nevertheless it wonderfully stirred up the bile and acrimony of a gallant, hot-faced man of London, who stood in the crowd with his hat on the back of his head viewing the scene with the steady dignity of a fat statue. Said the gallant, hot-faced man of London to me, "Aren't you hany manners? Wot are you a shovin' of 'im fer? Don't you see the gent must purtect 'is missus from bein' smashed? You a Hinglishman and do sich a thing!— fer shame!"

Now, this was too bad. It was sufficiently irritating for a passive recipient of injury to be denounced as an active aggressor, but for a citizen of the great and free Republic of America to be accounted a subject of the old, tyrannical monarchy of Britain was absolutely intolerable. As the reader of course knows, from what I have heretofore candidly told him of myself, I am a man pre-eminently possessing all the kindly traits and gentler virtues of humanity,—and it has been observed by the sages that the wrath of a long-suffering man is terrible. So the man of London found it, for I fell foul of him with a surprising force of language, denying utterly any complicity in the shoving, and especially repelling with almost inarticulate indignation his atrocious assumption of fellow-citizenship. He withdrew both charges, and was so captivated with the great spirit I had displayed as to propose that we should consolidate ourselves against the crowd who were pressing savagely in rear; but I declined the coalition, bidding him shove behind if he were so minded, but for my part, I told him, I now meant to push to the front.

In the mean time, those in the vicinity had taken the matter up in Italian, French, and English, and for a time it was as if the thunders of the Vatican had bursted amongst us. At this juncture the door opened, the concourse fermented violently, and the little Italian with the lady had another awful fit. In dancing about his charge with the intention of keeping me back, he missed his own opportunity of entering, and at the same time bestowed upon me an auspicious side-long butt with so much heart-felt energy as to knock me clean to the door, through which I passed triumphantly; and, as the portal closed, I saw him dancing with undiminished vigor.

CHAPTER XXII.

The Relics of the Ancient City.

HAVING acquitted myself in some sort of my obligations to the ecclesiastical structures, I propose now to cast a glance at some of the objects whose glories are of another day. And, first of all, let us betake ourselves to the Capitol. Climbing the steep we are confronted by an assemblage of statues and monuments, including two lions, Castor and Pollux holding their horses, the first and seventh milestones belonging to the Appian Way, and the admirable bronze equestrian statue of Marcus Aurelius, a relic of ancient art which has been spared to us from the anti-pagan zeal of the middle age professors of our faith by the fortunate hallucination that induced the good people to revere it as the semblance of the Christian emperor Constantine. We now find ourselves in a square which is surrounded on three sides by massive but unimpressive buildings; and we wonder which of these three edifices is the Capitol. We conclude that the central one is,—firstly, because it is in the middle, and secondly, because it has a high tower sticking out of its roof. And then we sorrow to behold so poor a representative of the ancient structure,—that stately pile whose grandeur we have so often pictured to our imagination, and which, mayhap, in our enthusiam we have even denationalized ourselves so far as to conceive almost as resplendent as our own unmatchable conglomerate at Washington.

But, in sooth, it appears that neither of these three is the Capitol, there being no such edifice now in existence. If there be any which is worthy to be deemed such, it is the central building aforesaid, both on account of its position and tower aforesaid, and especially on account of the fact that therein sits the solemn court of police to try drunk and disorderly Romans. Yet, though it is not the Capitol itself, it may be assumed with as much certainty as we can ever attain to in Rome that it at least occupies the site of the Capitol; and in poking about in its cellar we were shown certain stones which we were positively assured were the substructions of its illustrious predecessor. As we wandered about the spot, therefore, we experienced something of a sensation from the tolerable certainty that beneath our feet was ground made famous by great men and great deeds; that here the long line of the three hundred laureled victors had come one by one to consummate their triumph, and that where we stood historic Gaul and Goose had stood before us.

The central building is known as the Palace of the Senator. Excepting its tower, which affords a grand and instructive panoramic view of the surrounding country, it has nothing of especial interest about it. On the right-hand side of the space stands the Palace of the Conservators, these Conservators being a species of City Fathers. Herein is a suite of rooms devoted to illustrious Italians, where their busts are displayed for the titillation of the natives and the dumbfounding of such foreigners as have rashly concluded that Italy has been decaying since the glorious old Roman times. And, really, I was not prepared for the magnitude of the spectacle, for it indicated that this ancient land has always been as full of great men as a superannuated cheese is of skippers. The Palace also contains a fair supply of heads, hands, and feet pertaining to bronze and marble worthies, as well as entire busts and statues of other worthies—most of which have been identified by the antiquarians, generally by intuition. It boasts, also, an accumulation of old vases and pots, and a gallery of pictures, comprising scriptural subjects mostly; but though the pictures are numerous, they are said by those versed in such things to be of indifferent execution. The rooms, nine in number, especially set apart for the City Fathers are decorated with frescoes representing events in early Roman history, and are enlivened with busts of the departed, sarcophaguses, sculptures of the gates of hell, bronze ducks, etc., and in them are contained the *Fasti Consulares*, very interesting antiques, being a list of the office-holders of the ancient city; as, likewise, the standard measures of the present day, inclusive of the standard sturgeon, whose length limits that of such of this delightful fish as it is lawful for common fishers to take for their own behoof,—all in excess of the statutory dimensions being confiscated and devoured in the name of the Senate and People of Rome by the Fathers themselves.

The old pots and vases above mentioned are also a part of the adornments of these apartments; but, above all, they hold the Bronze Wolf of the Capitol. This celebrated relic of the olden time shows a she-wolf standing in a posture of defiant vigilance, with the little Romulus and Remus ravenously sucking the milk of conquest; and it at once awakens the active interest of the beholder independently even of its claims on the score of antiquity and the legend it illustrates, for, while the maternal ferocity exhibited rather chills us, our hearts yearn with tenderness as we gaze on the little black, upturned faces and little, rusty, outstretched arms of the poor, hungry innocents. A father of a family might well melt in sympathy with the touching picture; and, even I, contemplating the unwonted magnanimity of the wolf, was encouraged, and entertained a momentary thought of risking myself with a wife. Fearful have been the contests amongst the learned in the struggle to identify this image with all the images of wolves mentioned in ancient history. Some say it is that wolf spoken of by Dionysius and Livy. Some say nay, it is that wolf referred to by vainglorious Cicero in detailing the marvelous works wrought in his consulship by the immortal gods—among the marvels a prominent one being the striking of the said wolf with lightning; and these point triumphantly to the marks yet visible, especially a fracture of the leg, as irrefragable proof of the solvency of their opinion. Some say, again, that it is neither of these wolves separately, but both of them conjointly; and there are not wanting others who say that the fracture of the leg was not done by lightning at all, but is attributable to the natural frailty of legs under undue stress and pressure. Dense-brained and thick-headed men have gone mad and burned to tear the eyes out of their adversaries' sockets for misuse of their vision in discussing this momentous topic; sure, therefore, it is not meet for me to say what I think of it.

On the opposite side of the square from the Palace of the Conservators is the Museum of the Capitol. This is filled with statues, busts, altars, sculptures, sarcophaguses, inscriptions, urns, vases, nondescript stones, and such like, in mass and pulverized, too numerous and diverse even to be mentioned. I will specify only that renowned work, the Dying Gladiator, so called—he that Byron saw before him lie. He has a rope around his neck, and a horn is near his hand. He is down and about to die, but he holds himself up for a little while. In all respects the attitude and expression of the figure are most truthful. There is no difference of opinion amongst the critics concerning this statue except the everlasting and inevitable one as to what it is intended to portray. Our fathers died in the absurd belief that it was a dying gladiator, as its name betokens; but we, wiser in our generation, have positively settled it to be an expiring Greek, a herald by profession,—as witness his horn. There can be no manner of doubt that our children will establish it on an immovable basis to be something else,—as witness the rope. I know nothing better fitted to impress the salutary lesson of the mutability of human affairs than these Roman relics. As we meditate upon their transversations from age to age and year to year we are irresistibly borne down by the overwhelming realization that this is, indeed, a world of change, and that, of a verity, not anything is certain.

I had a vehement yearning for a sight of the Tarpeian Rock, the brink of the Roman rebel's last ditch, which it is claimed is somewhere in this neighborhood. More complaisant than usual, the guide showed me two of them. The one I saw to most advantage was approached by raiding into some man's back-yard, and to his manifest surprise. He came forth and stared hard at me, and so did his wife and family of small children. Under their rigid surveillance, I stretched my neck and gazed diligently up as directed; but, if I saw anything, I have forgotten what it looked like.

In the valley at the foot of the Capitoline Hill was the Roman Forum, occupying the site now called—alas, for the degenerating power of time!—the cow-lot (*campo vaccino*). It is inexpressibly mournful to think of this degrading change of nomenclature, and it becomes yet sadder as we feel that this example proclaims what may in the lapse of time be the fate of our own high places. How lamentable is the apprehension that in future ages the site of our own most glorious Capitol may be known as the ass-fold!—and yet, who can doubt the reasonableness of the fear? Somewhere in this cow-lot—but the antiquaries have whipped the boundary marks hither and thither so often that nobody knows exactly where—the Clays, and Websters, and George Francis Trains of the period thundered; and in this cow-lot the Sovereign People again and again assembled to pass resolutions, adopt platforms, nominate candidates, and save the country; and since an assembly of the Sovereign People has been the same thing from the foundation of the world to the present epoch, we cannot question that over and over again, in expressing the sense of the meeting, the families residing in the vicinity were howled into distraction, lamps demolished, stove-pipes torn down, and the lot inundated with tobacco-juice. The Sovereign People, or some other malign agency, has made a thorough wreck of it, and no man now is certain of the location of anything excepting the Signors Roriborialli and Pochinozi and their disciples, who, indeed, know everything, but, unfortunately, are as diametrically as the poles opposed in their knowledge. A few battered and time-worn columns and fragments of stone, giving forth ambiguous responses to his questioning, are all that remain for the general observer to note, but the bare place itself is all-sufficient to evoke recollections which will speak to him with an eloquent power that needs no visible aid to enforce it.

From the Forum we may pass to that other and stupendous wreck, the Coliseum. Despite the demolitions and neglect to which this enormous structure has been so long subjected, and the fact that time after time, for a space of nearly two centuries, its walls were resorted to for building materials, a third of it yet remains to startle the mind with the idea of what it must have been when it stood in all its vastness and splendor. It covers an area of almost six acres, and, as was the case with amphitheatres generally, is elliptical in form, the arena being two hundred and seventy-eight feet long in the greater diameter and one hundred and seventy-seven in the lesser. As applied to the whole building these dimensions become five hundred and eighty-four and four hundred and sixty-eight feet respectively. It has four stories, three of them formed of arches, and with a tier of seats to each story, and it is stated that it could accommodate eighty-seven thousand persons.

The performances here were inaugurated by Titus with a brilliant season extending over more than three months. His exhibitions on this opening occasion were gotten up with a lavish expenditure of money and beasts, five thousand of the latter having been disbursed. His successors were not behind him in zealous catering for the public amusement. Under their management lions, bears, boars, elks, zebras, ostriches, and men were kept continually fluttering, fussing, and fighting in the arena. But while slaughter was their ultimate aim they made some effort to have it done in a scientific and æsthetic manner. With this view they brought into requisition what little mechanical art the rapidly degenerating period could afford. Thus, at times, they had the arena set forth with an artificial forest, that the animals might feel at home and so be nerved to the acme of combativeness by the beguiling thought that they were striking for their altars and their fires. At another time the vast space was transformed into a lake, on whose surface a ship would be made to sail, so contrived that it would presently open and turn out a multitude of ferocious monsters, mortal enemies of one another, and then shutting itself up quietly, move off, leaving them adrift to settle it amongst themselves.

From all accounts the slaughter of varmints at these exhibitions must have been prodigious. But the prime attraction was the gladiatorial combats. At times the sacrifice of men almost vied with that of animals. The emperor Probus set three hundred pairs of fencers to fighting, and kept them at it to the death. But while the recollection of these things stirs the mind of the traveler as he treads the arena, most impressive of all is the knowledge that these walls have witnessed the agony and this earth has drunk the blood of countless Christian men and women; and he will not resist the feeling of reverence and thankfulness excited by the sight of the cross that rises in the midst to consecrate the place where they were butchered to make a Pagan holiday and show the triumph of the faith for which they died.

For four or five hundred years the Coliseum continued the scene of these disports with man and beast. Many of the animals that figured in the lists were of a sort seldom seen in Rome, and of which very little was known; hence it has been reasonably surmised that these shows were countenanced by the respectable and intelligent portion of the community purely with a view to the furtherance of the study of natural history—just as in our day many irreproachable Christian ladies and gentlemen attend the menagerie-circus altogether, as is well known, to perfect themselves in zoological knowledge. When at length an itinerant preacher, bent upon doing good out of season, was slain in the arena, whither he had penetrated for the purpose of admonishing a couple of red-hot gladiators on the impropriety of their conduct, the sentiments of the authorities underwent a radical and most salutary change, and the brutal exhibitions were forever abolished. The glory of the Coliseum having no longer any patron to foster it departed, and the building itself was left to battle unaided against the assaults of time.

One of the most celebrated relics of ancient Rome is the Pantheon, remarkable alike for its architectural beauty and grandeur and for its invincible tenacity of existence under the persistent efforts of man and the elements to destroy it. Fire, water, wind, and dirt have exhausted their malice upon it, and it has time and again been robbed of its metal- and marble-work by Goth, Vandal, and Pope. Houses have been built against it and shanties in it, and the architects of these hovels scrupled not to break away any part of it that interfered with the symmetry of their edifices. Yet, it has withstood all this. Its beauty has in all ages commanded for it protectors and adorners, each one protecting and adorning it according to his own notions of how this should be done, the consequence being an awful conglomeration of styles and tastes. It has withstood all this, too; and now remains the best preserved as well as one of the most imposing of the ancient structures.

In the Pantheon are the tombs of several noted artists. It had been stated for a long time that the bones of the illustrious painter Raphael rested here,—all except his skull, which was preserved and exhibited with religious veneration by the Academy of Fine Arts, otherwise of St. Luke. The antiquaries, however, were not satisfied with this statement, and they proceeded diligently to work to investigate and rectify the matter. The upshot of this rectification was that men's minds were so unhinged that common people knew not what to believe about it. As for the antiquaries themselves, of course there was no cloudiness in their ideas,—one set being as certain as that they were alive that Raphael was buried there, and the other being as sure as that they would die that he was not,—and under these respective convictions they argued powerfully with each other.

There is nothing more deplorable than disputes between learned men, for it is impossible to set a limit to the evil that directly and indirectly springs from them. On the present occasion the most honorable Society of Antiquaries contrived, unwittingly I am sure, to deal so grievous a blow upon a sister society as to leave it sore and touchy even to this day.

The admirable science of Phrenology was then in its infancy and eagerly seeking facts in every quarter to sustain itself. It had ransacked all the anatomical museums in Europe, and fingered every skull it could lay its paws on. It had pounced upon Raphael's in the Academy of St. Luke among the very first, and to its joy found it to yield absolutely irrefragable proofs of the soundness of its doctrines. Had there been given to it power to make a painter's skull in perfect accordance with the principles of the new philosophy it would needs have modeled it identically after this one. There was the bump of Ideality to conceive the subject, of Form to limn it down artistically, and of Color to daub it glowingly,—all as prominent and bulgy as if they had been raised by the thump of a ten-pound muller. Nothing was ever seen more conclusive, and the advocates of Phrenology held the skull aloft in triumph, and the opponents turned their eyes from it in dismay.

Now it fell out at last that the functionaries of the city became so worked up, bewildered, and uneasy, through the argumentation of the antiquaries that to calm their nerves they were impelled to open the reputed tomb and settle the dispute by ocular inspection. It was knocked to pieces accordingly, when behold! there lay Raphael, skull and all!—and all susceptible of identification beyond the shadow of a doubt even of an antiquary. We may well suppose that the academicians of St. Luke were distressed by this unhappy annihilation of their venerated relic; but how can we realize the feelings of the unfortunate phrenologists, the innocent victims of a miserable wrangle in which they were never implicated! And will it be believed, that on top of this enormous injury, which, as I have said, I am willing to think unintentional, the antiquaries have actually gone to work and wantonly proved that the academical skull belonged to a man with really next to no gifts at all!

When an old Roman had done with the business of the Forum and the pleasures of the Coliseum, and his days were numbered, it was a great point with his relations and friends to have him decently interred; and there are numerous monuments remaining to show how sumptuously and substantially those who died seized of much possessions were laid away. But Time the Everlasting Gnawer, beneath whose adamantine fangs even files give away, has made havoc with these grand mausoleums. Of the majority of them scarce more than a vestige is left. Some have come to base uses, as that of Augustus, where once reposed the ashes of many a mighty and honored personage, which has dwindled away, degenerating as it dwindled, first into a fortress, then into a bull-ring, and now what is left of it is employed as an exhibition hall for acrobatic feats on the tight-rope and jim-crow performances. The tomb of Hadrian, likewise, was put on a war-footing at an early period, the statues which adorned it having been used as ammunition against the heads of Gothic besiegers, and it has remained a military stronghold ever since, being the Castle of St. Angelo of the present day. What has become of its original owner it would be hard to say, but Pope Innocent II. laid violent hands on his porphyry ash-urn and made off with it for his own behoof. Of all these sumptuously-lodged defuncts Caius Cestius has been much the most fortunate in his tomb, for his executors were men well versed in sepulchral architecture, who had it built in the fashion of a pyramid, whereby its stability under the destroying operation of natural agencies was provided for, and upon a plan that afforded no facilities for diverting it from its legitimate purpose, whereby mischievous interlopers were kept out. As a consequence it stands in good order and well-conditioned to this day. As for Caius himself, as of Cheops, his illustrious predecessor in a pyramid, not a pinch of dust remains, and so of all the rest of those rich and honored men—their urns are empty.

One of the most interesting of the tombs is that of Cæcilia Metella, wife of Crassus, situated about two miles from the city on the Appian Way. It remains almost perfect, at least externally. It, too, was at times held as a fortress, for which its construction was well adapted, it being in the form of a circular tower, and built with extreme solidity and strength. The garrison surmounted it with a battlement, which still exists to show the warlike purposes it has subserved. To some it may seem in a measure unbecoming to be brawling and fighting in a woman's grave, but we survivors of our own war, of both political complexions, to whom was occasionally vouchsafed the unspeakable mercy of contending with the enemy from behind the tombstones in a graveyard, will ask for time to consider before expressing an opinion on the point. I went in and inspected the interior of the structure. There was nothing to see but a round hole filled with rubbish. In coming up out of the hole I was waylaid by two vicious old women, who sternly demanded to be reimbursed for the sight I had taken; but holding that every man has an inalienable right to descend into the tomb gratis, I put myself in a posture of offense and fought my way through them.

Besides the famous monuments of antiquity of which I have now made mention, there are numerous others at Rome,—arches, temples, columns, palaces, circuses, aqueducts, baths, sewers,—which I must ignore lest I should be tempted to say too little, or else too much of them, and so endanger this beau-ideal of travel-books by the reproach of plagiarizing the plain preciseness of the house-for-sale advertisements, or the ornate sentiment of the Young Lady's Select Extracts. A word or two about that melancholy chaos, the Palace of the Cæsars, and I have done.

Begun by Augustus, the palace was enlarged, contracted, remodeled, and transformed in various ways by succeeding emperors, till Nero hung up his fiddle and his bow, after burning it down, as they say, and started it afresh, when it attained its acme, being made to take in an immense extent of ground. Then it became one of the most sumptuous of edifices. He formed of it a grand treasure-house, inestimably rich, where were gathered the most precious productions of his empire. Of this "Golden House," as it was rightly called, the visitor will now behold hardly more than its primordial atoms that make the dust beneath his feet; and if he be a thoughtful man will gladly turn away his eyes from the sad spectacle, and, approaching the verge of the mount, relieve his burdened mind by contemplation of the extensive and impressive prospect that the point commands. Among the edifying objects included in the range of vision he may mark the gas-works and the Circus Maximus—a spot full of tender reminiscences, for here occurred the gobbling up of the Sabine virgins. Truly, he may as well look afar as near, for very little satisfactory knowledge will he get from peering at the Palace of the Cæsars.

The wrecks and crush of matter here scattered round past all identification have, of course, given rise to quantities of surmises, and we are constantly told that this dirt pile is supposed to be so-and-so, and that, thus-and-so,—but always with an air to impress us that the supposition is merely a modest mode of expressing a well-settled fact. Naturally, this has been a great battle-ground of Roriborialli and Pochinozi the aforesaid. Peter Rose, otherwise Signor Pietro Rosa, one of the most distinguished followers of Pochinozi, now holds absolute possession of the heights, and with consummate skill he has intrenched himself against all prospective assailants by the singularly efficacious plan of staking the place all over with sign-posts bearing his own designations, which are faced and strengthened with formidable references to the ancient writers.

For terseness and beauty, and no less for accuracy, no description of these ruins can equal Byron's comprehensive summary:

> "Cypress and ivy, weed and wallflower grown
> Matted and massed together, hillocks heaped
> On what were chambers, arch crush'd, column strown
> In fragments, choked up vaults, and frescos steep'd
> In subterranean damps, where the owl peep'd
> Deeming it midnight:—Temples, baths, or halls?
> Pronounce who can; for all that Learning reap'd
> From her research hath been, that these are walls—
> Behold the Imperial Mount! 'tis thus the mighty falls."

CHAPTER XXIII.

Of Rome in its Modern Relations: its Squares, Fountains, Picture-Galleries, Palaces, etc.; including Short Disquisitions on Art and Cotenancy—Of certain Great Rejoicings going on thereat, and a Vision of the Woman of Babylon—Concluding with the Sorrowful Story of good little Santy Tudwolley.

Some of the Sovereign Pontiffs during their domination in the City of the Cæsars have suffered the ancient monuments to go quietly along to decay; some have vigorously assisted them on the road to ruin; but many have generously stretched forth their hands and interposed to stay the cruel ravages of time. Besides looking after the old city, the more enlightened Pontiffs have paid some attention to the new. In their efforts they have had the powerful co-operation of the French, who at different times have associated themselves with them, sometimes as their very efficient friends and sometimes as their very disagreeable tormentors. This singular nation, as is well known, has an incurable penchant for fixing up and tricking out every people they overwhelm. The moment they have finished demolishing a place they set to work to bedeck it in the most tasteful manner,—a trait in which it must be confessed they display a delicacy and refinement of sentiment akin to that which impels us to strew flowers upon graves. The Pontiffs, as is fit, have confined themselves mainly to the religious improvement of the city,—that is, they have built and repaired vast numbers of churches; while the French have directed their attention mostly to secular matters, such as the laying out of squares, walks, etc., and the promotion of the public health and comfort.

One of the squares much indebted to the French for its improvement is the Piazza del Popolo, and this being close to my abode was the one I most affected while I sojourned in Rome. It is situated at the edge of the modern city, in that quarter which foreigners generally occupy, and at the foot of the Pincian Hill, which connoisseurs in the sublime and beautiful ascend to see the glorious orb of day decline in the west. From one side radiate three streets, whose vistas the eye can take in at the same glance—the centre one being the celebrated Corso, which, commencing its career under the sanctifying influence of a church at each initial corner, proceeds for a mile or more till it stops at the Capitol. The right-hand one of the trio goes to the classic yellowish-dirt-colored Tiber, only a short distance off, and the other penetrates into the depths of the city. The great object of attraction, however, presented by the piazza is the Egyptian obelisk towering in the midst of it, which originally belonged to the Temple of the Sun at Heliopolis, but which was brought to Rome by Augustus, as heretofore mentioned. Since his days it had fallen and become buried, but it was dug up and re-erected in this place by one of the Popes in 1587. It is cut from red granite and is about a hundred and twelve feet high, and is liberally bepictured with hieroglyphics. As appears from an inscription upon it, Augustus when he set it up dedicated it afresh to the sun; but the Popes have abrogated and nullified this heathenish proceeding completely and confirmed it to our faith by planting a cross firmly on the apex.

In former days, and more particularly in former nights, this square was a most abominable place. It was well known then, though the lapse of time has caused it to be not so well known now, that the reprobate Nero was buried here under a big chestnut-tree; and we have the best authority for saying that his grave was a famous old doggery for sundry old crony evil spirits of his, where they used to meet to kick up and carouse, and that citizens passing thereby were incessantly holloed at, made fun of, and insulted by these unprincipled rowdies. The citizens complained of this thing very much, representing to Pope Pascal that it was a shame, now that the city was regenerated to the true faith, for Christian people to have their feelings hurt in this way by a gang of low-bred heathens. Pope Pascal said he agreed with them, and would see if he could not put a stop to it. Accordingly, he marshaled his ecclesiastical army, equipped it with crosses, holy-water, and axes, and sallied forth in battle array against the enemy's tree. With his own hands he made the first dig at it, and the rest seconding him powerfully, in a little while the tree was demolished root and branch; and then something underneath it that looked very much as if it were Nero's ashes being hauled out, uplifted, and slung harum-scarum in the air, the work was done. The evil spirits, appalled by this majestic exhibition of the indignation of a righteous people, got away from there as fast as they could, and have never been back since. The spot was purified and an altar erected upon it,—and this was the beginning of the present church of Santa Maria del Popolo.

Many of the squares are furnished with fountains, which are, indeed, very numerous, and form a conspicuous feature of modern Rome. Some of them are of very elaborate design, and, as a general thing, the more show they make the less the taste they display. A few are harmonious and imposing, and not a few are incongruous and tame. They all utter forth a sufficiency of water, of whose detergent properties there is no reason to doubt, and it is a pity and a shame that more of it is not made use of.

It would be well worthy of reprehension were I, while treating of the existing characteristics of the Eternal City, to utterly ignore the galleries of paintings for which Rome is renowned and which make such a figure in the writings of my masterly predecessors. But, in truth, after all, the most I feel authorized to do is to give them a mere mention—an honorable mention. Whether I am actuated by real ignorance of art-matters, or only by false modesty in thinking myself ignorant,—whether by one or the other,—I have hitherto strongly intimated, and, in fact, said in so many words, and do now repeat most emphatically, that I know nothing about such things. It is, methinks, a little anomalous that this is so, for I am certainly not deficient in the poetic faculty,—as witness my "*Lament*" on receiving full thirty-nine lashes for disorderly demonstrations in the school-house; nor do I lack imagination, for I have seen a good quality of ghost. It is so, I believe, nevertheless. Doubtless it is unwise in me to make this acknowledgment. I should do as many an eminent critic has done before me—imagine inconceivable beauties in this picture, and point out imperceptible defects in that, and do it in high-sounding mystical technicalities. I should do this, and I am honestly certain that I could do it as effectively and with as much of the semblance of genuineness as most of the *dilettanti;* and you may be sure I would do it, but that I am a plain, honest man, wanting in discreetness and worldly wisdom,—as you will readily credit when you know that I am poor—dog-poor. I looked at all the masterpieces because I fully realized that it was my solemn duty to do so, and I have never shirked my solemn duty. Not entirely comprehending what I was expected to do or how I ought to feel, I conscientiously imitated those who were proficient. I saw the experts plant themselves before a picture, generally of a woman, —the men delineations, even when saints and martyrs, were not so much stared at,—fold their arms, drop into a catalepsy, and gaze, and gaze, and gaze, for untold minutes. I cannot doubt that this proceeding gave them pleasure, for to think one's self pleased is to be pleased; but I was not able to delude myself to the same extent. On adjusting my legs, arms, eyes, and hat to the orthodox positions, it would presently befall that my nether jaw would be irresistibly hauled away from its fellow, and then a cubit would seem to be added to my stature by the malignant elongation of a fit of the stretches. This peculiarity of impression made upon me by art-treasures was occasionally marked by some deep-dyed connoisseur, and with an air which showed that his mind was not altogether at ease about it; still, this circumstance did not deter me from discharging my duty,— though, indeed, I discharged it with all seemly haste, and having done it came away with a great buoyancy of feeling, such as one always experiences when he has manfully acquitted himself of an obligation.

To the wealth of pictures and sculptures left us by the old masters more is being constantly added. New masters and mistresses, too, from all the quarters of the globe turning Romewards like needles to the pole, are now camped there in droves, all daubing and chipping away for immortality. Their mode in general is to conceive an idea, please Heaven they can do so, or, if they cannot, to lay hands on one conceived by Shakspeare or Milton, or some other fertile man, and then hire somebody to materialize it. The daubers, it is true, from the peculiar requirements of their specialty are mostly under stress to do their own daubing; but the chippers can readily procure professional stone-masons to chisel out anything they can imagine. It is a source of national pride to know that a very great many pounds and yards of the productions of the new masters are secured for the galleries of our own country,—for there is no such patron of the arts as an American when he has got himself free of the sordid necessity of working for a living; and it is pleasing to add that he becomes an unprejudiced patron, encouraging the arts for their own sake alone—any lump of stone that is symmetrical, and any bundle of canvas that is pictorial, eliciting his favorable consideration—a remark that I must, however, limit to some extent by the qualification that the lump be hewn and the bundle be smeared in Italy—Home of Art.

The new masters are a most amiable and affable set of people, perfectly willing to receive visitors at their studios and to listen to commendations of their works. I paid my respects to several of them, and can speak highly of their urbanity and readiness to unveil their treasures and whirl them about on revolving pedestals for my satisfaction. I also gratefully acknowledge the edifying insight I obtained into the manufacture of statuary by inspection of myths in their inchoate state of mud, and in their advanced condition of plaster of Paris. Some of their finished pieces were really very beautiful. At one or two studios I noticed several works on the stocks which had been ordered by certain patriotic citizens of our land, who, fearful lest the remembrance of the late aggravating rebellion might die out from among men, had taken steps to perpetuate the recollection thereof in marble. Mr. Lincoln figured colossally at one place in plaster of Paris, depictured with a copy of the emancipation proclamation on his knee and a vast reed pen uplifted in his hand, and with an air of the profoundest preponderation upon his countenance—showing that he well merited the title of "Honest Old Abe" by the careful deliberation he exercised before disposing of so many million dollars' worth of other folks' property. If I were to say of this mass of plaster that it is a hard-looking production, the assertion would be attributed to partisan prejudice; or, were I to say that it is admirable in conception and faultless in execution, I would not be trusted, for I have already confessed my unfitness to pronounce on such matters. I will, therefore, say nothing —and the more willingly because I understood that when the embodiment should be perfected it would be planted on the top of a house high enough to enable it to hold its own against all adverse critics who did not resort to the mean advantage of bringing it down with a spy-glass.

Rome is richly supplied with palaces, wherein reside the over-plentiful magnates of the land. These magnates while very illustrious are also usually very economical, contenting themselves with a few of their ancestral halls for their own use, and renting out the rest as lodging-places for mankind, as well as stables for brutish beasts. As I have tested by experience, the abiding of sundry and distinct persons and animals in the same house does not inure to the highest development of that house. When, in the earlier days of my professional career, I had my office under the same roof with Mrs. Wodkins,— with Mr. Wodkins, commonly spoken of as the poor, old afflicted creature by Mrs. Wodkins,—with John Bunyan Wodkins and Patsy Geliny Wodkins, their son and daughter,—with Mrs. Ramshorne, otherwise the Old Reprobate; so invariably styled by Mrs. Wodkins, who waged everlasting war with her, on account of her belligerent and aggressive nature,—with Mrs. Rams-horne's small son and cat,—with Madam Oliphant, always called Elephint by Mrs. Wodkins, Astrologist, Phrenologist, and Ladies' Botanic Physician,—and with many more besides of lesser note, I well remember that the pulverization of window-glass, the deplastering of walls, the transmutation of wash-boards and banisters into fire-wood, the volatilization of the tops of chimneys, the mysterious disappearance of the back porch bodily, etc., moved our landlord at last to take the extraordinary step of making proclamation that whoso of his tenants would depart into some other habitation should have entire remission of his or her arrears of rent,—amounting in most cases to full two years,—and I remember further that this proclamation being derided and scouted, he was in the end obliged to sell the tenants along with the house to the highest bidder. Were it germane to the subject I might mention in addition the domineering of the terrible Old Reprobate over the feebler portion of the co-tenantry —especially her occasional overthrowing of poor, old afflicted Mr. Wodkins and frequent putting to flight of Mrs. Wodkins, as well as the intolerable hinderances she threw in the way of Madam Oliphant's quiet contemplation of the heavenly bodies on the house-top and of her peaceable prosecution of the study of the occult sciences generally; the regular incursions of the police, and the weekly presentation of the premises as a nuisance; the anguish of spirit of the landlord, helplessly beholding his property jumping to destruction; the flat denials of his integrity morally, and the indecorous likenings of him to unclean beasts physically; the shakings of fists in his face; the threats of kicks and projection from the summit to the base of the stairs, and grievous maimings and disfigurements, and other despiteful entreatments to which he was subjected when, making bold, he ventured thither to ask for his just dues; my own mortal and ever-present dread lest I should somehow become an unwitting victim of the universal anarchy around me; the periodical ruination of the stock of Moses Vhroghenschticher, drygoods and merchant tailor, occupying the store below, by the bursting of the water-pipes from overstuffing with old rags, potato-peelings, and such like; and a thousand other evils and calamities that sprang from this heterogeneous congregation. All of these things I might mention but refrain, hoping hereafter to give some little account of them in a large volume. The Roman palaces with their variety of occupants, it is true, have not suffered as much as did our habitation under similar circumstances; nevertheless, we find within them but an imperfect realization of the princely elegance and splendor which their grand and imposing exterior has led us to expect.

The houses of Rome are generally tall, and the balconied window which is so much affected in Southern Europe is rife here. The majority of them are built in a plain but substantial style of architecture, such as in our newer country is approved of for jails. Some, however, are quite ornate, and tolerably free and airy. The streets are narrow and tergiversating, with scarce ever a sidewalk; and while I saw on them an overwhelming abundance of priests I met exceeding few beggars,— though there be some who would have us believe that these two classes of our fellow-creatures do increase and multiply *pari passu*. If the inhabitants engage in any heavy commercial transactions they do it in a very clandestine way, for their shops present a decided passivity of aspect, the most prosperous of them apparently having less stock on hand and doing less business than one of our flourishing retail groceries. A perambulator about the city is obliged to conclude that Rome is dead, and that, unless his nasal organ be playing him false, she is rotten into the bargain. I would not speak aught of the afflicted but good. I deeply sympathize with the lone mother of dead empires and reverence her in her widowhood, and nothing would I utter that could anguish her aged brow. I therefore restrain myself and merely say that she is about the dismalest, nastiest, dirtiest, worst-flavored old hole I ever set foot in in all Christendom.

At the period of my stay in Rome the city was in a notable state of commotion and jubilee. The performances going on were part in honor of the saints and part in glorification of the Pope's own self,—certain great church festivals and fasts falling due at this time, and this also being the fiftieth anniversary of his Holiness's induction into the priesthood. Being myself a mere sojourner in the city and poorly skilled in churchly things, I found it difficult to discriminate between the divine and human phase of the ceremonies. I will, however, give some account of them as far as they came under my observation, and let the reader determine which was which for himself.

I have already in recounting my journey to the city made reference to the snap-judgment that was served on us in the matter of the illumination of St. Peter's by doing the lighting up on Saturday night instead of Sunday night, as per mutual understanding. The most noticeable feature of the Sunday celebration was the shutting up of the shops. In addition to this, when night came, several street-lamps had the usual plain gas-jets substituted by ornamental burners giving circular and spiral lines of flame, and looking very pretty. Some churches, also, had a sprinkling of paper lanterns hung to their fronts, and a few other places were in a measure illuminated. On the whole, however, the exhibition was very partial and imperfect, and seemed to indicate a serious diversity of opinion as to the intent and meaning of the programme.

Monday was the great day. The Pope's army, consisting of a brigade or so of French troops, all turned out to be reviewed, marching hither and thither up and down the streets, with an immense quantity of martial music, and with all the vagabonds in Rome at their heels and the aristocracy, resident and foreign, ourselves included, chasing them up in carriages,—making an intolerable rumpus and giving a magnificent idea of the power of the church militant. They subsided about three o'clock and we had peace for the space of an hour or two. But at the end of this time the Pope set forth on his annual thanksgiving journey to the church of St. Agnes without-the-city, where he had been miraculously preserved in the going down of the floor thereof, as hereinbefore related.

Immense crowds collected to do reverence to his Holiness in his progress. We ourselves went forth to see him. We proceeded some distance out of the city till we reached a part of the road where we could have an unobstructed view. There we stood alone—my companion, the guide, and myself—and waited. Presently came rushing by a cardinal in a red blaze, and then another, and another. Next there was a surpassing dust and to-do in front. And now, behold, the Woman of Babylon herself has hoven in sight! There she comes down the road, sitting upon a chariot drawn by four horses, and glorious exceedingly, being clad resplendently in a white nightgown, clean shaven, and methought, of the semblance in a manner of the Hon. John Letcher, whilom governor of the Commonwealth of Virginia, though of a superior fatness. She came over green leaves strewed in her path, amid incantations intoned in Latin by a great multitude of orphan children collected in a choral band, and bestowing her benediction freely as she passed. As she neared us we removed our hats, and in return she stretched forth her hands and gave us a whole blessing to ourselves. Really wishing to testify my respect in a becoming fashion, I did what was perhaps not the most rational thing I might have done, but the only thing that occurred to me on the spur of the moment—I uplifted my arm and in reciprocation of her benediction waved her the military salute, as I had been wont to wave it in my fighting days when doing honor to the magnates of the rebel host. We subsequently ascertained that on reaching St. Agnes' Church she was prevailed on to allow her toe to be kissed, but, unfortunately not being aware that this privilege would be accorded we failed to pursue her, and so missed participation therein. She went her ways, and we went ours, and that night when we were ensconced in bed the fleas, drawn to our newly-sanctified carcasses in unparalleled numbers, fell on with thrice-envenomed tooth and wellnigh destroyed us from the face of the earth.

That night there was a most gorgeous display of fireworks and illuminations. The partial exhibition of the preceding night was now completed in all its details, and much more than that had promised was done besides. All the street-lamps flamed in circles and spirals. The church-fronts generally were hung with paper lanterns, and so were numbers of the private buildings. Enormous frames representing façades of temples had been erected in the squares, and now had all their architectural features delineated by thousands of little lamps.

The fountains were in a blaze, and the obelisks were festooned and wound from top to bottom with fillets of light. Ingenious and beautiful pyrotechnic devices were set off at various places both on the land and water, and on the Tiber especially, near our flea-ridden lodging-house, there was a grand farago of aquatic fireworks of peculiar splendor. The whole population was out to see the show,—the poor and rational on foot, the rich and irrational in carriages,—and the narrow streets were crammed, rammed, and jammed with people and vehicles. The city seemed freshened by the shower of light, everything was orderly and everybody was happy, comparatively few persons were run over, and those who were shoved into the river, by virtue of the lowness of its banks, were pulled out readily.

Other pageantries occupied the remaining days of the week, but their nature was mostly of a sort not easily grasped by the uninstructed mind. They were hidden mysteries to me, wherefore I shall not say aught concerning them.

Much to my regret circumstances prevented me from cultivating the distant acquaintance I had formed with His Holiness when on his way to the church of St. Agnes. I therefore can give but little information respecting him of my personal knowledge. But I have been assured by Englishmen—unexceptionable authorities—who have been thrown in contact with him that he is one of the most amiable of men,—beaming, benevolent, and waddling when he walks, and praying daily for the return of wandering Britain to the fold. His greatest fault is being too religious, despising worldly affairs altogether and setting his thoughts exclusively on heavenly things. Thus, he neglects Old Rome for the New Jerusalem, and cares not a copper how a citizen fares in the one so he can secure for him the freedom of the other, and if he gets it for him thinks the sooner he vacates his old and moves into his new quarters—why, the better for him. Hence he supplies his children abundantly with churches, and holds out inducements to any pestilence that wishes to settle amongst them,—paying all heed to the cleansing of the inner man and none at all to the outer. The bulk of the children are, however, not sufficiently spiritualized to appreciate his motives. According to their drossy conception of things the old man does not act well by them, and they meditate mischief against him. There is great and lamentable reason for surmising that but for the extraneous protection that has been thrown around him they would in their blindness turn unfilially upon the Holy Father and chase him out of their midst.

I am now about to take leave of Rome, and in doing so let me, peradventure, shock my reader by the honest confession that I was very little affected by the sight of this renowned city, and have no vehement desire to see it again. How different would have been my feelings could I have trod its streets when I was some years younger—when my mind and heart were not so engrossed with the realities of the present as to be careless of the phantoms of the past! Amongst the saddest experiences of life are the changes of feelings and tastes that we undergo as we creep on in age,—made yet more sad, and unspeakably provoking withal, in that very commonly it happens so soon as we have lost a particular taste the means are thrust upon us for gratifying it. When I wanted to go to Rome, above all things in the world, I was utterly debarred from it; now that I had no care whether I saw it or not I was surfeited with the sight of it. Sad, indeed, and, alas, ofttimes momentous, are these changes of taste wrought by the lapse of years, as an occurrence of this very day has brought forcibly to my mind, and the circumstances of which I yearn to relate; for, albeit I tell a sorrowful thing, I yet in a manner am heartened by it, because I find in it assurance that this mournful alteration is not all of it in me alone.

Many years ago, when I was treating good little Santy Tudwolley for the cholera-morbus, how well I remember with what delighted interest I used to sit and listen to the relation of his constancy and fervor in virtue's ways as recounted by his admirable mother. She told me how, awaking to a realizing sense of the exceeding enormity of sin in which he had been conceived and the appalling mass of iniquity in which he had been born, he had recently become converted and joined the church; and also how, seeing an inebriated fellow-creature singing songs of rejoicing and dancing the double-shuffle in the public highway, he had been moved to associate himself in brotherhood with the Sons of Temperance, and was now become the Most Grand Worthy Patriarch of all the junior divisions of the order in the district. She told me further of the horrible temptations and dreadful persecutions to which he was subjected on account of his religion—how his fellow-boys strove night and day to subvert his faith, cajoling, urging, and commanding that they might procure him to utter the ensnaring word "mill-*dam*," and how he held out steadfast, even unto hootings most diabolical, chastisings most intolerable, and the splitting of the back of his roundabout most irreparable. Moreover, she told me how, for temperance' sake, he had forsworn apples, because of the cider that lurks within them, and how, when he learned from Kornstork's Elements of Chemistry that alcohol was an inevitable concomitant in the making of light-bread, he had that instant renounced light-bread forever and taken to batter-cakes; and, indeed, it was this change of diet that had brought him under my care. It is impossible to describe how I was affected by the recital of these traits. What a future is before this extraordinary youth, thought I! He will never go to Congress or disgrace himself in any way, but will become a blessing to his race, and will finally go down peacefully to his rest in the bosom of some cannibal in a beautiful far-off isle of the sea,—a model and example for all the rising generation to imitate and follow. Nay, I debated with myself whether it might not be imputed to me as something of righteousness to cancel my charges against so exemplary a patient. At any rate, I summoned all my skill, gave him double rations of calomel, and cured him with dispatch.

Time has flown since then over poor mediocre me and good little Santy Tudwolley, and the revolving years have rolled to-day's newspaper into my hands. My eye falls upon this item in the local column: "*Still at it.*— St. John Gough, *alias* Grognose, Tudwolley, young in years but old in crime, was again before his Honor yesterday for the fortieth time on the standing charge of being drunk and disorderly in the streets, cursing the officers in heaps, and trying to tear their uniforms off their backs. He stated to the court that he had got his liquor by cutting up his mother's family Bible and selling it to the barbers for shaving-paper. He is evidently a gone case, and sat during his examination very unconcernedly munching an apple, and with a large roll sticking out of his shirt-bosom. Our readers will remember that only recently he was arrested in the Rev. Dr. Fatpotrick's church, while that eminent divine was delivering his annual sermon on missions, for rising in the gallery and magnifying the heathen above his own Christian countrymen, wishing he was a Fecjeean, and be-hounding that he would eat up every missionary that came to convert him. He is an excellent sample of the abominable political horde with which he associates; though if they intend to bring him out as their candidate for Congress, as is currently reported, they must do it on bail, for his Honor sent him to jail in default of security."

On the whole, I perceive little to make a visit to Rome desirable, or, indeed, agreeable, but its associations. It oppresses the mind with the obtrusive marks of desolation. No invalid *compos mentis* would think of it as a suitable residence, for the activity of nature and the passivity of man are combined to make it a favorite dwelling-place for disease. None but the local doctors venture to speak in its behalf; and it may be that they—for even medical human nature is somewhat frail—speak thus to seduce sick men to come, knowing that a request for their services must needs be the consequence. Even these couple their commendations with a formidable list of precautionary injunctions concerning sun, shade, wind, damp, etc. True it is that the Popes and high functionaries have found the climate reasonably wholesome; but then, as is well known, office-holders are physiologically and pathologically an exceptional class everywhere, invariably living very long and dying very hard.

My last day in the Eternal City was a dull and gloomy one, and my parting visit was to the Capitol and the Roman Forum; and there, standing in the rain, I looked and pondered. As I beheld the once omnipotent city, as she now lay prostrate before me, and contemplated her wrecks, her ruins, her decay, her degeneracy, and her dirt, I could not refrain from sorrowfully joining in the invocation of the poet to old Tiber—

"Rise, with thy yellow waves, and mantle her distress."

CHAPTER XXIV.

Relates how we went from the Eternal City to Civita Vecchia by Rail, and how we there took Shipping for Marseilles—Of our Bark, her interior Economy, and how she was navigated to her Port, and the Quality of the Skipper thereof.

WE were now prepared to go. A few days before we had gone to reclaim our passports, which had been taken from us on our entry into the town, and been astonished to find that the Head of the Church, regarding us in the exalted character of holy pilgrims come to worship in his city, had graciously seen fit to discharge us of the accustomed dollar levied on reclamations of these documents, so that we parted on the best of terms with the Pope and his cardinals. We had likewise gone to the office of the I-know-not-what great international steamship company, whose vessels plied between Civita Vecchia and Marseilles, and procured our tickets for that route. This corporation was somewhat unique. In the course of a tolerably extensive traveling experience it was the only transportation company I had ever known whose fares could be made a matter of bargain between them and the passengers. I would certainly as soon think of trying to beat down the tax-collector in his charges as to attempt to obtain a railroad or steamboat ticket below the advertised rates; but this company, I was told, sold theirs at prices to suit the market, being always anxious to strike a trade, and offering great inducements to purchasers. We ourselves paid full fare, not being aware of these facts at the time, but on the steamer became acquainted with passengers who had dealt with them on accommodating terms.

On Sunday morning we hied away to the railroad station, and there got our hearts rankled and minds embittered at the outset. Baggage was charged as freight. My trunk was as heavy as lead, being fit to burst with packages of ruined temples and towers that I had been gathering all along, and the weighmaster rated it at the uttermost grain. Not only this; for, unlike the steamship company, the railroad authorities were straight-laced even to bigotry in adherence to their charges. After raking out of our pockets all the change we could scrape together, we yet lacked one poor, pitiful cent of the amount assessed against us; and the miserable, old strict-constructionist holding dominion at the station rigidly refused to give us quittance till the one cent was forthcoming. The matter was aggravated terribly by the cursed necessity of having to discuss it in French. A real primitive Christian of a gentleman, standing by, seeing our tribulation, magnanimously gave us a cent, and so put himself everlastingly in our debt, for he modestly withdrew immediately after doing the benefaction, and we never did and never will see him again to pay him back.

In the midst of showers we glided along through a trim-looking country for about two hours, stopping at eleven o'clock in an extensive mud-swamp, which proved to be the suburbs of Civita Vecchia. We now debarked in the mud, where we stood for a time up to our knees, at a mighty nonplus, for not a soul could we find who spoke English. Presently there came to us a desperate villain, tall and terrible to look upon, who proposed to take possession of us in French. He was too desperate, and tall, and terrible for us to demur at his proposition, so we suffered him to pack us into a carriage and take us to the town. He drove us all over it, took us to a hotel against our will, and sought to make us eat dinner in spite of our repletion with a recent breakfast; and when we summoned up sufficient courage to object to this, he whisked us off to the seashore, and there turned us out of the carriage, bag and baggage. The steamer, which was to touch here on her way from Naples, had not yet arrived, and we had nothing to do but to wait patiently for her till she should come—the desperate villain sticking close to us and watching us all the time, and we watching him with an equal scrutiny.

It was excessively doleful. The wind was blowing cool, and the rain would come drizzling and pouring down upon us in frequent showers. There were a few solemn-looking vessels in the harbor for us to contemplate, and a little pleasure-steamer belonging to some noble personage, which had been hauled up in the mud and freshly painted, whose propeller we studied till we became smeared all over with cadaverous-colored paint. A few melancholy wharf-rats were lounging round, seeking how they might devour us. To mitigate the dreadful tediousness we now and then made short excursions into the town, one of us at a time, the other remaining with the baggage to act as a check upon the desperate villain and the wharf-rats. It is one of the meanest and most forlorn of little towns,—the last place in the world where a man would choose to spend a rainy Sunday. It is enough to make a philanthropist weep to know that twelve thousand of his fellow-creatures are condemned to reside here. It is a conceited little hole, too, as I judge, from the fact that it is provided with fortifications—affecting to think that somebody might want to take it; and above its towers float in amicable juxtaposition the flag of France and the banner of the Pope.

When three miserable hours had crept away the longed-for steamer came and delivered us. She was a dirty little craft, all lumbered up with heterogeneous merchandise ill bestowed about the decks, which were begrimed with coal-dust, grease, and foul waters. The crew had more the look of brigands than of true mariners. We had a small quantity of freight to take on at this port, but the genius of this crew did not lie in the line of vessel-loading. Never did I see men do this kind of work at such wanton disadvantage. Unless I grievously mistake them, they had never done any loading before in their lives, except, forsooth, it were the loading of guns up among the hills. The captain himself was by birth and education a wine-merchant, but the owners of the ship conceiving an exalted opinion of his maritime capacity had secured his services as commander,—this being his first assumption of the responsibilities of navigation. With all his maritime capacity he was more distrustful of the water than I was myself,—and, of a verity, I had no overweening confidence in the element,—and he jumped with amazement whenever the ship gave an extra toss. He was of grave and sober port, as is proper to him who moves in apprehension of ever-impending shipwreck. At times, however, he would force himself to relax, and then would crack an awful smile, when his mouth looked like it had been mashed to pieces with a brick-bat.

In this auspicious bark, then, we took passage for Marseilles. In three hours' time the brigand crew had done their twenty minutes' work of loading, the anchor was tugged up, and we were on our way. This was the turning-point in our travels. We had now fairly set our faces homewards, and we were glad of it. Driven away so frequently and so long by his malady my companion regarded home with more than ordinary affection, and was willing to forego everything in order to return to it at the earliest period consistent with prudence. The season was now sufficiently far advanced for him to hurry on with safety. As for me, I was surfeited with sight-seeing, and had, moreover, begun to be tormented with misgivings as to how far the machinations of my professional brethren had carried them during my absence into the small and not over-resistent circle of patients I had left behind me. We, therefore, agitated not our minds with anticipations of further pleasure on that side of the Atlantic. Even Paris and London held out but slender inducements to us, and, like staid and knowing travelers who had happily passed beyond the point of astonishment and admiration, we were well inclined to go straight home and to get there as soon as might be.

The sea was boisterous when we set out and soon became more so. When it seemed to have attained its acme, the master of the pantry sounded his bell and summoned us to dinner. On board this vessel dinner was solemnized at half-past five and breakfast at ten,— nominally so, though in fact these hours were unscrupulously varied to facilitate the perpetration of that besetting crime of the navigators of these waters, the serving of meals on a high sea,—by which abominable device they seek to economize their provisions, and I regret to say generally succeed. On this occasion we were furnished with a very sumptuous feast, and the entire passenger list was represented at table. But ere the soup had given way to the fish an ominous discomposure was visible in our midst; soon evident marks of disgust appeared on the countenances of the guests everywhere around the board, and many rose and departed,—some with a becoming air of dignity and self-respect, but most of them abjectly and with precipitation. Ere the feast was half over not one remained except my companion and myself and a tall, thin, weather-proof veteran of the seas. Our commander, too, though he looked very wild, and stretched his neck, and rolled up his eyes at every palpitation of the waves, stuck out manfully, slinging out his legs and holding fast to the head of the table, and even favoring us now and then with one of his mashed-mouth smiles,—his stomach maintaining its tone possibly by virtue of that pathological law which beneficently provides that fright and sea-sickness shall counteract one another.

The passengers were a sickly, sentimental, reserved set, with no disposition to make acquaintance with each other. The tall, weather-proof one, however, was very sociable, being an enormous giggler and liable to fits of violent cachinnation from inappreciable causes. We communicated much with him, though the pleasure and profit of the communion was sadly interfered with by lingual obstructions. There were, fortunately, two young Englishmen on board, and with them we became very intimate. They had been making a rapid holiday tour in Italy and were now returning laden down with great bundles of walking-sticks, masterpieces of modern painters in tin canisters, and quantities of precious mementos of divers sorts. They were in great haste to get back, the elder one having to fulfill a theatrical engagement at home as one of the *dramatis personæ* in an amateur performance of "Boots at the Swan." He had the playbook with him, carrying it about in his hand, and studying it at every opportunity, but at great disadvantage, for he was wretchedly prone to sea-sickness, so that we apprehended he must ultimately throw up his part. He was mercilessly down on this steamer, pronouncing her blarsted, bloody, and deadly for her untoward influence on his digestive apparatus,—which influence he regarded as highly anomalous and marvelous, seeing that he felt nothing like it during a long cruise he made the preceding summer in a small yacht, and above all, seeing that he had come unscathed across that most baleful of all waters to a true Briton, the English Channel. He attributed his discomposure to a criminal understanding between the master of the pantry and the steersman by which the latter personage was to inflict upon the ship the singular jerks and twitches that tormented her,—though, in my opinion, he judged that functionary too harshly, for I am persuaded that no one on board was sufficiently conversant with the philosophy of steering either to cause or to cure these vexatious manifestations.

The ensuing morning was ushered in with much bawling and confusion, growing out of the fact that there were no conveniences for ablution in the staterooms, but, instead, a public washing-tank in one corner of the cabin, where each washer in turn became frenzied with ignorance how to dispose of his predecessor's dirty water or how to obtain clean for himself—all the waiters having disappeared to attend to matters of more importance—probably to assist in navigating the ship. The air was calm and the sea smooth, and the passengers generally were filled with peace and joy at the prospect of eating their breakfast in quiet—the two young English gentlemen being especially elated, for they were monstrous hungry. Never were confiding people more basely betrayed. Ten o'clock came, but no breakfast. The elements were not propitious. But as time wore on a favorable change of weather occurred. A stiff breeze began to blow and a heavy swell commenced to flow, and then the tocsin sounded. The scene at dinner was repeated. There was the same happy gathering together and sorrowful separation. The two Englishmen sat down but rose instanter, and going on the upper deck obtained a measure of comfort by poking their heads through the skylight, peering at their stouter-stomached companions, and showering down denunciations not only upon the ship but upon the victuals.

On coming together when breakfast was finished to chat and smoke, as voyagers at sea are wont to do after meals, and comparing notes, it was ascertained that some villainies were perpetrated on this bark yet more heinous, if possible, than manœuvring a man out of his provender. The Englishmen complained that in the dead of night some one entered their room with robbery in his heart, and when detected in the act of carrying out his fell intent sought to evade the consequences by declaring that he entered merely to close the diminutive window,—being driven by mortal dread that the ship might else founder through that aperture. Even worse than this, the stopper was drawn out of our medicine vial and full a pint of the invaluable medicament was swallowed down by the servitor of the stateroom.

The commander was excessively assiduous in the discharge of his duty, posting himself determinedly on the lofty perch appropriated to his use, and staring above, below, and all around with might and main. Whatever flaws nautical critics might think they could detect in his system of sailing, they would be compelled to acknowledge that he was eminently gifted with one admirable trait which is by no means universally possessed by more pretentious navigators—and that was cautiousness. He was thoroughly well aware that in the event of any disaster he must depend on the land for ultimate safety, and he sagaciously acted on the knowledge by keeping just as close to it as he possibly could, faithfully following all of its juttings and indentations, so that he was in condition to run the ship ashore at the first indication of a gale or other untoward occurrence. He secured another most important object by thus hugging the land. While it is likely that he would have been found in a measure deficient in the sublimated learning insisted upon by boards of naval examiners, he had a good share of that mother wit or hard common sense which so often proves an efficient substitute for laboriously acquired science. He had acumen sufficient to perceive that if he struck out straight for Marseilles, depending on the compass and sextant as the vain writers of books would have him to do, he would of a surety never get there; at the same time he saw intuitively that if, on the contrary, he coasted steadfastly along it was next to impossible for him to miss it. He coasted, therefore, all the way, never for an instant losing sight of land, and the event triumphantly vindicated the soundness of his perception. By this scheme of sailing the compasses were rendered of secondary importance and the helmsman was spared the introduction of an additional perplexity in a business already sufficiently abstruse,—still, they might have been made of considerable service, even under these circumstances, by those who knew how to use them. The usual complement of these instruments had been furnished to the ship by her English builders and stood up boldly on the deck on highly ornamental metal supports. They seemed to be regarded by our captain and crew as intended to give an air of finish to the vessel rather than for any practical purpose. They were therefore allowed to remain, though much in the way, but no use was made of them except to lean against; and so the craft wobbled along, the bow pointing now to away over there, and then of a sudden whirling around to away over here.

About half-past two in the afternoon of the first day out we were so fortunate as to get to Genoa, all safe and sound, though most of us very empty. We anchored in the harbor some little distance from shore. The crew went to sleep and all the passengers but my companion and myself went off to see the city. We were sight-worn and loth to put ourselves to the trouble of going ashore, notwithstanding that here Columbus is reputed to have been born. We had already seen where he was unequivocally buried, and that was enough for us. We therefore contented ourselves with what was to be seen from the deck of the vessel, and thought the city presented a fine appearance, resting at the foot of a chain of hills. For three blessed hours we sat and gazed, solemnized by the stillness prevailing on board and relaxed by the warmth of the weather, at the end of which time the crew woke up and went to work discharging and receiving freight with a vigor not to be expected of them. At six o'clock we were off again.

A glorious opportunity was here afforded to the master of the pantry to show the rectitude of his intentions, for the advertised dinner hour came while we were lying quietly in port, and, indeed, the repast was partly spread upon the board. He, however, cast his eye to seaward, and the sight of the beautiful billows rolling and tumbling there was too much for his better impulses; and, as usual, he stifled the utterance of his bell till we were rolling and tumbling amongst them. Some of the passengers, tormented beyond endurance by the continual trifling with their feelings, had held it to be no breach of the etiquette of the table to anticipate the formal announcement of the meal by clandestine nibbling of the crackers and pickles and walnuts while we were yet in harbor,—and it was as well they did, for there occurred the same old tumultuous rising as soon as they received lawful notice to sit down.

We coasted quietly along all night, nothing unusual occurring, and next morning all rose wonderfully freshened at the prospect of reaching Marseilles some time during the day. So marked was the tonic effect of this prospect upon us that though the incorrigible demon of the pantry again displayed his deviltry at breakfast, I do heartily rejoice to record that his machinations were mightily shorn of their power, only one woman, a man, and a child falling victims to them.

Our commander was tremendously fidgety all this morning. He had every reason to believe that Marseilles was somewhere about, and armed with a spy-glass gazed into the heavens above and the waters beneath, almost straining his eyes out looking for it. The helmsman was scarcely less excited, causing the ship's bow to bob in and out till our track shone behind us as if made by the great sea-serpent. At length as we proceeded it befell that we got into a terrible quandary, which came near culminating in a disaster. A little island rose right in our way, and the quandary was whether to go inside of the island between it and the shore or outside of it. The latter was clearly the safer course *per se;* but then it would have carried us full two hundred yards farther from the mainland,—a venturous distance, which the captain was not inclined to risk if it could be avoided. As we drew nearer and nearer to the point where it was necessary to make choice between these alternatives the wobbling of the ship grew perfectly awful under the indecision of the captain and the steersman. As evil fortune would have it, just at this crisis a small sail-boat whipped around the little island. This raised our perplexity to its acme on the spot. We wobbled worse than ever. And now the boatmen became perplexed, too, being confounded by our manner of steering and finding it impossible to get out of our way, for no matter which direction they took they would see us coming right at them exactly as if we were aiming at their destruction with malice aforethought. And of a certainty we would have destroyed them, but that of a sudden the captain received a heaven-born inspiration to order the engine to be stopped and the helmsman simultaneously forbore to steer.

At length we were happily delivered from the quandary, and the captain was again at liberty to direct all his genius to the search for Marseilles. He had manifestly hoped to get some insight into its whereabouts as soon as he should have cleared the island, but the air was hazy and it was nowhere visible. He now grew deeply depressed in spirits and seemed to be cogitating the prudence of sending a boat ashore to inquire where we were. But by-and-by on the distant horizon there appeared an extensive conglomeration of something that looked like houses. If that really be houses, reasoned the captain, it is possible that it is a city, and if it be a city it is probable that it is Marseilles. I will seek counsel in the matter. He therefore summoned up on his lofty bridge one of the passengers—that tall, thin, weather-proof one,

—who in his time had already been to Marseilles, and besought him to resolve the question. The veteran stared strenuously through the captain's spy-glass, and deposed that that was certainly Marseilles,—and at once brought a glow of happiness over our commander's countenance which irradiated that sober visage from ear to ear. In his gladness he actually abandoned the coast, turning sharply off from it and heading right across the dread expanse and through the mighty depths of ocean for the city. The captain was, however, yet imbued with his habitual caution and realized all the horror of that most melancholy of disasters—being wrecked in port. To diminish to the uttermost the chances of so direful a catastrophe, therefore, while we were yet a great way off he caused the engine to be worked at its minimum and eternal vigilance to be observed fore and aft. In this way, exercising the most trying care and deliberateness in our every movement, we crawled along, and in the fullness of time were fairly inside the harbor.

It oftentimes happens that the most uncertain and troublous period in the progress of an undertaking is when we are just about to put the finishing touch to it. So it was now. Our commander had been miraculously endued with unexpected wisdom as long as he had been going, but now that it was incumbent on him to stop he knew not where to do it. The quantity of shipping scattered about bewildered him grievously, and in his tergiversations among it he presently became so involved that he had to stop perforce, right or wrong. The pause afforded him opportunity to make investigations, and he found he was wrong, and that it was necessary for him to move to another locality. But he was afraid to evoke the slumbering power of the engine to aid him. He resorted to the somewhat slower but rather safer expedient of summoning all the idle boats that could be gathered together to tie on to the steamer and to tow her into her berth; and in this graceful style, amid the groanings of the toilers of the sea, who tugged tremendously and vociferously, we gradually got to our allotted station.

Under the influence of a temporary aberration of

memory the commander had the side steps promptly lowered to permit the debarkation of his passengers, and the elder of the young English gentlemen, too eager to leave this wretched craft, was upon them immediately with his bundles of canes and canisters of the new masters. But the captain of a sudden recollected that he had forgotten to attend to certain indispensable preliminaries with the people of the custom-house, and ordered the steps up again with a jerk,—to the utter amazement and disgust of the elder of the young English gentlemen, who perceived that himself and canes and new masters were being lifted back in an unpleasant and unseemly fashion to the abominated deck which he hoped he had quit forever. After awhile, however, the steps were let down in finality, and we were received in boats and conveyed ashore. To our infinite astonishment no charge was made for this transportation. This circumstance, together with the fresh and neat appearance of everything about us, and the quiet and systematic way in which affairs were conducted, so opposite to all our previous experience, constrained us to believe that of a truth we had at last got into Europe. We were thankful and took courage.

A mighty cargo of people from Algeria had arrived just before us, and all the mind and strength of the custom-house was now concentrated upon them, so that we had to wait. But though it was full an hour and a half before our turn came we were not cast down, nor even measurably wearied, so buoyed up were we by the improved prospects before us. When at length we were summoned to unpack, we were treated with exceeding courtesy and dismissed without loss or detriment. We were next bestowed into a capacious omnibus whose function it was to take us whithersoever we listed. The two English gentlemen and ourselves listed the Hotel of the Louvre and of Peace, and there we were deposited.

CHAPTER XXV.

A Brief Mention of the City of Marseilles, and how Hostilities broke out between us and the Hotel of Peace—A Cursory View of Paris, interspersed with Episodic Observations upon, first, the Excellences of the Military Law; and second, the Inconveniences of Sunday-Clothes.

WE spent only a few hours in Marseilles, so that I am not in condition to say a great deal respecting it. We padded over as much of the place as we could in so short a space of time, and stared unremittingly in our wanderings, and the result is that I esteem it a very handsome and pleasant city. The streets that we traversed were wide and shady and lined with fine houses. There was none of that stagnation of industry which we had so generally noted in our travels hitherto, and which is so oppressive to a man from our energetic land. Everybody seemed busy and everything wore a look of thrift and prosperity. And well might this be so, for its three hundred thousand people are earnest manufacturers of Fez caps, indefatigable smelters of lead, powerful expressors of olive oil, furious constructors of steam-engines, and mighty makers of soap and sugar.

We started for Paris in the eleven o'clock morning train along with the English gentlemen;—but before leaving were so unlucky as to get involved in war with the powers of the Hotel of the Louvre and of Peace. Publicans, I have reason to believe, are pretty much the same all over Europe, especially in the more refined countries, this sameness being particularly pronounced in the matter of getting the last possible stiver out of their guests; in which design they are materially favored by the preposterous system of charging for all those trivial comforts or necessaries that publicans in our country would shudder to put in their accounts. All the charges of this Hotel of Peace were at regular war prices. Besides that those which were legitimate were shamelessly high, others were inserted in the bill purely constructively. Some of these last we took the liberty to dispute. Thus, we demurred to the three and seven-eighths wax bougies (*Anglicè* stearine candles) recorded against us, which we had not lighted, being, nevertheless, perfectly willing to be assessed one whole one by virtue of the eighth of it we had actually consumed. The clerk, however, a most independent and high-minded personage, sagaciously pointed out to us that the said bougies being set in our apartments thereby became our own property,—that we had the option of doing whatever we chose with our own property,—and that, of course, we could not think of holding the house responsible because we had failed to make the most judicious use of it. This argument was unanswerable and we said no more. But furthermore, we saw ourselves mulcted for two glasses of cognac which we could by no means remember to have taken. The clerk essayed to lubricate our intellects on this matter, also, and in a decidedly more independent and high-minded manner than before. "Did not your English friends just now order liquor to be brought?" asked he, curtly. We admitted that they did. "Did they not invite you to participate with them?" asked he again yet more curtly. We admitted this likewise, but added that we had declined, having no relish for spirituous potations at that time. Said he in effect, and very peremptorily, "It was brought for you to drink in accordance with the invitation; if you refused, it was your own affair. We did our part and will positively not be answerable for the caprices of people." This argument did not strike us as being altogether as lucid as that concerning the bougies, and we proceeded to demonstrate its weak points. This led to a multiplicity of words, and he grew indignant at our low-mindedness and we waxed wroth at his high-mindedness and his incorrigible propensity to steal. It was a little thing pecuniarily, but was so much the greater psychologically; for there is nothing more harassing to the mind than to be the subject of small pilferings. He persistently clung to his view of the case, and as he would not take the cognac off—why, we took the candles off,—packed them up in our valises and took them clean out of France, leaving them with our compliments at the first hotel we stopped at in England. This excellent counterstroke of ours cut the high-minded clerk to the very chine, for though the candles were our property purchased at his own price, he had the most flattering hopes of being our legatee and selling them again many times over. So embittered did he become against us that he actually refused to bestow upon us a bottle of water to take on our journey; wherefore we shook the dust of our shoes into his countenance and departed, invoking confusion to light upon the bureau of this place of Peace.

At the railroad station so many kilogrammes, hectogrammes, decagrammes, etc. weight of trunks and contents were accounted baggage, every gramme above this being rigorously charged as freight, and at a pretty round rate, too. Here we successfully negotiated the purchase of a bottle, and, having filled it with water, we felt that we had now completely circumvented the malignant clerk and were ready to depart in peace. The French are great economizers of space in their railway carriages. Our coach was supplied and kept supplied all the way to Paris with its full quota of passengers. Among them were two of the reverend clergy, grave and decorous men, who rode soberly along to their journey's end. The others were your commonplace travelers, with no hook or crook whereon to hang an observation. Soon after starting we plunged into a long, dark tunnel, and scarcely were we out of it before we were in another, and then in another, and so on till we were disgusted with them. Finally we got fairly and squarely above-ground, and then we poked our heads out of window and took a circumspective view of the landscape; but seeing nothing particular in it drew them in again and laid ourselves back in the hope that something striking would turn up after awhile. Nothing did, however, and the whole company betook themselves to introspection to beguile the time, the majority falling asleep under the process. At times we would be exalted to a very vivacious and merrisome mood, but in a brief space would sink back into thoughtfulness and profundity. The reverend clergy nibbled a good deal at a cold collation of sugar-cakes and like temperate sustenance which they bore about them, assuaging its aridity with an occasional mouthful or two of feeble wine; while the elder of the young English gentlemen—he of histrionic intent—betook himself to his dramatic labors, toiling studiously at his book, and every now and then arousing us from our lethargy by bursting into an agony of despair at the treachery of his memory, accompanied by the bitterest complainings that the screw of the Civita Vecchia steamer was in his head.

There was no fault to be found with the road. It was very smooth and pleasant to ride over. The coach, too, was an excellent one. True, it had no water-vessel, no stove, no nothing that we have in our coaches, but it was upholstered and fixed up in the topmost height of their fashion. Every time we stopped, each wheel was subjected to a thorough and determined tapping with a hammer to ascertain whether its normal molecular constitution was still maintained,—a judicious custom whose utility is not unknown to our railroad managers, who occasionally adopt it when they can spare a hand for the purpose.

Traveling all day through a thrifty and prosperous country, we arrived about half-past seven in the evening at the important city of Lyons, where we were allowed thirty minutes for dinner. This was procured at the *buffet*, or eating-house, at the station, and was a good one, well and promptly served, the host taking no ungenerous advantage of the terrible power conferred upon him by the railroad time-table. As it was dark when we arrived and time was precious and monopolized by the duties of the trencher, we saw little of Lyons but the beef and pie of its buffet.

Punctually at the expiration of the allotted thirty minutes we resumed our journey, the coaches being first supplied with iron cylinders containing hot water,—the substitute of the wretchedly behindhand nations of Europe for our stoves. On these cylinders we planted our feet, and, feeling materially refreshed by our repast, fell into an animated discussion with our English friends concerning the union of Church and State. Before either party could convince the other of heterodoxy, we sank into a doze, which condition of semi-repose we would fain have maintained till morning. But in the nature of things this was not possible. There can be no permanent slumber with the body oscillating in the perpendicular; nor yet when the frame is so contracted and rounded that the crown of the cranium is jammed in between the knees. Those who essayed the former mode were forever on the topple, besides being constantly at the point of death with the snorts; while those who tried the latter were delivered up body and soul to the nightmare. Every sleeper either groaned, or snored, or both, while taking his rest, striking a chill to the bones of him who chanced to be in a state of consciousness. Every now and then the whole company woke up simultaneously with one accord, putting themselves in a posture of offense and eyeing one another with deadly malice, the reverend clergy looking particularly truculent. Our animosity was greatly augmented by the cooling down of the hot-water cylinders, and our consequent tendency to congelation, till at length we grew so irritable that a touch was sufficient to provoke a kick in return; nay, we would let fly our feet at a venture without any tangible provocation at all, sincerely trusting that we might mortally mash somebody thereby.

At last the eastern sky, which we had watched with wistful gaze off and on all night long, began to be irradiated by the blessed gleams of day, and the glorious news being instantly proclaimed to every one we woke permanently, and in an excellent frame of mind. Passing through a rapid succession of towns and villages, and by fine houses and grounds, and, taking now a lively interest in everything we saw, we sped along till seven o'clock, when we made our final stop, being now in Paris, the beautiful, the wonderful, where dwell the wisest, brightest, meanest of mankind,—the paradise of fools, the Mecca of the seeker after wisdom.

Under the guidance of our English friends, who were familiar with the city, we betook ourselves to a hotel, where they got rooms but we did not, the house being full. The same fate awaited us at another hotel, but we finally gained admittance to the Grand Hôtel du Louvre, where we obtained one room at four dollars a day, which included the customary brass clock, oil paintings, etc., but not soap, candles, or anything to eat.

It would be a shame for me to assume to describe Paris who saw so little of it. It is a place that might afford study for a sage for years, yea for a lifetime, seeing with what deliberate slowness sages study. Those who are not sages do not exhaust even its superficial features by months of experience of them. The eye and the ear and the understanding find it impossible to heed all the appeals here made to them. Enough can be gathered, however, to make plain the fact that in many respects this great and wonderful city should be a warning to the rest of the world, and in as many others should be a model for it. How unfortunate it is that in neither of these capacities has the good it is capable of accomplishing been commensurate with its influence! for though its sway is exercised to a greater or less extent over every civilized people on the globe they heed not its warnings, and where they follow its models they have too often taken only those they should have avoided.

Since, then, I saw comparatively little of Paris I shall say comparatively little about it. I had tolerably fair reasons for not seeing much of it. There was but a week at our disposal before the sailing of the steamer for America, which we were obliged to divide between Paris and London, giving to each about three days—a space of time hideously disproportionate to the magnitude of the enterprise. Again, we were now at the tail end of our travels, with soul, mind, and body aweary, and could not prosecute sight-seeing with the enthusiasm of those who enter Paris in the full flush and heat of traveling fervor. Moreover, on top of this, we were crushed to the earth and restrained by a terrible financial crisis impending over us. This calamity had come in this wise. As it was nearly an even chance when we set out from home whether we would go to South America or Europe, we had concluded to defer completing our money arrangements till we should reach Havana, having no doubt that we should find all the facilities there for doing so. But we were mistaken, and on appealing to New York for a letter of credit found it was necessary to apply in person, in order that the party might be identified, or for some other abominable formality. It was out of the question to journey to Gotham for any such purpose, and the only alternative left us was to lug over all the money we expected to spend in our pockets. We made what we thought a very liberal calculation of the probable expense, but not having the light of experience to instruct us we failed to make a sufficient allowance for those innumerable ever-flowing small drains to which we were to be subjected, which while the least conspicuous are amongst the surest depleters of the purse. Therefore, what with boat hire, porter pay, donations voluntary and enforced, differences every fifty miles in the coinage and the rate of exchange, —which was invariably against us, whether we traveled backwards or forwards,—to say nothing of grievous losses sustained by counterfeit money, here we were at last in Paris reduced almost to penury.

It was necessary to husband our resources by retrenching our outlays. The four dollars a day for lodging was fixed beyond recall, but the expenses of the table were happily somewhat under our control. The breakfast was so conducted that the eater paid for what he called for, no more nor less; consequently we called not redundantly at this meal, but showed ourselves patterns of frugal feeding. The dinner, however, was provided at one dollar a head, no stint being put upon the guest, who was permitted to eat anything and everything if so minded. We availed ourselves of this liberty to the uttermost extent, making ourselves at the repast a wonder and a terror in the endeavor to consolidate three meals into one.

Under this state of constrained economy we had, likewise, to be wary in the use of wheeled conveyances. In truth, I bore this deprivation remarkably well, for except for the saving of time it effects, this mode of progression is to me of very secondary importance. For my part, it is greatly more gratifying to walk about a strange city than to ride about it; and it was one of my chief delights in Europe to saunter at my ease through the streets, with the privilege of stopping or going on as the humor took me. In Paris, therefore, I endeavored to find where the principal objects of interest were situated, and then worked my way to them on foot to the best of my ability. Under the best of circumstances Paris is an overlarge place for a pedestrian to compass in three or four days. In the mood that actuated me I felt far more disposed to loiter than to do steady walking, and in consequence can lay no claim to that deep knowledge of its mysteries which American visitors do so generally affect.

A source of undying interest to me was to gaze into the shop-windows. The Parisians themselves do this —a circumstance that heartened and comforted me mightily, forasmuch as it banished all apprehension of the dreadful reproach of being an inhabitant of the rural districts. Nothing can exceed the dexterity with which the shopkeepers manage to make a grand display with scanty materials, and their enticing manner of arranging jim-crackery. In many of the windows hung the encouraging notification that "English is spoken here." As a general thing the attendants were cunningly selected from the beguiling sex, and when they were Frenchwomen, were disastrously affable, though occasionally they were English-born, and in this case were apt to conduct their shopkeeping on the English model, which is not over and above remarkable for conciliating courtesy. Inexpressibly various were the things for sale, and good round prices were asked for them. I bought a hat—an atrocious ugly hat of the latest style—for five dollars in gold that I found I could buy for three dollars in greenbacks when I got home. Jewelry, especially, was superabundant. In the Palais Royal, where the jewelers appear to be centralized, the quantity of it on exhibition is positively appalling; and in the course of my nightly strolls through this place, when it was resplendent with gaslights, I was almost dazed with the glitter and coruscation that assailed my eyes, at the same time being quite befuddled with conjecturing how it was possible for so many of a trade to subsist together, and the more so since, according to my observations, purchasers were far from plentiful. One of our days in Paris being Sunday, we had the opportunity of noting that most of the shops were kept open the same as on week-days—at least in the morning. In fact, I may say here, there was nothing particular in the aspect of the city to indicate the arrival of the day of rest. In the afternoon, however, there was a general shutting-up and a universal turn out of the attending nymphs and everybody else, who, rigged to kill, were perambulating the streets and gardens, giving the whole place an exceeding gay and gladsome air.

The streets of Paris are kept in the best order, every appliance that science and art can supply being made use of to accomplish this object. They are eternally watered by hose scientifically mounted on little wheels, and I saw a stupendous piece of mechanism worked by steam whose function was to roll down all asperities. Shade-trees are nurtured with a mother's tenderness and a father's care. The wayfarers you encounter on these highways, if they regard you, do so in a highly respectful and courteous manner. I bestowed but little attention on the male portion of the inhabitants, who, to the best of my recollection, are generally a thin people, sallow and frisky, with beaver hats, and more or less whiskers; but the female portion I scrutinized somewhat closely,—more closely, I have sometimes feared, than did well comport with my habitual severity of thought and character. It concerns me to have to say that, in my humble judgment, beauty is not the rule among the Parisian ladies. They possess a vivacity of manner which is engaging, and whatever advantages dress can confer they know how to extract from it to the last atom, but in the charms of person, methinks, they are deficient. The handsomest ones I encountered were those retained in the shops to fascinate the susceptible and bully the close-fisted customers.

It is some comfort in walking the streets of Paris to know that as far as human foresight can provide, no harm can be done to you, and neither can you do any to anybody else. There are guardian angels, it may be, invisible, but who have an eye to you, and who will appear the moment their services are needed. If you be a man of wrath and get involved in a fight, you may show as much spirit as you choose, assured that before your enemy can do his worst he will be separated from you. If your animation should become suspended from any cause, you will be immediately attended to, and aspersed with water, rubbed, turpentined, mustard-plastered, "pinched, and burnt, and turned about," and indefatigably treated in the latest scientific style till you are restored; or, if in spite of every effort you give up the ghost, you will be stripped, and stretched nicely on a table before the public, with your clothes hung over your head for identification, and in case any one can tell who you belong to, you will be religiously handed over to your friends for their disposal. If you should drop down dead-drunk, your carcass will be kindly trundled from under the feet of the passengers into a corner, and be protected against the malevolence of the boys, who, in our country, do show such devilish pleasure in devising torments for the unfortunate beings upon whom this calamity has fallen.

All these advantages arise from the admirable system of polity prevailing in this model city. The authorities constitute a species of provost-guard, with powers nearly equivalent to those of a court-martial. The management of affairs, therefore, approaches very closely to perfection; for your court-martial is perhaps the best government the world ever saw—as I judge from my experience in the Confederate army, and afterwards, under different auspices, when my native town was overthrown and passed under the yoke. Some people object to courts-martial, especially those whose ideas have become relaxed by the latitude allowed in a republic; but while these tribunals may well be a terror to evil-doers they are not obliged to be excessively over-formidable to such as are unimpeachably upright and irreproachably circumspect. They are the only courts of genuine justice, indeed,—their proceedings being uncontaminated with any of that weakly quality, mercy, but being short, sharp, and decisive, as legal proceedings ought to be. In their eye every prisoner is presumed to be guilty till he proves himself innocent, and the burden of proof being thus shifted, they move unincumbered by a load under which the prosecution so frequently breaks down in other courts. With them flaws in the indictment amount to naught, the true intent and meaning of the statute is not a matter for argument, and alibis are flouted and scouted. We have no tedious references to precedents, no wearisome procrastination for the judge to consult authorities and look into the law governing the case, no provoking insufficiency of evidence. As a consequence, though an objector might possibly complain that there was something of the insolence of office, Hamlet himself, were he on trial before one of these tribunals, would utter never a murmur about the law's delay. On the contrary, apprehension, trial, conviction, and execution follow in rapid and certain sequence, for there is no obstruction to the Juggernaut car of justice, which having free course runs and is glorified.

Not the least meritorious characteristic of the military law is the plenary power it possesses to determine not merely the degree but the kind of punishment to be inflicted,—matters in which the civil law is so miserably restricted; for, whereas the latter is obliged to confine itself to such old and threadbare devices as fines and jails and gallowses, the latter is at liberty to give full scope to its inventive faculty and strike out into the domain of originality. And surely nothing can be more ingenious, and at the same time pregnant with salutary warning, than some of its essays in this direction. What, for example, when we consider the horror of our colored fellow-citizens concerning things pertaining to mortality and their sensitiveness on the score of their complexion, what could be more appropriate than to incase one of them in a coffin and set him out in the sun with his countenance irradiated with a handful of flour,— as was done by our worthy provost-marshal of Richmond a month or two after the surrender? I have seen nothing to surpass it even in the annals of the slaveholders—no, not in that notable collection of contrivances against the African people which Mr. Charles Dickens in the softness of his heart displays in his "American Notes," and where in the softness of his head he attributes all the piercings of ears for ear-rings, amputations of toes for frost-bite, extractions of teeth for toothache, and tush-marks of the guardian dogs of the hog-pen and chicken-house to the barbarism of slavery.

Certain it is that this anomalous spectacle wrought a deep impression on the minds of the newly-enfranchised population, who marveled greatly as they looked upon it, and, paying full tribute to the unmatchable genius of their deliverers which had devised it, betook themselves to redoubled vigilance in their operations to guard against detection. Yet cannot I help allowing that in some of its forms of punishment military law in a measure oversteps the bounds of what is strictly judicious and seemly; and in the name of a large and deserving class of the community I must plainly protest against the custom of shaving the heads of malefactors, as calculated to exert an injurious influence on the ideas of the rising generation and others of ill-regulated judgment, by bringing the reverend attribute of baldness into discredit and contempt.

It is true that errors will be occasionally committed even by these courts, for no human institution is absolutely perfect. The wrong man (or woman) will sometimes be hung, or something be done to the prejudice of outside parties. Thus, a patient of mine who was on the point of liquidating his indebtedness of ten dollars was apprehended for something, convicted,—he was not tried, the case being too plain to require it,—and fastened hermetically in the penitentiary by our post-bellum provost-judge's court,—all in the space of one little half-hour, with too much expedition for me to become cognizant in time to enter my bill in bar of the proceedings; and, since he was bestowed hopelessly beyond the reach of any collector, I lost my money. But when such a case occurs it is clearly the part of wisdom to comfort ourselves with the reflection that it is better for ninety-and-nine innocent to suffer than for one guilty to escape,—a maxim of the military law which it would not be altogether amiss were the civil more frequently to adopt.

But while the city government of Paris is endued with powers almost as extensive as those I have been lauding, it is proper to add that it does not consider it necessary to exercise them to their full limit. No very striking innovations have been made in the everyday modes of punishment, nor is the celerity of legal proceedings so great that a man may not be late in coming home to dinner without terrifying his family with the well-grounded fear that he has begun a term of service in the state-prison,—as was the case in our good city of Richmond under the auspices I have mentioned. Nevertheless, in many things the government is sufficiently arbitrary. Thus, a man, albeit as thoroughly saturated with healing power as is the seventh son of a seventh son, is not permitted to sell his infallible pill or potion to a suffering fellow-being without giving the sufferer a clue to what he is taking,—a proviso which, as all who are in the habit of prescribing medicines well know, is competent to blast the virtue of the best remedy that ever was concocted. Neither is a confectioner at full liberty to consult his own tastes in selecting the colors wherewith he would adorn and glorify his handiwork. He is ruthlessly compelled to abstain from such as contain copper and lead and ratsbane. In fact, in no business is one allowed to conduct it to suit himself alone; but, instead of being left to look after his own interests exclusively, he is forced to consider those of other people too. An American is struck with astonishment at a system so much at variance with that which prevails in his own country, where buying and selling are done with the understanding that every man is for himself and God for us all, and which is so inimical to the exercise of our most idolized national trait of "smartness;" and he wonders how a people can prosper under it.

The interference with private affairs here goes yet further, even to the restriction of man's inherent right to dispose as he chooses of his own body and bones. Should these mortal concomitants become a burden to the possessor—a case that not unfrequently happens to Frenchmen—all kinds of obstacles are thrown in the way of getting rid of the incumbrance. It is with the greatest difficulty that a quantum of poison can be procured. The inviting bosom of the Seine is likewise guarded against him; or, if perchance, he can throw himself upon it, ere he is fairly nestled there like enough he will be jerked away and restored to the abominated upper world by the implements and appliances scattered thick along the river's banks, and which are put into assiduous operation under stimulus of the liberal reward paid to those who save lives. To elude this vexatious watchfulness of the government therefore it is that the tired denizen resorts to charcoal fumes and other outlandish, unsuspicious agencies for gaining rest. Let freedom-shriekers scream as they will, great blessings spring from this despotic surveillance. The very hackmen are subdued by it. It is a matter of some concern to them whether or no they run over you in the streets; nay, they will actually hold up and notify you of your peril if it threatens; while in the matter of fares the regulations to which they are subject render it very difficult for them to swindle. How to deal with this intractable class has ever been one of the sternest problems of legislation. No other city that I wot of has accomplished anything worth the mention towards its solution, and the fact that here so near an approximation has been made to this desirable end speaks volumes in behalf of the municipal government of Paris.

The Gardens of the Tuileries were but a short distance from our hotel, and in this convenient retreat we were frequent loungers. It is needless to say that these gardens are artistically laid out, neatly kept, and in all respects a delightful resort. They could not be in Paris and be otherwise. Among the pleasant features are multitudes of little birds, whom kindness has made trustful, and who hop down before the visitor and confidently appeal to him for charity, which is most willingly bestowed, many good people bringing provision with them expressly for almsgiving to the amiable little pensioners. Here we spent all of our Sunday morning, and with great pleasure and profit, especially from beholding the trim citizens as they passed by arrayed in their Sunday-clothes. The Parisians are notoriously tasty in dress, and to any one fond of witnessing the pomps and vanities of the world it is a treat to see them in full feather.

We were mightily taken with one particular pair of the promenaders, comprising a credulous father and a lowly son. To the eye of a disinterested observer the son certainly appeared to be yet very far from maturity, but in the estimation of the fond parent he was a little man; and in this belief he had been decked out in man's attire, and of the most pronounced description, being provided with a long split-tailed coat, a stove-pipe hat, kid gloves, and a walking-stick. The poor child did not share his father's infatuation, but, crushed beneath the greatness thrust upon him, pulled the narrow brim of his hat over his eyes, tucked his walking-stick under his armpit, and curved his spine till the waist of his split-tailed coat rested on his shoulder-blades;—his general bearing being one of most desolate sheepishness. The parent, mortified at this ignoble port, essayed to readjust him, instructing him in the approved swing of his stick, restoring his hat to its proper poise, and almost pulling him backwards to the earth by tugs at the tail of his coat, in the attempt to coerce that garment into its rightful position, at the same time loading him with reproaches and remonstrances; but all to no purpose. As fast as he was restored he relapsed, till at length the parent's shame was swallowed up in sorrow, and he, too, hung his head, sore stricken by his offspring's incorrigible littleness of soul.

This unfortunate youth had my fullest sympathy in his afflictions, for the sight aroused the recollection of my own earlier days, when I too was a living sacrifice to the demon of dress,—though, thank Heaven! not on anything like so pretentious a scale. Vividly did he recall to my mind the desperate efforts exerted to make me look a neat and pretty little boy;—all utterly futile, except to excite in me bitterness of heart and rebelliousness of spirit at the restraint upon my natural proclivity for free and easy clothing and playing in the dirt. Had I continued a child all the days of my life, I fear these vexations would have at last driven me to infidelity, for the Christian Sabbath had become an abomination in my eyes because of the scrubbings, and combings, and brushings, and buttonings, and pinnings, and trickings which announced its advent. With what disgust I regarded the finery wherein I was that day endued, which was to be worn till blessed eventide, and religiously guarded against spot or blemish, and with what joy unspeakable I laid aside the sacred vestments! The love of freedom in matters of the toilet has not been entirely left behind in my advance in years, and chief among the few gleams of comfort which in my army experience tempered the grim asperities of war was that derived from the inestimable privilege of wearing a shirt from moon to moon with unimpeachable reasons for doing so, and, in addition, no public opinion demanding a daily washing of the face.

We had not been long in Paris before we were assailed by an individual who insisted strenuously upon being engaged as guide. We felt no great need for his services, but he gave such glowing accounts of what it was in his power to show, and was withal so intolerably pertinacious that we employed him in self-defense. He was a little plumpish wanderer, or, most probably, refugee from England, with the flavor of the Cockney lingo rich upon his tongue, and thoroughly unfit for the function he professed. His first essay was to get us admitted into the halls of legislation, in which he failed egregiously, getting us no farther than an ailing hydrant in the yard afflicted with incontinence of water, which when we would drink from it doused us from head to foot. Baffled here he squired us to the Hôtel des Invalides, where there being no opposition whatever to our entrance, he claimed great credit for successfully engineering us therein. On the way thither, to indemnify us for our exclusion from the Legislative Palace, he gave us a comprehensive sketch of French politics, with an exposition of the true motives underlying the ostensible policy of Louis Napoleon, and prophecies of momentous public events which must assuredly come to pass;—all of which we listened to because we could not help it, and all of which we would have treasured up had we had the least idea that he knew anything in the world of what he was talking about.

Under the splendid dome of the Hôtel des Invalides lies the dead Man of Destiny, piously brought from the far-off alien sea-girt rock to repose in the midst of the people that he loved so well. The dome is the crown of a magnificent church, all of the central space of which is occupied by the large circular crypt where stands the tomb. Numerous paintings and tasteful architectural devices adorn the church, and about it are several sepulchral monuments dedicated to French worthies. The tomb is a massive block of porphyry, elegantly but plainly sculptured, which covers the sarcophagus,—the whole supported by means of two plinths upon another massive block of green granite. Around it and confronting it stand in solemn state twelve colossal statues, images of twelve great victories. In the pavement is worked in mosaic a crown of laurels, and upon the balustrade are sculptured eight laurel wreaths, each circling the name of some fierce battle of the hero's. No cost has been considered, no labor has been spared, to make this monument of a people's veneration worthy of the nation and the man; and while it is magnificently grand its grandeur is withal the grandeur of simplicity.

When the tomb had been inspected, the guide would fain have us go through the hospital. But my companion being an invalid himself turned up his nose at the very thought of invalids, and, for my part, I relished hospitals "no better than a grocer does figs." Accordingly, we turned back, making for the Louvre, where the guide professed to be able to show us great things. Like all guides I have ever seen, his specialty was paintings. When, therefore, we were at the renowned palace, he hurried us past the vases and mummies and minor objects generally, and pioneered us to the picture-galleries. On all the masterpieces he descanted with the usual eloquence and erudition. Now it chanced that sundry of these were Scripture subjects, and, while we made no boast of art-knowledge, we at least felt ourselves to be measurably well grounded in the rudiments of biblical history. In these particulars, however, we found that the guide was exactly the converse of us; he was a connoisseur in light, shade, and perspective, but a tyro in Moses and the prophets. We were shocked at his heathenish ignorance, and outraged that he should hold our scriptural acquirements so low as to presume to pass upon us his profane versions for gospel facts; and when to top it he spoke of our old friend and first acquaintance in art, Murillo, as an

Italian, we were fit to burst. It was intolerable and we discharged him at once.

As we were domiciled almost under the shadow of the Louvre, it was easy enough to visit it, and we occasionally strayed through it subsequently under our own auspices. The building itself is an imposing piece of architecture externally, and the interior is richly and appropriately adorned, while considerable regard for the comfort of the visitor is evinced,—a point on which institutions of the sort do not generally much concern themselves. No half francs are demanded for anything. No canes are taken from the feeble and the weary, leaving them perchance to drop exhausted somewhere in the depths of the vast pile. On the contrary, there are divans where one may sit and poetically meditate, or prosaically catch his wind. Moreover, he may stand upon the floors without apprehending the refrigeration of his marrow, for they are of wood. Last but not least, the thoughtful custodians have provided spit-boxes, so that the despised but devoted chewer of tobacco can indulge the habit which does so solace and assist him in his labors in these places without having to trot all around semi-strangulated by nicotine, looking for some secret spot to hide his shame.

What is to be seen in the Louvre is altogether too various to specify. It has enough of all the staples kept in a well-furnished museum and to spare, and a vast deal the like of which is to be found nowhere else. Here are many interesting souvenirs of the great Napoleon. The collection of Egyptian mummies, sphinxes, seeds, spoons, brooms, shoes, pieces of bread, etc. of the Pharaohs' days is unrivaled. The specimens of Gobelin tapestry are most magnificent, representing subjects with the fidelity and vividness of oil paintings; in fact, we took them to be paintings till certified of their real nature by our guide; and truly it would puzzle any one not a connoisseur like him to detect the difference. It is needless to say there are vases; of course there are vases, Greek and Roman vases, Egyptian vases, African vases, all kinds of vases. Its paintings in quality and in quantity are not behind those of any similar institution in Europe, and this despite the fact that it has been obliged to disgorge all those which the first Napoleon, who loved art not wisely but too well, stole from other museums to enrich it. The same may be said of its statuary. This is displayed in its naked beauty, and from it I was forced to draw the inference that many of the old worthies, whatever might be said of them morally, were physically condescending and candid enough ; even emperors and rulers of nations having no concealments to make, but permitting themselves to be hewn out exactly as they were, *viz.*, of the identical make and fashion of common mortals, and without even so much as a fig-leaf to hamper the inquiring mind.

One afternoon I sought out the Morgue,—the repository in which the poor waifs of dead mortality are gathered to wait for claimants. It is a low building near the riverside, with a wooden screen before the door. Within it is a long glass partition, behind which are ranged twelve tables for the reception of the dead bodies. On these they are laid confronting the spectators with their heads raised, and naked, except a cloth across the loins. A vast quantity of clothing, the accumulations from many subjects, is suspended behind the partition. The place is neatly kept and is entirely free from odor. There were two subjects on the tables the day I visited the Morgue : one a man, rather coarse looking ; the other either a fair, delicate young man or a woman,—I could not by the fading light well determine which. Both had their arms extended by their sides and looked exquisitely placid, exactly as if asleep. Many persons lounged in to gaze at them, mostly trifling men and slattern women, people of the neighborhood, some having babies in their arms. Children came in, too. All performed the inspection very unconcernedly, and, their curiosity being satisfied, they idled off without apparently laying the scene much to heart. A thoughtful man might, however, draw some useful reflections from a visit to the place, which is in a manner the register of the gayety of Paris, for it is said that in seasons of universal joy and merriment then does the Morgue appear in all its fullness.

If means of pleasure could save one from the Morgue, no Parisian need ever get there. There are amusements innumerable, and to suit all sorts and conditions of men. I am myself a man who can be satisfied with very few and simple enjoyments, and it was my custom, after the perambulations of the day, to recreate my spirits at the nightly out-door shows about the Champs Elysées. These shows were particularly numerous and well patronized on the Sabbath-night. The more pretentious of them consist of thrillingly ludicrous dramatic representations, interspersed with singing and dancing. The spectator sits under the trees, no charge being made for admission, though he is not suffered to go away till he has purchased some refreshment, which is put at a figure high enough to cover all incidental expenses. My glass of beer, which was the shape in which I elected to liquidate my obligation, was assessed at forty cents.

Of all the performances I witnessed, the most meritorious was a drama vividly portraying the omnipotence of woman's wiles. An unlucky man is beset by an insidious charmer who seeks to cajole him out of his garments. He strives against her, but hearkens, nevertheless. How true it is that the man who deliberates is lost! He yields up his coat. She urges him further, and he gives his waistcoat Yet further she presses him—she wants his shirt. Now he begins to struggle in earnest, but too late—he parts with this, too. Will it be believed?—the insatiable monster now demands his pantaloons! Upon this the wretched victim is in an agony; his strivings are terrible, and he has already retired behind a friendly screen to hide his emotions. The audience is in a fever of anxiety to know if he will surrender this wellnigh the last refuge of manhood. Alas! who that has gone so far can stop? The vestments come protruding from behind the barrier. And now the audience is almost crazed with anticipation of what will come next. But, blessed be woman! in her most remorseless moods she still retains somewhat of her inborn compassionateness and tenderness of heart, yet mingled with it a spice of her natural waywardness; for, though at this crisis the persecutrix relents, she pulls down the screen from before her denuded and abashed dupe and in token of her triumph makes him dance a hornpipe with her in his drawers.

CHAPTER XXVI.

How we went from Paris to Calais, and how we passed over the English Channel with due Observance and landed at Dover—How we went to London—A Cursory View of London, with some Facts that militate against the Assertion that the English are a Nation of Shopkeepers.

CONTRARY to what we should expect of a people so practically æsthetical as the French, it is their custom to confine the wayfaring public in a saloon at the railroad station, barring them out from the train till a very few minutes before it is time to start, causing tremendous agitation, trepidation, and frenzy in the crowd of expectant voyagers when the gates are opened and they are turned in pell-mell to look for places. We found ourselves thus cribbed and kicking our heels impatiently early on the cool, dull, drizzly Monday morning terminating our brief survey of Paris. When the floodgates were raised we surged madly along with the current, coming to rest in a coach with a quota of pure Frenchmen, who spoke not nor understood aught of English, and at the appointed moment rolled smoothly and rapidly away, bound for London town.

The journey to Calais, which we made by way of Boulogne, was very void of interest. The weather was dispiriting, and we were deprived of the solace of conversation with our fellow-travelers, who had too great a command of French for us to dare to provoke them. Every now and then a tunnel would shut from us the sight of an unattractive country, mostly flat in its character, and bearing some resemblance to our Western parts, but relieved by numerous villages and an abundance of windmills. Nothing, whatever, as far as I remember, occurred to us, nor do I recollect anything we did more noteworthy than yawning and stretching ourselves.

At ten minutes past one o'clock we reached Calais.

The cares of transshipment of self and baggage to the steamer engrossed my attention to the exclusion of all things else, so that if I passed through the town, which I doubt, I did not see it; and consequently, on second thoughts, suppress the description of it I had prepared. Great was the bustle about the boat for half an hour, at the end of which time we cast loose our fastenings and struck out for Dover.

We were now traversing that renowned artery of the sea which is the pride and terror of the Cockney voyager, and his infallible gauge and measure for all troubled waters; over whose bouncing bosom he delights to bear his new-made bride to show his prowess, and for the maintenance of whose nauseous name and reputation he feels it incumbent on him to make oblation of his beef and ale. The steamer, which was small and ill arranged but of much horse-power, was well filled with this kind of travelers. The hazy, drizzly weather grievously distracted them, and they could be seen chasing the steward from stem to stern anxiously seeking his opinion concerning the prospects of a propitious passage. The moment the wheels began to revolve they commenced to grow sea-sick, and numbers of them with wise forethought lay down even before we started; they and their baggage, which was in all the national redundancy, monopolizing so much of the limited space that it was difficult for sound persons to move about. Much of the illness that prevailed, I am quite persuaded, was attributable to the patriotic tenderness for the Channel's fame, for there was not enough sea on to account for it. The ladies were particularly demonstrative; and as the construction of the boat did not readily permit privacy, they reaped whatever benefit could accrue from the public recognition of their sacrifices. The proprietors of this line of steamers are very considerate of this delicate class of passengers. Instead of intrusting them in these emergencies to the puny care of a waiting-woman, as would be the case were it an American line, they are placed under the stalwart guardianship of a man. The steward himself attended them, assisted by two sturdy little sailor-boys, and certainly displayed all the assiduity, and apparently all the loving-kindness, of a female. This steward was a most notable-looking person. At the first blush of his grandeur I presumed him to be the captain, being misled by a cursory glance at the golden blazonries upon his coat, which, however, upon narrower inspection showed so much the semblance of wash-basins that I stood corrected, interpreting them to be insignia of his true office. My illusion was greatly aided by the transcendent straightness with which he held himself and the stupendous importance of his general carriage. However, he was assiduous and tender, as I have said, keeping his boys continually on the tramp with their crockery equipments, so that he certainly entitled himself to honorable mention.

Be it known, tobacco-chewing is a subject little understood by Europeans. According to their benighted idea of it, it is practiced only by the refuse of the earth, and they cannot conceive that a gentleman traveler would indulge in it. The sick people, therefore, stared with amazement at the complacent countenance with which I every now and then tripped to the vessel's side and expelled a mouthful of tobacco-juice overboard. They took the fluid to be bile—the darned fools!—imagining me to be afflicted like unto themselves, though with a kind of latent form of the malady, and wondering how on earth I bore it so philosophically.

When two hours' time had passed we were over this portentous Strait and in the town of Dover. I saw almost as little of this place as of Calais, having deposited myself promptly in the train, which shortly set out for London. In deference to the seclusive and secretive tastes of their countrymen, managers of the English railways are not prone to fill every coach to its maximum capacity, as they are wont to do in France, consequently we had abundance of room to sling our legs about in our compartment; nor were we disturbed by idle chattering, our two or three companions having a masterly command of their tongues. We flew smoothly along through a lovely undulating and verdant country, well besprinkled with sheep, passing through divers villages on the way,—

the whole panorama pleasing me vastly, for it vivified many a fascinating idea of English scenery and life and manners long before implanted in my mind by communion with the revered men of the land who had made these things their theme, and whose pirated thoughts I even then had in cheap editions in my trunk. Speeding thus for an hour and three-quarters, we finally penetrated a mass of vapor, rode over the tops of divers houses, and worked through sundry topographical mazes, ultimately coming to rest at the Charing Cross terminus of the railroad, being now in London.

From some unaccountable impulse of benevolence towards travelers, the custom-house authorities had so arranged affairs that the examination of baggage coming from France might be postponed till it reached London. I trembled to know that this ordeal was now at hand. Both by reading and hearsay I had been assured that of all custom-houses that curse the fair earth the English was the most bloodthirsty and inexorable ; and I was painfully conscious that it would find me an exquisitely succulent morsel for its cruel craw by reason of the good store of tobacco, the great mass of American reprints, consisting of the Bible, the works of Byron, Dickens, etc., and many other articles which are deadly abominations to the revenue officers, which were conspicuous components of my traveling equipment, constituting, in fact, much the most considerable portion of it. Knowing, too, how bitter are the customs against articles of virtu, I thought I had especial cause to fear for the fate of my inestimable collection of weeds, lumps of rock, brickbats, etc. that I had gathered from famous places, of which things of price I had a peck and a half or two pecks.

But, after all, these distressing anticipations came absolutely to naught. It has long been a maxim that a man's appearance is fully competent to carry him smoothly over the rough places he will encounter in his pilgrimage through life. The soundness of this observation was evinced on the present occasion, for to my looks alone am I to attribute the successful and easy tiding that I accomplished over this truly ominous trouble.

The fact is, that being none of your holiday tourists, but a pure and simple traveler after wisdom, I had burdened myself with no superfluity of apparel, and so in process of time had come to have something of a dilapidated, hoary, and amorphous guise as to the garments. Moreover, not having shaved nor trimmed my hair since leaving home, I had now gotten an eldritch look about the dome of thought and palace of the soul, and, taken altogether, had right smartly the seeming of a demon or wild man of the Western prairies. On the other hand, my companion, from the fact of being an invalid, had been forced to bring many changes of raiment, and accordingly was in condition to always shine forth exceeding spruce and gentlemanlike. It came to pass, therefore, that the functionary of the custom-house, affected by his good clothes, gave him full credit for his station in society, but instead of according me my deserts as a learned and reverend professor of physic, he set me down as the valet.

Well do I know there are abundance of my republican fellow-citizens who would have resented such an indignity as this, even to the sacrifice of their tobacco, and Bible, and everything; and who expect to read immediately that I snapped my fingers at the functionary's nose and peremptorily convinced him that he was the victim of an optical delusion. But, no—my temperament is too philosophical for anything of that sort. He might have burst with ignorance ere I had enlightened him; for so long as I myself *know* what I am, knowing nothing to my disparagement, I care not the value of a canceled revenue stamp what the custom-house folks or any other folks *think* I am—and especially when it is to my advantage that they should think wrong. Therefore I let him retain his hallucination, under the influence of which he proceeded to inspect my companion's trunk, which he did in a most courteously cursory manner,—though, in truth, there was very little of a contraband nature in it,—and then, his hallucination obtunding him thoroughly, he suffered my trunk to pass without any inspection at all, taking it as well as myself to be the property of the well-dressed gentleman, and being too polite to subject a person of his figure to further detention. Thus, it will be seen, how greatly I was indebted to my appearance; for had I been respectable-looking, my baggage would have been thought to belong to me and been examined likewise, when, unless the functionary had chosen to be guilty of misprision of perjury, I must have been wellnigh ruined. Highly elated at the satisfactory issue of our encounter with the great bugbear of the traveling public, we departed from the domains of the custom-house, and going a very short distance reached Morley's Hotel, where we proposed to sojourn during our stay in the metropolis.

The obstacles that impeded us in our exploration of Paris operated equally in the case of London. We had little time, little money, and little curiosity. The very close approach of the Atlantic steamer's day of sailing made us too restless to be very persevering sight-seers. For my part, it was pleasure enough to walk up and down the streets, observing men and things as shown on these great thoroughfares. It is true I had to be circumspect in doing this, for the passengers here are not as polite and considerate towards one another as they are in the streets of the Continental cities. The footmen will walk over you without scruple, and the hackmen will run over you most willingly. My spinal column was repeatedly jarred as I sauntered along by the intrusive knee of some heedless pedestrian coming impulsively behind me. The people are brisk, and shop-windows are fine, and the placards and posters are gigantic and glaring. To my eye London looks like New York magnified,—magnified very much—much more than the New Yorkers themselves are disposed to believe.

By far the most satisfying and substantial part of the pleasure I felt in London was from being once more in oral communication with the human species after so many months of practical dumbness. The change that a few hours' journey had wrought was marvelous and supremely delightful. It seemed really too good to be true that I could actually understand what people were saying around me, and I would stand still ofttimes merely to let my ears wanton in the luxurious melody.

It is not possible to convey an adequate idea of the thrills of rapture that shot through me when I discovered that I had an intelligent conception of the announcements of things for sale and their prices in the shop-windows. Oh! thought I, as I read "Hot joints," "Half-and-half," "Pot-pie," "Hair brushes," "American drinks," "Only 2s. 6d. a yd.," "1s.," "6d.," and so on,—this is the language of Shakspeare, and Milton, and Byron, and blessed be the day that permits me to see and hear it again! Yet more delightful was the fact that I could talk now without peril of unhinging my mind in the effort to make myself understood. I could scarcely have been more overjoyed at the release of my tongue had I been a woman. One of the most precious advantages that it guaranteed to me was that I could now walk the streets in security and peace of mind, knowing that when I got lost I was able to ask to be set right. In the Continental towns when prospecting through their intricate streets it was my prime care to take my bearings with mathematical exactness, but when in spite of this I missed my way, as often happened, and the impotency of my condition appeared to me, I was prone to collapse in wild panic and be fit to drop. Many times in the Spanish and Italian cities had I been sunk into mute despair at finding myself in some obscure and dreary nook from which were half a dozen ways of egress, but only one of deliverance. It would have been a mockery of Heaven's good gift of speech had I attempted to ask any one to unravel the mystery, and my sole resource in such circumstances was to walk unintermittedly till I would be led back to the hotel providentially by a way I knew not of; and I may as well mention further, that inasmuch as I invariably reached my objective point in the end, I did sometimes get in a measure puffed up with the conceit that I was a marvelous proper topographer and a pathfinder of a right crafty skill, though, for all this, I must confess my collapse and demoralization recurred none the less surely under the appropriate provocation.

Besides indulging in street-walking, I idled away much of my time in sauntering with my companion through the parks and gardens, of which there were several within commodious reach of Morley's. These, though they are not of surpassing elegance and beauty, are, nevertheless, tastefully arranged, well kept, and very pleasant places of resort. Our enjoyment of them was greatly enhanced by the delightful weather prevailing at that time, which was as fine as I ever experienced and utterly at variance with the current notions of London weather. The atmosphere was hazy, it is true, for this is an inevitable condition of it in London, but the temperature was as genial and comforting as any reasonable creature ought to ask. And yet, so querulous and exacting is human nature, and especially English human nature, that I heard certain of the natives denouncing the meteorological status for being by no means what it ought to be. An abundance of respectable-looking vagrants lounge about these parks, and others a shade less respectable looking, with their legs alternately drawn up and extended, loll upon the grass. A plentiful quantity of nurses with children contribute to give variety to the grounds, and feathered songsters ruralize the scene; but I observed that, unlike them of Paris, the birds here, taught I question not in the school of experience, keep sedulously aloof from the people of this latitude and trust nobody.

Cursory as was my inspection of London, I yet took a glance at a few of its most noted objects of interest. Prominent in my recollection stands the British Museum. Of course I shall not attempt to describe all that is to be seen there. He would be an impetuously bold man and a voluminous writer who should adventure upon such an undertaking. I shall not attempt to give even a skeleton description of the stupendous collection. Let it suffice to say that there is a vast quantity of materials pertaining directly and indirectly to sundry Rhamses and Nebuchadnezzars and other mighty men of the East, and relics of Greece and Rome without number. There are printed books by the hundred thousand, and manuscripts in proportion, with autographs of almost every famous and infamous dead and living man and woman gifted with the art of fingering a pen. There are mineralogical, geological, and botanical specimens by the cart-load, and a truly appalling array of preserved birds, beasts, and fishes. There are—I know not what not. All this heterogeneous mass is admirably discriminated and arranged, there being one feature in the arrangement in particular of such singular merit that I cannot omit to mention it with the heartiest approbation, for it was one which I was grieved to find neglected in the otherwise well-ordered museums of Naples, Rome, and Paris, and, indeed, in all the Continental museums I had visited—*viz.*, the names and descriptions affixed to the objects are expressed in the English language.

There is one circumstance connected with this Museum that I would not on any account pass over. In exploring the ornithological department, I was unable in the time at my disposal to discover any sample of the Great American Eagle; but in place thereof what should I see but a feathered monster ostentatiously labeled "Great American Turkey-Buzzard!"—perched up and fixed off with the identical sweep of wing and cock of head which our artists love to give to their portraitures of the Fowl of Freedom. I do not suppose that anybody can fail to see in this another British outrage. Something ought to be done about it; and I hope that, at the least, the honorable Senator Sumner will include it in his Alabama account along with the blood and treasure and sweat, wear of shoe-leather, detrition and fracture of teeth by hardtack, blasphemies (the army swore terribly in Dixie), and the other items embraced by specification and implication in his comprehensive bill of charges against Great Britain.

Another object very prominent in my recollection of London is Westminster Abbey. It was with a feeling of solemn interest that I traversed this ancient pile. Graves of kings were about me, but I lingered not long at these. My footsteps turned more readily to "Poets' Corner." This is a small nook in the stately temple; but what precious dust is gathered here! Chaucer, Shakspeare, Ben Jonson, Cowley, Milton, Dryden, Addison, Prior, Congreve, Gay, Thomson, Gray, Goldsmith, Garrick, Sheridan, Southey, Campbell, Wordsworth, Macaulay, Thackeray, lie within its precincts, or are commemorated by memorials. Some of them have unconsciously penned their own epitaphs, for their monuments are inscribed with words appropriately selected from their writings. It is so with Shakspeare; so it is with Campbell; and so it is with Gay, though his epitaph was penned consciously and selected, some think, very inappropriately, being couched in this hideously humorous phrase :

> " Life is a jest, and all things show it—
> I thought so once, but now I know it."

Since I trod this hallowed ground it has opened to receive another of England's worthies, Charles Dickens— fit company for the worthiest there.

Several others of the noted objects of London I saw, but as of the majority of them I saw only the outside, I shall not tantalize or deceive my reader by professing to describe them.

I am none of your penetrating travelers who can stop a day in a place and know all about it and be qualified to give you an exact analysis of the character of the people. If I were I should not make a favorable report of those that dwell in London. Those I had dealings with were for the most part a very unceremonious, discourteous, snappish set of curmudgeons. But I am far from judging the whole by a part. I have no doubt there are some excellent persons somewhere in London,— there must be in so populous a place,—but very few of that class came within the scope of my observation. Probably they keep themselves close to avoid contamination by the rest. The very morning after reaching the city, on our first venturing forth, we were shamefully insulted by a red-coated miscreant, of a villainous saltpetre countenance and bearing, and with a gun in his hand, who, seeing us with our feet on the railing round a curious kind of cannon which we were inspecting in one of the parks, bade us take our feet off-o'-ther in such a short, hoarse, truculent voice that we did not understand him; whereupon he repeated his injunction with so great augmentation of emphasis and such snapping-up and putting into position of his firelock as greased our ears for the quick reception of his words and caused us to draw off from him, hating him in our hearts. Now had this been a French warrior, in all probability he would have entreated us to do him the pleasure and honor to remove our feet from the railing if we could possibly make it consist with our convenience to do so, and most likely he would have been at a present-arms the whole time he was making the petition.

Napoleon Bonaparte, among other remarks of his which have been recorded for our admiration, is reported to have declared that the English are a nation of shopkeepers. With all the deference due to so great a man, I think he spoke without adequate knowledge of the subject, if the shopkeepers of London are fair exemplars of the class. Had he ever gone a-shopping here he would have speedily found that they are wofully deficient in the prime element in shopkeeping, which is the courteous treatment of the customer. They may be tolerably conciliatory if they have the article you want; but if you ask for anything they happen not to have, the response in the negative is apt to be made very peremptorily and superciliously. The honor of your patronage may be accepted, but they are above soliciting it. In one of the shops where they did not have a certain book which I thought they would be likely to have, when I inquired politely where I would probably find it, I was told that I might get 'em where they made 'em, wherever that was, —an answer, methought, sufficiently correct in matter but something coarse in manner. Another of this nation of shopkeepers, an optical dealer, upon whose premises I had been seduced by his advertisement of stereoscopes for sale, denied having any such instruments on hand with such acrimony as almost terrified me. Indeed, had I not usually been armed with a cane or umbrella, I question if I could have summoned enough valor to do any shopping in London at all. In Paris I had had a shopwoman to patiently overhaul hundreds of photographs in search of the low-priced picture I had asked for, and she would have gone on to overhaul thousands of them had not my own convenience obliged me to beg her to stop. Nothing approximating to this ever befell me in London.

My companion was much addicted to ornithology, having in his stronger days devoted a good deal of his time to the shooting of partridges and such like. His interest in this branch of science induced him one afternoon, as we were walking out, to pause before a bunch of defunct birds lying upon the pavement and to inquire of the man in whose custody they were to what order and genus they might belong. The custodian, a burly, straddle-legged, firm-footed wretch, raised the birds aloft, and says he, "Do you want to buy 'em?" "No," says my companion, "I don't want to buy 'em, I only want to know what they are." "Well," says he, "if you don't want to buy 'em, I want to sell 'em;" and with this he slings the bunch of birds down, puts his arms akimbo, describes a quadrant of a circle by centreing himself on the heel of one foot, and kicks up the other to an angle of about a hundred and ten degrees. No further communication was had with him.

Almost the only person I encountered in London who had a well-defined genius for business was the operator in a certain barbering saloon. As I have already had occasion to mention, I had not cut my hair or trimmed my beard since I left home, and the consequence was a wildness of growth of these appendages desirable to be curtailed, and an accumulation amongst them of sea-salt, dust of empires, remains of antiquity, etc. that I did not care to lug across the Atlantic with me. Seeing a promising place in the Strand where these alterations could be effected, I entered and commanded that they be done. The operator put me in position and at once began as minute a fingering of my cranium as if he were a phrenologist. "You 'ave fine 'air," said he, "remarkable fine 'air, sir. It is a pity you 'av'n't more hof it." "It is," returned I; "it is a great pity." "We 'ave a Preparation," said he, "wich we gorontee to prejuce it hout again as thick as hever." This Preparation I ascertained was "The Juice of Lime;"—the juice being, I would fain hope and believe, that of the fruit and not of the earth of this name. "You should hallow me," he continued, "to recommend it to you." "Certainly I will," replied I; "recommend it to me, by all means."

"He-he!" tittered he; "you are jockler, sir." He, however, complied with my injunction and went on to deliver a powerful eulogium of the Juice of Lime as a fertilizer of the scalp. In the course of conversation he put himself in possession of the knowledge that I had been on the Continent. "The Continent," said he, "is hinjurous to people's 'eads. The salt gits in 'em in crossin' the Channel, and them countries is 'ot—the hair dries hup the 'air. Our customers always comes back with their 'eads hall brashy and split at the bends like yours is, but they begin with our Preparation, wich smooths 'em hoff and puts a new glossh upon 'em at the first happlercation. You 'ave wery fine 'air, hall it wants is glossh." "Yes," said I, "it wants glossh." "Your 'ead is much soiled," he went on to say; "dandriff is acumerlated, the scalf looks un'ealthy, and the pores of the skin is stopped hup with prespreration. We 'ave a little treatus on the use and abe-use hof the 'air, showin' 'ow it may be preserved in youthfil lustrer to hextreme hold hage, wich we put in the wropper round our Preparation, wich is just the thing for you. 'Er Majesty and the Royil fam'ly happlies it to their hown 'eads and says there never was nothin' like it." After much more discourse of the same tenor, perceiving what little progress he was making in converting me, he brought his operations to a close by declaring that he would anoint my head with some of his Preparation, anyhow,—which he did, rapturously directing my attention to its exquisite odor and ecstatic lubricity; and then, hitching a big outlandish-looking cylindrical brush to a pulley, which caused it to fly around equal to the drum of a thrashing-machine, he proceeded to brush my hair therewith. This was the first time my hair was ever brushed by machinery, and the impression made upon me was very great. Seeing me ready to depart he took a bottle of the Preparation in each hand, and, planting himself before me, made the most eloquent and able appeal in behalf of it that I have ever heard from mortal lips on any such topic. Simple courtesy would have dictated some notice on my part of such an oratorical effort, but its fervor and power compelled a formal reply. "Friend," said I, "for years I have diligently used 'Dolbibby's Concentrated Compound Comminuted Extract of Guano, Highly Perfumed, for the Promotion of the Growth of the Hair,' and 'Professor Chinch Shadd's Natural Detergent, or Rational Combination of Soap, Soda, and Sandpaper, for Purifying the Scalp, Cleaning out Chicken-coops, Polishing the Teeth, and Removing Rust from Old Iron.' In spite of these my fine hair, as you yourself have discovered, has seriously diminished in quantity and has become brashy and split at the ends and deprived of its gloss, while my head is much soiled, dandruff has accumulated, the scalp looks unhealthy, and the pores of the skin are stopped up with perspiration. All this wreck and desolation has come in spite of the use of the best preventives that the genius of man has ever devised; for, mark you!—Dolbibby's and Shadd's preparations are both compounded after recipes of my own invention. It would be stultifying myself to admit that anybody else's preparations are better than my own, and your proposition to purchase the Juice of Lime is respectfully but firmly declined." His jaw dropped and we parted.

Of the vices and of the virtues of London, is there not enough written in other travel-books? It would seem that there dwell here the worst of villains—they who, after assassinating a fellow-man, will grind up his remains and put them upon the market done into sausages—and the best of Christians,—who send out flannel waistcoats to the tropical heathen. The social contrasts have also been thoroughly talked about. Some writers moralize with great power upon the vast distance that intervenes here between the top and the bottom rounds of the ladder of life—a marvelous thing, which they appear to have realized for the first time on arriving in London. For my part, I did not have to go to the great city to recognize this. I can see it plainly enough in my own little town. I have known, I think from my childhood, that very rich folks are better off than very poor ones, and I must honestly admit that to my mind it is not very surprising that this should be so. Of a truth, London has its penury and its wealth, its disgraces and glories, its abasements and exaltations, its pains and pleasures, its woes and joys, like every other spot on this Hell-cursed Heaven-blessed earth. Of the kind and degree of all these circumstances I could not walk its streets without obtaining some inkling, but if I were to presume to make specific mention of them, as well as of many other things, it could only be after another visit made under more propitious auspices.

CHAPTER XXVII.

How we set out for Liverpool to embark for America, and of the agreeable Companion we journeyed with—A few Observations on Liverpool—A Glimpse of Ireland, and the Passage Home, with an Account of the Principal Passenger and of my Shipwreck, and the Conclusion of the Volume.

ONE day more and we were to be upon the sea, homeward bound. We employed this day, or three or four hours of it, in journeying to Liverpool, where lay the steamer that was to take us over. It was a pleasant journey, for we happened to be quartered with an unusually communicative old English gentleman, who, finding we were from America, set us down for barbarians, who knew nothing, and availed himself of the circumstance to make himself great and glorious in our eyes. Thus, he related an interesting anecdote of how adroitly on one occasion he had reserved a whole compartment of a railroad carriage to himself and friend by feigning to be conveying the said friend to a lunatic asylum. He told it with great minuteness and particularity, and caused us to laugh with a heartiness which would have astonished him had he known that we had not heard it above fifty times before in our own country. He also drew forth his watch, a hunting-case affair, and directed our especial attention to the singularly great improvement effected by making a little circular aperture in the centre of the case, by which the face could be seen without the trouble of springing the cover. He informed us that he was the inventor of this admirable device, the idea having occurred to him of a sudden on his present trip to London. We lauded it as a real advance in watch-making, and, to show that the appreciation was genuine, my companion pulled out a time-piece with identically the same improvement, which he had bought some time before from an horologer, who had scores of them. The inventor was stunned for a little while by the sight of it, but rallied under the remark that coincidence in invention was not very uncommon. At one of the stopping-places we thought the old fellow was in a fit; but he explained that he was merely recognizing his friend the brother of the Premier; and, from the very decided commotion under which he was laboring, we thought that it was really probable he had seen the apparition of some great man or other. On the whole, our friend was a very agreeable person, talking much on many topics; and, with the limitation that we could not believe a word he said, we got a vast deal of information out of him. We thought, indeed, he was a little too ancient to be carrying on so; but, as it did us no harm and him so much good, we took no step to dash his joy.

The district of country through which we passed was, for the most part, level and sprinkled with trees, and thickly settled and highly cultivated. We reached Liverpool early in the afternoon, being let down into it along an inclined plane through a tunnel by means of a rope, an operation which we underwent with admiration not unmixed with awe. Upon the recommendation of our fellow-passenger, we repaired to the hotel called after the Father of his Country, namely, Washington, and, in this particular at least, found that he might be depended upon; for, though it may possibly not be the best of hotels, it is good enough for one who is going to leave the country the next morning. In this establishment they observe the good old English custom of having a maid to keep bar, and a lady also presides in the office.

Having dined, I strolled forth to get what idea I might of the place in the few hours I could devote to it. I do not believe there is much of general interest to be seen in Liverpool. It is a business town, and the inhabitants are a practical people, more disposed to accumulate money for their own proper good than to waste it in making displays for the benefit of strangers. I came across a monument to the Duke of Wellington, and another to His Royal Highness Prince Albert, which had that cold, gloomy, lonely look which runs in the family of monuments. I also contemplated St. George's Hall, hard by the monuments, which is the great hall of the town; and afterwards stumbled into and walked through the Roscoe Arcade, which is a kind of caravansary for the sellers of sere-and-yellow-leaf furniture, and where I was treated with open contumely and profound contempt because it appeared not to me judicious to traffic for an old buggy bedstead and a bureau with the varnish all rasped off. Liverpool is a smoky place, and for so important a one presented, it seemed to me, no very prepossessing aspect, though, in truth, I inspected it only in the vicinity of the hotel.

When I came forth the next morning I was astonished at beholding all the horses in town discharging their duties gloriously arrayed in gay cloths and crowned with flowers. Upon inquiry I ascertained that this was done in honor of May-day, it being the praiseworthy custom of the place on this festival to gladden the hearts of the quadrupeds with the delights of finery, that they too might participate in the rejoicings incident to the occasion. Another astonishment awaited us when we came to settle our bill. In this document we found recorded against us between thirty and forty drinks, potations of the preceding night. They were all specified minutely on the authority of the bar-maid, and comprised a few ales, some gins, several whiskies, and very many brandies. We stood appalled at this stupendous catalogue, and as soon as we could recover breath flatly denied the charges. The lady of the office scanned us, and clearly perceiving that we were not of a stomach to take in these things and live to dispute the bill, was pleased to remit the items from us and set them to somebody else's account.

In a few minutes we were on the tender and making our way to the steamer, which was awaiting us out in the river. We now had the opportunity of contemplating the magnificent docks, works of solid stone, miles in extent, and justly the pride of Liverpool. Our eyes were also refreshed by the view of the river itself; for the Mersey is here a fine stream, whose broad expanse conforms to the American idea of what a river ought to be. Presently we were on board the steamer, where, for our own parts, owing to our moderation in baggage, we were comfortably domiciliated at once and at leisure to observe our English fellow-passengers, who were straightway flung into a tremendous pother and perspiration, and remained so for a long period, by reason of the perplexing multiplicity of their packages. About one o'clock we set out, steaming along in gallant style, but shortly slackened speed to receive the mails and three or four of that strange sort of travelers who inevitably start by the last opportunity instead of the first; after which we went fairly and squarely on our way.

After passing a dreadful night, occasioned by the hideous noises on board, especially those arising from the cleaning of ashes from the boilers and the songs with which the mariners beguiled their labors, at nine o'clock next morning we came to anchor before Queenstown, where we were to stop till the afternoon to take on the latest mails. The little mail-steamer coming off to us soon after, several of the passengers took the opportunity of going ashore in her to get a peep at old Ireland,— among them a fat and facetious German gentleman long resident in England and myself. Between him and me a strong friendship had already been established in consequence of the congeniality of our dispositions, both of us being irrepressible commentators on men and things and terrible jabberers at meat, and we associated ourselves together on this expedition.

The harbor of Queenstown is a very fine one and strongly fortified, and the scenery around it is really lovely. Queenstown itself is a picturesque and small place, which would be an exquisitely dull one into the bargain were it not enlivened to the last degree by beggars.

This active class of the Queenstown community were as numerous as at Cadiz, and far more tormenting, from the fact that they could put themselves in verbal communication with us. No sooner did we touch terra firma than we were beset by them in shoals. The large majority of them were widows, according to their own showing,—old widows and young widows, each provided with a preternatural quantity of children. They welcomed us in the most enthusiastic manner, blessing the day that brought us to their shores, and giving glory that they had been spared to see our honors. Unbounded encomiums were showered not merely upon our moral but our physical loveliness. Never before did I know wherein my comeliness consisted, but these acute observers pointed out my lurking beauties at first sight; and as for my fat friend, had he not been a philosopher indifferent to these vanities, he must have become puffed up to bursting with the commendations lavished upon the shapely rotundity of his body and the symmetrical massiveness of his head. Clamorous with compliments, the widows pursued us high and low all over town, trooping with their menagerie of children close upon our heels when we walked and camping round about us when we stopped to rest. In time, however, they began to see that we were men of obdurate hearts which were not to be softened by blandishments; and now the innate delusiveness of widows began to display itself. Their compliments were suspended, and in place of them came the most derogatory declarations and most opprobrious comments. Somehow they had imbibed the idea that I was a man of natural benevolence, passing friendly to widows and willing to relieve their distresses, but that my amiable intentions were kept from fructifying by the malign interposition of my fat friend. In this supposition they certainly did him gross injustice, but it had the good effect, at any rate, of preserving me from the heaviest of their fire and concentrating it upon him. Their remarks were exceeding pointed and peppery, and very painful to hear. "Be gorra," said an old widow, "the worrums will have fine atin' av him, blissed be the sints in glowry!" Said another old widow, "Down't ye ax the ould divil inny mowre—his hid an' his billy's too big to hiv innything good in 'em." Harassed out of his wits by the everlasting homily of a young widow concerning his duty to take care of the fatherless, my friend was so indiscreet as to ask her why she had so many children. The young widow blazed up terribly at this question, and among other dreadfully disparaging things screamed to him that he might break his very shin-bones in trying to get only one and would fail. The persecution was now getting too fierce and fiery to be borne, and we were compelled to retreat to the mail-boat and hide to save ourselves. Terror of the captain prevented them from following us, and here we remained, cowering behind the machinery, till at last to our great joy the mails came down and were taken on board and we were ready to return to the steamer. The body of widows collected in force on the wharf to see us off, chattering and clamoring and commenting upon us in the most ungentlemanly terms, my unfortunate fat friend being singled out for the cruelest of their animadversions. And so it came to pass, that whereas beggars welcomed me into Europe, so did beggars hustle me out of it.

At four o'clock the engines were put in motion to be stopped no more now till we were on the other side of the world. We were done with mankind for a time, or forever,—who could tell?—and must rely upon ourselves. We watched the receding land, those of us who were going home, cheerfully—those of us who were leaving it, sorrowfully—as long as it could be seen, and when darkness came we watched a far-off lighthouse. Its benignant light was still gleaming upon us late in the night when I retired to rest, and this was the last I saw of Europe.

Our steamer was constructed on the same model as the Guipuzcoa, the Spanish ship that bore us over from Cuba, but was larger than that worthy old craft. From what I had heard of the line to which she belonged I was prepared for better accommodations than were furnished. With proper allowance for the difference between Spanish and English cookery, the fare was inferior to that of the Guipuzcoa, inferior in the variety, profusion, and general "make up" of the dishes. The flesh and fowl were prone to be indifferent well flavored, and were oftentimes pestilently sturdy in resisting the teeth. Neatness was, however, in higher esteem on this vessel, except in one important particular—there were no table-napkins. Some of us with beards and moustaches who were soup-eaters, perceiving what great embarrassments this neglect would entail, made bold at the outset to seize each for himself a waiter's towel, notwithstanding the earnest protestation of the steward against the proceeding, and contrived to maintain possession of it during the whole voyage—one or two being so fortunate, indeed, as to be able to secure a second towel towards the last. One of the most reprehensible features in the management was the attempt to crowd all the passengers at one table. In this they nearly or quite succeeded, and the consequence was that we ate at immense disadvantage, being eternally in one another's way. This state of things could not but hinder the growth of the kindly feelings amongst us, for we could not but rejoice when our neighbor was laid low by sea-sickness and lament when he rose again, seeing that our own comfortable feeding was involved in his presence or absence. Our first dinner together was a disastrous botch, no man knowing his rights or respecting those of other people. The waiters, too, may be said to have been all at sea, trotting hither and thither taking orders and forgetting to execute them. After this, however, things gradually began to adjust themselves, and by the time we reached New York were getting into quite a promising state. By that time all the loquacious portion of the company had gravitated to one end of the table, having driven away the quiet eaters, and especially frightened off what ladies had quartered there at first. The fat and facetious German gentleman was one of this band, and so was I, and the uproar they made at meal-times was stupendous.

Our passengers were of the general run of decorous, unostentatious, companionable passengers, with nothing about most of them particularly characteristic. There was a lady who had crossed the ocean twenty-seven times. There was also an old gentleman with an incurable organic disease of the eyes which had impaired his sight so that he had to be led about the deck, who had been treated unsuccessfully by the best oculists of London and Paris and was now journeying to New York to put himself under the care of one of our celebrated "natural healers,"—an interesting case, since it showed the recognition of American talent abroad, and pitiable, too, in that a sensible, amiable, feeble old man should be deluded into adventuring all this weary way on a fool's errand.

We had, however, one pretty prominent character amongst us—a gentleman spoken of and addressed by his wife under the appellation of Mr. Richard. He was English by birth, but had been naturalized in the United States, and had resided for a great many years in one of our large Western cities, where he had become thoroughly impregnated with American ideas and principles, and now esteemed himself as perfect an American as if he had been born in the country. He was an exceedingly knowing gentleman, versed in any topic that could be started, and quick to enter into conversation, which he had the most admirable knack of speedily transforming into a controversy. He clipped the king's English freely, and was greatly addicted to metaphor and substantial portly words, speaking in a strain sometimes trenching closely upon the poetical. By all odds his most favorite field of argument was the political. On this account especially I held him to be an inestimable acquisition to the ship, for he kept us continually in the current of national politics, which is the *pabulum pabulorum* of enlightened Americans. He was of the sect which is called "Copperheads," being one of the worst amongst them. It made the nerves curdle to hear him detail the enormities which had been and were yet being perpetrated by his ravening enemies the Radicals, which had reached so sanguinary a pitch as to preclude him from ever speaking of the land of his adoption in any other form of words than "Our bleedin' country." When not debating or expounding, he could usually be found on the upper deck, sitting with a thick stick in his hand, looking straight out to sea, with his aged black beaver hat well on the back of his head, and with his mouth puckered up and his visage wearing a cast of the mournfulest reverie, and when his meditations would be brought to light, they would invariably prove to be grounded upon the woes of our bleedin' country aforesaid.

I early became acquainted with Mr. Richard, the acquaintance being brought about ere we were yet out of sight of Liverpool by a surmise of mine that we might have a safe passage,—with which surmise he immediately took issue, advancing several reasons why we might not. A discussion ensued and then other conversation, by which he learned that I was from the South. He now warmed to me at once, regarding me in the light of one who had suffered in an especial manner from the persecutions of the public enemy. "I mourn for you," said he; and then imposing his massive hand with a paternal flop upon my shoulder-blade he bade me cher *rup*, for, he continued, "at the next election we will root down them who're gnashin' their bloody fangs over a hopeless pipple." I expressed to him what a weight he had lifted from my heart by this assurance, and he went on to tell me privately, with the request that I would not mention to any one that he had said so, that in his opinion the Radical party were Nerios bent on destroyerin' the liberties of our bleedin' country, and next let me into some of their villainies in the matter of the tariff, and in other matters which I did not entirely understand, but agreed that it was indeed but too true. All this led to a review of the war, which he criticised with great severity. "They tried to force my son in," said he, "but they couldn't git him to fight you." And he related an incident which displayed the magnanimity of the young man's character in a striking light. He had been drafted and the officers went forth to take him in his slaughter-pen, where he was peacefully pursuing his regular avocation of killing hogs. When he was apprised of their errand, as quick as lightning he uplifted his reeking butcher-knife, and exclaimed he,—"Before I will be taken to the army I'll plurnge this weepin' through and through me—by Gum!" They were too nimble for him, however, for ere he could execute his threat they had secured him inextricably. "But," added the father, triumphantly, "he was as good as his word,— he wouldn't fight aginst you,—he bought a substoot."

Mr. Richard then proceeded to recount a mass of revolting barbarities inflicted on the soldiers themselves, particularly how they were robbed of things sent to them. I was in full accord with his feelings on this point, being cognizant that similar atrocities were wrought on our own side during the war, and I became equally hot in venting my wrath against the perpetrators of them. And, indeed, what outrage can be more villainous? Amongst civilians universally the robbery of a church is held to rank with the basest of crimes, but as a warrior I protest that the robbery of a soldier's box sent him by the loving ones who have stinted and starved themselves to give a son or brother a little taste of home comforts is worse than sacrilege. Ah, me! the shrieks, and roars, and tears, and curses that I have seen and heard over the scraps of paper, the empty bottles, and desolate tin pie-plates revealed upon the raising of the box-lid,—and all without avail, for never on any occasion within my knowledge could justice be got to overtake the demons who wrought the ravage.

There were some of the opposing sect on board, and it would have been against reason had so blatant a reviler of their principles as Mr. Richard was been permitted to go long without an attempt to check him. In fact, so soon as the second day, while we were yet lying at anchor in the harbor of Queenstown, a Radical champion went up against him in his camp on the upper deck, where a terrible battle of words was at once joined. The Copperhead declared that the Radical party was a conglomernation of vill'ny, and that he was for liberty. The Radical replied that he was for country. The Copperhead rejoined that shoulder-straps and shoddy had been the ruin of his bleedin' country. The Radical retorted that the Copperheads were in favor of paying the Rebel debt. At this Mr. Richard waxed wroth exceedingly and notified his adversary that since he had commenced to throw epithrets he himself could throw epithrets, too; and straightway began to do so. The Radical finding that he was unable to withstand the jagged and shapeless verbal masses that now came showering upon him, and being incapable of replying in kind, fell back,—to the disgust of the triumphant Copperhead, who complained that it was invariably the case that as soon as he cornered one of them he would run away. This encounter diffused around such a just conception of Mr. Richard's calibre that though there were many passages of arms between him and the rest of the company afterwards, it was always understood by everbody but himself that they were merely feints, and that no one cared to cope with him in serious argument.

As a whole, the passage was a dull one. The captain, unlike him of the Guipuzcoa, neither laughed, nor screamed, nor played on the gourd for us, but, on the contrary, was a grave, sober, reserved mariner, who devoted his attention exclusively to the navigation of the ship, leaving the passengers to their own devices. Neither did these sing and dance of nights, as did our Spanish fellow-voyagers, but betook themselves to such sedate pursuits as whist and checkers. The earlier portion of the day would be worried through by the sedentary in yawning over the books of the library, and by the active in distressing efforts to play a species of croquet and other games, wo-begone sea-faring adaptations of earthly pastimes. Meal-times were the most pleasant seasons, and much jocularity prevailed on these occasions, at least at our end of the table, where the fat and facetious German gentleman would lead off and be ably aided and abetted by the rest till the inappreciative steward would break us up by lugging off the dishes and dragging away the table-cloth. After dinner this roistering segment of the company would concentrate in the cuddy to smoke, recount adventures, and mayhap to sing. At these convocations the Copperhead usually attended to refresh us with his exhaustive disquisitions, and once or twice he was induced to unbend sufficiently to volunteer a song. This song was a naval ditty, setting forth the exploits of the immortal Nelson, and was enriched with a chorus whose curious collocation of "yilly-yilly-yum-yio" and "tilly-tilly-tum-tio" would have irresistibly struck the auditor whoever might have been the chorister, but, as rendered by the present executioner, filled every soul with unimaginable emotions. Such, however, was the recognized merit of the performance that, although no one could tell for certain whether the melodist was singing or crying, and he had, moreover, to come to a dead halt at the end of the first two lines of every stanza to consider what were the last two, the assembly received it with unbounded applause and rapturously demanded a repetition.

It was at one of these cuddy meetings that I gained an opportunity to unburden myself of a matter which I was never able before to satisfactorily discharge. The subject of shipwreck was introduced, and, getting the ears of the convocation, I was for once in a position to detail fully to an intelligent and sympathetic audience a disaster of the kind which it had been my fate to be called upon to endure.

Pause we right here for a moment. It is a maxim continually enforced by moralists that it is in our power to profit ourselves by every stroke of adversity that befalls us, and they cogently inculcate it as a solemn duty we owe to ourselves to do so. This is my own sentiment in the matter, and, indeed, I am not one to suffer gratuitously if I can help it. But, up to this time, I have not derived one iota of benefit from my shipwreck, and this I conceive is attributable to the fact that it has never become generally known, there having been no one with common charity enough to talk about my calamities and get them into profitable circulation. Nay, I know some people so selfish as to deprive me of the comfort and advantage of my sufferings by slurring over and smothering the subject even after it had been broached, and when I was hopeful of achieving therefrom a goodly degree of repute and consideration among my fellow-citizens. I am determined that this state of things shall stop. I have suffered from silence long enough, and I mean to suffer no longer. My shipwreck would certainly be worth something to me if it were properly brought before the public, and, since no one will do this paltry service for me, now that the opportunity offers I shall summon my manliness to my aid, beat down my modesty, and do it for myself. I beseech of the reader, therefore, as a simple act of justice to a man whose name has been unrighteously kept out of the newspapers, to peruse the following succinct narrative, which is in substance what I related in the conference above mentioned; and let him not niggardly keep it to himself, but let him show at least a spark of magnanimity by bringing it to the attention of the females of his family:

Some years ago it chanced that I was tarrying in Jerusalem, of Southampton, in Virginia. While there abiding I made acquaintance with that admirable old salt, Captain Sylvester Drake, commander of the A No. 1 river craft, the Jane Eliza, who, taking a fancy to me, was pleased to tender me the hospitalities of his ship on my way home. The Jane Eliza was then at the port of Smithfield, on James River, a few miles distant, where she was loading with jugs for the Richmond market. I gratefully accepted his kind proffer, and at the proper time repaired to Smithfield and embarked.

In the middle of a pleasant day, some twelve hours after we were all ready to go, we gradually set sail and departed with the benedictions of the citizens and a full cargo. The ship's company consisted of Captain Drake, who also acted as cook and anchor-dropper, and a reflective man, whose duty it was to abut against the tiller and bring the vessel up whenever she showed a tendency to veer more than forty-five degrees from the direct course. There were no passengers other than myself. We moved demurely along without the occurrence of anything particular till sunset, when we ran ashore, and, dropping anchor at the bow, tied our stern to a tree, and so reposed in quietude all night.

Next morning, after breakfast, we set out again and traveled on pleasantly, the captain beguiling the hours by eating peanuts, and I by picking oakum. The afternoon was a remarkably fine one, and this circumstance, conjoined with the fact that we were now arrived at a famous oyster-ground, induced Captain Drake about four o'clock to knock off for the day and lay by. A pair of oyster-tongs was a portion of the normal furniture of the Jane Eliza, and albeit it was in the summer season, when this species of fish has lost its obesity and is withal in ill repute as to wholesomeness, we lowered the boat and betook ourselves for the remainder of that pleasant afternoon to the extraction and the cooking and eating of oysters.

It was most delightful. Alas, what a disastrous day was to follow this festive night!

We started rather early the ensuing morning, for the captain had hopes, Providence permitting, to get somewhere in the neighborhood of Richmond that evening. I was still abed on the cabin-table and a bacon-box (for though the captain had most politely insisted on giving me his berth I positively refused to deprive him of it), my whole strength employed in digesting the oysters I had eaten, when of a sudden the Jane Eliza received a blow which seemed to shiver her timbers, and which was accompanied with a rushing of waters and the most appalling rattling of jugs that the human mind can conceive of. I was on my head in an instant and as soon as possible on my feet, and forthwith hurried on deck. The horrid truth loomed high before me in the shape of one of those gigantic plain matter-of-fact structures which by an outrageous misnomer are called Lighters, being in truth heavier than any other specimen of naval architecture. It appeared that our reflective steersman, intent on introspection, had failed to look out, and so had suffered the Jane Eliza to be run down by the lighter,—to which, of course, no blame could be attached, since this kind of craft does not profess to steer and is too self-sufficient to have the inclination, even if it had the power, to get out of anybody else's way. A great hole had been staved in the Jane Eliza's bow, her doom had been inexorably pronounced, and it was clear that no human power could save her. All that remained for us was to endeavor to save ourselves. By a prodigious effort, Captain Drake and myself mounted into the lighter, being generously assisted by the colored navigators of that portentous craft, but the steersman, true to his nautical instincts, remained faithfully abutting against the tiller, and would probably have gone down at his post had not Captain Drake from the lighter's side screamed to him, "Come out o' thar, you darned lubber!" He obeyed orders and came, being encouraged all the way by such expressions as "A divil of a mess you've made of it, ain't you?" and "Darn you!" frequently repeated.

And now from the lighter's side we saw and heard the

good ship Jane Eliza and her precious freight of innumerable jugs struggling with the pitiless element. It was an awful scene, utterly indescribable, but never to be forgotten. High above all was the dreadful gurgling of the jugs as they drank in their death potion. "Iggle-iggle-iggle," squeaked the little jugs,—"oggle-oggle-oggle," moaned the medium jugs,—"uggle-uggle-uggle," groaned the big jugs. For yards around the water boiled and bubbled in a way only to be paralleled by the seething pool of Phlegethon. Let the reader look within and picture for himself, if he can, this tremendous spectacle, for what pen can adequately describe the shipwreck of a bark laden with jugs?

The direful sights and sounds gradually became stilled, but for a long time after the accustomed calm had overspread the scene there would at intervals come forth the last bubblings of some long-enduring jug, tenacious of its vital air, which had at length succumbed. We gazed in a sort of fascination upon the spectacle, watching it intently to the last, and I think our heads must have been turned by its horrors, for we—that is, the colored navigators and myself—frequently broke into wild peals of laughter. The Jane Eliza was gone forever, and with her were gone my hat, coat, vest, pantaloons, and shoes and stockings; but I myself had been mercifully delivered from the dangers and inconveniences of submersion, and I was tolerably thankful.

The lighter people were as kind as they could be to us, though their kindness was necessarily restricted by their circumstances,—there being nothing to eat, drink, or wear on board. They, however, cordially permitted us to walk about in the water in the bottom of the lighter and to sit on the beams. I was pained to see that Captain Drake and his reflective steersman, instead of being united by calamity, now began to fall further and further asunder. A distressingly contentious argument arose between them in discussing the theory of the catastrophe, which culminated on the part of the steersman in a positive declaration that he would never give Captain Drake the benefit of his services again.

We drifted hither and thither on the lighter till the

Norfolk steamer on her way to Richmond hove in sight. We hailed her and she stopped, and the commander, when we had told our sad story, moved by that generous sympathy which actuates mariners towards their shipwrecked brethren, granted us a free passage,—Captain Drake lending me his pea-jacket in order that I might present myself before the deeply interested passengers of the steamer with something of that seemliness befitting a man of my station and function. On the steamer I procured a full outfit of sailor-clothes, and so reached home, greatly chastened and sobered by the momentous scenes through which I had passed.

Return we now to the main current of our narrative. The weather for most of the time was good and the sea smooth. For the first day or two we suffered from a mild visitation of sea-sickness, all the ladies having to lie down below, except the veteran of the twenty-seven crossings, who came manfully up to time at every meal. We soon became acclimated, however, and only a few sporadic cases of the malady occurred during the rest of the voyage. As we advanced westward, we began to be notably disturbed by the roosters on board, who having but a poor conception of longitude persisted in crowing by Liverpool time and broke us of our rest of nights. When we got on the banks of Newfoundland, we were beset by tremendous fogs, compelling us to extraordinary circumspection in navigation and a lavish blowing of the whistle. The weather, too, in these regions grew piercingly cold, freezing the convocation of the cuddy out completely. On the second Sunday we had divine service in the cabin, my professional brother, the ship's surgeon, officiating, and with an edifying impressiveness not to be expected from one who was so nimble a swearer as in my communion with him I had noted him to be. After prayers this same Sunday we had a series of little whirlwinds, typhoons, and other aerial gymnastics, which caused the wind to whip about ahead, astern, and abeam, discomfiting landsmen and making the mariners stand by their ropes. And on the ensuing morning it was darkly whispered about ship that that night we had by a handsbreadth escaped colliding with another vessel.

But thanks, hearty and sincere thanks, to the beneficent Power which had blessed me with the opportunity of enjoying so many new and interesting scenes, and had mercifully guarded me amongst them all, when I arose on the morning of the tenth day from Liverpool my eyes were gladdened by the sight of my native land. In a few hours we were in New York. In two days I was at home, and the journey was ended.

THE END.

www.ingramcontent.com/pod-product-compliance
Lightning Source LLC
Chambersburg PA
CBHW020303240426
43673CB00039B/690